Men, Women, and Issues in American History

VOLUME II

The Dorsey Series in History

Men, Women, and Issues in American History

VOLUME II

Edited by

HOWARD H. QUINT

MILTON CANTOR
Both of the
University of Massachusetts

Revised Edition   1980

 The Dorsey Press
Homewood, Illinois   60430

Irwin-Dorsey Limited   Georgetown, Ontario   L7G 4B3

© THE DORSEY PRESS, 1975 and 1980

ISBN 0-256-02312-3
Library of Congress Catalog Card No. 79–56088
Printed in the United States of America

1 2 3 4 5 6 7 8 9 0 ML 7 6 5 4 3 2 1 0

LEARNING SYSTEMS COMPANY—
a division of Richard D. Irwin, Inc.—has developed a
PROGRAMMED LEARNING AID
to accompany texts in this subject area.
Copies can be purchased through your bookstore
or by writing PLAIDS.
1818 Ridge Road, Homewood, Illinois 60430.

For our sons and daughters
—scholars all—
May they have inherited our strengths,
not our shortcomings.

Janet and David Quint

David, Elisabeth, and Daniel Cantor

Introduction

College and university undergraduates are often as interested in the characters on the stage of history as in the historical process itself. For more than anything else it is the dramatis personae who bring history alive and make it not only the record of what men and women have thought and done but, in most instances, an exciting story in itself. Many are the students unfortunately who find history uninstructive and irrelevant, but rare are these same students who do not find themselves absorbed by historical biography, particularly when it presents people as they were and not what mythologizers have made them.

The essays in these volumes seek to place individual men and women within the context of their age, and, at the same time, to explore what contributions—political, economic, social, or intellectual—they have made to their society. In attempting to understand their values and goals, it is essential to understand those forces that shaped them; namely, family traditions and background, friendships which influenced them, religious and educational attachments which had an impact, economic commitments to which they may have been devoted, the social class to which they were seamlessly wedded, the changing historical circumstances that formed the backdrop against which they played out their lives. Knowing this congeries of attitudes and events, we know the men and women themselves; and, knowing them, we throw a spotlight on the society itself and the historical period that bounded their time on earth.

Contributors to these volumes include men and women of all academic ranks, from professors emeriti to assistant professors, as well as the distinguished former director of the Folger Library. They come from private and tax-supported colleges and universities and without exception are highly respected for their work in the fields of American history and American studies. They represent a wide spectrum of viewpoints, though on the whole we should have to say that their approach is essentially in the so-called Whig tradition of historical writing that has been the dominant one in this country. In the planning stage for *Men, Women, and Issues in American History,* the editors suggested a general format for the organization of the individual essays, but the reader will quickly realize that it has not been followed in all instances. We have accepted the departures because we endorse Carl Becker's dictum that every man must be his own historian and because we believe that every historian must organize the ideas presented in the manner most satisfactory to himself or herself.

The editors wish to acknowledge here, with appreciation, the assistance given them in various ways, large and small, by their colleagues in the Department of History at the University of Massachusetts/Amherst. Equally, they want to express publicly and thus for the record their gratitude for the secretarial help of Mary Reddington, Sandra Mailho, Susan West, Barbara Einfurer, and Jane Marino.

February 1980   HOWARD H. QUINT
                                                   MILTON CANTOR

Contents

1

Organizing and Rationalizing American Capitalism

JOHN D. ROCKEFELLER
ANDREW CARNEGIE
J. PIERPONT MORGAN

by John G. Sproat
University of South Carolina

It was almost as though two men were swapping a bushel of corn for a new harness at some crossroads country store. Andrew Carnegie, the undisputed lord of the steel industry, scribbled a few figures on a scrap of paper and sent it to J. P. Morgan, the undisputed lord of investment banking. The figures represented Carnegie's price for selling out of the iron and steel business—a bargain at $492,000,000—and they evoked from Morgan one quick glance and two words: "I accept." No questions, no haggling, not even a signed formal agreement: one of the great financial transactions of history took place with almost studied casualness. Several weeks later, Morgan acquired a vast range of iron ore from John D. Rockefeller; then, in a matter of days, he merged his new holdings with mills and factories already in his hands and brought forth a colossus. On March 3, 1901, the House of Morgan announced the formation of the United States Steel Corporation, a giant of a company with a total capitalization of just under a billion and a half dollars.

Andrew Carnegie, John D. Rockefeller, and J. P. Morgan: the brief interaction of these three regally rich and powerful men at the beginning of the 20th century resulted in the birth of the first supercorporation. The event marked the end of one economic era and the start of another. Industrial capitalism, that stage in economic development wherein individual entrepreneurs built and operated basic industries largely for personal profit and power, gave way to finance capitalism, the culminating stage of corporate consolidation, wherein powerful banking syndicates sought to bring the entire economy into some rational order. Successful business tycoons retained considerable importance, to be sure, if only as public symbols of the importance of individual enterprise. But the complex bureaucracy of the supercorporations inevitably overwhelmed the highly personalized entrepreneurial ventures of the 19th century. Where once the name Rockefeller had automatically been identified with control of the Standard Oil Company, in the new economic dispensation it became impossibly difficult to pinpoint corporate ownership beyond the vague entity known as "Wall Street." Where once it had been possible to comprehend the business methods of an Andrew Carnegie, the manipulations of a J. P. Morgan in the lofty world of corporate finance were a deep mystery to the average person.

This complex corporate economy had begun to take shape even before the Civil War. Its dimensions revealed themselves first in the steady expansion of the railroads; then in a proliferation of manufacturing enterprises that produced the metals, machinery, lubricants, and other staples of an industrial society. During the war, the economy behaved erratically, with some industries fattening on war contracts, while others lagged behind because of shortages of capital and raw materials. After 1865, the entire economy literally "busted loose." Interrupted only by a few brief spells of sluggishness, economic growth proceeded at a furious pace throughout the rest of the century.

By 1900 the statistical and visual evidence of an economic revolution was overwhelming. Railroad mileage had grown since the Civil War from 35,000 to nearly 200,000. The production of coal for industry had increased in short tons from 13 million to well over 200 million. The amount of capital flowing into industrial enterprises had risen from a billion dollars to almost ten billion. New sources of energy tripled the supply of power available to factories, cities, and farms. A national market had developed; it was made up of eager consumers, who gobbled up better than 90 percent of the goods American factories produced and inspired industry's leaders to set ever higher goals of production. Wages climbed and purchasing power rose significantly. To be sure, many people— unskilled workers, small farmers, racial and ethnic minorities especially—knew the period only as a time of nagging insecurity or outright privation. But the millions of white Americans who made up the middle class enjoyed a steadily rising standard of living and a sustained prosperity.

As in all revolutions, the ingredients that fueled such a titanic economic change were many and complex. After the long ordeal of the Civil War, Americans generally basked in a climate of unity and national purpose.

The dominant middle class eagerly reaffirmed its faith in progress by investing its savings in economic development. To augment this native capital, European and British investors poured a steady stream of gold into the underdeveloped American economy. Another Old World resource—people—also streamed across the Atlantic (and, to a lesser extent, the Pacific) to provide industry with a pool of labor. Vast stores of natural resources were readily available and freely exploitable, while a sprawling transportation network linked all the elements of the complex and fed the finished goods into the marketplace. Economic nationalism, a political doctrine the Republican Party had brilliantly translated into legislation during the Civil War, committed the federal government firmly to the cause of industrial growth and development; while all agencies of government—local, state, and federal—outdid themselves in catering to the needs of business enterprise. Both common law and juridical practice, moreover, enabled the corporation to evolve as an ideal legal device for organizing large-scale business operations in a coherent fashion. Underlying the revolution—and indeed, sanctifying it—was a congenial philosophical outlook that, in typically American fashion, fused self-interest and idealism. An ideological mishmash, it owed something to the Puritan ethic, something to Adam Smith, something to Poor Richard, and a very great deal to expediency.

Finally, there were the revolutionaries themselves. As the political revolution in 18th-century America had generated a crop of superb politicians, so the economic revolution a century later begot a group of entrepreneurs of extraordinary vitality, imagination, and ability. Doubtless, the revolution would have come without them, for there was a self-generating quality about industrial development that always limited the influence of individual industrialists in the process. Still, the entrepreneurs of the Gilded Age stamped the revolution indelibly with the marks of their personalities and methods. They were a varied lot, to be sure. Some were scoundrels who never pretended to be otherwise. Others were pillars of church and community. A number were super-bookkeepers, who overwhelmed their competitors with their single-minded attention to the most minute details of business. Still others simply bulldozed their rivals into oblivion in a ruthless, compulsive reach for power. Heroes or villains, they were all supremely self-assured men; and even the most inconspicuous of them played the game with apparent relish. They were the primeval planners of a new society, the true radicals of the industrial era. They paid lip service to traditional values and codes of conduct; but in their everyday business they seldom looked to the past for guidance or precedent. The industrial complex they helped to create literally transformed the face of a nation and the lives of a people.

In the process, some of these entrepreneurs themselves underwent an ironic transformation. Driven from the start by a fierce competitive spirit, many of them came in the end to loathe competition. The inefficiency, waste, and destructive conflict that marked the competitive struggle appalled them; and as their ranks thinned, the survivors sought ways to curtail the competitive factor in business or, better still, to eliminate it altogether. From the moment he entered the oil business, John D. Rockefeller undertook systematically to bring his far-flung industry as a whole under rational control—his control. In the steel industry, Andrew Carnegie enjoyed the competitive combat; but the combat was constant, and the powerful company he created had to expand constantly to hold its position against its competitors. J. P. Morgan, it was rumored, dreamed at night of the horrors of competition; and at the turn of the century it was this tough-minded, tight-fisted baron of high finance who turned his organizing genius and the immense power of his position in the banking world to the noble and imperative task, as he saw it, of bringing order to the entire industrial complex. The debilitating, wasteful effects of an archaic competitive economy could no longer be tolerated. It was time now, in Morgan's view, for each productive unit in the economy to take its place in an orderly, highly-integrated system and contribute to the smooth functioning of the whole. But if the competitive system was archaic, Morgan reasoned, so were the competitive entrepreneurs. Having attained maturity, American capitalism henceforth would be organized and rationalized by the ultimate capitalists—the bankers.

*   *   *

"I cheat my boys every time I get a chance," William Rockefeller once boasted. "I want to make them sharp. I trade with the boys and skin them and just beat them every time I can." William's oldest boy, John Davison Rockefeller, must have enjoyed these paternal "skinnings"; for years later, when he was the richest man in America, he wrote appreciatively of the lessons his father had given him in the "practical ways" of doing business. Certainly the lessons were well-learned. In the classic age of business enterprise, John D. Rockefeller set the pace for his fellow entrepreneurs in the game of "skinning" the competition. Indeed, in a remarkably short period of time, his genius at absorbing or eliminating rivals enabled him to create America's first great industrial combination, the Standard Oil Trust.

"Luck and pluck" played a part in Rockefeller's life, as they did in the legendary lives of Horatio Alger's heroes. But the similarity between reality and fiction ended there, for Rockefeller's life followed no pattern of rags to riches. Born in 1839 into a comfortable family in upstate New York, he knew affection and security throughout his childhood. His father, an itinerant and modestly successful vendor of patent medicine, was a lively extrovert who enjoyed exposing his children to the "real world" he knew so well from his travels. John's mother, Eliza Davison, was a serene and deeply religious woman, who passed on to her son her looks and many of her personality traits. Both mother and son were tall, handsome individuals, with a serious, thoughtful mien that sometimes bordered on dourness. Eliza also imbued young John with her faith, and there was no false piety in Rockefeller's lifelong commitment to his Baptist religion. His famous remark in 1905 that "God gave me my money" rang with hypocrisy for many of his skeptical contemporaries; but in his own mind, at least, he was quite convinced that he was only a steward of God's will on earth and that his power to make money was a gift from God.

Even as a boy, Rockefeller displayed the qualities of shrewd good judgment and prudence that helped to make him a success in business. "When it's raining porridge, you'll find John's dish right side up," his sister quipped of him. Although he admired the life of the mind and later translated his admiration into princely benefactions to institutions of higher learning, for his own formal schooling he chose his father's "practical ways." After high school, he studied double-entry bookkeeping, commercial law, and principles of banking at Folsom's Commercial College in Cleveland. "I was very sedate and earnest, preparing to meet the responsibilities of life," he recalled of his school years. At the time, too, he started his first account book, Ledger A, in which he dutifully recorded his earliest venture in philanthropy: 15 cents to a "Missionary Cause."

In 1859 young John D. and a friend formed a commission firm that was a success from the day it started. Rockefeller's conservatism showed in the attention he paid to the smallest details of business and in his exacting, methodical supervision of the account books. But he also revealed a bold, daring streak that pegged him as a gambler, ready to follow his own instincts in striking out for new territory, even at considerable risk. Borrowing so heavily from the banks as to alarm his less ambitious partner, he expanded the business and put it in a splendid position to profit from the Civil War. Like many ambitious young men of his time, Rockefeller managed to avoid military service. Under his deft supervision, the firm prospered so handsomely in selling supplies to the Union armies that he soon had sufficient capital of his own to begin looking for other investment opportunities. He found one in a new, high-risk industry—oil. A bawling feverish infant at the time he discovered it, the oil industry matured under his stern guardianship to become a mainstay of the modern industrial order.

An element of luck in Rockefeller's career surely was his good fortune at being in the right place at the right time, namely, Cleveland in the early 1860s. Discovery of oil in nearby western Pennsylvania in 1859 touched off a regional boom that found its natural financial and trans-

portation focus in the lakeside Ohio city. Better than any of his contemporaries, Rockefeller saw the larger significance of the boom and
turned it to his own advantage. Investing in a small refinery as "a little
side-issue" in 1863, he soon became completely caught up in the new
venture. As the Civil War came to an end, he and his brother organized
their own refinery and began immediately to expand its operations.
Rockefeller early perceived an unlimited future for the oil industry, if
ways could be found to refine and transport its products cheaply, efficiently, and in great quantities. That a vast market existed for petroleum
products—an international market—he was sure. Once committed to the
industry, he set about methodically, often ruthlessly, to create the op-
timum conditions under which that market could be controlled and
exploited.

At the time Rockefeller entered the industry, thousands of small
producers and marginal refiners cluttered the oil fields of Ohio and
Pennsylvania, struggling furiously among themselves for position in
what was still a highly speculative venture. It was a ruggedly competitive
situation, quite in keeping with the best traditions of a free enterprise
society. But it was also a volatile situation, plagued with glutted markets
and wildly fluctuating prices and profits. To Rockefeller, such volatility
was intolerable and demanded correction. Competition was the villain,
he concluded; it tolerated inept and mediocre operators, while encouraging waste, inefficiency, and disorder throughout the industry. Openly and
deliberately, he launched an attack not only upon his individual competitors, but also upon the competitive principle itself.

In 1870 the Rockefeller brothers joined with another gifted entrepreneur, Henry M. Flagler, to incorporate the Standard Oil Company of
Ohio. In the next five years the Company grew to become the largest
unit in the oil industry and one of the biggest business operations in
America. With Rockefeller as its president, Standard Oil used every device
and opportunity at its disposal to create a monopoly within the industry.
The Company itself became the most efficient and centrally managed
operation in the oil fields. By vertically integrating many of the industry's
component parts, Rockefeller and his gifted associates sharply reduced
their dependence upon outside suppliers and services. Standard Oil
contracted for its own crude oil, coopered its own barrels, built its own
refineries, laid its own pipelines, merchandised its own products, and
ultimately even sailed its own fleets of tankers. At the same time, Rockefeller moved to absorb his rivals into a vast horizontally integrated and
centrally directed operation. One after another, he forced them into a
corner, where their only choice of action was to surrender or take a
"skinning." Those who gave in were absorbed methodically, even in-
differently, into the growing giant. Those who resisted usually ended up
broken and driven from business.

By itself, Rockefeller's genius as an organizer and manager probably would have gained him quick ascendancy to a dominant position in the oil industry. Never one to take all power and credit for accomplishment unto himself, he had a talent for identifying ability in his associates and for utilizing their gifts to the utmost. Notwithstanding an occasional and sometimes affected waspishness of mind, Rockefeller's breadth of vision had wide sweep, especially as it encompassed the industrial revolution. The movement toward consolidation in industry, he once observed, was really the "origin of the whole system of modern economic administration." It developed because the time was ripe for it: "It had to come, though all we saw at the moment was the need to save ourselves from wasteful competition." Whether or not Rockefeller ever systematically studied or took seriously the works of Herbert Spencer, he found the sophistries of "social Darwinism" a congenial explanation for the growth of giant business. It was all historically and biologically inevitable. Indeed, the survival of "fit" businesses was comparable in his view to the development of a magnificent flower, say the American Beauty rose, which survived in its splendor only because the early buds around it were sacrificed. "This is not an evil tendency in business," he insisted. "It is merely the working-out of a law of nature and a law of God."

Yet Rockefeller was never content in his business career to let the law of nature, the law of God, or the flow of history work themselves out without some help from him. Impatient and grimly determined to achieve his ends by any means at hand, he freely engaged in ruthless price-cutting, industrial espionage, and other censurable tactics. For instance, shrewdly alert to the crucial importance of costs in the competitive struggle, Rockefeller mastered the art of manipulating railroad rates to his advantage. In secret deals with the railroads, he offered them impressive shares of his considerable traffic in exchange for rebates—"kickbacks" of as much as 50 percent of his transportation costs. Incredibly, too, he even persuaded the railroads to give him rebates on the rates of his rivals. In 1872 Rockefeller led a group of large producers in a conspiracy aimed at assuming control of Pennsylvania's entire oil industry by using the rebate as a bludgeon against their rival "independent producers." He failed on this occasion, though later achieved the same goal by other means. In any event, Standard Oil continued to receive preferential treatment from the railroads throughout its early history, a factor of singular importance in explaining Rockefeller's spectacular success as an oilman.

Expansion alone, however, could not bring the kind of order to the industry Rockefeller envisioned. Centralization and consolidation were needed as well. Some entrepreneurs relied upon voluntary arrangements among themselves—e.g., "pools"—to control production, prices, and marketing areas, and thus to bring a measure of order to their industries. Rockefeller had no use for such "gentleman's agreements," probably because he took a hard-headed view of human nature and knew they would fall apart under pressure. Instead, he sought some legal device through which to refashion the oil industry. He found it in the trust, an arrangement wherein the companies comprising the sprawling Standard Oil empire in 1879 turned over their capital to a board of trustees that, in turn, coordinated and directed the affairs of the resultant huge accumulation of capital. The Standard Oil Trust was a model for other industrial combinations in the 1880s and a milestone in the movement to organize the new economy in a systematic fashion. At its peak it brought some 20 constituent companies together in a powerful, centrally-directed consortium—producers, refiners, pipelines, merchandisers, and tankers. In an industry where technology and convulsive shifts in demand made adaptation to change a way of life, Rockefeller through his trust managed to introduce an element of stability without sacrificing progress. In the 1880s Standard built a network of pipelines throughout the oil regions, established a comprehensive national marketing organization, and introduced manifold economies in production—all at a cost, of course, of eliminating much of its competition.

And that was the rub, in the opinion of Rockefeller's critics. For the Standard Oil Trust aroused anew the historic American distrust of unbridled bigness and monopoly. To a generation still confused by the dawning realization that competition and economic growth might not be compatible partners, Rockefeller's empire symbolized an awesome threat to traditional laissez faire individualism. Battered by an increasingly hostile public opinion and a series of court actions aimed at destroying its charter, the great combination in 1899 abandoned the trust device in favor of a vast holding company, Standard Oil of New Jersey. But the new corporation did not abandon Rockefeller's dream of order, and it continued the consolidating and centralizing thrust of its predecessor until it, too, ran afoul of the antitrust laws and was ordered by the Supreme Court in 1911 to disband.

Much of the public's suspicion of Standard Oil doubtless reflected distrust of Rockefeller himself. A man of single-minded interest, utterly devoid of any visceral feeling for public relations, he projected an image to the world of a sharp Yankee trader, ever on the hunt for unsuspecting victims. Disdainful of emotions in business, he shunned any public display of feeling as well. As a consequence, his enemies found it easy to depict him as an austere, humorless machine, intent only upon getting what he wanted from life. His very conventionality—his plain manner of dressing, his prudish piety, his economy of expression—made him a figure readily parodied and caricatured. Even after he retired from business to enter upon a new career of giving away his millions, a quality of meanness pursued him, at least in his public image. In the depths of the Great Depression of the 1930s, an ever-popular newsreel subject was the aged

Rockefeller, tottering about on the golf course, and handing out thin dimes to those he encountered, rich and poor alike.

In truth, Rockefeller had little to contribute outside his world of business, except his money and some occasional advice on golf. Content to live a planned and orderly life, in a sense he only projected his most intimate self into the business world when he sought to impose rationality upon his industry. In business and in life generally, what he enjoyed most was harmonious organization. And there can be little doubt of his brilliance as an organizer—a superorganizer, indeed, of a very disorderly industry. In that sense, he was the outstanding business genius of 19th-century America. For capitalism in the post-Civil War era was really a self-sustaining phenomenon, that needed more to be controlled and disciplined than to be stimulated by mere men, and John D. Rockefeller was above all a master disciplinarian.

He was also a master moneymaker, of course, who retired from business in 1912 with a personal fortune of a billion dollars. But in the great game of business enterprise, he had never sought solely or even primarily to make more money than his rivals. Rather, Rockefeller had relished most the opportunity business gave him to evoke his genius in bringing an industry to maturity. In philanthropy, too, the same passion for order guided him. With characteristic attention to detail, he gave money to churches and charities from the day he earned his first dollar. As his fortune grew, so did his donations; and after 1912 he took up philanthropy with much the same careful, persistent zeal he had brought to the oil business. Superbly conceived and organized, the great foundations he endowed, the universities he underwrote, the research hospitals he founded all became models of efficiency and productivity for other philanthropists to emulate. Together with the industrial empire he molded, they stand today as monuments to an authentic American hero, albeit a rather dull one. They also testify to the truth that in American society at large, as in industry, the drive toward consolidation and centralization that Rockefeller epitomized had destroyed the myth of free competition.

By the time he died in 1937, Rockefeller had divested himself of some $600,000,000. God gave him his money, made him its trustee, and guided him in using the money wisely and well. For the son of Eliza Davison, it was a life well lived.

* * *

Andrew Carnegie never believed God gave him his money, because Andrew Carnegie never believed in God. Not, at least, in the wrathful personal Jehovah of his friend Rockefeller and most other American Protestants. Oddly enough, one of his many philanthropies was the giving of pipe organs to churches—7,689 pipe organs, in all. Churches, after all, were maintainers of social stability. But on the rare occasions when he ventured inside a church himself, it was more to find confirmation of his skepticism than to offer thanks to the Lord or ask forgiveness for his sins. How, indeed, could one ask forgiveness for sins never committed?

Not that he was a confirmed unbeliever. In a life devoted almost as much to romantic speculation about the human condition as to selling more iron and steel than anyone else on Earth, he could hardly have avoided giving some thought to the eternal mystery, if only to help him understand his own extraordinary career. Alone among his fellow entrepreneurs in the Gilded Age, Carnegie found the time to dabble in such esoteric—and highly unbusinesslike—activities as the study of Oriental cultures and religions. It was superficial study, to be sure; but Carnegie even visited East Asia to investigate for himself what effects the contemplative religions of China and India had on the masses of people in those huge countries.

For himself, ultimately, he came only to acknowledge the existence of some "Supreme Force" in the universe, which he credited with having fashioned a grand design for mankind. In effect, he made a religion of Progress—a ripening faith in the inevitable movement of all things toward perfection. For Carnegie, a religion of Progress confirmed everything he wanted so badly to believe about the "inevitability" of his own accumulation of worldly wealth and power. Moreover, he liked its simple litany—"All is well since all grows better"—which fit so comfortably into his enthusiastic, if wrongheaded, reading of his idol Herbert Spencer's "social Darwinism." Unlike Rockefeller's stern faith, the religion of Progress did not press unduly for an explanation of how one acquired wealth. But it tapped insistently enough at one's conscience to elicit some accounting for wealth once acquired. Carnegie's response to this moral imperative was the Gospel of Wealth, a self-serving injunction upon men of wealth to become "mere trustees" of their riches for the benefit of their poorer brethren. The Gospel of Wealth differed from Rockefeller's notion of stewardship only in its lack of heavenly supervision, and it moved Carnegie also to make a second career of giving away his money.

But only after his remarkable first career had given America one of its great success stories. Indeed, of all the entrepreneurs, Carnegie came closest to epitomizing the myth of rags to riches. Born in 1835 in Dunfermline, Scotland, he grew up in a respectably poor family, but also in an environment vibrant with the radicalism of Chartism (an English workingmen's social reform movement) and tinged with literary pretensions. Both the radical and literary influences remained with him for life, although neither ever developed beyond a level of superficiality. Carnegie thought of himself as a profound thinker and serious reformer. He was neither, largely because he was never able to distinguish between means and ends, in either a moral or a practical sense. This confusion accounts for many of the contradictions in his life. As one of his biographers observed, his sympathy with Chartism made him "a rebel with a cause but without any understanding of effect"; and this flaw spotted his character for life.

Hard times in the Lowlands drove the Carnegies to America in 1848, where they settled in the grimy industrial boomtown of Pittsburgh. While not really "rag poor," the family had only its labor to sustain it, and Andy was sent out to work at once. That suited the ambitious towhead fine, for already, at age 13, he was eager to make his mark in the world. After a brief stint as bobbin boy in a mill (at $1.20 a week), he became a messenger for a local telegraph office. There his restless curiosity and compulsive drive took hold: he quickly mastered telegraphy and became one of the first operators in the United States to take messages by sound. He also found time to study double-entry bookkeeping; and, if he was never quite the equal of Rockefeller as a master of the account books, his skill at accounting was unquestionably one key to his success in business.

Luck came his way in 1853 in the person of Thomas A. Scott, a rising power in the Pennsylvania Railroad. Scott liked Andy and made him his personal telegrapher and private secretary. In effect, he set the young immigrant lad on the track that would take him, with astonishing rapidity, to the very pinnacles of economic success. "Mr. Scott's Andy," as Carnegie was known in those early years, moved up the railroad hierarchy with his benefactor, then went with him to Washington in 1861 when Scott became Assistant Secretary of War. Scott gave Carnegie free play to develop his genius as a salesman, sending him to Europe and Britain to peddle the railroad securities that underwrote much of the postwar expansion of the American rail network. With his handsome commissions from these sales, Carnegie invested widely and wisely—usually with Scott's advice —and by 1868 he was earning $50,000 a year and talking of retiring. But it was talk only, for the lure of capitalism and the excitement of moving in ever higher business and social circles were not to be shaken so easily. Instead of retiring, he moved to New York, a city that provided him with a wealth of opportunities to exercise his insatiable curiosity, while it also put him at the very center of the developing American industrial-financial complex. Gradually, too, he began to focus his investments on the iron industry, especially on those companies that were feeding the ravenous appetite of the railroads for iron products. In 1872 he built the J. Edgar Thompson Steel Works, a giant Bessemer process plant that netted him huge profits, even during the depression years of the mid-1870s.

One of Carnegie's contributions to 19th-century entrepreneurship, indeed, was to upend the notion that businesses should contract their operations during hard times. Maintaining that steady production was cheaper than shutting down operations, even if it meant that prices fell below costs, he kept his plants "running full" when business was poor and built up a productive capacity and a surplus of products with which he undercut his competitors, both at home and abroad, when good times returned. Totally unafraid of innovation, he equipped his plants with the most modern and efficient machinery and unhesitatingly abandoned machines and processes as they became obsolete. Determined to keep costs at a minimum, Carnegie familiarized himself with every operation in the steel industry; nothing escaped his attention, and he had a gift for spotting precisely the point at which economies could be effected or efficiency increased. But he was not so much a great ironmaster, really, as a superb marketer. Developing an aggressive sales force and technique, he built up the demand for his products, especially among the railroads, then followed through by delivering products of the highest quality to his customers. No industrialist in America knew more about world market conditions, and his uncanny ability to anticipate demand kept him always ahead of his rivals. In 1887, sensing the impending end of the railroad boom and the onset of a great upsurge in the building industry, he shifted the bulk of production at his mills from rails to construction steel. That bit of foresight alone insured him enormous profits over the next decade.

Fearing that the big bankers would wrest control from his hands, Carnegie studiously avoided incorporating his enterprises. Instead, he built a limited, but expandable, partnership in which he held the majority of shares. Nothing served him better as a business leader than his genius for picking good men to work for him, then stimulating them to perform incredible feats of production and marketing. As a good "social Darwinist," he set them to competing among themselves, and the "fittest" who survived the struggle he took into the partnership. They chafed under his tight control and yearned for a bigger share of the profits he so stubbornly insisted upon plowing back into the business; but they learned from him, too, and many went on later to luminous careers of their own.

Carnegie himself relished the competitive struggle. In 1872 he built the Lucy Furnace in Pittsburgh, a huge blast furnace clearly capable of outdoing the prevailing production average of 50 tons of pig iron a day. When his rivals built another giant, the Isabella Furnace, he accepted the challenge eagerly; and over the next decade, Lucy and Isabella engaged in fierce competition, breaking record after record, until both were producing over 300 tons a day.

Never as distrustful of laissez faire as most other successful entrepreneurs of his time, Carnegie honestly extolled the virtues of free enterprise, even as he built an industrial empire that helped in the end to cripple free enterprise. He always thought of himself as a self-reliant individualist, governed only by the imperatives of the marketplace. Although he was not above entering into an occasional pool or agreement to restrict competition by manipulating prices, he disliked such arrangements because they denigrated the element of individual enterprise. "Whatever I engage in I must push inordinately," he confessed, and there was, indeed, always a reckless, highly personal, quality about his business operations that sometimes alarmed his partners and sent shudders through the massive frame of that champion of order, J. P. Morgan. Like the oil business, the post-Civil War iron industry presented a picture of chaotic competition, characterized by price-gouging, cutthroat rivalries, and miasmic uncertainty. From the chaos, Carnegie emerged as the dominant figure; but, unlike Rockefeller, he was never driven by a passion to impose order for its own sake or create quiet harmony throughout the industry. Rather, he simply did with uncommon zeal that which he knew best how to do—organize men and machines, anticipate demand, publicize products, create markets.

In the process, of course, he imposed his will upon much of the steel industry, if only because he understood so clearly that growth and modernization were the keys to survival in the explosive economy of the Gilded Age. As his horizontal structure grew during the 1880s, his control over such outside factors as raw materials and finishing processes became a matter of increasing importance and concern. Thus, a major development in the growth of his empire was his absorption of the thriving Frick Coke Company. That move insured him a supply of coke, a critical raw material in the making of steel, while in the person of Henry Clay Frick it brought a cold, hard-headed entrepreneur into the highest echelons of the Carnegie enterprises. Possessed of a "positive genius for management," in Carnegie's words, Frick led the great combination in an aggressive campaign of vertical expansion and integration in the 1890s. In 1892 all of Carnegie's holdings were consolidated into the Carnegie Steel Company, a move that set the stage for other gigantic industrial consolidations in the 20th century. Then, in a fruitful deal with Rockefeller that reflected the shrewd good sense of both men, Carnegie obtained from the oil magnate a promise not to enter the steel business, in exchange for his own pledge to lease only Rockefeller-owned properties in the great Mesabi iron ore fields of Minnesota. With his access to this vast reservoir of raw materials thus assured, Carnegie carried ore in his own ships to a port he built on Lake Erie's south shore specifically to receive it, then transshipped it to his smelters at Pittsburgh over a railroad line he laid out and operated. Nor did he neglect the other end of the production line, for the Carnegie Steel Company also began to manufacture finished steel products.

Perhaps Carnegie did all this with the lofty goal in mind of bringing some rational order to the entire steel industry. More likely, he was simply strengthening his defenses in the seemingly endless competitive struggle among steel producers. Other large steel combines emerged in the 1890s, and Carnegie had little choice but to expand, consolidate, and integrate, if he wished to maintain his strong position. In any event, the campaign was a brilliant success, and at the end of the century Andrew Carnegie was the world's largest producer of steel and clearly master of the industry.

Carnegie likely went to his grave convinced that his business career had been a succession of blameless moves for the benefit of mankind. As a young man, he had made a remarkably swift and thorough assimilation to his adopted country, and as he grew older he tended increasingly to identify his own achievements with the manifest superiority, as he saw it, of the United States. "The old nations of the Earth creep on at a snail's pace; the Republic thunders past with the rush of the express," he wrote in his strange book, *Triumphant Democracy*. He conceived the book as a defense of American democracy; in reality, it was an uncritical justification of American capitalism and, by implication, of one very successful American capitalist, Andrew Carnegie. Indeed, it was one of many manifestations, albeit an elaborate one, of his lifelong compulsion to justify himself and his actions to the world. Carnegie wanted desperately to be remembered as what Robert G. McCloskey calls a "moral humanitarian," and his great philanthropies gave him a substantial claim to the title. But both his morality and his humanitarianism were flawed, the imperfection residing in his puzzling inability—or unwillingness—to reconcile cause and effect, means and ends. Truly a rebel with many causes, too often he was insensitive to effects, especially as they touched the lives of other people. Doubtless, his craftiness in manipulating the careers of his partners was offset by the benefits they derived in other ways from their association with him. But there was downright cruelty in his calculated refusal to come to the rescue of his benefactor Tom Scott, when the older man was slipping into financial ruin.

Above all, the streak of insensitivity showed in his relations with the working class. Himself a mere transient in poverty, he somehow convinced himself later that to be poor was to know true dignity. Life in the "humble cottages" of the poor, he insisted, was greatly to be preferred to life in the palaces of the rich. If the poor knew what terrible responsibilities wealth imposed upon its owners, they would happily rest content with what they had. In all the literature of uplift, few passages compare for sheer self-righteousness with the advice Carnegie offered to the young during the depression of the 1890s: "We should be quite willing to abolish luxury, but to abolish honest, industrious, self-denying poverty would be to destroy the soil upon which mankind produces its virtues which enable our race to reach a still higher civilization than it now possesses." During the same economic crisis, his romantic radicalism, as well as his moral humanitarianism, were put to a test which both failed miserably. Earlier, Carnegie had written an extraordinary essay for a national magazine, defending the right to strike, deploring the conditions in industry that drove men to strike, and condemning the use of strikebreakers: "Thou shalt not take thy neighbor's job." But when workers at his Homestead plant called a strike in 1892 to protest drastic wage reductions, Carnegie gave Frick a free hand to provoke a confrontation with the union and drive it from the plant. The result was the bloody Homestead Massacre, a pitched battle between strikers and strikebreakers, which claimed ten lives and effectively crushed unionism in the steel industry for half a century.

At his castle in Scotland, where he had gone to vacation after approving Frick's plan to break the union, Carnegie grieved over the loss of life. But he could never bring himself to acknowledge moral responsibility for one of the worst outrages in American labor history. Nor did he comprehend the hypocrisy that struck like a cleaver at his standard of values, sharply dividing what he said from what he did. But, "all is well since all grows better"; in the solace of "social Darwinism" and its celebration of the survival of the fittest, Carnegie could rationalize the unfortunate Homestead affair.

Ironically, the restless, aggressive expansionism of the Carnegie forces in the 1890s convinced the great bankers that the time had come to take the steel industry out of the hands of such strong-willed individualists as Carnegie and bring it under unified, systematized control. At the very peak of his success, Carnegie had become a threat to order. But he had also come to a realization himself that the evolutionary process had brought the day near when unbridled entrepreneurship must give way to a more orderly system. Resigned to the inevitable, he authorized his agents to open the negotiations that led, in 1901, to the formation of the supercorporation, United States Steel. At the time he turned his business over to the Morgan interests, the Carnegie works were returning an annual profit of $40,000,000, of which his own share was $25,000,000. His life was a great American success story, but his Chartist forebears in Scotland would never have understood it.

*   *   *

J. Pierpont Morgan liked yachts, solitaire, beautiful women, and power. Among his pet dislikes, after competition and democracy, were Andrew Carnegie and John D. Rockefeller—the brassy little Scot for calling him Pierpont to his face, the pious oil titan for having what Morgan thought was a cold lust for money. From time to time he had to do business directly with mere millionaires of this sort, but he much preferred dealing with them through intermediaries to spending time in their company.

Morgan was very choosy about the people he permitted to come into his presence, and those blessed with the privilege almost always came entirely on his terms. Almost everything he did, indeed, was on his terms. To be sure, an occasion or two arose when he was forced to bend to the will of others, as when a president of the United States ungraciously spurned his suggestion to call off an anti-trust suit against a Morgan holding company, or when a committee of Congress was so insensitive to his privacy as to make him testify publicly about his money. Situations of that sort were distasteful in the extreme to him, and he could never understand how others could be so "ungentlemanly" as to let them come about. Few men in American history ever were so blandly accustomed to having their own way about so many things as this coldly impressive giant of the financial world.

In the international imperium of banking, John Pierpont Morgan was born to the purple. His father, a banker with interests on both sides of the Atlantic, was instrumental in starting the flow of European capital into the developing American economy, and the family wealth went back several generations in New England. On the maternal side, a streak of impetuous romanticism, coupled with religious mysticism, came down through the generations to touch Morgan's character with certain strange qualities that were utterly alien to the image of nerveless strength he projected as a financier. Young Morgan grew up in an urbane and supremely confident environment, one in which he might naturally have assumed early in life that Morgans were a very special breed of people. Still, as a youth he was morose and sluggish, lacking in friends and seemingly without much talent for anything. His schooling began in Boston and ended at a German university, where he studied mathematics briefly and excelled at accounting. In 1856, at the age of 19, he entered his father's London banking house and a few years later settled in New York as the firm's American agent. During the Civil War he paid a substitute to serve for him, while he foolishly involved himself in several shoddy war-profiteering schemes. But these indiscretions only momentarily sullied his reputation. After the war, Morgan quickly established himself as a dominant and prestigious figure in American business and a powerful member of the world banking community.

He made his name chiefly through his skill as an organizer and integrating force in the disorderly American economy of the postwar years. Like Rockefeller, Morgan had a passion for order: the spectacle of railroads and other corporations squabbling among themselves, engaging in insane price wars, and threatening the whole economy with disaster, genuinely appalled him. As an internationalist, he perceived better than most Americans of his day that foreign investors would not long continue to underwrite an economy that tolerated the banditry of buccaneers like Jay Gould and Jim Fisk, while it showed no signs of developing in an orderly, rational manner. The interests of his growing transatlantic banking business alone demanded that he do something to end this competitive madness, especially in the railroad industry, where near anarchy had come to prevail in the 1870s. After a few preliminary thrusts, he took a bold step in 1879. In a brilliantly successful negotiation for William H. Vanderbilt, he secretly disposed of 250,000 shares of New York Central stock in Europe at an enormous profit to the railroad baron. Together with $3,000,000 in commissions, the deal netted Morgan a seat on the railroad's board of directors. Traditionally, bankers had played a passive role in economic development, serving as the financial agents of businessmen, but taking little part in matters of basic organization and management. As a director of the New York Central, Morgan signaled a change in this state of affairs. From being mere intermediaries, henceforth the big bankers would become the principal organizers of the economy, imposing their rules upon management and injecting at last an element of rationality into the industrial picture.

The change did not come overnight, as Morgan moved into his new role slowly and with meticulous care. It was never his method to buy up companies indiscriminately and throw them together in some scattershot combination. Rather, he assumed control of them in subtle, discreet ways, using his access to vast reservoirs of capital to force financially troubled businesses to come to him, where he dealt with them on his terms. And his terms were little short of revolutionary, in the results they effected in the railroading industry. If he deemed a company worth saving, he imposed three conditions upon its managers as central to its refinancing and reorganization. First, they must guarantee future solvency by slashing fixed charges to a bare minimum, even if this meant foregoing dividend payments on common stock. Second, they must enter into a general "community of interest," in which the competitive drive that had brought them to ruin would be replaced by cooperation among all units within the industry. Third, the board of directors of the reorganized company must be dominated by members appointed by the House of Morgan. In the 1880s, most railroad leaders were still sufficiently solvent that they could evade the net Morgan and other large bankers were setting for them.

One memorable encounter in 1885, however, underscored the growing influence of the financial wizards over even the most powerful industrialists. Chafing under the monopolistic conditions imposed by the Pennsylvania Railroad in carrying his steel from Pittsburgh to the east coast, Andrew Carnegie proposed to build a competing line and lured Vanderbilt into supporting his scheme. "Carnegie is going to demoralize the railroads just as he has demoralized steel," Morgan fumed, when he learned of the plan. Dismayed at the prospect of a ruinous competitive war between two giant railroads, the Pennsylvania and the New York Central, he mobilized his capital resources and, at a "peace conference" aboard his yacht *Corsair*, he not only scotched the plan, but even managed to turn the affair to his own financial advantage. The encounter left Carnegie deeply distrustful of the banker, while it convinced Morgan that Carnegie was an "irresponsible" man. The two titans would deal again in the future, however, and for vastly higher stakes.

When the Panic of 1893 struck, the power of the House of Morgan swept through the railroads like a reaper. In the epidemic of bankruptcies that was a legacy of two decades of speculation and overcapitalization, the railroad men had no choice but to turn to Morgan and the other big bankers for their financial salvation. A wave of reorganization ensued, leaving at the end of the decade three great combinations in effective control of the nation's railroad systems, and one of these combinations was Morgan's.

This sweeping power was by no means confined to the railroads, moreover. Alert to the general drift of the economy, Morgan was instrumental in developing such industrial giants as International Harvester, American Telephone & Telegraph, and General Electric. He was an early backer of Thomas A. Edison. His stubborn insistence on dealing only with "gentlemen" sometimes cost him dearly, in the sense of golden opportunities lost. But the Morgan influence—subtle, often undiscernible, but always real to those who encountered it—penetrated every sector of the economy.

Inevitably he turned to the steel industry, which had become, by the 1890s, the key industry in the new economy. Morgan's first sally into the business was to organize the Federal Steel Company, an ultramodern plant that he put under the general management of Elbert Gary, a Chicago lawyer who knew absolutely nothing about making steel. That small deficiency bothered Morgan not at all, however, for he trusted Gary and "trust" was the chief criterion by which he judged the men who worked for him. Using Federal as a base, he set out to do for steel what he had done for railroading: reorganize the industry along rational lines, eliminate the competitive factor, impose management that would insure orderly development and sound finances. But he could achieve his grandiose goal only by coming to terms with the master steelmaker of them all, Carnegie. When the opportunity at last arose to buy out the Carnegie empire, Morgan was at first uncertain that he could raise the required capital. But the need to put a harness on the restless Scot once and for all was so imperative that he worked his genius overtime and brought together the stupendous sums that closed the deal. At a meeting of the two men some months later, Carnegie commented: "I made one mistake, Pierpont, when I sold out to you. I should have asked for a hundred million more than I did." To which the laconic response was: "Well, you would have got it if you had."

The photographer Edward Steichen once likened meeting J. P. Morgan's gaze to confronting head-on the headlights of an express train approaching at full throttle. Much of the banker's power, doubtless, stemmed from his commanding personality and presence. He was a man of decision and concentration, capable of overwhelming other men with the sheer force of his mental vigor. In business affairs he was abrupt and dictatorial, brooking no alternatives to the ultimatums he laid down. He scarcely understood the meaning of compromise; and in his presence, one either quaked or surrendered complete confidence in his judgment. He knew the precise point in a negotiation at which to lose his temper—or, at least, to appear angry—and few men could stand up to his anger. His very physique was commanding: massive frame, broad shoulders, large head, piercing eyes. Throughout his life he suffered from an uncomfortable skin disease, that ultimately turned his naturally powerful nose into a bulbous, discolored monstrosity. He was painfully sensitive about it, but some observers thought the affliction only heightened the impression of power he projected. A man of strong and often violent feelings, he was brutally insensitive to the feelings of others, especially if he sensed what he thought was weakness in them. For all his blunt prejudices, he had a talent for picking able men to work for him. But he worked them almost to death and was totally oblivious to the terrible strains he subjected them to.

The private Morgan had qualities somewhat less severe, though no less impressive. At his Hudson River estate he lived the life of an English country squire, raising dogs and blooded cattle, doting on his children and grandchildren. Religion was a profound and everyday part of his life. At times, indeed, Morgan withdrew into spells of deep solitude and melancholy, when religious contemplation expelled all other considerations from his mind. He loved the ritual and orderly conservatism of the Episcopal Church, to which he contributed lavishly of his time and money, and he regularly attended the triennial Episcopal Conventions, debating with clerics and fellow laymen minute points of church governance and litany. A man of slight intellectual bent, he was nonetheless a voracious reader of church history. Had he not given himself to the world of finance, he would have made a splendid archbishop, albeit an utterly authoritarian one.

As it was, he was a latter day Renaissance prince. Morgan disliked the epithet "Pierpontifex Maximus" some wag coined for him, but he rather enjoyed being compared to Lorenzo the Magnificent. Like a Medici prince, he lived to the hilt: lavish parties, beautiful women, fine wines, good food. Nothing pleased him more than his yachts, of which he had three in succession, all named *Corsair* and each one longer and more magnificently appointed than its predecessor. On them he traveled in kingly fashion to the smart places of the world. As he grew older, Rome and Cairo became his favorite haunts, probably because they evoked a pervasive sense of past grandeur that appealed to his romantic streak. He was a great collector of art; indeed, he aspired to dominate the field of collecting as he dominated entire industries. Downright undiscriminating in his tastes, he dispatched raiding parties throughout Europe to buy up whole collections of books, manuscripts, paintings, bronzes, snuffboxes, watches—anything of value that was for sale. His philanthropy, too, reflected a quality of impetuosity that might have produced disasters in his business affairs. Rather than dispose of his wealth in a systematic fashion for the considered good of society, Morgan gave much of his money away in spur of the moment gestures, often emotionally inspired.

Obviously, a man of such temperament had no use for the masses. Indeed, Morgan was contemptuous of ordinary men and totally oblivious to the social ills of his time. One contemporary, stung by an encounter with him, described him as a man "so swollen with pride and a sense of his own power that it never occurs to him that other people have any rights." Morgan required no elaborate "social Darwinist" rationale for his public life, and he considered his private life to be no one's business but his and God's. He saw his business ventures as acts of high responsibility, which contributed to corporate stability and served to drive "dangerous elements" out of the economic picture. Moreover, Morgan considered himself a true patriot. After all, had he not responded faithfully to President Cleveland's plea in 1895 to save the credit of the United States by lending the Treasury $65 million in gold? It mattered little that he made a commission on the transaction—just how high a commission he refused to reveal. His sole aim, he insisted, was "to secure the gold that the government needed and to save the panic and widespread disaster that was sure to follow if the gold was not got." Again in the panic of 1907, Morgan saw himself as a stabilizing force in the economy, using his prestige to inspire confidence among other financiers and channel money to trouble spots.

Thus, it was with acute pain and genuine puzzlement that Morgan found himself, in his late years, a public symbol of a grasping, insatiable money trust. According to investigators for the Pujo Committee of the House of Representatives, Morgan and several other banking syndicates had a stranglehold on the American economy by reason of their vast financial holdings and interlocking directorships in the nation's largest corporations. Called to endure the ordeal of public testimony before the committee, Morgan acquitted himself well. He simply denied everything, portraying himself as a simple banker who had always made "character," not money, the primary factor in his business.

Morgan never understood why the public distrusted him or how the government could have been so ungrateful as to humiliate him publicly. Shortly after his appearance before Congress, he sailed *Corsair III* to Cairo, where he died a few months later. Article I of his will affirmed his complete faith in the doctrine of atonement: J. P. Morgan died with the same self-assurance with which he lived.

*   *   *

The "new order" in industry Morgan and his fellow bankers introduced never worked the way they hoped it would. Part of the problem was traceable to the type of management they instituted. Morgan never thought in terms of the people who worked in industry, or even of the machines they operated. His sole concern was with the officers who oversaw the enterprise and the investors who financed it, and he was quite content to leave matters of administration in the hands of "honest gentlemen." Into positions once held by steelmakers, railroad men, and experienced manufacturers, he put a new breed of manager—bankers, lawyers, and other men of "character." Utterly beholden to him, these men typically lacked imagination and boldness, not to say expertise. Unlike the great entrepreneurs, they were timid when it came to innovation, inexpert in technical matters. None displayed the inventiveness or willingness to take chances of a Rockefeller. None had the restless curiosity of a Carnegie or the sweep of vision that had made the Carnegie works the most modern in the world. Ironically, the supercorporation of which Carnegie's plants became a part soon fell behind its competitors, at home and abroad, in producing the steel demanded by industry in the new century.

Moreover, the very fact that United States Steel still had competitors testified to the persistence of "irrational" factors in the economy. Despite their best efforts and enormous financial power, Morgan and his allies never succeeded in making their system foolproof against disruption and discordance. Doubtless, their efforts were doomed from the start. To bring the industrial equation into genuine harmony required unerring, unchallengeable, control of raw materials, transportation, basic manufacturing processes, the labor market and wages, the creation and exploitation of markets, techniques of distribution, price structures, and sources of capital. No individual or group—not the heroic entrepreneur, not any consortium of bankers, not even government, to which businessmen turned in the 20th century for both capital and direction—could master each element and bring them all together in some rational whole.

The most successful businessmen in the age of enterprise were always driven, to some degree, by a vision of order. At its most utopian, the vision contemplated a time when panics and depressions would become outmoded, because rational men would not permit such violations of good order. The imperatives of the vision accounted in considerable measure for the compulsive drive of the entrepreneurs and financiers of 19th century business and for the startling rapidity with which the modern industrial complex came into being. But the achievement of harmony also required stability within the overall economy, and the American economy simply refused to stand still long enough for any measure of rational control to take full effect. This central problem plagued Rockefeller as he tried to make sense out of a chaotic industry; it kept Carnegie immersed in an endless competitive struggle; and it frustrated the imperious designs of the most powerful banker in the world, J. P. Morgan. It continues to defy the best efforts of governments, businesses, and men and women in our own time.

2

Social Science and the New Industrial Society

WILLIAM GRAHAM SUMNER
LESTER FRANK WARD
THORSTEIN BUNDE VEBLEN

by Howard H. Quint
University of Massachusetts, Amherst

So much do we take the social sciences as a matter of course today that we may not realize that they came into existence in the United States a short hundred years ago and achieved academic acceptance and respectability only after the beginning of the 20th century. Then as now, social scientists took upon themselves the task of analyzing their own society. Then as now, they lived in a period characterized by extensive and often revolutionary changes in technology and economic organization, scientific knowledge, political ideology, social structure, religious and philosophical assumptions, and ways of understanding man himself. Though most innovations in social science theory and methodology in the half century, 1875–1925, originated in Europe, the United States was not without contributors. Among the most prominent of them were William Graham Sumner, a clergyman turned economist and anthropologist; Lester Frank Ward, a natural scientist turned sociologist; and Thorstein Bunde Veblen, a philosopher turned economist.

The erudition of these men was breathtaking, and their understanding of contemporary affairs stands up well in historical retrospect. They worked without the various technical aids that facilitate modern social science research, and this very fact may account in part for the human emphasis in their writings as against the mechanical and methodological. One need not be a mathematician or statistician to understand what they wrote, although both Ward and Veblen invented some pretty atrocious social science terminology.

Sumner, Ward, and Veblen all taught in American universities. Academe was good to Sumner, as indeed it should have been, for he was a strong scholar and a great teacher during his lengthy career at Yale. It was less appreciative of Ward who did not receive a professorship at Brown until comparatively late in life, despite his previous universal recognition as both sociologist and natural scientist. It was more hostile than friendly to Thorstein Veblen, albeit his difficulties at various universities were probably more the result of his personality than his unorthodox approach to economics. But scholarly recognition sometimes comes post mortem and in not completely expected ways. Today Sumner's social analysis is substantially rejected, although his strictly anthropological work continues to stand up quite well. Ward's sociology is out of date and largely forgotten, although recently women liberationists have "discovered" his writings in behalf of sex equality. Veblen's institutional economics is of little interest to our contemporary economic theorists and model builders, although his diagnosis of the new industrial society, unlike those of Sumner and Ward, has remained as fresh and trenchent as the day it was first written.

*   *   *

Romanticism and William Graham Sumner had very little to do with each other. From the time of his birth in 1840 to the time of his death in 1910, Sumner had no Emersonian affection for the world he lived in or for his fellow men. And this despite the fact that he began his career as a minister of God. Sumner was the ablest spokesman for the social conservatism and the materialism of the Gilded Age. He was America's foremost intellectual advocate of Social Darwinism which, simply stated, held that the same evolutionary laws that applied to nature and other animals likewise governed man. Few rivaled him in defending laissez faire as a general policy for social and economic deportment, although few were also willing to be as consistent as he in adhering to it. Sumner bluntly justified an economic order based upon the jungle law of the tooth and the fang, held that poverty and want were "an essential part of the social order," and consigned the poor and the weak—those who were not "adapted" to the demands of a capitalist-dominated society and hence "unfit"—to social extinction. He made culture heroes of the new class of industrial capitalists who could hardly pass muster if measured against the criteria of Jeffersonian democracy. Sumner likewise denied the desirability of a society premised on the idea of equality and refused to accept the traditional American belief in the wisdom and rightness of "the people" as expressed at the polls.

Sumner's origins were humble. He was the son of a Paterson, New Jersey, machinist, Thomas Sumner, who had emigrated from England. Hard-working, hard-headed, frugal, and largely self-educated, Thomas Sumner imparted to his son his own Puritanical belief in thrift and personal self-discipline. There is reason to believe that Sumner's boyhood was drab and lonely. He and his brother and sister went their separate ways with a minimum of intimate communication. His mother died when he was eight; his stepmother, an austere woman, bestowed little attention on her adopted brood, let alone affection. Sumner consequently grew up in a home atmosphere that catered little to human feelings or sympathies. It was a brand on his own psyche and personality that he bore throughout his life.

Thomas Sumner, after trying his fortunes in the West, settled permanently in Hartford, Connecticut, where he worked as a machinist for the Hartford and New Haven Railroad. He somehow saved enough money to send his son to Yale College in 1859. At that bastion of Congregationalist orthodoxy and conservatism, young Sumner concentrated on theology and the study of ancient languages; he avoided such frivolities as reading fiction and participating in athletics. Among his small circle of friends were some rich young men, one of whom induced his brother not only to defray the cost of three years of post-graduate theological study for Sumner in Europe but also to pay for a substitute to serve for him in the Union army during the Civil War.

Upon Sumner's return to the United States, he accepted a tutorship at Yale from 1866 to 1869. But he was also preparing for the Episcopal priesthood, into which he was ordained in 1869. For the next few years the new clergyman edited a religious paper and served as rector of the Episcopal Church in Morristown, New Jersey. It is difficult to think of Sumner engaged in pastoral rounds or to imagine him bringing comfort to those in dire distress. Then in 1872, President Noah Porter, remembering Sumner's sterling academic record at Yale, brought him back to the College as Professor of Political and Social Science. He and the clergymen who constituted the Yale Corporation subsequently were to rue this appointment, when the new professor assigned to his students Herbert Spencer's *The Study of Sociology*. Along with many other American divines, Porter considered the panjandrum of Victorian social science an infidel or worse and wished to keep Yale free from his contaminating influence. But in a direct confrontation with Sumner on the issue, it was Porter who backed down, not his gruff, young colleague. Moreover, Sumner, while properly conservative in social and economic matters, was actually quite radical in his academic views. He wanted less attention given to the classics and more to the sciences, and even went so far as to recommend abolition of the study of philosophy from the College's curriculum. "Philosophy," said Sumner, "is in every way as bad as astrology. It is a complete fake . . . unworthy of serious consideration. It is an anachronism. We might just as well have professors of alchemy or fortune-telling or palmistry."

The more Sumner became involved in the study of social institutions, the less patience he had for abstract speculation of every kind—"gush," he called it. What interested him was objective fact. His empirical approach to knowledge as well as his crisp and dogmatic style of teaching appealed to students and before long, Sumner, though personally cold and forbidding, was the most popular professor at Yale. He also became the undisputed leader of the College's faculty and its most articulate commentator on public issues. For over 30 years he bombarded popular journals and newspapers with letters and articles, and frequently spoke from the public lecture program. Yale's alumni were not always pleased with Sumner, especially when he attacked protective tariffs.

Sumner's early teaching career was largely centered in political economy in which he earned a national reputation through his writings in defense of free trade and in opposition to the Populist monetary heresy of free silver and bimetalism. His later years at Yale were focused on the study of social institutions. Sumner taught the first course in sociology offered in an American university. He preferred to call it "the Science of Society," since he believed the still infant discipline of sociology to be dominated by humanitarian reformers who were more concerned with redesigning society than in studying it. Large-framed, bald, with steely eyes and drooping mustache, Sumner's physical presence pervaded the classroom. Likewise, his erudition was overwhelming; he was widely read in the natural and social sciences as well as in religion and the classics, and he possessed a working knowledge of at least a dozen languages. His lectures were meticulously organized and were devoid of the anecdotes that professors so often use to awaken the flagging attention of student audiences. For their part the students did not attend Professor Sumner's lectures to be amused or to challenge his presentation of the "facts." Sumner was one of the truly great teachers in American academic history, and few students went through Yale without taking one or more of his courses.

As often as not Sumner's ideas rested on unorthodox premises. Like most Americans, he was a moralist and a democrat. But his morality blended a curious mixture of materialism, relativism, and Calvinism, while his democracy was atypical in its rejection of the natural rights hypothesis, which he considered anthropologically unsound and historically unsupportable. Sumner's economic views were consistent with the laissez faire doctrines of the English Manchester School but, no less significantly, they were an integral component of his over-all analysis of social structure; he well might have arrived at them independently of any organized body of economic theory. In an era of militarism and imperialism, Sumner stood forthrightly in the ranks of the opposition. But again his position was unconventional in that it was based less on humanitarian concerns than on the wasteful and corrosive effects on those nations that resorted to them.

Sumner's unshakeable belief in natural law (contrary to his denial of natural rights), his own anthropological investigations, and Herbert Spencer's social determinism, all convinced him that competition was the law of life. In this competition, which prevailed equally in the primitive jungles and in the most advanced civilizations, the fittest survived and prospered. And along with Spencer, Sumner insisted it was best that they did, for the alternative was the survival and perpetuation of the unfit.

In the competitive struggles of modern life the sole obligation of organized society was to guarantee individual citizens the civil liberty necessary to the working out of their destinies. But, said Sumner, such liberty was not easy to maintain, since there were always those who would use the power of the State in efforts to achieve what they deemed to be a more equitable society. Here Sumner came down hard. It was not for the State, he asserted, to interfere in the competition among men. Nor was its function to make men happy in the "absurd effort to make the world over." Men sought happiness at their own risk. Sumner, thinking of self-reliant men like his father who asked little or nothing of society, asserted that every man was "expected to take care of himself and his family, to make no trouble for his neighbor, and to contribute his full share to public interests and common necessities."

Sumner reviewed the long evolution of mankind and concluded that whatever progress had been made over the centuries in the relentless struggle against the brute forces of nature was primarily the consequence of the application of human intelligence to technology. Indeed, man's earliest forms of social organization resulted from the desire to utilize technology more efficiently for industrial ends. A thorough-going materialist, Sumner, like Marx, held that a society's industrial sophistication determined the nature of its entire set of institutions and beliefs. It followed that those in whose hands industrial power resided also controlled all of the other elements of modern society.

Unlike Spencer, Sumner did not believe that the evolutionary process was synonymous with progress. Civilization had its periods of both advance and retrogression, depending on man's success in his struggles with nature and in his ability to live peacefully and harmoniously with his fellow man. The slow but steady accumulation of capital and the expansion of Europe to the four corners of the globe since the end of the 15th century had carried civilization to its highest stage of development, though Sumner was by no means sure that the forward march of mankind would continue. For he saw ominous clouds on the horizon that could destroy civilization in its totality.

Surveying his own country, Sumner was satisfied with the progress it had made. While readily acknowledging the courage and hard work of those men and women who had brought the United States to its present state of development, he also took note of their relative freedom historically from political and economic restraint. Equally important if not more important, had been the generosity of nature to Americans in terms of land and resources, a luxury that few of the other peoples of the world enjoyed. Sounding much like the historian Frederick Jackson Turner, a contemporary, Sumner ascribed American democracy more to a highly favorable man-land ratio than to any given set of ideological assumptions.

Indeed, Sumner saw the increasing resort to ideology as one of the most portentous forces in the late 19th-century American society. He thoroughly distrusted ideology as a kind of verbal legerdemain that had little if anything to do with reality. It was "easier to imagine a new world," he wrote, "than to learn to know this one." Ideology, framed in the sentimental rhetoric of humanitarianism and egalitarianism, was used to appeal to the masses of men by those seeking to exercise the power denied them by the working out of the evolutionary process.

Sumner had been a member of a group of "visiting statesmen" sent by the national Democratic Party to Louisiana for the purpose of observing the operations of a special board entrusted with validating the state's electoral vote in the disputed presidential election of 1876. There he had seen firsthand the venality of working politicians. He also had served three years on the Board of Aldermen in New Haven and was not overly impressed by the wisdom of his colleagues. Practical experience, then, had given Sumner reason to have strong doubts about popular government in the Gilded Age.

Sumner had other reasons to be uneasy with a political system that confused vox populi with vox Dei. What few Americans realized, he observed, was that their vaunted public opinion was often manipulated by designing men who obfuscated the real issues with the camouflage of democratic ideology. Or, conversely, when these same men were not affecting public opinion, they were responding to the clamor of popular majorities. As a consequence, they invariably enacted arbitrary and "speculative" legislation detrimental to the property rights of the hard-working middle-class citizen, Sumner's "forgotten man." It was he who paid the taxes that underwrote "paternalistic" legislation on behalf of the "poor and the weak."

Sumner had kind words for the great captains of industry, the new elite in American society. In his mind millionaires differed from the members of the middle class only to the extent that they were shrewder businessmen, more skilled organizers and entrepreneurs, and better accumulators of capital. Millionaires deserved respect rather than the public opprobrium they consistently received and accepted, so Sumner maintained, with "good humor." While admittedly millionaires got high wages and lived in luxury, the bargain was a good one for society since there was "the intensest competition for their place" at the top. "Where is the rich man," he asked, "who is oppressing anybody? What harm has ever been done by the Rothschild fortunes or those in America?" Sumner in effect was saying that the relentless pursuit of acquisition was not only morally right but that unrestrained capitalism was the economic correlative of political democracy.

As for the poor and the weak in society, there was no sensible reason for the State to ameliorate their condition. In the end it was better for society to allow them to go down the drain. Sumner conceded that there were victims of misfortunes beyond their personal control, and in such instances it was incumbent on private charity to extend aid, a practice he himself quietly followed. But he had no patience with the Biblical injunction that the poor and the meek were the blessed. People were poor and badly off, he maintained, because they were shiftless and unwilling to save themselves: in short, unable to adapt to the requirements of modern life. "The fact that man is here is no demand upon other people that they shall keep him alive and sustain him," Sumner wrote. But could poverty be eliminated? Yes, he replied. Simply "let every man be sober, industrious, prudent and wise and bring up his children to be so likewise." Yet Sumner also knew that this injunction would not be followed and that the poor would always be with us.

Sumner not only opposed using the power of the State for purposes of social reform but he also predicted that the extension of this power would have a baleful consequence unforeseen by democratic reformers. Once the State could determine the very life and death of all social and economic institutions, every special interest group would seek to obtain either partial or complete control of its political and administrative apparatus. Prominent among these special interest groups was the new industrial and financial plutocracy, which could use its wealth to corrupt the people's political representatives. While Sumner admired those rich men who ostensibly had gained wealth by their skill in the struggles of the competitive market, he scorned the plutocrat as a capitalist gone wrong. For the plutocrat corrupted the democratic political process by his persistent attempts to obtain monopoly control over the economy through protective tariffs, public charters and franchises, and other special favors from the State.

The American democracy could prevent the State from being taken over either by utopian reformers or by avaricious plutocrats, counselled Sumner, by pruning its functions so carefully and thoroughly that special interest groups would no longer care to control them. In brief, the State should confine itself to maintaining peace and public order. But Sumner did not take the extreme position of Herbert Spencer. For example, Sumner believed in tax-supported public schools and, as a good Victorian moralist, he thought it the State's duty to protect the condition of women against male predators ever poised to take advantage of their weakness and helplessness.

While Sumner disapproved of corporate monopolies created largely through government assistance and favoritism, he condoned industrial consolidation by business entrepreneurs. If the large corporation provided the best means of economizing in the production and distribution of industrial goods or in financing industry itself, businessmen would be foolish not to resort to it. The corporation, he held, was part and parcel of the development and refinement of capitalism. Once again Sumner's economic analysis is not unlike that of Karl Marx.

Logical consistency, one of Sumner's hallmarks, dictated that he accord workers the same right to organize as businessmen. Workers, he agreed, were entitled to improve their lot in the great competition of life if they could. Thus, Sumner, unlike most apologists in American capitalism in the late 19th century, did not condemn trade unions. He thought some were "exotic" and more attuned to English industrial conditions than those in the United States, but on the whole he deemed them "right and useful" and perhaps "necessary."

Sumner did not like strikes, but neither did he oppose them when conducted in such a way as not to disturb the public order or affect unduly the lives of innocent third parties. Strikes fell directly within the context of his belief in freedom of contract as well as in continuous competition in the industrial world. If workers individually or collectively were forced to enter into contracts that were not the best they thought they could obtain for themselves, "the relationship might serve as a definition of slavery." The ultimate test was whether strikes were successful, said Sumner, sounding very much the pragmatist.

Freemarket competition, constantly endangered by reformers and plutocrats, was also imperiled, said Sumner, by the growth of militarism and imperialism in the United States. Jingoist sentiment, exemplified by Theodore Roosevelt, had led to the construction of a costly new navy and to the Spanish-American War with its aftermath of overseas territorial expansion. Witnessing this development with dismay, Sumner brilliantly expressed his disapproval in a biting essay entitled "The Conquest of the United States by Spain." The war, he asserted, signalized the entry of the United States into the world of power politics and the diversion of its vast resources from peaceful to militaristic and imperialistic ends. The political and economic progress made over three centuries of historical development would henceforth be risked in saber-rattling confrontations with other imperialistic powers. "It is the essence of militarism," he noted, "that under it military men learn to despise constitutions, to sneer at parliaments and to look with contempt at civilians. . . ." It is militarism that forbids people to give their attention to the problems of their own welfare and to give their strength to the education and comfort of their children.

With the advent of the 20th century, Sumner's pessimism deepened. In declining health, he faced death without fear or regret. Convinced that he had lived during the best years of his country's history, he saw only decline and retrogression. Moreover, his perspectives had modified appreciably. While still a believer in "rugged individualism," his anthropological research had revealed to him the importance of the group, as against the individual, in social dynamics. Sumner's famous study *Folkways*, published four years before his death, revealed the full extent of his intellectual growth as well as the moral relativism that had come to dominate his thinking.

If earlier in his career Sumner had found the major danger to American democracy coming from misguided reformers who were attempting to thwart the laws of social evolution, he now saw the ever powerful plutocracy posing the greatest threat to the nation. In a ringing jeremiad he declared: "Every year that passes brings out this antagonism more distinctly. It is to be the social war of the 20th century. In that war, militarism, expansion, and imperialism will all favor plutocracy. . . . War and expansion will favor jobbery both in the dependencies and at home . . . they will take away the attention of the people from what the plutocrats are doing . . . they will cause large expenditures of the people's money, the return of which will not go into the treasury, but into the hands of a few schemers . . . they will call for a large public debt and taxes, and these things especially tend to make men unequal, because any social burdens bear more heavily on the weak than on the strong, and so make the weak weaker and the strong stronger."

Finally, Sumner, predicted that the nations of the world would fall under the sway of despots and that the world itself would be engulfed in the ruinous conflagration of continuous war. All of this would occur he said, because men would subordinate their individual judgments to ideological doctrines and submit to injustice and cruelty "for reasons of state." Sumner died on April 12, 1910; Joseph Stalin was then a young man of 30 and Adolf Hitler had just celebrated his twenty-first birthday.

Sumner's ideas go down hard today, as indeed they should. Few Americans are willing to accept his intellectual premises, his repudiation of our tradition of social reform, or his remorseless determinism. Whatever may be their shortcomings, Americans, by and large, have not surrendered their belief that society has an obligation to help out its less fortunate members. Yet Sumner also had some important things to tell us. Perhaps he understood what was happening to the country far better than most of his generally optimistic contemporaries. His forebodings merit attention in an era when the military-industrial complex has become a fact of life, when plutocrats, business corporations, and monopolistic labor unions unduly influence state and national governments, and when the country's enormous military power has been crudely and cruelly used to interfere in the internal affairs of smaller and weaker nations.

*   *   *

Historians have largely made Lester Frank Ward what he is today. With the growth of social planning in the United States during the second quarter of the 20th century, liberal scholars sought an ideological heritage to give their beliefs historical respectability. In their quest they discovered Ward. Conceivably they made too much of the man since in his own time he was virtually unknown outside a small circle of scholars. Yet despite his failure to achieve popular acclaim among his contemporaries, he is not without importance in this country's intellectual history. For he was, in truth, a distinguished scientist. Equally significant, it was he who developed what was probably the ablest refutation of William Graham Sumner's negativist social determinism.

In a world caught up in the Darwinian intellectual revolution, Ward attempted to create universal laws that would guide mankind to ever higher levels of civilization. To this end, he not only aspired to bring all realms of human knowledge under his personal command but also developed a theoretical system, "sociocracy," which he believed contained the formula for social advancement. That he found few followers to march to his drum left him disappointed but undaunted. Unlike Sumner, he had great faith in man's rationality and educability and equally great hope in the future.

Ward's was the kind of life that elicits considerable sympathy and admiration. His dogged efforts to achieve an education were little short of heroic, and his total dedication to learning and social meliorism was in the best tradition of the 18th century Enlightenment. After spending almost all of his adult life working in the scientific bureaucracy of Washington, he finally received an appointment as professor of sociology at Brown University in 1906. In the same year, he was elected first president of the American Sociological Society, although paradoxically, his influence on most of the new generation of sociologists had already become tenuous at best.

Born in the frontier community of Joliet, Illinois, in 1841, a year after Sumner, Ward also came from a lower middle-class economic background. But whereas Sumner's immigrant father provided his family with stability and security, Justus Ward, a mechanic and jack-of-all-trades, was something of a rolling stone who moved his family of ten children from one small middle western community to another in search of a change of luck and fortune that never came. Both Justus Ward and his wife, Silence, the daughter of a clergyman, were of old Connecticut Yankee stock. Fortunately for young Frank, as his family called him, Silence Ward was a strong woman who made the best of a fecund but otherwise questionable marital bargain. In a frontier environment that placed little premium on education, she imparted her literary interests and her religious piety as best she could to her children in those moments when she was not producing or weaning them.

Not all of the Ward children were as eager to learn as Frank, the youngest, and his brother Erastus, who was three years his senior and his inseparable boyhood companion. What formal schooling the boys obtained in one-room rural schools in Illinois and Iowa was rudimentary at best. But even had the schools been better than they were, the Ward children would have attended them only fitfully, since they were constantly employed doing odd jobs for neighbors or helping their father on one of his various undertakings. Frank was a healthy and vigorous youth (he was rarely if ever ill until his 70s) and while he could exult in hard physical labor, he also learned quite early that it did not necessarily produce riches.

Much of Ward's early education came outside the schoolhouse and the home. He and Erastus had a genuine love of nature and an intense curiosity regarding the flora and fauna of the prairies. In the introduction to his diary, Frank was later to write: "Roaming wildly over the boundless prairies of northern Iowa in the '50s, interested in every animal, bird, insect and flower I saw, but not knowing what science was, scarcely having ever heard of zoology, ornithology, entomology, or botany, without a single book on any of these subjects, and not knowing a person in the world who could give me the slightest information with regard to them, what chance was there of my becoming a naturalist? It was 20 years before I found my opportunity and then it was almost too late." In addition, young Ward embarked on the study of foreign languages with little help from teachers or anybody else. Once while working for a French-Canadian farmer with the unlikely name of Smith, he found a French grammar in the farmhouse and immediately began to learn the language as best he could. Eventually he mastered it. From French he went on to study Latin, Greek, and German —again largely on his own.

When Justus Ward died in 1857, the family gave up its Iowa homestead. Silence returned to Illinois to live with her one daughter, and Frank and Erastus went out into the world to seek their fortunes. After a year of odd jobs in Illinois, Frank hiked to Myersburg, Pennsylvania, where another older brother, Cyrenus, owned a factory that manufactured wagon-hubs. Cyrenus was the only other of Justus Ward's brood who had a scholarly bent, but he also inherited his father's bad luck in business. Two years after Frank came to work for him, he went bankrupt. At the age of 20, Frank was again adrift and still hungering for a formal education.

In 1861 the door opened to him when he enrolled at the Susquehanna Collegiate Institute of Towanda, Pennsylvania. The institution's name was far more impressive than the quality of its academic offerings or the talents of its students. Despite his lack of preparatory training, Frank Ward was quickly outdistancing his fellow students and, for that matter, probably his teachers. Lack of money limited his education to one term at the Institute and he did not return. Moreover, the Civil War had broken out, and the next year he enlisted in Mr. Lincoln's army. Unlike Sumner, he had no one to pay for a substitute, but even if he had, he would have joined up, for he believed fervently in the righteousness of the Union's cause and in the perfidy of the rebels. Five days before marching off to fight in Virginia, he secretly married Elizabeth Vought, a young woman who shared his thirst for knowledge.

Private Ward was quick to learn that military life was anything but glamorous, and at the disastrous Union defeat at Chancellorsville, he suffered leg wounds that were to remove him from further combat duty. As he recuperated at the Fairfax Seminary Hospital, he began to re-assess his views on the war and on society in general. The enemy, he concluded, was not the Johnny Rebs or any other group of human beings but rather just plain ignorance and superstition. He decided then and there to devote his life to their eradication. His wife, a kindred spirit and militant free thinker, provided strong moral reinforcement.

To crusade for humanity was noble, but there also was the problem of earning a livelihood. This was resolved in 1865 when he obtained a clerkship in the Treasury Department in Washington. Thus began Ward's long and varied career in the federal bureaucracy. In 1881 he moved on to the Bureau of Statistics and subsequently to the Bureau of Immigration and to the United States Geological Survey. He also became a highly regarded associate of the National Museum, the Smithsonian Institution, and the Biological Society of Washington. And as a paleobotanist, ge-ologist, and paleontologist, Ward would have few peers in the capital's scientific community.

Assiduous intellectual endeavor had carried the knowledge-hungry Illinois farmboy to positions of increasing importance in Washington. Like many other government workers in the capital, Ward attended college at night. In quick succession he received from Columbian Uni-versity a B.A. degree (1869) and an M.A. (1872) in botany, qualitative chemistry, and practical anatomy and from Johns Hopkins University an LL.B. (1871) and a diploma in medicine (1872). Ward never practiced medicine or law, although he was admitted to the bar. His "conscience," he said, "would not allow it."

Ward's rise to prominence had its bittersweet aspects and even its moments of profound personal tragedy. As a youth, he had been a devout Christian, but the more he learned about science, the more he became a sceptic. Like the "great agnostic" Robert Ingersoll, a contemporary, Ward maintained that all religion was based on superstition. "Our civilization," he wrote in 1870, "depends wholly upon the discovery and application of a few profound scientific and philosophical principles, thought out by a few great minds who hold the shallow babble of priests in utter con-tempt and have no time to dabble in theology." This statement appeared in a little paper, *The Iconoclast*, which Ward published with the aid of his wife. *The Iconoclast* had a brief life of a year and a half and then ceased publication, little lamented and quickly forgotten. Vastly more crushing to Ward were the deaths of an infant son and then in 1872 of his wife. By the next year, however, and not without a twinge of guilt, Ward had married Rosamund Simons, a widow, and was again absorbed in the research and writing of what would be his major scholarly opus, *Dynamic Sociology.*

Published in 1883, *Dynamic Sociology* was the pathfinding treatise of modern American evolutionary sociology. It represented Ward's effort to synthesize all areas of knowledge within a sociological framework. In one way, he did not differ from Herbert Spencer: both men believed in the guiding force of evolution on social development. This similarity is understandable. Ward was, after all, a product of the great scientific revolution of his time. Where he differed from Spencer were in his conclusions regarding the outcome of the evolutionary process.

William Graham Sumner believed all animals, man included, were subject to the same evolutionary forces that made for the survival of the fittest in the relentless struggle for existence in the world of nature. Ward went part way with him. True, he agreed, the sorting-out process prevailed in nature, and man himself was one of its results. But Ward made a fundamental distinction between man and other living organisms. Possessed of intelligence, reason and memory, only man had the ability to give direction to his own social evolution and to control the biological evolution of plants and animals.

For that matter, said Ward, there was a fallacy in the idea that competition was constructive and beneficent even in nature itself. Two forces governed the natural world: the *genetic,* which operated blindly on flora and fauna, and the *telic* wherein man, by his knowledge of science, harnessed the energy of evolution and subjected it to his own will. Ward's far-ranging biological investigations convinced him that the genetic force was extraordinarily wasteful. As illustration, he pointed to the millions of eggs required to hatch a small number of fish and the similar millions of seeds and seedlings needed to bring forth a tree in the forest.

When man interfered with, or, better yet, removed such genetic competition he inevitably produced superior species. The improvements in modern agricultural and horticultural products and in scientifically bred farm and domestic animals resulted from man's *artificial* control of the environment. What survived where raw genetic force prevailed independent of man's intervention might well have been the *fittest* in the competition of nature but not necessarily the *best* insofar as man's own needs were concerned. Artificial selection rather than natural selection was the key to biological progress. But Ward refused to apply the principle of artificial selection to man. His strong democratic sensibilities and his own first-hand knowledge that self-educated proletarians like himself could share no less than the rich and the well-born in the "aristocracy of brains" made him wary of human eugenics. He saw in it a subterfuge through which the so-called upper classes hoped to perpetuate their own kind and to insure their social positions.

Having swept Sumner and Spencer from the battlefield of biological science where they were no match for him, Ward proceeded to attack their social assumptions. The fact was, he wrote, "that man and society are not, except in a very limited sense, under the influence of the great dynamic laws that control the rest of the animal world." On the contrary the dynamics of human society were the antithesis of those of animal life. Whereas in the great struggle for existence in nature, the weaker of the species, though not necessarily the poorer qualitatively, were destroyed, man progressed "through the protection of the weak." For the "animal economics of life," Ward substituted the principle of human economics. Based on man's intelligence, human economics permitted the survival of both the strong and the weak. No one had to go down the drain.

Surveying the existing state of man's ethics as well as the record of his accomplishments with physical and mechanical phenomena, Ward noted that progress in both had resulted from man's "telic" response to the challenges he had been forced to confront. "The ethical code and the moral law of enlightened man," he wrote, were "nothing else than the means adopted by reason, intelligence, and refined sensibility for suppressing and crushing out the animal nature of man—for chaining the competitive egoism that all men have inherited from their animal ancestors." Similarly, "every implement or utensil, every mechanical device, every object of design, skill, and labor, every artificial thing that serves a human purpose" was "a triumph of mind over the physical forces of nature in ceaseless and aimless competition."

But man's ethics and his material gains had fallen far short of his potentialities. Even this limited progress had come at the price of allowing individuals to make random, helter-skelter decisions in much the manner of the genetic method in nature and usually with little concern for their social consequences. Among the results of such lack of concern were despoliation of the environment and natural resources, overcrowding of cities and growth of slums, gross maldistribution of wealth, deplorable conditions of labor and unemployment, disastrous industrial warfare, and general social dysfunction. Given these circumstances, the future had one overriding priority: to expand "individual telesis" into "social telesis," in short to direct the collective will and intelligence of men and women more effectively toward the betterment of society as a whole. Social telesis, Ward predicted, would make the achievements of science and technology available to everyone rather than to the privileged few. It would serve to eliminate existing social inequities and bring about new and improved social norms.

Ward described his society of the future as a "sociocracy." Its concerns would extend far beyond those of the contemporary American democracy. Its entire ethos would be different in that it would seek to eliminate those competitive aspects of social organization and human activity that benefited the few but retarded the many. Ideologically, it would be in the Jeffersonian tradition in emphasizing man's rationality, educability, and trustworthiness. It would recognize man's essential morality and justice in dealing with his fellow men as well as his willingness to act for the social good. On the other hand, it would be decidedly un-Jeffersonian in that it would take a highly positive view of the role of the State.

Ward had no interest in Marxism nor did he believe in an all-powerful state. But he had no fear of political power exercised through democratically constituted government. Having labored diligently in various Washington agencies, Ward had a healthy appreciation of what government could do to assist its citizens. Consequently he had no hesitation in expanding the scope of its authority. He disagreed vigorously with those who claimed that the bureaucracy was less efficient than private enterprise and that government workers did not put in an honest day's work. Nor did he think that the legislative branch of government was naturally prone to corruption, even though such was the case in his own day. Government would operate for the public good when properly oriented and capably led. Every lawmaker in Ward's sociocracy would be, in effect, a social scientist willing to experiment in solving social problems.

Law was the foundation of government and the means man used to control and transform his social environment; therefore, the correct formulation of legislation was of the utmost importance. Critics like Sumner maintained that social legislation in reality harmed those whom it ostensibly was intended to benefit. But intelligently conceived and scientifically formulated social legislation, said Ward, would serve the public good. The problem of democratic government was to devise laws that were as scientific in their way as those of physics and astronomy.

How could this best be done? Here Ward, the master of several fields of knowledge, answered as might be expected: through trained intelligence and reliance on experts. Like George Washington and John Quincy Adams, he called for the founding of a great national university in Washington where students would be educated in the science of government. Its graduates would help staff the administrative branch of government and their knowledge and expertise, particularly in the realm of statistical information, would be called on when legislators were confronted with the need to frame new laws.

Heretofore, Ward noted, most statutes were negative and coercive in character: they told citizens what they could not do. But law could also be "attractive" or affirmative, and he pointed to legislation that served the welfare of financial, manufacturing, and industrial interests. Ward observed that many American apostles of laissez faire, who clamored against "paternalistic" legislation in behalf of the weak, the poor, and the downtrodden, were conspicuously silent when government enacted laws that catered to their own special interests. Was it not the "rugged individualists," he asked, who were in the forefront of those seeking protective tariffs, government land grants, railroad construction subsidies, special mailing rates, and public utility franchises? "The charge of paternalism," Ward wrote, "is chiefly made by the class that enjoys the largest share of government protection. Those who denounce state interference are the ones who most frequently and successfully invoke it. . . . Nothing is more obvious today than the signal inability of capital and private enterprise to take care of themselves unaided by the state."

Ward maintained that competition in the economy was no more beneficent than it was in nature. He had a simple, if not simplistic, answer to those Social Darwinists among American businessmen who prated on the advantages of an unregulated free market. Pointing to the likes of Andrew Carnegie and John D. Rockefeller, he observed that such tycoons had accumulated their vast fortunes by *destroying* competition through business combinations and monopolies that controlled the market. They had recognized the inefficiencies involved in small business enterprises as well as the wastes in the competitive process itself and had sought to eliminate them. The long-range prospect for American capitalism, Ward predicted, was the elimination rather than the perpetuation of a free market economy.

Education was for Ward the "great Panacea" for the problems of society. As one whose own education had been agonizingly acquired, he had a touchingly naive faith in the collective wisdom of a thoroughly educated citizenry. In his sociocracy citizens would take an intense interest and an active role in their government and society. And they would make the right decisions in the end precisely because they were educated. Ward was convinced, moreover, that men, women, and children of all classes, nationalities, and races were equally educable. Hence the great problem for both the present and future was to equalize intelligence by putting "knowledge in the possession of every human being." Equal access to education would afford children of the poor the same opportunities in life as those of the rich. Ward was also an early advocate of women's liberation. His two marriages were to women of clearly superior intellect, and he early concluded that women were the equal of men and in some respects their superiors.

Whereas Sumner tremendously admired those who had achieved business and pecuniary success, Ward identified with the underdog, "the hated paupers and the worthless invalids" whom Sumner "would turn over to nature." Both attitudes are characteristically American: we admire winners but we also like to see the favorites upset. And whereas for Sumner it was every man for himself "root, hog, or die," for Ward every man was his brother's keeper and society as a whole had a direct responsibility for the well-being of all persons, rich and poor, high and low. Once again, each man was expressing an aspect of the American character: Sumner spoke for individualism and Ward for humanitarianism. But it was on their prescriptions for the future that they stand in most marked contrast. Whereas Sumner sociologically assigned society to a blind and purposeless negativism, Ward offered the hope that an enlightened citizenry could attain its ethical imperatives through both individual and socially organized efforts. Contemplated from our vantage point of today Ward may have expected too much from his fellow citizens, but then Sumner perhaps expected too little.

*   *   *

It was hardly a treat to attend Thorstein Veblen's lectures in economics at any one of the several universities at which he taught. The shaggy browed and bearded professor would sit at a desk on the lecture podium with his head turned away from the class. He would speak in a low voice that ran the gamut from "a drawl to a mumble." On occasion he did drop a pearl of wisdom, but if he was asked to repeat or to explain a point, he would usually reply that he didn't recall what he had said or that it was of no importance anyway. Seemingly the only questions that he welcomed were those which he could use to show up the student's ignorance or to demolish his opinions. Veblen certainly knew what constituted good classroom teaching, for he had studied at Yale under William Graham Sumner whom he greatly admired. But classroom teaching obviously bored him. Not a few of his students suspected that Veblen never read the papers they submitted to him; he rarely gave any indication that he had. Moreover, he refused to give examinations and awarded every student the grade of "C" at the end of the course. He considered the entire grading system worthless and productive only in pitting students against each other in grubby competition. In granting "Cs" he was merely complying with the letter of academic regulations. Students knew Professor Veblen was immensely learned, but they couldn't understand why he seemed to deprecate his own scholarship, as, for example, when he referred to his classic book, *The Theory of the Leisure Class,* as "that chestnut."

Small wonder that Thorstein Bunde Veblen never received tenure at any of the three universities at which he taught, although in two instances his amatory scandals with an assortment of accommodating females were probably as decisive as his poor teaching performance. And yet the morose and unhappy Veblen had a coterie of followers that included some of the nation's most distinguished economists. Many were his former graduate students. Moreover, Veblen himself was to be recognized as probably the most original and provocative social scientist that the United States produced during the first quarter of the 20th century.

One of 12 children, Veblen was born in 1857, nearly a generation after Sumner and Ward. His boyhood was spent in physically and culturally isolated agricultural communities in Wisconsin and Minnesota. These were inhabited almost entirely by Norwegian immigrants like his father, Thomas Veblen, a master carpenter and a skilled farmer. Although the elder Veblen had come to the United States as a young man, he never learned English. Among his fellow Norwegians, however, he was recognized as a man of towering intellect. Hard-bitten and taciturn, Thomas Veblen was a confirmed agnostic and Darwinian and looked on life as a remorseless struggle in which one neither asked for quarter nor gave it. In the hostile environment of the prairie frontier, he harbored a thoroughgoing populist suspicion of small-town bankers, merchants, and lawyers (a Yankee claimant with a superior knowledge of land law had euchered him out of his first farm which he had hacked out of the Wisconsin wilderness). Like Sumner, Thorstein Veblen considered his father the single most important influence in his life. Thomas Veblen had not only honed his mind but also served as an example of the individualist who stood on his own two feet and resolutely faced the world.

Veblen's mother was of a different cast. Outgoing and warmhearted, she was ever loving and protective toward her children. A practitioner of folk medicine, which was about all there was on the frontier, she frequently left her large brood to attend ailing neighbors. Unlike her freethinking husband, she read the Scriptures faithfully. While Veblen was impressed by his father's personal strength and power of intellect, he was no less affected by his mother's gentleness and humanity. There was a soft side to Veblen that escaped the notice of his contemporaries but which quietly made its way into his writings.

Veblen might just as well have grown up in Norway. Among his family and neighbors, English was virtually a foreign language. Both his father and mother had read deeply in Norse literature, and he himself became a translator of Icelandic sagas. This was probably his only hobby as an adult. Veblen never lost his "Norskie" accent which he sometimes purposely exaggerated in order to watch the reaction of both acquaintances and strangers.

When in 1874 Veblen finally left home at the age of 17 to attend Carleton Collegiate Academy, an outpost of Congregationalist culture and piety in Minnesota, it was almost as if he were enrolling as a foreign student. Thanks to his own precocity and his father's rigorous educational training, he was far more widely read and better prepared academically than his fellow students who did not know quite what to make of him. Already exhibiting the withdrawn personality as well as the spells of indolence that were to characterize his behavior during the remainder of his life, he did little to conceal his disdain for the other students and consequently lacked friends among them. Ellen Rolfe, daughter of a railroad magnate and niece of Carleton's president, was an exception. Sharp of mind but underdeveloped of body, she too was a loner. In Veblen she found someone who shared many of her intellectual interests. Several years later, in 1888, they were married, her parents vainly disapproving, and Veblen entering into the union with the same general lack of enthusiasm that he displayed in nearly everything he did. Their childless marriage ended in divorce several years later, although Ellen was reluctant until the very end to separate from her husband.

Veblen spent six years at Carleton, three in its preparatory school program in which he finally learned English properly and three in college. Avoiding the theological courses in which Carleton specialized, he concentrated on philology, philosophy, biology, and economics. He had the good fortune to study economics with John Bates Clark, then at the beginning of an academic career that ultimately would carry him to Columbia. Clark, who taught straight out of the English classical school of economics, recognized Veblen's intellectual prowess and encouraged him to go on to graduate school. Veblen proceeded to do so, first briefly at the new and innovative Johns Hopkins and then at the venerable and stodgy Yale where in 1884 he received a doctorate in philosophy under Sumner's old adversary, the Reverend Noah Porter. Interestingly enough, Veblen got along well with Porter, and the two often took long walks. Sumner, too, admired Veblen and thought his prize-winning essay on the 1837 panic was brilliant. On the other hand, Veblen once again irritated his fellow students.

Although strongly endorsed by Porter, Veblen could not secure an academic position. Four years of graduate study seemed utterly wasted. He returned dejectedly to the family farm. Home, noted Robert Frost, is where they have to take you in, and Veblen spent the next seven years either there or at his wife's father's farm in Stacyville, Iowa, doing light farm chores, inventing farm machinery, and loafing. An illness contracted at Yale provided him with a convenient excuse for avoiding heavy work, at least so believed some of the less sympathetic members of his family. Veblen and his wife spent most of their time reading whatever books they could obtain.

Finally in 1891, Veblen decided to return to academe, this time to Cornell as a graduate student in economics. Again he worked under a highly conservative mentor, J. Laurence Laughlin. Certainly, no two men could have been further apart in their approach to economics, but once again the teacher acknowledged the abilities of the student. When Laughlin moved on the next year to the new University of Chicago to become chairman of its Economics Department, he not only brought his student with him as a teaching fellow (not as a member of the faculty) but also made him managing editor of the new *Journal of Political Economy*. For his teaching and editorial services, Veblen received the unprincely annual salary of $520. Nonetheless, there were advantages in being at Chicago. Veblen taught a course on socialism in which he concealed his own true feelings from his students (he was a socialist), and he also became acquainted with such intellectual giants as John Dewey, Franz Boas, Jacques Loeb, and George Herbert Mead. None of them, however, impressed him as much as had William Graham Sumner.

In the stimulating atmosphere of John D. Rockefeller's new university Veblen produced some of his most important early work including *The Theory of the Leisure Class* (1899) which solidly established his reputation among scholars. Written as a satirical metaphor and in an anthropological vein, the book struck hard at those social institutions Veblen considered worthless as well as at the men who had achieved success in the existing "pecuniary culture"—the industrial, mercantile, and financial capitalists. Rather than being the fittest and finest products of natural selection, as Sumner and the Social Darwinists proclaimed, this new breed, said Veblen, had attained its status through "predaciousness," "shrewd practice," and "chicanery." In the pecuniary culture, he added, "It is only within narrow limits, and then only in a Pickwickian sense that honesty is the best policy."

In his anthropological analogy, Veblen observed that there was little to differentiate the barbarian warrior chieftains of by-gone times from the modern masters of wealth. They were brothers under the skin in what they esteemed to be most important in life. To both the possession of wealth mattered as much for what it symbolized as for the actual power it conferred. It permitted them to advertise their privileged status, or "invidious distinction" to use Veblen's term; to emulate their peers through display of "conspicuous leisure"; to indulge in acts of "conspicuous consumption" and, above all, "conspicuous waste."

While ostentatiously abstaining from doing useful work, the modern day "leisure class" was not necessarily idle. It engaged in such ego-building, "nonproductive" pursuits as the military, government service, religious office, charity work, the arts, and sports. It was preoccupied with its mansions, furnishings, servants, yachts, jewels, fashions, racehorses, hunts, parties, sports, etc. That such concerns might be fraudulent and downright silly rarely crossed the collective mind of the leisure class.

Veblen was only one of a legion of turn-of-the-century American social critics that included the novelist Edward Bellamy and the California journalist-turned-reformer, Henry George. Bellamy, whose utopian romance *Looking Backward* (1887) was "the turning-point of our lives," according to Ellen Veblen, saw in the "trustification" of American industry the cancer that ultimately would destroy it. George ascribed the malfunctions of American capitalism to private ownership of land. Veblen had a different answer. He gave it initially in *The Theory of Business Enterprise* (1904) and then developed it more fully in *The Instinct of*

Workmanship and the State of the Industrial Arts (1914), *The Engineers and the Price System* (1921), and *Absentee Ownership and Business Enterprise in Recent Times* (1924).

America's industrial economy, Veblen explained, suffered from a kind of schizophrenia. Pitted against each other were those who determined industrial policies and those who actually operated the industries. The former were the industrial and financial tycoons whose sole interest in production was "pecuniary gain" or the absolute maximizing of profits. The latter were the technicians—engineers, foremen, and ordinary industrial laborers—all of whom were accustomed to the "discipline of the machine" and possessed what Veblen called "the instinct of workmanship," a pride and satisfaction in what they did. Their goals were industrial efficiency and full production. Given free rein, they would scientifically reorganize the structure of the present industrial system, improve technology, and turn out better as well as cheaper products.

Cheaper prices benefited the general public, but in their calculations, those who owned or controlled industry were not inclined to consider the social good. Always seeking quick and windfall returns, they rarely took note of long-term consequences. Therefore they did not hesitate to command production cut-backs in order to create market scarcities. These, they hoped, would elevate prices and bring large and immediate profits. But such "capitalistic sabotage" could have baneful results. Because of the interdependent character of the modern industrial system, disruption of the natural flow of production, if extensively practiced, would throw the entire economy out of kilter, opening the way for sharp downswings in the business cycle, recessions, and depressions.

Unlike the Marxists, Veblen had no clear answer to this dilemma of modern capitalism. Implicit in his analysis, however, was the need to replace the existing "price system" with one dominated by scientific experts—engineers and technicians—and not by Marx's proletariat. Such a change would doom the leisure class, which was inextricably tied into the pecuniary culture. But Veblen saw no prospect that either would occur as long as traditional economic theory continued to be popularly accepted and while the predatory barbarian ethos pervaded every class of modern society. "The sentimental deference of the American people to the sagacity of its business men," Veblen wrote, "is massive, profound, and alert."

Veblen's criticism of the "pecuniary culture" and his institutional approach to economics had little or no relationship to the classical economic theory espoused by Clark, Sumner, and Laughlin, with its *a priori* assumptions about hedonistic "economic man," natural rights and natural law (used to justify existing property arrangements), and ideal marketplace competition. Small wonder that among orthodox American economists, he was a disturber of the peace.

"Publish or perish" did not apply to Veblen at the University of Chicago. *The Theory of the Leisure Class* and the *Theory of Business Enterprise* as well as articles in scholarly journals failed to advance him beyond the rank of Assistant Professor or to gain him tenure. His morose personality, slovenly teaching, and extra-marital affairs did not endear him to the University administration. Thus when David Starr Jordan, president of the 15-year-old Stanford University, offered Veblen an Associate Professorship in 1906, he accepted with alacrity.

But Veblen did not improve his teaching or decorum at Leland Stanford's "Farm." Once again he got into "woman trouble," which forced him to resign in 1909. For a year he was jobless. Then one of his friends, H. J. Davenport, obtained a lectureship for him, not a professorship, at the University of Missouri where he spent the next seven years, living in Davenport's cellar, ungraciously criticizing his benefactor's textbook in class, and writing what he thought was his best book, *The Instinct of Workmanship*. Veblen, who despised the Germans, also published *Imperial Germany and the Industrial Revolution* (1915). In a sense a prophetic study, it found many of the ingredients of Nazism—racism, imperialism, militarism, and industrial efficiency—in the Second Reich.

With the outbreak of war in 1917, Veblen went to Washington to work in Herbert Hoover's Food Administration. Ostensibly he was "on temporary leave" from Missouri "by mutual consent"; in reality, he had bid farewell to academe. But Veblen was as much a "misfit" in the bureaucracy, where his talents went unused, as he had been in the university. The next year he bitterly paid his disrespects to academe, in *The Higher Learning in America: A Memorandum on the Conduct of Universities by Businessmen*, which he mockingly described as a "study in total depravity." (Here indeed is a book that should be read by all academic bureaucrats, but one wonders how many even know of its existence.)

Until Veblen left for Washington he had always eschewed the role of activist and reformer. He was a driven man who refused to commit himself to any ideology, organization, party, or cause. Like Thoreau, he felt that he had come into the world to live in it, not to change it. In Washington, however, his almost Olympian detachment weakened under the stimulus of wartime idealism and hope for the future, and he became absorbed in furthering his plans for postwar social and economic reconstruction which he had outlined in *An Inquiry into the Nature of Peace and the Terms of Its Perpetuation* (1917). This book had been well received by the country's pro-war liberal intelligentsia who praised Veblen's attack on German autocracy. But few in policy-making positions in the capital listened to the aging Veblen, and nothing came of his plans. Again he returned to living in the world, leaving the efforts to change it to others.

The post-war years found Veblen in New York, still writing about the "pecuniary culture" that became even more pronounced in the twenties; briefly editing the resurrected Transcendentalist magazine, *The Dial;* and lecturing at the New School of Social Research where students habitually dropped out of his classes. In declining health, the old man was a prophet without honor in his own land. When in 1925 his friends sought to gain him the recognition that he deserved by nominating him for the presidency of the American Economic Association, he declined the honor and declared sardonically, if somewhat petulantly: "They didn't offer it to me when I needed it." The following year Veblen moved back to California where he spent the remainder of his days in an isolated mountain cabin. He died in 1929 on the eve of the greatest economic depression in the country's history.

Probably no 20th-century American social scientist has received as much scholarly attention as Thorstein Veblen, unless it be his friend John Dewey. Brilliant, perverse, enigmatic, Veblen was a marginal man who perched on the outer periphery of his own society—ever peering in and always failing to find what his mother had personified to him: probity, diligence, friendship, altruism, and peace. Veblen, of course, did not always meet his own standards, and his personal ambivalences make him a fascinating subject for psychological analysis.

Insisting that economics was an evolutionary science without teleological ends, Veblen refrained from prescribing for the future. He was content to expose the divergence between abstract economic theory and concrete economic fact and to show the institutional shoddiness of a society dominated by leisure class values and driven by a deeply internalized need to "keep up with the Joneses."

To Veblen the new industrialism with its emergent class of technicians portended grave problems. While he found the scientists and managerial experts timid and easily satisfied, he thought them infinitely superior to aggressive and manipulative captains of wealth. Yet Veblen opposed social control by any elite group. The prospect of a bureaucratic-structured and corporate-dominated society pleased him no more than one that took its direction from business entrepreneurs or "captains of education." In either case, the creative individual found himself submerged in the amorphous and impersonal group.

Finally Veblen early recognized that industrialism harnessed to a politically autocratic state spelled a larger tyranny. Kaiser Wilhelm's Imperial Reich was merely the beginning of a development that would culminate in Stalin's Russia while Veblen was still alive and in Hitler's Nazi Germany shortly after he died. Like the equally pessimistic Sumner but unlike the optimistic Lester Frank Ward, Veblen despaired of the future.

3

Three Faithful Skeptics at the Gate of Modernity

HENRY ADAMS
WILLIAM JAMES
OLIVER WENDELL HOLMES, JR.

by Cushing Strout
Cornell University

When he was in college before the Civil War, Mr. Justice Holmes recalled, explanations "meant a reference to final causes." After the war, he said, they came to mean instead "tracing origin and growth." A tracer himself, he wanted "life history" of rules, however, "to get the dragon out of his cave on to the plain and in the daylight" where you could kill him or tame him. Similarly, his contemporaries the historian Henry Adams and the psychologist-philosopher William James were vanguard intellectuals in their estrangement from traditional religion, their contempt for Andrew Carnegie's gospel of wealth, and their complex mixture of a familiar liberalism and an unorthodox conservatism that was deeply personal.

Realists as well as idealists, the three men complemented their skepticism of traditional absolutes with their own passionate beliefs. They struggled to mediate cultural conflicts between tradition and revolt, belief and disbelief, reason and feeling, finding footholds of certainty in an uncertain universe. Like the Roman god Janus, who was connected symbolically with a gate that opened both ways, they faced in two directions. Friends of the same class and professors together at Harvard in the early 1870s, they were, nevertheless, sharply divided by insistent differences of character and shaping experience.

* * *

In his autobiography Henry Adams noted that he as the fourth child, "being of less account, was in a way given to his mother," who named him "after a favorite brother just lost." Affection between mother and son was long lasting, and something deep in her personality appeared also in him, for she was said "to have delighted in the dark side of anticipation" and "the forecast of evil." At 24 he speculated that the human race might "commit suicide by blowing up the world." Much later he liked to think that he had inherited his alienation from Boston through his half-English grandmother, whose own displaced life in John Quincy Adams' career of politics had made her "weary of being beaten about a stormy world." Women made heroines for Henry Adams' novels, and in his biography the deaths of his sister, his wife, and his mother were events of great import. In his avuncular years, as private tutor in medievalism to his affectionate "nieces," Adams would compose a literary prayer to the Virgin, historically celebrate the cathedrals she had inspired, and ponder over the social meaning of the new American working woman.

In women, actual and mythical, Adams found some of his own qualities of artistic feeling, imaginative empathy, and teasing wit, which tended to be regarded by his culture as "feminine" in contrast to the supposedly "masculine" virtues of scientific control of nature, making money, and wielding power. Yet he was also deeply attracted to making history scientific, and he was a self-styled "pilgrim of power" who had been secretary to an Ambassador, a muckraking journalist of the Washington political scene, and a friend of John Hay, Republican Secretary of State. As a writer, he developed various forms to take account of art, science, and politics, seeking mastery of the conflicting impulses of his restless mind. From earliest childhood memories of the polarities of a Quincy summer and a Boston winter, of "sensual living" and "compulsory learning," Adams believed he had developed the feeling that "life was double."

At 13 Henry Adams wore a white armband to school to show his support for the election of Charles Sumner, an anti-slavery Senator who in five years would be caned about the head by a Southern Congressman. Adams' own grandfather, John Quincy, was the "Old Man Eloquent" of the anti-slavery cause in the House, and the young man's father, Charles Francis, was once the vice-presidential candidate of the Free Soil Party. When Sumner, a family friend, went abroad to recover from his beating, Henry Adams suggested, in a letter to his hero, that they go to Siberia; he would be Sumner's devoted nurse.

At Harvard Adams had been a writer, actor, orator, and club member. He was also an idealist who thought "this nation of ours furnishes the grandest theater in the world for the exercise of that refinement of mind and those high principles which it is a disgrace to us if we have not acquired." So he had told his contemporaries in his address as Class Orator in 1858. Rushing off to Europe, Adams studied German, enjoyed American

friends in Dresden, and ran a mailman's errand for his government that
gave him a glimpse in Palermo of the revolutionary Garibaldi. Adams' moratorium from responsibility was over when his father was elected to Congress. He believed in his father's politics and was eager to help. Back home,
he cast his first vote—for Abraham Lincoln.

Adams soon went back across the Atlantic with his father, as secretary
to America's Ambassador at the Court of St. James. Writing reports for
American newspapers, Adams offended English sensibilities at a time when
the English, irritated by the American removal from a British vessel of two
Confederate agents, needed a scapegoat. Stung by scorn and the loss of his
reportorial job, he amused himself by undertaking a historical investigation
of the story that Pocohontas had saved Capt. John Smith's life. Because she
had married a white man from whom Southerners were often proud to be
descended, Adams thought that depriving the Indian girl of her legendary
nobility would be "in some sort a flank, or rather a rear attack, on the Virginia aristocracy, who would be utterly gravelled by it if it is successful."

Adams then gravitated to Washington as an independent journalist, anxious to use his literary talent in the cause of reforming a government increasingly sinking under Grant into a system in which "great corporations
whose wealth and power were now extending beyond limits consistent with
the public interest, found no difficulty in buying whatever legislation they
wanted from State Legislatures. . . ." His brother Charles was documenting railroad corruption in the same journal, the *North American Review,*
and Henry published in an English magazine his untangling of Jay Gould's
attempt, with the help of Grant's brother-in-law, to corner the gold market, thus inducing a stock-market crash.

Escaping to England to "wash the dirty linen" from his mind, he learned
of his sister's illness and hurried to Italy to see her through to her courageous but horrible death from tetanus. Stunned, he returned home to accept at his family's urging the job offered him by Harvard's President
Charles A. Eliot, who was bent on turning the college into a modern university. As a teacher of medieval, English, and American history, Adams
characteristically innovated in method, spurning textbooks, emphasizing
primary sources, provoking dialogue, and stimulating thought. He eventually derided his professorial career on the ground that teaching boys was
"mean work" because it was "distinctly weakening to both parties." Even
so, with his students he produced a book, *Essays in Anglo-Saxon Law,* that
lent itself to the current fad of finding German roots for representative
government.

Adams was still an active reform journalist as editor of the *North American Review,* busily working with other liberal Republicans who also were
interested in civil service reform and scornful of regular party politics.
Much like the founding fathers, they believed that parties were the source
of corruption. The Independents shared the optimism of the editor of the

Nation, E. L. Godkin, who boasted that "the Lord is delivering the politicians into our hands." But at their own convention in 1872, they were outmaneuvered by politicians, and in a notable anticlimax nominated Horace Greeley of the *New York Tribune*. Four years later the Independents failed to hold together, and Adams himself voted for the Democrat Samuel Tilden, reform governor of New York. When Adams and his brother Charles used the *North American Review* to campaign for Tilden, their publisher repudiated the manifesto and Adams quit his editorship.

Adams consoled himself for political defeats by affirming that "literature offers higher prizes than politics." Asked to edit manuscripts of New England Federalism and of Albert Gallatin, Jefferson's Secretary of the Treasury, he saw an opportunity to devote himself to writing without the burdens of his university routine. In 1877, seeking a wider world in a capital city, Adams and Marian Hooper, whom he had recently married for her "intelligence and sympathy," set up housekeeping in Washington. Still preserving "great faith in this country" and enjoying the "expectation of the coming day," he set to work on a nine-volume history of the formative years of the Republic, published between 1889 and 1891 and based on a combing of European and American archives. Modelling himself on the English historian Edward Gibbon, Adams completed his project in half the time it had taken his hero to chronicle *The Decline and Fall of the Roman Empire*.

Adams dramatized his own version of decline and fall in his novel *Democracy*, published anonymously in 1880. Painting a satirical portrait of Washington as a corrupt political city, he contrasted it with an elegiac image of the home and tomb of George Washington, symbol of the incorruptible gentleman. Adams made his heroine a widow of a descendant of Robert E. Lee (who had married the daughter of Washington's adopted son), and she characterized her suitor, a Southern gentleman-diplomat, as "George Washington at Thirty" because of his probity. The heroine is attracted, however, to a powerful Midwestern Republican Senator and is disenchanted to discover his moral obtuseness and her own vulnerability to the corrupting magnetism of power. "I bade politics good-bye when I published *Democracy*," he later said; but actually he urged Carl Schurz to lead a free-trade movement of Independent Republicans. For his pains Adams was offered a humiliatingly minor diplomatic post (which his wife refused for him), rather like the fate of his novel's Southern gentleman.

In Washington Adams found congenial company among the scientific members of the Cosmos Club, such as the explorer Major John Wesley Powell, the geologist Clarence King, and the paleontologist-sociologist Lester Frank Ward. His other novel, *Esther* (1884), participated in a current debate over the relation of science and religion. His friend William James had urged "the stifled soul" to take the risk of faith. Adams replied by making Esther a rationalist who was constitutionally unable to believe, even at the cost of losing the man she loves. In Esther (reminiscent of Hawthorne's

Hester) he projected an artistic, agnostic young woman, wooed by a minister and befriended by a young scientist. Esther's refusal to be intimidated by men recalls Adams' lecture on "The Primitive Rights of Women" (1876). Then he had attacked the conventional Victorian image of woman as the idealized "silent and tender sufferer," in contrast to her status in primitive and Roman times when the "defiant heroine of the heroic age" was not mere property. Esther was intellectually a "defiant heroine" of her own age.

The story also acutely forecasts the neurotic side of his agnostic wife's attachment to her father and her disabling depression after his death. In similar circumstances Esther, torn between a wish to submit and to defy, hating the church because it cries " 'flesh-flesh-flesh' at every corner," and "feverishly" proposing to a girl friend that they "elope together" on a "wedding journey" to escape the problems thrust on them by their suitors, is much like a patient in one of Sigmund Freud's case histories. A friend wrote Adams that he had left his heroine no alternative but suicide. In 1885, when he was 47, his wife tragically proved his point with chemicals from the photographic hobby he had taught her.

Desolated with self-punishing guilt and self-pitying grief, which he hugged to himself, Adams increasingly wore a mask of self-protective witty cynicism, which Justice Holmes disapprovingly called Adams' "old cardinal" tone. For recuperation he toured Japan with the artist John La Farge, studied Buddhism, and commissioned the sculptor Augustus Saint-Gaudens to carve a Buddhistic gravestone for his wife. "In the midst of gloom and depression," he confided to his diary, "I have come to the last page of my history." In 1890, as a release from the long discipline of completing his *History,* he set out with La Farge for the South Pacific on a two-year voyage. Characteristically, its fruit was a privately printed history of Tahiti that he had gleaned from his warm friendship with a native grandmother, a former chieftainess.

The History of the United States during the Administrations of Jefferson and Madison linked Adams' concern for democracy and his aspiration to do for history what Darwin had done for biology. Mixing elements of social history and speculations about national character with a close-grained diplomatic, military, and political narrative, he told a story that culminated by fixing a new mold of men on non-European lines. By 1815 Americans, he concluded, had raised the average standard of intelligence, comfort, and wealth in a more easy-going optimistic society. With little capacity for skill in national political administration, they had best shown their talents in the clipper ship, the torpedo, and the screw propeller.

During the panic of 1893, which threatened the family's investments, Adams worked closely with his brother Brooks who was spinning out a grand historical theory about the victory of an economic age over more imaginative times when soldiers, priests, and artists had been dominant types. Henry also visited the Columbian Exposition and "looked like an owl at the dynamos and steam-engines." Increasingly, he felt that his country was divided into money-lenders and money-borrowers. "As I have a foot in both stirrups," he confessed, "I am alternately kicked off on both sides." Politically, he preferred the agrarian People's party whose ideology drew on the 18-century republicanism that Adams had admired in his biography of Albert Gallatin (1879) and that had been perverted by doctrinaire Jeffersonians, as Adams had shown in his biography of John Randolph (1882). But increasingly he had an apocalyptic sense of catastrophe: "it recurs to me every November, and culminates every December." These were the months when depression had overwhelmed his wife.

In 1895 he found a new focus for his life in enthusiasm for the cathedrals of northern France. The medieval world of art and religion became his passion, and he paid it a loving tribute in *Mont-Saint-Michel and Chartres* (1905), a learned travelogue for his "nieces," celebrating the Virgin and St. Thomas. Medievalism linked up his artistic sensibility, his nostalgia for a coherent world, his idealization of women, and his ambition to find a "great generalization that would reduce all history under a law as clear as the laws which govern the material world." The Gothic cathedral fascinated him by its "visible effort to throw off a visible strain," its joyful aspirations qualified by "the pathos of its self-distrust and anguish of doubt . . . buried in the earth as its last secret." While Adams admired his father for having the only "perfectly balanced mind" in the family, in the Gothic style the historian saw the precarious poise of his own anguish of doubt.

Adams' "The Rule of Phase Applied to History" (1909) was a hybrid. It applied physical laws to history—which was understood as phases of energy in an expiring universe. And it found a cultural benchmark in the medieval world as a symbol for man's sense of himself as "a unit in a unified universe." Modernity was the result of an acceleration of multiplicity and disorientation. An amateur reader of science, he had also stumbled upon the historic shift from classical mechanics to quantum mechanics, from a picturable, certain Newtonian nature to an unpicturable, uncertain nuclear family of strange little particles, and it gave him a bewildered sense of having lost his foothold. Only in international relations could he still find a sense of purpose in modern history. He believed John Hay had forged an "Atlantic system"; fear of Germany "effected what Adamses had tried for two hundred [years] in vain—frightened England into America's arms." American intervention on England's side in the year before he died convinced Adams that his dream of a "great community of Atlantic powers" had finally been realized.

In his privately published *The Education of Henry Adams* (1907), he presented himself and his Harvard education as failures. The tactic drew from Justice Holmes, to whom he had made "a noble present" of his German law books, the proper rebuke: "I for one have owed you more than you in the least suspect. . . . Of course you may reply it is also futile—but that is the dogmatism that often is disguised under scepticism." His friend William James uncovered another of Adams' dogmatisms. James admired *Mont-Saint-Michel and Chartres* for its rare "frolic power"; but he also saw the fallacy in Adams' "scientific" theory of decline. Maybe the *ultimate* state of the universe was extinction, but "the penultimate state might be the millennium." Adams was delighted at this spirited response, and when James died, he was moved to write Henry James about the group they had known: "We all began together, and our lives have made more or less of a unity, which is, as far as I can see, about the only unity that American society in our time had to show." To this extent Adams had found compensation for the lost coherences he admired in Chartres and Mount Vernon. Shortly after the *Titanic* sank in 1912, he suffered a stroke, treating the shipwreck as proof of his pessimism about modern civilization. He survived for six years, enjoying hearing his nieces sing his favorite 12th-century songs, which he dug out of Paris archives with a still-eager historian's curiosity.

*   *   *

A historian of Victorian intellectuals, Gertrude Himmelfarb, has pointed out that if madness has varied habitats for different types of intelligence and sensibility, then English intellectuals of the 19th century "dwelled, for the most part, upon the plains of madness." Here rationalists suffered inexplicable illnesses, novelists of domesticity made unhappy marriages, libertarians were puritans, and moralists lived in the shadow of sexual improprieties. William James was of their company: a philosopher of freedom and "the will to believe" who felt trapped in science and "suffered from incredulity." He had been suicidally depressed in his 20s and in his 60s had been disturbed by dreams that seemed to divide his identity in three. Like so many of the great Victorians who suffered a crisis of belief, he found in it the impetus to a major achievement of original work.

In moving from science to metaphysics through the detour of medicine, the shape of his career was like Freud's, finding its way back to his "earliest path" of theoretical speculation "after a long and roundabout journey." As a philosopher, James influenced American psychology, religion, education, and historiography; this cosmopolitan patriot was also a creative force on European thought in the decade preceding the first World War. Like Adams, James had to seek some balance in himself of the competing attractions of science, art, and philosophy. His ideas grew out of his personal history, providing escape-hatches from the oppression of being, as James put it at age 53, "a victim of neurasthenia, and of the sense of hollowness and unreality that goes with it." When it would end with him he did not know. That summer he gave his popular lecture on "The Will to Believe," concluding that "the whole nature" of both skeptic and believer went into their respective attitudes. "Which of us is the wiser, Omniscience only knows."

James's story begins with his grandfather William, who emigrated from Northern Ireland to America in the early days of the new nation. A severe Calvinist, successful entrepreneur, and public-spirited citizen in Albany, he lived a life that was a textbook case for Max Weber's theory of the connection between Protestantism and capitalism. His son Henry grew up resenting the Calvinist vision of a God "exceedingly jealous of the hypocritical homage we paid to his contemptuous forbearance." At 13 he twice suffered the shock of amputation when his leg was burned in a fire. Something of a rebel, he once ran away from Union College, and his strict father punitively left him with only a small annuity from a very large fortune. Henry brought suit, broke the will, and was thus rich enough to spend his time in compulsively restless European travel, theological writing, and utopian social speculation. He could even afford rooms at the posh Astor House, in New York City, where William James was born in 1842.

At that time William's father was puzzled about what to do with his life. He asked Emerson: "shall I learn science and bring myself first into men's respect, that thus I may the better speak to them?" When William was four, his father was rescued from his doubts and "insane and abject terror" by a conversion to Swedenborg's supernaturalism, which Mr. James infused with Fourier's utopian socialism. "The children were constantly with their parents and with each other," as William's son later put it, "and they continued all their lives to be united by much stronger attachments than usually exist between members of one family." As the eldest son, William enjoyed the special interest of his father and reciprocated by his fascination with his father's mind. "What a passion your father has in writing and talking his religion!" exclaimed the skeptical Oliver Wendell Holmes, Jr. After his father's death in 1882, the 40-year-old son confessed that he was "learning every day now how the thought of his comment on my experience has hitherto formed an integral part of my daily consciousness, without my having realized it at all."

In William the father saw an opportunity to realize the unchosen path he had mentioned to Emerson. Himself a little-read theologian without a church, he posed a troubling model for a dutiful son who found "something disheartening in the position of an esoteric philosopher." An advocate of spontaneity and love, William's father, nevertheless, could be brusquely implacable. When the son sought independence to study painting at William Morris Hunt's studio in Newport, his father decided to "break that up" because he "hoped that his career would be a scientific one," and so William was whisked away to Europe. When his father relented, William abandoned art school within a year, probably still feeling his father's disapproval. When William and Henry tried to enlist in the Union army (as their two brothers did), their father wrote, "I have had

a firm grasp upon the coat tails of my Willy and Harry, who both vituper-
ate me beyond measure because I won't let them go."

In 1861 William gave his father his plan to study chemistry, anatomy,
and medicine as preparation for working with Louis Agassiz in natural
history. In 1863 he entered Harvard medical school and the next year went
to Brazil with Agassiz as a part of an exploring and collecting expedition.
He found in his "isolated circumstances" in the jungle more sympathy than
ever with his two brothers who had joined the Union army. One of them
had been honored as a badly wounded hero of the assault on Fort Wagner
by the regiment of free Negroes commanded by the martyred Brahmin,
Robert Gould Shaw. Hospitalized by a mild form of smallpox, William decided that, unlike military heroes, he was "cut out for a speculative rather
than an active life." He returned home with new resolve: "When I get
home I'm going to study philosophy all my days." Privately he read philosophy voraciously, but publicly he resumed his medical studies, including
a brief internship at the Massachusetts General Hospital. Yet he thought
there was "much humbug" about the practice of medicine. In 1866 he complained of digestive disorders, eye troubles, weakness of the back, and
acute depression, symptoms similar to those he had felt in Brazil when his
scientific collecting career had gone sour. One winter he felt on the "continual verge of suicide." In the suddenly remembered image of an epileptic
idiot, which reduced him to panic fear, James saw himself—*"That shape
am I,* I felt, potentially." This image was very like the one Victorian doctors conjured up to warn young men about becoming a "lunatic victim"
to the vice of masturbation. Moreover James was unsuccessfully courting
Fanny Dixwell, who married his friend Holmes in 1872. The hideous figure
also dramatized his unconscious fear of being trapped in the medical career he despised, a kind of psychic suicide. The epileptic was greenish-
hued like the "green darkness" he described as the void into which a suicide would step.

James could not find himself in medical materialism. He felt "swamped
in an empirical philosophy," believing "not a wiggle of our will happens
save as the result of physical laws." His father wanted him to be a scientist yet boasted: "I am sure I have something better to tell you than you
will be able to learn from all Germany—at least all scientific Germany."
The son could not follow both his father's advice and his example without
suffering intense conflict. Reading through his father's books, the despairing young James made himself a parody of his father—a crippled philosopher without a job. "The crisis in such a young man's life," as the psycho-
analyst Erik H. Erikson has remarked about Martin Luther, "may be
reached exactly when he half-realizes that he is fatally overcommitted to
what he is not."

He gradually climbed out of the depths of 1870. Poetry—Goethe, Words-
worth, Browning—helped, and James was excited to find in the French phi-

losopher Charles B. Renouvier a credible defense of free will. That a person could sustain a thought *because he chose to* was no illusion. James declared: "My first act of free will shall be to believe in free will." The point was important to him because determinism blotted out the reality of evil as well as the power to resist it. "I can't bring myself, as so many men seem able to," he shortly wrote his brother Henry, "to blink the evil out of sight, and gloss it over. It's as real as the good, and if it is denied, good must be denied too. It must be accepted and hated, and resisted while there's breath in our bodies."

In 1872 James accepted an appointment at Harvard to teach physiology, but he confided to his diary: "Philosophy I will nevertheless regard as my vocation and never let slip a chance to do a stroke at it." Meanwhile he needed "some stable reality to lean upon" and did not feel prepared yet "to strike at Harvard College" for a professorship in philosophy. In the year of his marriage, 1878, James signed a contract to write *The Principles of Psychology* on which he spent 12 years.

The book was a bridge from physiology to his deeper philosophical interests and had little to do with the laboratory work he always hated. The thought of "brass-instrument and algebraic formula psychology," he confessed, "fills me with horror." Written with a painter's eye for detail and a poet's feeling for immediate experience, the two volumes inspired John Dewey to express his indebtedness to James's demolition of the "superstition" that "a scientific book ought to be a corpse." *Psychology,* incorporating James's vision of man as a *"fighter for ends"* of which cognition was a servant, emphasized the presence of selectivity in sensation itself.

By 1899 James had with relief surrendered all psychological teaching to Hugo Münsterberg and was wondering if he had strength enough to prepare and deliver the Gifford Lectures at Edinburgh, published as *The Varieties of Religious Experience* (1902). More popular than the widely used *Principles of Psychology,* the *Varieties* harked back to that work in its probing psychological emphasis and pointed forward to his epistemological and metaphysical studies in *Pragmatism* (1907), *A Pluralistic Universe* (1909), and *Essays in Radical Empiricism* (1912).

James felt that his father's experience, peculiar as it was, illustrated the familiar story of conversion among "saints and mystics" who kept religion alive. "The experience in question," he wrote, "has always been an acute despair, passing over into an equally acute optimism, through a passion of renunciation of the self and surrender to the higher power." Anxious to vindicate the message of his father's life that "religion is real," James also wished to make way for his own pluralism.

Audaciously, James combined what he knew of the idea of the subconscious "subliminal self," developed in Frederick Myers' investigations of spiritualistic phenomena, and of the unconscious in Freud's recent studies of "whole systems of underground life" in the shape of painful memories in hysterics. When he met Freud at Clark University in 1909, he told him, "the future of psychology belongs to your work," even though he himself could "make nothing" out of Freud's dream theories and thought symbolism "a most dangerous method."

James was always crossing back and forth over the borders between psychology and religion, his passport stamped with the credentials of his own experience. In the year of his death he published "A Suggestion About Mysticism" that related "the most intensely peculiar experience" of his life, a dreadful sense of belonging to three different dream-systems at once, none of them connected to his waking life and giving him the eerie feeling of "getting into other people's dreams." Contradicting his title, he conceded that the event was "the exact opposite of mystical illumination," and it filled him with "a new pity towards persons passing into dementia." This border had also been crossed by his father in 1844 on his way to the New Jerusalem of Swedenborg. Like Adams welcoming St. Thomas and the Virgin at the back door through his historical study of Gothic architecture, James, a fellow-agnostic, was inclined to greet Methodism through the scientific study of morbidity, "mind-cure" therapies, and the mediums of spiritualistic circles.

James made much of the difference between the "tough-minded" and the "tender-minded" in philosophy; he was the same in the world of his day. A proponent of "the strenuous life," he defended home rule in the Philippines against the Republican administration's imperial passion for military conquest. A mountain-climber who strained his heart and relished "life's more bitter flavors," he urged formation of a peace corps into which "our gilded youth" would be drafted to do painful work as a "moral equivalent of war."

Pragmatism (1907) spoke for a new view of truth but its purpose was to sponsor a shift to minds "more scientific and individualistic in their tone yet not irreligious either." As a good evolutionist, he repudiated the traditional argument justifying design in creation, because "Darwin opened our minds to the power of chance-happenings to bring forth 'fit' results if only they have time to add themselves together." Though *design* was worthless as a rationalistic principle, it could be, for theistic exercisers of the will-to-believe, "a term of *promise,* nurturing confidence and hope that "we may reasonably expect better issues." Thus did the problem have *pragmatic* meaning. Appropriately, *Pragmatism* was dedicated to John Stuart Mill, whom he had often discussed with Charles Peirce, Chauncey Wright, and Wendell Holmes in the Cambridge "metaphysical club" of the '70s.

The French philosopher Renouvier, who first confirmed James in his identity as a philosopher, told him that he was "called to found an *American philosophy.*" But he also saw the personal roots of the American's thought: "Your thinking springs from a source that is original and profound, and bears the stamp of what you yourself feel—of something that comes, indeed, from your very self." In his old age James was moved by the inspiration of Renouvier's continuing energy to think of writing "a somewhat systematic book on philosophy—my humble view of the world —pluralistic, tychistic, empiricist, pragmatic, and ultra-gothic, i.e., non-classic in form." But he died of heart trouble in 1910, four years after resigning from Harvard, convinced that it was an "aesthetic tragedy" to have left his philosophy "too much like an arch built only on one side."

Pragmatism has been called American because it stresses the practical. But James was something of an artist and a scientist, a patient and a psychiatrist, a religious man and a skeptic; and he made his philosophy a mediation of all these polarities.

*   *   *

Oliver Wendell Holmes, father of the jurist, once remarked that he kept his "cellar door open for 'Science,' " and his "attic skylights open for unclassed and as yet unclassifiable statements about the imponderable." So did his son, who had an even greater gift of phrase, thus proving his father's point that the term "Brahmin caste" ought to stand for a continuity of "learned labor" in some New England families. The most learned of the Supreme Court justices during his long tenure from the first to the second Roosevelt, he was robust where James was frail, sanguine where Adams was pessimistic. Though he had known them both in "The Club" of young Harvard professors, he was proud to leave academic groves for more worldly business because (as he would much later tell his disciple Felix Frankfurter) it makes "more of a man of one who turns it to success." Like Theodore Roosevelt's cult of "the strenuous life," Holmes's morality insisted that "the line of *most* resistance is the one to choose."

Though Emerson first started the philosophical ferment in his mind, Holmes put no stock in democratic dogmas and was a social Darwinist, finding "the final test of energy" in "the fight for mastery in the market or the court." No more than William Graham Sumner did Holmes believe in "the absurd effort to make the world over." Yet because of his self-limiting doctrine of judicial review, he wrote many opinions that endeared him to the very people who were busily engaged in that reforming effort. "An aristocrat in morals as in mind," the novelist Owen Wister admiringly observed. He had "a touch of both Puck and Ariel." Holmes mocked true believers of all kinds, but he had his own "fighting faith." Much more single minded than either Adams or James and never devastated by inner conflict or tragic losses, Holmes matured early and kept senility at bay in his 90s, thus living "in that state of grace we call maturity," as Richard Rovere has put it, "as long as any man in the history of this republic."

Holmes's father was a man of letters, as well as a professor of medicine, and his son showed the family literary bent when he was at Harvard, edit-

ing the literary magazine, writing a prize essay on Plato, and being designated Class Poet. He loved Sir Walter Scott because in his stories "the
sword and the gentleman were beliefs," a sentiment that many Southerners, worshippers of Scott, would have endorsed; but Holmes thought the
South "ignorant of all the ideas that make life worth living to us." Holmes
in old age remembered that he had been "a pretty convinced abolitionist
and was one of a little band intended to see Wendell Phillips through if
there was a row after the meeting of the Anti-Slavery Society just before
the war." He was also idealist enough to be invited to become a major in
the regiment made up of free blacks, commanded by officers from families
of high social status and led by Robert Gould Shaw.

Holmes, however, joined the Twentieth Massachusetts regiment, and
suffered wounds in three different battles before being mustered out as a
Lieutenant Colonel. Believing he was close to death from a chest wound,
Holmes kept true to his father's agnostic opinion that it would be a "cow-
ardly giving way to fear" to be "guilty of a deathbed recantation." He sustained himself by a gentleman's code, feeling indifferent to the sight of
death. He was proud to say that his moustache grew well because it was
"nourished in blood," and he once told Emerson that the army was learning to avoid panics and excitements by acquiring a professional feeling.
Holmes thereafter blended in his character a proud professionalism with
an aristocratic pride and a romantic feeling for action. The war became, in
his edifying speeches on public occasions, a metaphor for the agnostic's
plight: a soldier who has not been told the plan of the campaign, but who
would fight anyway out of his own sense of power, leaving to the unknown
"the supposed final evaluation of that which in any event has value for us."
Holmes was a very cultivated man, who collected etchings, loved to phi-
losophize, and read widely in the classics, but it was military experience
that first gave him a feeling that "life is a profound and passionate thing."

Anxiety over "the collapse of creeds" never disturbed Holmes because
he never doubted "that the faith is true and adorable which leads a soldier
to throw away his life in obedience to a blindly accepted duty, in a cause
which he little understands, in a plan of campaign of which he has no notion, under tactics of which he does not see the use." James, in contrast,
celebrated the *civic* courage of Robert Gould Shaw in leading a Negro regiment, drew the lesson from the war that "evils must be checked in time
before they grow so great," sought a "moral equivalent of war," and complained that "mere vital excitement" was "an immature ideal, unworthy of
the Supreme Court's official endorsement." But Holmes found an equivalent for morality in the fact that his generation had been "touched with
fire" in battle. In the 1880s and 1890s when Holmes preached this doctrine,
martial heroism was for him, as for many others, a critique of the commer-
cialism of his day. It was linked to his aristocratic admiration for sports like
fencing and polo because such "rough riding" was needed "for the breeding of a race fit for headship and command."

Holmes and James as young men were friends who enjoyed twisting the tail of the cosmos together in philosophical debate about Herbert Spencer and John Stuart Mill, and they both admired the same girl, Fanny Dixwell. The despondent and doubtful James was understandably miffed to see Holmes get the girl and hit upon his vocation with such a sure touch. Holmes said he had been "kicked into the law" by his father, but his Harvard classbook recorded his aim of studying law after the war. His maternal grandfather had been a judge on the state's highest court, and even Holmes's father had briefly studied at Harvard Law School. The choice of law was natural enough for a gentleman-veteran with a taste for intellectual debate and a profound belief in action. Even the drudgery of law school was acceptable to him if only because by comparison it made philosophy seem like "spongy stuff" that "goes down like macaroni." Ten years after graduating from Harvard Law School in 1866, he sent Emerson one of his first essays in law and explained his ambition: "It seems to me that I have learned, after a laborious and somewhat painful period of probation, that the law opens a way to philosophy as well as anything else, if pursued far enough, and I hope to prove it before I die."

Holmes believed that "if a man was to do anything he must do it before 40." Keeping right on schedule, he joined a Boston firm, accepted in 1870 an appointment to teach constitutional law at Harvard, and edited the *American Law Review* and Kent's *Commentaries on American Law*. When at 40 he published his masterpiece, *The Common Law* (1881), he was the first lawyer, English or American, according to his biographer, "to subject the common law to the analysis of a philosopher and the explanation of a historian."

Holmes had foreshadowed his perspective in an unsigned review of a casebook written by the Dean of the Harvard Law School. The Dean, he complained, was "a Hegelian in disguise" because he tried "to reduce the concrete details of an existing system to . . . logical consequence of simple postulates." A scientific method, he added, would emphasize changing experience as well as anthropology, and bring the law, much as James brought traditional philosophical notions of truth, down to earth. In *Pragmatism* James condemned preoccupation with crime, sin, punishment, and blame that "hang like a bad dream over man's religious history." He preferred instead to rely on "instinct and utility" to carry on "the social business of punishment and praise." In *The Common Law* Holmes defended the preventive theory of punishment and urged that civil and criminal liability be judged by an *external* standard. The importance of intent in criminal law, he maintained, "is not to show that the act was wicked, but to show that it was likely to be followed by hurtful consequences." Similarly, a contract should be viewed in terms of definable external requirements. His aim was behavioristic: "The law has nothing to do with the actual state of the parties' minds." The way to understand it, he claimed, was to look at it as "a bad man" might: "a prediction of the incidence of public force" that a court would bring to bear in a given circumstance. Holmes admitted that he and James started from "surprisingly similar premises," but he also branded Pragmatism "an amusing humbug," too much of "a sop to free-thinking Unitarian parsons and the ladies." Moreover, his religious skepticism was more aggressive. Finally, unlike James, he was a technocratic rationalist, believing that "the man of the future is the man of statistics and the master of economics." His own utopia was a positivistic one, "a commonwealth in which science is everywhere supreme."

Holme's masterly book earned him a professorship and three months later an offer to sit on the bench of the highest court of Massachusetts. Characteristically, he seized the chance at once with a quickness that scandalized some of his colleagues at Harvard. His reason was clear: "I did not think one could without moral loss decline any share in the practical struggle of life which naturally offered itself and for which he believed himself fitted." To refuse would have been to choose "the less manly course." He often idealized the heroic thinker, working in "a black gulf of solitude" and trusting to his "own unshaken will," but he also felt that "the professor, the man of letters, gives up one-half of life that his protected talent may grow and flower in peace." Holmes may have enjoyed reading Casanova as a relief from the strain of *The Common Law*, but his steady appetite for ambitious work provoked William James to call him a "powerful battery, formed like a planing machine to gouge a deep self-beneficial groove through life." He was solidly forging a career bound to end, James predicted, on the Supreme Court of the United States.

Holmes served from 1882 to 1902 on the Supreme Judicial Court of Massachusetts, testing out and developing his legal philosophy which remained remarkably stable for a half century. He urged that a constitution should be broadly construed as a document made "for men of opposite opinions and for the future." He spoke for the Court in upholding a Boston ordinance requiring a mayor's permit for public speaking on the Common; but he dissented from judgments upholding injunctions against peaceful picketing or demands for a closed shop by strikers because he believed competitive combination by both labor and capital was inevitable, regardless of any judge's social preferences.

Theodore Roosevelt, another ardent believer in "the soldier's faith," appointed Holmes to the Supreme Court of the United States in 1902 in the hope that he would be "a statesman of the national type." Holmes was at first one of the "Roosevelt Familiars" that included John Hay, Henry Adams, Augustus Saint-Gaudens, and Owen Wister, but he offended the President by refusing to support the government's case against the Northern Securities holding company, formed to control the merger of two railroad systems. Roosevelt did not realize that Holmes was as strict in construing a statute as he was flexible in construing powers under the Constitution. A partnership between formerly competing roads, he argued, was not illegal unless the Sherman anti-trust law was absurdly stretched to "disintegrate society so far as it could into individual atoms." However, a year later in *Swift and Co.* v. *U.S.* (1905) Holmes spoke for the Court in deciding that meat packers, charged with collusive bidding and pricefixing, had to be viewed realistically within a streaming "current of commerce" among the states and hence were subject to regulation by Congress.

Holmes knew that judges then were likely to be simple-minded men, frightened of socialism and inclined to take the conservative side of a burning question in the guise of finding law. He urged them to transcend their own social prejudices "to leave room for much that we hold dear to be done away with short of revolution." He reminded them that "the Fourteenth Amendment does not enact Mr. Herbert Spencer's *Social Statics*." He was inclined to believe that a majority has the right if it has the power to change things. In notable dissenting opinions, he upheld the legislature's right to pass maximum hours and minimum wage regulations, as well as laws against "yellow dog contracts" or child labor, positions not taken by the Court until well into the New Deal. Personally, he thought it was "empty humbug" to believe that "by tinkering with the institution of property . . . we should have women free and a piano for everybody." He took the luxuries of the few to be "a drop in the bucket," complacently believing that "the crowd now has substantially all there is." But he held too professional a conception of his function as a judge to think that his economic opinions had any constitutional bearing. A thoroughgoing empiricist, furthermore, had to consider cases "in the light of our whole experience and not merely in that of what was said a hundred years ago." Thus this conservative skeptic of all believers paradoxically was cherished by some radical believers, like the English socialist Harold Laski, with whom Holmes conducted an affectionate 20-year correspondence on literary, social, and philosophical matters.

Holmes's inflated reputation as a civil libertarian largely rests on *Abrams* v. *United States* (1919) in which he dissented from judgment under the Espionage Act against Russian emigrant radicals for disseminating leaflets urging a general strike to prevent capitalists and militarists from crushing the Russian revolution. The Espionage Act (1918) punished any intent "to cripple or hinder the United States in the prosecution of the war," and in Holmes's view "these poor and puny anonymities" in question had only intended to stop American intervention in Russia. His decision turned mainly on this technical point, though it was thereafter hailed for his liberal Darwinian flourish, "the best test of truth is the power of the thought to get itself accepted in the competition of the market." True, in 1925 (*Gitlow* v. *New York*) Holmes did cite the absence of a "clear and present danger" to uphold the right of radical speech; but it was more often his reform-minded colleague Brandeis who sharpened the phrase as a protection for dissidents. In the war-time cases against Debs and other socialists Holmes had not thought it unreasonable to say "we won't have obstacles intentionally put in the way of raising troops—by persuasion any more than by force." He was for tolerating the "aeration of all effervescing convictions" as a conservative tactic because "there is no way so quick for letting them get flat."

Having sharply turned away from the moral absolutism of abolitionist days, Holmes preferred instead the challenge of making "nice and doubtful distinctions." Neither conservatives nor liberals found consistent comfort in his decisions. In time of public danger he was willing in 1909 to yield "the ordinary rights of individuals" to the judgment of a Colorado governor that the "necessities of the moment" required preventive detention of a militant labor leader. He upheld compulsory eugenics legislation, a ban against German language-teaching in the Nebraska schools, and enforcement of peonage contracts with Alabama Negroes. But he would not sustain a Texas provision for a white primary for Democrats, nor would he deny to Negro petitioners a writ of *habeas corpus* when a trial had been infected by a "wave of public passion." And again in dissent, he opposed allowing the federal government to use "the dirty business" of wire-tapping in a state that made it a crime.

Holmes was fond of saying "certainty generally is illusion, and repose is not the destiny of man." He was unusually serene, nevertheless, because he was so certain of his own satisfaction in the exercise of his powers, so confident in his own laconic judgments on men, books, and issues, so willing to leave the weak and foolish to their fate. Scorning talk of altruism, he was determined to remain "one Philistine, egotist, unaltruistical, desirer to do his damnedest . . . while this old soldier lives." But like a good soldier, he wanted man to be "not merely a necessary but a willing instrument in working out the inscrutable end," and he characteristically added that such "vaunted egotism makes us martyrs and altruists before we suspect it." Like James, he affirmed that "to make up your mind at your peril upon a living question, for purposes of action, calls upon your whole nature." At the quiet storm center of the Court Holmes was privileged to fulfill this ideal of conduct. He was grateful at 82 to have gotten through without a breakdown and aimed to "keep producing" until he was 90. In legendary style he did, resigning on schedule in 1932, three years before he died. After 1937 the Roosevelt court would build his paradoxical monument by turning his dissents from dogmatic judicial nullifying of legislative reforms into majority decisions in favor of social experiments whose real merits he had always doubted. Facing backwards to the Civil War he had, nevertheless, solicited the future. James would have been pleased at the pragmatic result, and Adams would have appreciated its political irony. Standing at the gateway to modernity in the spirit of Janus, however, all three men would surely have cast an ambivalent eye on the territory beyond the gate.

4

Establishing a Philosophy for American Labor

SAMUEL GOMPERS
TERENCE POWDERLY
BILL HAYWOOD

by John H. M. Laslett
UCLA

"We have no ultimate ends. We are going on from day to day. We are fighting only for immediate objects—objects that can be realized in a few years. . . . We want to dress better and to live better, and become better off. . . . We are opposed to theorists. . . . We are all practical men." So testified Adolph Strasser, ex-Socialist, President of the Cigarmakers International Union, and friend of Samuel Gompers, before the Senate Committee on Education and Labor in 1883. They are words that most would probably still accept uncritically—and too readily—today, as exemplifying the labor outlook of most American workingmen throughout their history.

Historians have frequently puzzled over just why and when it was that the dominant labor ideology in America, unlike that in most European countries, became limited to the narrow, pragmatic, job-conscious form of trade unionism exemplified in the history of the American Federation of Labor and in the life of its most famous leader, Samuel Gompers, who was President with only one year's interruption from 1886 (the year of its founding) to his death in 1924. They have generally attributed the growth of the AF of L's hegemony to broad national developments that took place in the United States during the last quarter of the 19th century. These developments, which in themselves had little to do with the labor movement, were initially accomplished by a supposed psychology of abundance, induced by widespread opportunities for self-employment and the presence of an open frontier. Later there was a shift to a psychology of scarcity induced by urbanization, mass immigration, and the declining independence of the skilled artisan. Only relatively recently have historians troubled to ask themselves whether any other form of labor ideology existed in America, still less inquired as to its extent or popularity. "The American labor program" of job-conscious, business unionism, argued labor historian Selig Perlman in 1950, "has shown remarkable steadfastness through times of rapid external change. The objective . . . is unaltered from Gompers' day."

Was Perlman being fair? Certainly neither Grand Master Terence V. Powderly of the Knights of Labor, nor William D. Haywood of the Industrial Workers of the World, the other two labor leaders examined here, would have agreed with him. Cooperative, not capitalist, forms of production was the aim of the Knights. So, too, was resistance to the encroachments of industrialism, not an eager welcome for it. Or take the revolutionary preamble adopted by the 1908 convention of the Industrial Workers of the World, which had been founded at Chicago in June 1905 by Bill Haywood, Eugene Debs, Daniel DeLeon, and the then powerful Western Federation of Miners, as well as by dissident elements in the AF of L. "It is the historic mission of the working class to do away with capitalism," the Wobblies (as IWW members were called) boldly declared. "The army of production must be organized, not only for the everyday struggle with capitalists, but also to carry on production when capitalism shall have been overthrown. By organizing industrially we are forming the structure of the new society within the shell of the old."

In the end, of course, the job-conscious philosophy of the American Federation of Labor won out over both that of the Knights of Labor and the IWW, at least until the 1930s. The Federation's membership also became much larger than either of its rivals. The Knights of Labor tumbled from its peak of 750,000 in 1886 to relative insignificance by 1900; and the IWW, although far more persistent (it still exists today) in its attempts to organize the unskilled and semi-skilled, never acquired more than approximately 50,000 members at any one time. The AF of L, on the other hand, had organized two million workers by 1917, four million by 1921; and thereafter its numbers never fell below two and a half or three million, rising rapidly to more than six million in the 1930s under the competitive stimulus of the CIO. But these developments had far more to do with specific events taking place both within the labor movement and in American society at particular points in time—as well, as we shall see, with the outcome of conflicts among the three leaders we shall be dealing with—than they did with any overarching or readily predictable historical design. Neither the individual lives of Powderly, Gompers, or Haywood, nor even a brief survey of the organizations they led, can of course tell us anything absolutely conclusive about the reasons for these historical developments. Nevertheless, they can point to some highly important trends.

*   *   *

Although the broad, producer-oriented tradition of the Knights of Labor was both older and more deeply embedded in the history of American reform movements than either the revolutionary syndicalism of the IWW or the narrow business unionism of the AF of L, institutionally speaking it was the AF of L that appeared first. Such principles as exclusive craft jurisdiction over the workshop or factory, regulation of control over apprenticeship, or the sanctity of contracts can be found as far back as the Mechanics' Union of Trade Associations in Philadelphia in 1827. But it was with the rise of the so-called "new model" unionism of England's skilled workers and in particular with the high dues, extensive benefit system, and exclusive membership policies of the Amalgamated Society of Engineers and similar unions in the 1850s—all of which were later adopted by the AF of L—that the most familiar principles of craft unionism developed. Numerous skilled British engineers, glass workers, iron peddlers and other tradesmen emigrated across the Atlantic in the pre-Civil War period, and several of the American national or international craft unions, which later helped to found the AF of L—the Printers, the Moulders, and the Carpenters and Joiners International Union—were established in these years.

Samuel Gompers, principal founder of the American Federation of Labor, was too young to have had any direct experience with these ideas during his own residence in England, the country of their birth. He was born on January 27, 1850, in the impoverished Spitalfields silk-weaving district of east London, where his father and mother, Solomon and Sara Gompers, had come six years before from Amsterdam. On both sides of the family his forebears had included rabbis, merchants, inventors, even poets—surprising, perhaps for a man who is often thought of as anti-intellectual. Conceivably Gompers' later readiness, even eagerness, to collaborate as president of the AF of L with statesmen and business leaders, at some level reflected a desire to retrieve the fortunes of a family that had earlier been *déclassé*. But there is no doubt about the poverty and struggle of his earlier years. After four years picking up the rudiments of French and Hebrew (as well as a life-long love of music) at the Jewish free school near his parents' two-room tenement home, Gompers at the age of ten was apprenticed to his father's own trade of cigarmaking. Socially, if not geographically, the small, crowded cigarmaker's shop in Bishopsgate was a far cry from the respectable world of the London Trades Council where the carpenters' and engineers' leaders William Allen, Robert Applegarth, and George Odger (known collectively as the Junta) were then hammering out the craft-union policies that in 1868 would become the basis of the Trades' Union Council. And yet, as Gompers acknowledged in his autobiography, it was these same policies that two decades later "greatly influenced" the philosophy of the AF of L.

At the national level in America, for the time being at least, this philosophy was still far in the future. But its first step toward fruition were taken in 1863 when the Gompers family, oppressed by poverty and a growing number of children—Sam was the oldest son in a family of nine—migrated from London's east end to its equivalent on the lower East Side of New York. At first, little seems to have changed. For 18 months young Samuel helped his father roll and cut cigars in the combination kitchen, living room and workshop which, aside from a single bedroom, was all that the Gompers family could afford. At the age of 17 Gompers married Sophia Julian, another London-born Jewish immigrant, moved out of his parents' home to start a family of his own, and began to look about him. Employed now in a larger cigar factory instead of in a tenement workshop—and avidly studying history, science, and economics at night school—Gompers attended debates at Cooper Union on the nature and purposes of the labor movement. He sat around the long cigarmaking tables discussing them with his friend Sam Prince and his mentor Ferdinand Laurell, and in the winter of 1874 joined the great Tompkins Square demonstration of the unemployed. Six months later he was elected president of the largest Cigarmakers International Union local in New York City, Local 144.

The ensuing five years were fateful ones for Gompers, for the CMIU and, as it later turned out, for the American labor movement as a whole. During the depression of the mid-1870s, employers in New York's cigar industry had transferred much of their production from the larger shops to tenement houses, which were much more difficult to organize and where near-starvation wages were usually paid. In response Gompers, Adolph Strasser, and Sam Prince among others led a general strike of New York cigarmakers in the fall of 1877. Their goal was to abolish the tenement house system. From seven to ten thousand men walked out, supported by cigarmakers across the country. Gompers, dismissed from his job, pawned everything but Sophie's wedding ring and moved into even cheaper quarters in Brooklyn. But still the strike was lost. Leaders of Local 144 were finally convinced of the need to reform the CMIU along English lines.

Up to this point the union had admitted rollers and bunchers as well as skilled cigarmakers. There was no uniformity in dues or initiation fees, and strike benefits were paid only when there happened to be money available. At the 1879 convention of the CMIU, Gompers with Strasser in support, secured adoption of a wide range of changes designed to transform the union from a confederation of loose, sovereign locals into a tightly knit, financially sound, and stable institution primarily serving the interests of the skilled. The changes were most significant and suggestive: high dues to build a financial reserve during depressions; strike, sick, and death benefits that would provide a financial incentive for permanent membership; centralized control, especially in authorizing strikes; and, perhaps most important of all, the English principle of equalization of funds making money from one local available to others in time of stress. "Thus," as one historian observed, "there arose a new Cigar Makers International Union which became the model for many American trade unions and laid down the principles upon which the American Federation of Labor itself were to be based."

The significance of this development went largely unnoticed at the time. Most of the craft unions that were later to establish the AF of L had suffered severely during the depression of the mid-1870s. In 1872 they had finally failed in their first serious attempt to create a national labor federation, the National Labor Union. Moreover, in the early 1880s knowledgeable observers of the labor movement were understandably more impressed with the rapidly rising star of the Knights of Labor—already recognized then as a broadly-based national labor federation embracing unskilled workers, small town employees and even some farmers, as well as skilled artisans—than they were with the weak, fragmented Federation of Organized Trades and Labor Unions (the AF of L's immediate predecessor), which could boast the support of only a few, scattered east coast unions. Equally promising, at this early stage at least, was the short, but dignified and scholarly-looking figure of the man who would become the Knights's second and most famous Grand Master Workman, Terence V. Powderly. In three short years he had risen from the obscurity of a blacklisted employee on the Delaware, Lackawanna and Western Railroad to become Mayor of Scranton, Pennsylvania and then, in 1879 at the astonishingly young age of 30, he was chosen national leader of the Knights of Labor.

*   *   *

Although born on January 27, 1849, only 12 months before Samuel Gompers, and experiencing much of the same poverty and deprivation in his early years, this difference of one year symbolized a gap of at least a generation in terms of the overall development of the American labor movement. Gompers' formative years had been spent amid urban craftsmen struggling to defend their skills; and the solutions he advocated to the labor problem, although narrow and ultimately stultifying in their social consequences, appeared essentially modern and forward-looking at the time they were first advocated. Powderly's youth, by contrast, was spent in the rural atmosphere of the small, isolated, railroad town of Carbondale, Pennsylvania. His parents, Terence and Madge Powderly (the family was originally French Huguenot) were poor farmers who had emigrated from County Meath, in Ireland, to Ogdensburg, New York, in 1827. After two years of farm work, they walked the two hundred miles to Carbondale, where Terence Senior was employed by the Delaware Co. "With his axe my father assisted in chopping down the trees from which the first church in that part of the state was built," Powderly later recalled in his autobiography. "When it rained during the time of the service the congregation, although made up of strictly temperate people, was obliged to get wet." This remark, a pun on the leaky state of the church's roof, was also a reference to liquor: temperance, like other forms of self-help, was to be an important part of the Knights's philosophy.

Like his parents, Terence Powderly was a Catholic, and his Catholicism was important to him, and also indirectly to the Knights of Labor. Significant numbers of Catholics, many of them originally ex-peasants from Ireland, had joined the Knights in the 1880s, despite the fact that its Masonic ritual and oathbound secrecy (abandoned in 1881) were offensive to the Church. Powderly's Irishness was also important. His later insistence that public lands be no longer ceded to corporations and speculators derived partly from his parents' life-long commitment to the cause of freeing Ireland from the grip of the English landlord. Powderly's personal concern with land reform, moreover, helped inspire the Knights's political support for the Granger, Single-Tax and Populist parties on a scale far greater than that of the AF of L.

Land and currency reform, temperance, third-party politics, and a deep but essentially utopian and backward-looking commitment to rescuing the "independent producer" from the onrush of post-Civil War capitalism were thus the dominating influences in Terence V. Powderly's early life. He had left home at the age of 13 to become a railroad machinist, a member of the Machinists and Blacksmiths Union and, in 1877, Corresponding Secretary of District Assembly 5 in the Scranton-Reading area. In varying degree these ideas were also reflected in the national policies of the Knights of Labor. So, too, was a broad ecumenicalism with regard to organizing the great mass of working people, irrespective of race, occupation, and skill. The K of L made far greater efforts to implement ideals of social equality among its members than most American labor organizations, either before or since. True, several of its members were prominent in the anti-Chinese riots that took place in Rock Springs, Wyoming, in 1885; and in the South separate Local Assemblies for blacks were more the rule than mixed ones. Nevertheless the Knights had over 60,000 non-white members by 1886. Also a far wider variety of occupations—among them farmers and small tradesmen as well as semi-skilled and unskilled laborers—were encouraged to join both the "mixed" and the "trade" Local Assemblies of the Knights. Few of the aforementioned were permitted to enter into the skilled unions of the AF of L. For Powderly, as for many Knights, the slogan "An injury to one is an injury to all" was taken more seriously than either before or since in the American labor movement.

The corollary to this broad, humanitarian approach—and probably the most important ingredient in Powderly's social philosophy—was his hostility toward the wages system. "The aim of the Knights of Labor—properly understood—is to make each man his own employer," Powderly repeatedly stated. But this antipathy toward capitalism had no Marxism in it. Indeed Powderly was contemptuous of most socialists, only accepting a membership card in the Socialist Labor Party for a brief time in the 1880s out of friendship for its Secretary, Philip Van Patten. Unlike Haywood, Powderly was opposed to strikes or revolutionary violence as a means of solving labor disputes. And unlike Gompers (who was also strongly anti-Marxist, although for very different reasons), he had little understanding of or sympathy with a purely economic analysis of society.

Accompanying Powderly's antipathy to class conflict and his belief in education as a panacea for numerous social ills went an abiding faith in both producers' and consumers' cooperation, and this despite repeated practical disappointments. Such cooperation was a means of subverting the wage system and of returning to an economy more consistent with the human scale. Powderly, we have seen, had grown up—much like Uriah Stephens, James R. Sovereign, and other Knights leaders but unlike both Haywood and Gompers—in the pre-Civil War period when communitarianism, as propounded by Charles Fourier and Albert Brisbane, was still strong. This tradition left a permanent mark on him. Thus at the first General Assembly after his election as Grand Master Workman (held in Pittsburgh in September 1880), Powderly insisted that the delegates eschew such relatively "petty questions" as higher wages and shorter hours, and embark instead "on a system of cooperation, which will make every man his own master, and every man his own employer." Almost none of the cooperatives established by the K of L succeeded. Significantly, most of them were in western rural areas where cooperation was regarded as the first step toward establishing an independent business rather than promoting an alternate social order. Numerous rank-and-file members complained about the high-handed way in which Powderly and the Cooperative Board of the Knights attempted to make the establishment of cooperatives compulsory, while demonstrating a singular inability to raise money for their support. By the end of the decade inefficiency, lack of money, and the strong opposition of many elements in the business community had forced the Knights's leadership to abandon cooperation as the major tool of social reconstruction. Instead, they placed their hopes on organization, education, and third-party politics, and in particular on the program of the People's Party.

The picture of Terence V. Powderly that emerges from these early years as Grand Master Workman of the Knights of Labor is not an especially flattering one. He married Hannah Dever (about whom almost nothing is known) in 1872, and remained Mayor of Scranton until 1884. But the Knights's headquarters had been established in Philadelphia, which suggests Powderly's peculiarly ambivalent attitude toward the prominent office he held. His letters during this period show him to have been sharp-tongued, satirical, and sometimes vain—as, for example, in requesting John W. Hayes not to send him newspaper clippings critical of his leadership, but "to fish out a line or two of a complimentary nature." To be sure, he also showed a strong current of sympathy for the underdog and a steady desire to advance the cause of social idealism, something that often seemed to desert the AF of L's trade union leaders once they had established their official position in a craft. He was also an excellent propagandist and orator. Unlike Gompers, however, Powderly was an extremely poor administrator. He arrogantly attempted to impose his own version of arbitration and conciliation on the General Assembly of the Knights, but lacked the taste or the talent for making it work. Although admittedly not overstrong physically, he constantly complained of the demands of office—the need to travel extensively to conduct negotiations with employers. He much preferred to remain in Scranton where in addition to his duties as chief officer of the K of L, he held multiple jobs—as mayor, county health officer, and part-time manager of a grocery store. Powderly also conducted too much of the Knights's business by letter, causing one historian to dismiss him uncharitably as a "windbag whose place was on the street corner rousing the rabble to concert pitch and providing emotional compensation for dull lives."

This judgment is too harsh. The ethos of the Knights prompted resistance to the idea that American workers had become permanent wage earners who needed full-time labor leaders to guide them. Certainly it was no discredit to Powderly that he sought to maintain in his own life a position as an "independent producer." Less easy to condone, however, was his quixotic policy toward strikes. Witness, for example, Powderly's antagonism toward the highly popular Eight-Hour strike of May 1886. Or consider his ambiguous response to District 101's request in March 1886 for national K of L support of the Southwest Pacific Railroad strike, which was a disastrous defeat for the Knights. On this occasion Powderly refused to make any serious attempt to bind Jay Gould to a previous agreement. And then there was his undermining of the efforts of T. B. Barry, the Knights's own negotiator, to get a favorable settlement in the Chicago stockyards strike during the summer of 1886. Powderly, it is true, personally disapproved of the use of the strike weapon in these

1886 disputes much as he did generally. But his naive belief in arbitration as the only proper means for settling industrial disputes led him to ignore the fact that employers, then as now, rarely concede anything to the workers unless forced to do. Finally, his extremely ill-timed attempt to discipline the strikers in the middle of the 1886 walkouts brought grass-roots anger and resentment. It also produced a serious loss of confidence on the part of those who had been critical of the Order's failure to throw its weight behind the Eight-Hour movement and were now beginning to doubt the long-range effectiveness of the organization as a whole.

In turn, these losses greatly strengthened the hand of those skilled workers in the Order who had never approved the Knights's policy of encouraging Mixed Assemblies (enrolling all of the workers in a given area into one local irrespective of occupation or skill). Having joined the Knights only because their own craft unions had been temporarily overwhelmed by the mid-1870s depression, these skilled workers now seized upon the opportunity presented by the defeat of the Gould and Chicago stockyard strikes to demand the establishment of Trade Assemblies (groups of workers defined occupationally rather than geographically) and to reject the larger organizational philosophy of the Knights. With the sudden rise in K of L membership early in 1886, numerous craft unions—including the Molders, the Boiler-Makers, the Typographical Union, and the Granite Cutters—accused the Knights of stealing their members. Although accounts of such raiding were undoubtedly exaggerated on both sides, one such incident led to open warfare between them and ultimately to the downfall of the Knights. The main protagonist in the struggle was none other than Samuel Gompers' Cigarmakers Local 144.

Hostilities commenced in January 1886 when members of both Local 144 and the Progressive Union No. I of New York, a separate cigarmakers union composed mainly of socialists, were locked out for resisting a wage cut. In February, Progressive Union No. I, with the support of District Assembly 49 of the Knights, negotiated an independent agreement with the employers under which wages were restored. In exchange, the employers obtained the use of the Knights's white union label and permission to reintroduce bunching machines. Members of Local 144 were furious. Adolph Strasser denounced District Assembly 49's "bold and unscrupulous attack" against the Cigarmakers; Powderly and three other members of the K of L Executive Board journeyed to New York to investigate the incident; and Gompers himself went on a national tour to arouse other trades to the threat posed by the Knights and to urge a closer federation of the craft unions. In this critical moment Powderly refused to be conciliatory. Instead he accused the CMIU of treachery for boycotting the Knights's white label. Adding insult to injury, he claimed that intemperance was the only reason for such conduct: "Men who indulge to excess in the use of intoxicants cannot be expected to transact business with cool heads. . . . The General Executive Board," he concluded, "has never had the pleasure of meeting with Mr. Gompers when he was sober."

The fat was now truly in the fire. Although Gompers, unlike Powderly, was a gregarious, sociable man who enjoyed good food and wine (later on in life he sometimes drank to excess, enabling vaudeville comedians to raise a laugh by patting their stomachs and refer to them as their "Sam Gompers"), there is no corroborative evidence to substantiate Powderly's claim. Gompers was understandably angry. On May 18, 1886, the craft unionists proposed a non-interference treaty with the Knights, according to which the latter would refrain from organizing any trade already having a national union, expel those who acted as scabs or worked at lower than union wages, and establish no label in competition with one of a trade union. The treaty suggested that the Knights confine themselves to reform and educational work, while the craft unions would take over the main economic and collective bargaining functions of the labor movement. Quite predictably, the Knights of Labor rejected the proposed agreement. On May 25 the K of L countered by suggesting that it share equally with trade unions in labor's economic functions. Acknowledging that the craft unions contained in their ranks "a very large proportion of laborers of a high grade of skill and intelligence," it nonetheless argued that the organization of the unskilled was imperative. This body of workers must also be looked to, ran the Knights' practical explanation, "or in the hour of difficulty the employer will not hesitate to use him to depress the compensation of the skilled."

Open conflict was postponed for a few months by continued negotiations between the two groups. But at its 1886 General Assembly in Richmond, Virginia, the K of L brought matters to a head by adopting a resolution, proposed by District Assembly 49 of New York, ordering all workers holding cards in both the CMIU and the Knights to withdraw from the Cigarmakers International Union under pain of expulsion from the Order. Alarmed, the trade union negotiating committee, with Gompers well to the fore, issued a call for a convention to be held on December 8, 1886. Twenty-eight delegates from 12 national unions, six former Trade Assemblies of the K of L and seven locals, representing in all about 317,000 workers, met in Columbus, Ohio, and phased the existing Federation of Organized Trades and Labor Unions out of existence. They excluded assemblies of the Knights from membership in their new organization—the American Federation of Labor.

In the ensuing fight for control over the labor movement the tide ran quickly against the Knights. Employer hostility, the Order's virtually uniform lack of strike success after 1886, and the attempt by Mixed Assemblies to prevent their members from joining the craft unions alienated many of the skilled. Long-standing organizational weaknesses, the unwarranted assumption by the public that the K of L had supported the Haymarket riot of May 1886, and the depression of the mid-1890s did the rest. By 1895 the once-proud Knights had been reduced to less than 75,000 members, the bulk of them coming from the hard core of small-town mechanics, shop-keepers, petty employers and farmers to whom the organization's all-inclusive producer philosophy had made its first and most forceful appeal.

Throughout these final, crucial, negotiations with the craft unions Powderly again showed signs of the ambivalent and contradictory behavior that had marked his earlier career. His accusations concerning Gompers' drunkenness were in themselves trivial. There is even a suggestion in Gompers' own autobiography that they may have been inserted into Powderly's public statement without his knowledge. But they were symptomatic of a distressing lack of judgment that was also displayed on more serious occasions. Almost immediately after passage of the damaging Richmond resolution in October 1886, for example, Powderly sought to minimize its effect by promising dispensations to Cigarmakers International Union members who remained in the K of L, providing they would desist from attacks on it; and at Powderly's suggestion the resolution was in fact repealed the next year. But he himself contributed to the conflict by appointing the Knights's General Executive Board, which was dominated by District 49 "Home Club" anti-trade unionists, as its main negotiating committee with the unions. And in 1887 he took back his conciliatory gesture almost entirely by vesting Charles H. Litchman with authority to establish a Cigarmakers Trade Assembly within the Order.

Samuel Gompers, on the other hand, showed no such vacillation. Although participating in a number of conferences designed to effect a *modus vivendi* between the AF of L and the Knights—the last one taking place as late as 1894—he made it clear from the first that he would not compromise on AF of L control of the purely economic functions of the labor movement.

Contemptuously dismissing the broad, reforming purposes of the Knights as sentimental and unrealistic, he even accused the Order of deliberately acceding to the demands of the employers through its reluctance to use the strike weapon. In a speech at the founding convention of the AF of L, he unfairly alleged that the Executive Board of the Knights included grocery store keepers, ex-police chiefs, and others "floating like a scum on the top of a part of the labor movement, continually seeking to direct it to their own ends." Such men as Powderly, he declared, could not be regarded as legitimate members of the American working class.

Personal relations between the two labor leaders also continued to deteriorate. Faced by rising criticism of his authoritarian handling of the

Knights's internal affairs and by his inability or unwillingness to delegate responsibility to other officials, Powderly was forced out of office in 1893 by an alliance of western agrarians and eastern socialists led by Daniel DeLeon. His successor as Grand Master was James R. Sovereign of Iowa. When President McKinley appointed Powderly Commissioner-General of Immigration in 1897, Gompers called the choice an insult to the labor movement. And six years later, when Powderly had left the Bureau of Immigration and was seeking a new appointment, he wrote to Gompers asking him for help in obtaining a position in the Department of Commerce. "I hope you may see your way clear to say a good word for me," Powderly wrote on February 18, 1903. "Were the situations reversed I would do it for you." Gompers did not bother to reply.

With Powderly out of the way and the Knights of Labor in rapid decline, President Gompers of the AF of L, as he must now be called, together with Adolph Strasser, P. J. McGuire and others, proceeded to institutionalize at the national level the principles of high-dues–high-benefits, pure-and-simple, craft unionism that Gompers had first developed during his years with Local 144 in New York. At first it was far from easy. With almost no money, in a New York office eight feet by ten, and with a kitchen table, a child's writing desk, and tomato boxes for equipment, and with his second son, Henry, as his only helper, the 36-year-old Gompers needed all of his youthful energy and determination to keep the AF of L going. "My official duties are taking up my entire time and energy," he wrote to J. P. McDonnell in March 1887. "You may readily form an idea of the truth of this when I tell you that I have not had the pleasure of partaking of afternoon or evening meals (Sunday included) with my family for months." The hard work and single-mindedness would always be there. For all his bureaucratic methods, no one ever accused Gompers of neglecting his duties, or of lining his pockets at Federation expense, as some modern labor leaders have not hesitated to do. Unlike Powderly, Gompers seldom travelled less than ten thousand miles a year on AF of L business. His activities were varied and seemingly unending. He argued in favor of pro-labor legislation before state or federal committees, addressed labor picnics, chaired negotiating committees in major disputes, attempted to mediate jurisdiction disputes between the largely sovereign unions of the Federation. Affable, gregarious, and hail-fellow-well-met in private, Gompers in public was always "calm, dignified, and unapproachable." His was a commanding presence despite his short, stocky body, balding head and pock-marked complexion. He fiercely resented "anything and everything" that detracted from the dignity of his office.

Soon after Gompers' confirmation as President of the AF of L in 1886, he began that stream of articles, speeches, and addresses to labor conventions that would be reiterated continually over the next 30 years. All upheld the virtues of craft unionism. "I cannot impress upon you enough the importance of developing a system of high dues," he told a meeting of building trades workers in Pittsburgh in October 1888. "It is this which enables us to assist our fellow workers, and to preserve and extend the sovereignty of our trades." By "fellow workers," Gompers in practice meant skilled workers; and by "the sovereignty of our trades" he meant the autonomy and independence of the craft unions. This form of labor organization was not then the purely defensive form of business unionism it would later become. Unlike Powderly again (and in this respect like Bill Haywood), Gompers accepted the inevitability of conflict between employers and employees owing to their divergent economic interests, and he vigorously upheld the necessity for strikes. Indeed, contrary to the impression Gompers struggled to give in his autobiography, as a young man he was in many respects a Marxist. Several of his closest associates in the New York cigarmaking shops were members of the First International, Karl Marx's own revolutionary organization whose headquarters were moved from The Hague to New York in 1872. In fact, Gompers learned German so as to be able to read Marx's works in the original. And until the 1890s he conducted an extensive and often sympathetic correspondence on the nature and purposes of the labor movement with leading European Marxists, including Friedrich Engels and Wilhelm Liebknecht.

The central point is, however, that as time went on, for reasons not of logic but deriving partly from the developing character of the labor movement and partly from incidents in his own career, the radical implications in Gompers' class view of American society were progressively whittled down to two basic considerations. The first of these was a growing preoccupation with dividing up control over the terms of employment of the purely urban labor force between the AF of L and the employers. An example of this concern was the operations of the National Civic Federation, a body founded in 1900 by representatives of both labor and capital to minimize industrial conflict. (Not inaccurately, American Socialists saw this policy as one of class-collaboration.) This preoccupation evolved into a view of the labor movement as defensive and job-conscious rather than militant and class-conscious. Such a view not only ignored farmers and other petty-bourgeois elements but also made no attempt to challenge capitalist ownership of the means of production. Gompers' second consideration was based on the changes in technology, which increasingly threatened the position of industry's hand-skill workers. In response to this development, the AF of L limited its interests still further, ignoring not only farmers and petty-bourgeois elements but semi-skilled and unskilled workers as well. The reasons for these changes, which came out of the developing character of the labor movement, have already been touched upon. They derive essentially from the fact that the AF of L was born out of a reaction against the broad and inclusive character of the Knights of Labor, which was understandably unwilling to devote more than a limited share of its resources to defending the interests of the skilled worker.

The incidents in Gompers' own career that led him to reject Marxism were more idiosyncratic. But they originated, at least in part, in a series of disagreements with the policies of the Socialist Labor Party. These disagreements began with the SLP's refusal to support Gompers' campaign to get bipartisan support for a bill to abolish tenement cigar manufacture which the New York State legislature was considering in the fall of 1881. They ended with Gompers' total repudiation of the philosophy of socialism, both that of the SLP and of the more moderate Socialist Party of America. "I have kept watch upon your doctrines for 30 years," Gompers told the minority of socialist delegates to the 1903 AF of L convention. "Economically you are unsound; socially, you are wrong; industrially, you are an impossibility." Thereafter, although the radicals made several further attempts to unseat him from the presidency—the Socialist Max Hayes, for example, received a third of the votes at the 1912 AF of L convention—Gompers succeeded in confining the AF of L's official political role to lobbying for labor legislation and to supporting major party candidates who were favorably disposed toward such measures. After President Woodrow Wilson's election to the presidency in 1912 AF of L lobbying was increasingly on behalf of the Democrats.

But Samuel Gompers and the AF of L leadership were not to have it entirely their own way. Labor lost one strike after another in the 1890s. These disputes involved both unskilled and semi-skilled workers as well as craftsmen—steelmen at Homestead in 1892, railroad workers at Pullman in 1894, and coal miners nationwide in the same year. Numerous other critics joined Socialists in attacking the AF of L's exclusive preoccupation with the interests of skilled workers as narrow, self-serving, and ultimately futile. The introduction of mass-production techniques, they argued, with its attendant destruction of craft lines, had already placed the unskilled into competition with the skilled for a wide range of jobs. The influx of new immigrants from southern and from eastern Europe that took place in the 1880s simply worsened matters. The proper answer was to open up the unions to the entire labor force and not, incidentally, on the basis of the Mixed Assemblies of the old Knights of Labor. Rather there should be modern industrial unions—with each incorporating all of the wage workers in an industry into a single, coherent, and militant mass union. AF of L policies, had been hopelessly outmoded by the development of industry, complained an 1898 correspondent to the *Typographical Journal,* and Federation leaders "are only anxious to have sufficient organization of labor to guarantee themselves positions."

*   *   *

It was in this context that a second great labor leader arose to challenge the hegemony of pure-and-simple trade unionism—William D. Haywood of the Industrial Workers of the World. He must be seen against such a backdrop and as a product of industrial conflict in the trans-Mississippi West, a region where labor violence had become even more endemic than it was in the East and where the AF of L had so far done little organizing.

On June 27, 1905, at Brand's Hall in Chicago, the 36-year-old Haywood—a tall, powerful figure of a man, of ample girth but with a handsome face set off by a patch over his right eye (the result of a childhood accident)—brought the IWW's 200 founding delegates to their feet in a ringing denunciation of the labor philosophy of the AF of L. "The American Federation of Labor," he argued, "which presumes to be the labor movement of this country, is not a working class movement." "It includes organizations which prohibit the initiation of a . . . colored man; that prohibit the conferring of the obligation of foreigners." And, he continued, "The Industrial Workers of the World will be formed, based, and founded on the class struggle, having but one object and purpose and that is to bring the workers of this country into the possession of the full value of the product of their toil." Following Haywood's advice the IWW adopted a form of organization (Father Thomas J. Hagerty's celebrated Wheel of Fortune) in which all American workers—skilled and unskilled, native and immigrant, black and white, and even Orientals, an earlier target of labor's hostility in the western metal mines—were to be grouped into five main "industrial departments," with low dues and free, universal union transfer cards. The whole organization would be under the general aegis of a central IWW administration in Chicago.

Bill Haywood had taken a considerable time to come to this revolutionary position. Haywood was born in Salt Lake City, Utah, in 1869—20 years after either of our other two labor leaders and less susceptible, therefore, to labor ideologies that had been fashionable before the Civil War—but his early life bore more resemblance to Powderly's than it did to that of Gompers. His father, who died when he was only three, was native born. His mother was of Scots-Irish parentage and had been brought up in South Africa until her family was attracted by the California gold rush, only to stop short at Salt Lake City. Like Powderly, Haywood's formal education was brief, and he had a variety of odd jobs in the sparsely settled rural districts around Salt Lake before taking an apprenticeship in hard-rock mining at Winnemucca, Nevada. He also acquired his first knowledge of the labor movement from Pat Reynolds, an Irish fellow-worker who had earlier been a member of the Knights. Like Powderly, Haywood was a brilliant orator, while at the same time being more direct in his language and much more forceful. Although well-read, Haywood was in many respects anti-intellectual. Essentially a man of action, he was at his best when addressing a crowd, debating with opponents, or leading a strike demonstration, as in the famous Lawrence textile strike of 1913. There was no air of the effete intellectual about him, still less that of the pompous labor bureaucrat.

And yet, like Gompers, Haywood was also a good administrator. The period between 1914 and 1917, when he was working full time for the IWW, was one of the few in which the organization achieved a modicum of stability. To be sure, he also had qualities that would have shocked the Victorian moral code of his elders in the labor movement. An unhappy marriage to Nevada Jane, a crippled, care-worn, frontier woman, frequently drove him to the solace offered by saloons and brothels. Indeed, in January 1906, when he was arrested—along with President Charles A. Moyer and Charles A. Pettibone of the Western Federation of Miners—on trumped-up charges of murdering ex-Governor Steunenberg of Idaho, Pinkerton detectives found him in a Denver house of prostitution, virtually within walking distance of his family home. Despite these lapses as well as an often-exaggerated reputation as a no-good layabout and as a sinister subversive, Haywood at his best was a hero to ordinary working people in a way that Powderly and Gompers never were. "He is the embodiment of the Sorel philosophy, roughened by the American industrial and a civic climate, a bundle of primitive instincts, a master of direct statements," wrote a perceptive foreign observer, J. Ramsey MacDonald, after the 1910 Copenhagen Congress of the Second International. "I saw him at Copenhagen, amidst the leaders of the working class movements drawn from the whole world, and there he was dumb and unnoticed; I saw him addressing a crowd in England, and there his crude appeals moved his listeners to wild applause. He made them see things, and their hearts bounded to be up and doing."

In view of Haywood's later reputation as a syndicalist, it is paradoxical that he first came to the fore as an efficient trade union administrator. In 1896 he went to work in the mines of Silver City, Idaho, where he met Ed Boyce, then President of the Western Federation of Miners, and became Secretary of the Silver City local. For four years he led this local cautiously and efficiently along the now standard American trade union route: job security, shorter hours, and higher wages. Haywood became Secretary-Treasurer of the WFM in 1900. What in fact turned the moderate Socialist reformer into a militant and a rebel was the ruthless, bitter, and—from the WFM point of view—disastrous 1903–1904 Cripple Creek strike. Before walking out, over a matter that in its origin was nothing more alarming than the eight-hour day, the WFM locals had offered to negotiate with the gold mine owners. But the Colorado Mine Owners Association, in conjunction with state Governor James H. Peabody and numerous Citizens Alliances, were determined not only to categorize the WFM as an un-American, seditious and even as a criminal organization but also to smash it. In a naked display of power the State sent in militia, made illegal searches and seizures, and forcibly deported over 400 miners from Colorado. Deputies openly attacked Haywood himself on the streets of Cripple Creek. He wounded one of them severely, but was freed soon afterward since the deputies were clearly to blame.

The Cripple Creek strike represented the culmination of a long series of bitterly fought struggles that had all the characteristics of class war. It was a turning point in Haywood's career just as the 1877 general strike of cigarmakers in New York City had been for Samuel Gompers, but with diametrically opposite consequences for the development of their respective ideological views. For Cripple Creek prompted Haywood to reject conventional labor tactics in favor of militant industrial unionism as the only proper form of labor organization (whereas Gompers retreated into a defensive position involving only one section of the working class). It also caused him—and many of those who would join him in founding the IWW 18 months later—to doubt even the value of Socialist political action as a means of affording protection to the worker. Again, interestingly enough, Haywood, like Gompers, rejected Socialist politics. Gompers had done so on the ground of voluntarism: compulsory social legislation such as old age, sickness, or unemployment insurance, he believed, would make the worker less dependent on his union and more upon the state. Haywood, on the other hand, had come to see the union not as providing a substitute for the liberal state, but as offering the means for fashioning a revolutionary alternative to it. The only direct experience of state power for many Wobblies had been at the receiving end of a policeman's club; but they nonetheless feared that even members of their own class, if elected to political office would become corrupted by participation in capitalist politics. Hence direct action in the form of strikes, demonstrations, sit-downs, and even sabotage (although the degree to which the IWW actually practiced violence was predictably exaggerated by the press) was preferred to voting as the only sure means of asserting economic control over the means of production. In theory at least, the culmination was the general social strike.

The character of its membership influenced the IWW's hostility towards political action. Before 1908 its members were largely western metal miners or disaffected AF of L members working in industrial occupations. Following the withdrawal of the WFM from the IWW in 1908, IWW membership came to be drawn, with some exceptions, from a sub-proletariat of lumbermen, wheat farmers, migratory fruit pickers, unnaturalized immigrants, or southern Negroes. Since many of these workers could not vote, the IWW's ideological move towards syndicalism was thereby reinforced and encouraged.

At the time of the IWW's founding in 1905, however, much of this syndicalist doctrine was still in the future. Haywood himself was a member of the Socialist Party Executive Committee from 1909 to 1913; and it was not until the latter year that he was recalled from his position on the Committee because of his alleged advocacy of violence. But this did not discourage President Gompers and other AF of L leaders. They denounced the IWW as a dual union along the lines of the Socialist Trades and Labor Alliance. (The STLA had been established by Daniel DeLeon as a rival to the AF of L in 1895, and it associated briefly with the IWW.) The IWW's goal, they charged, was not to promote industrial unionism, but "to direct, pervert and disrupt the whole labor movement." If the trade union movement were to be based on the fatuous "scheme" of industrial organization, Gompers told a Pittsburgh audience in August 1905, "the tinker, tailor, and the candlestick maker would legislate upon every minute detail affecting the interests of the workers." In other words, the labor movement would revert back to nothing more than "the old K of L idea." Haywood himself returned the dislike for Federation officials, suggesting the depth of the mistrust that now separated the radicals from the craft unionists in the labor movement. "Looking at him," Haywood later wrote of an encounter with Gompers in 1898, "one could realise that he might even refer jokingly to the defeat of a great labor struggle, if it were being conducted by an organization that was not strictly in accordance with his views." This was an apparent reference to the WFM's defeat in the 1897 Leadville strike. In this instance, the AF of L had declined to help the metal miners, a refusal that had been one of the original catalysts in the formation of the IWW. "Sam . . . had small snapping eyes," Haywood concluded, rather maliciously, "a hard cruel mouth, wide with thin drooping lips, heavy jaws, a personality vain, conceited, petulant, and vindictive."

Gompers himself, however, was also unfair in dismissing the IWW simply as a dual union out to destroy the AF of L. Undeniably, it had been founded in part by disaffected locals of Brewery Workers, Coal Miners, Garment Workers and others who sought to persuade members of existing AF of L unions to join them. Moreover, despite its industrial-union rhetoric, one of the long-term weaknesses of the IWW lay in its inability to establish a viable basis of its own in any of the standard industrial occupations, once the Western Federation of Miners had withdrawn in 1908. Except for a limited number of railroad, copper, and textile workers who joined briefly in the period just before and after the First World War, its membership continued to be confined to marginal elements in the labor force. Their occupations had little prestige or bargaining power, and their transiency was often such that they were unable to provide any stable organizational base. Gompers' assertion, however, that success for the IWW would have simply meant a reversion to the "old K of L idea" was wide of the mark. True, the IWW reasserted the Knights's old spirit of solidarity among all the workers, its antipathy towards craft-union exclusiveness, and its hostility toward capitalism as an institution. But it looked forward to a revolutionary general strike as the ultimate means of changing capitalist society and not backward to the recreation of a pre-industrial order. It upheld direct action and even violence as the catalysts of change, rather than arbitration and political action. And although its membership was organized into general unions that were more like the Mixed Assemblies of the K of L than the industrial unions later organized by the CIO, it accepted fundamental Marxist notions concerning the inevitability both of industrialization and of revolution. It did *not* seek to resurrect utopian ideas of a cooperative universe.

Bill Haywood's leadership may be measured by his degree of responsibility for the IWW's progressive retreat into the fringes of the labor force. It must be remembered that he never dominated the organization to the same extent that Gompers did the AF of L, or Powderly the Knights. He was, for instance, in jail for a year after its founding on the Steunenberg murder charge; he had no direct association with the IWW between 1907 and 1910; and he jumped bail to flee to the Soviet Union in 1921 after his arrest and conviction (along with virtually all other national IWW leaders) on charges of obstructing America's efforts in the First World War. He can hardly be found culpable for the IWW's attrition in the 1920s, for the tactically questionable "free speech" fights of the Wobblies in the years 1907–10 or for the crucial quarrel between political activists and direct actionists at the 1906 IWW convention, a quarrel that led ultimately to the withdrawal of the WFM. There were certain errors of judgment and some confusion over goals—whether to cooperate with the Socialist Party and whether to organize a mass base in the cities or concentrate on migrant workers. Nonetheless, it is less easy to assess the role of leadership in contributing to the IWW successes and failures than it is about either the Federation or the Knights. First of all, it was far more of a grass-roots kind of organization than either of the other two, thus tending to reduce the role of national leaders. Moreover, the IWW, almost from the first, was subject to such hostility from the press, from employers, from state agencies, and from Gompers and the AF of L itself (the AF of L willingly joined in the federal government's wartime persecution of the organization as subversive), that it is dubious whether any leader could have significantly altered the IWW's place in history.

And yet in Haywood's very first speech to the 1905 founding convention, he himself appeared to reflect the Wobblies' ambivalence about their role which was to dog the IWW in its subsequent development. "We are here for the purpose of organizing . . . an organization broad enough to take in all the working class," he asserted, a purpose which, had the IWW been allowed to carry it out successfully, might perhaps have generated a mass labor movement of industrial unionists two generations before the CIO appeared. "What I want to see from this organization," however, Bill Haywood added, "is an uplifting of the fellow that is down in the gutter." Organizing fellows down in the gutter is what the IWW came largely to be remembered for. It was a noble ideal, but it certainly did not make for organizational stability.

Death came to each of our labor protagonists in a way that was fairly consistent with the manner of their earlier years. After being dismissed as Grand Master Workman of the Knights of Labor in 1893, Terence V. Powderly, to his credit, did not immediately seek to exploit his fame but instead sought employment as a machinist or a railroad conductor. Failing in both because of his reputation as a labor agitator, he then took up the law. And his later career as a federal official included various posts in the Bureau of Immigration from 1907 onward. He also tried his hand at a number of commercial ventures in coal, oil, and real estate, thus in a sense preserving his reputation as an "independent producer" until his death at the age of 75 on June 24, 1924. Six months later, on December 13, 1924, Samuel Gompers also died, in San Antonio, Texas, after attending the inauguration of President Plutarco Calles in Mexico City. He survived every challenge to his presidency from Socialists and industrial unionists, the last one coming in 1919 from John L. Lewis, the youthful President of the United Mine Workers of America, who was to inaugurate the CIO in 1936. And he ended his career still a defiant believer in voluntarism and trade autonomy, even though such views were becoming increasingly anachronistic.

On the other hand, Bill Haywood, consistently cold-shouldered throughout his career by every official American institution (including the official labor movement), died lonely, sick, and unmourned in a Moscow hospital on May 18, 1928. He had tried to make a new life for himself in the Soviet Union, marrying a Russian national and working for a time as leader of the Kuzbas Mining Colony. But Haywood, unable to adjust to Soviet society, died disillusioned in the Communist system. Half of his ashes were buried alongside those of John Reed in the Kremlin wall; the other half were interred in Chicago's Waldheim cemetery near those of the Haymarket martyrs.

Biographical sketches such as these can illuminate the movements out of which the dominant labor ideology in America ultimately came. But they do not, of course, tell why the conservative AF of L officials, despite the increasingly anachronistic character of many of their views, managed to retain control of the labor movement of this country until the 1930s. History after all, especially the history of social movements, is more than a record of the actions of great men. It used to be fashionable to say that the AF of L won out in this three-way contest either because job-conscious trade unionism was "natural" to all industrial workers when left alone by interfering intellectuals; or, as we noted at the beginning of this essay, because 19th-century developments in the American economy were such as to displace a prevailing psychology of opportunity with one of scarcity (defined as a decline in the opportunities for self-employment). Neither of these propositions will hold up under sustained analysis. It should be clear from what we have said that the Knights of Labor —which had a producer-conscious, not a job-conscious, form of labor ideology—was just as much a response to the growth of this alleged psychology of scarcity as was the AF of L. And if the central issue for labor at the end of the 19th century was to devise a response to the problem of diminishing opportunities, there was no logical reason why it should have chosen the job-conscious accommodationist response of the AF of L rather than the revolutionary, class-conscious response characteristic of the IWW. The fact that labor did so is partly attributable to the three leaders whose careers we have examined—and, of course, to other union spokesmen and rank-and-file members whose lives we have not touched upon.

But profound internal developments in the nature of American society also determined labor's choices. The creation and preservation of a form of labor aristocracy was central to Gompers' efforts. This form also appeared in most European countries during this period (in England, most notably), but was later successfully challenged from below on the Continent. A comparable challenge did not succeed in America—at least insofar as such can be seen in the efforts of the leaders of the Knights of Labor and the IWW. This failure can be attributed partly to Gompers' own good fortune and astuteness, and partly to weaknesses of leadership displayed by Powderly and Haywood. But it was due more to the presence of other factors—government and big business preference for AF of L unionism; the suppression of left-wing alternatives; and, perhaps most importantly of all, the ethnic and racial fragmentation of the labor force. Such developments enabled the AF of L to identify the preservation of an aristocracy of craftsmen with fear of unskilled immigrants and non-whites —for an understanding of which the reader must look to the lives of the three labor leaders discussed here as well as to the forces that transcended them.

5

Removing the Welcome Mat: Changing Perceptions of the Immigrant

CHARLES W. ELIOT
HENRY CABOT LODGE
EDWARD A. ROSS

by Hugh Hawkins
Amherst College

If by some miracle the United States had refrained from major restriction on immigration until the 1960s or 1970s, it is easy to imagine that restriction would then have come with ecologists leading the activists, insisting that Congress "do something." Demonstrations of the unnatural prolongation of individual life, the limits of space, the limits on energy sources, denials that growth automatically means improvement, talk of quality rather than quantity, descriptions of the benefits of Zero Population Growth, such arguments might well have dominated immigration restrictions in the last third of the 20th century. Questions about the rest of the world ("Aren't we all on spaceship Earth together?") would have been answered with the notion of America as an example of ecological balance and offers to subsidize birth control programs abroad. Such talk is heard today in connection with immigration policy, but since the basic decision to set a ceiling was made in the 1920s, it lacks the fervor of the earlier drive for restriction.

This imaginary scenario for American immigration restriction lets us put ourselves in the picture. It suggests how a restrictionist might think of himself as a reformer and not a killer of the dream. Similarly, the following discussion, by dealing closely with three individuals who concerned themselves with immigration policy, shows human beings with mixed vices and virtues, not one hero (an anti-restrictionist) and two villains (restrictionists). These men were tragic mixtures.

Tragedy, in fact, is the central theme of the growth of restrictionism and its triumphant establishment as law in the 1920s. Restriction was achieved in a spirit of racism, one of the most sinister beliefs in the modern world. Science, which should have been a corrective to racism, was instead used to support restriction, suggesting how easily the scientific method and the tentative findings of science can be abused.

* * *

Appropriately, it is the oldest of the three men, Charles W. Eliot, whose ideas fit most closely with what in the 19th century would have been properly called the traditional American attitude toward immigration. That attitude was rooted deep in the national experience. Immigrants filled an economic need, it held, and the more who came, the faster the country could be built up. The American environment was considered so immensely assimilative that "foreigners" rapidly became "Americans." Almost as strong was the belief that America had a mission to be a sanctuary for the oppressed of the world.

Born in Boston in 1834, Charles W. Eliot grew up amid such ideas. His Puritan ancestors had been among the 17th-century settlers of Massachusetts. The economic opportunities of the nation had been demonstrated by his grandfathers, both import merchants whose wealth increased with the growth of the new nation. In a spirit of noblesse oblige, his father, Samuel A. Eliot, also a businessman, devoted himself to prison and educational reform and served as Mayor of Boston and as a Congressman. The Eliots were a conservative but tolerant family. In fact, Samuel was ghostwriter for the autobiography of the fugitive slave Josiah Henson (a major source for *Uncle Tom's Cabin*), and his children recalled with pride that black men had dined at the family table. The Eliots were theological liberals; they were pillars of Boston's patrician King's Chapel, usually considered the oldest Unitarian church in the country.

Charles Eliot was an only son. A beloved though unpampered child, he had early instilled in him a powerful sense of duty and self-discipline as well as respect for those who worked with their hands. From boyhood he was tall and erect, enjoying wonderfully good health which preserved him until his 93rd year. (His life spanned American history from the Age of Jackson to the Jazz Age.) Amid all this good fortune, the boy had one heavy cross to bear: his face was disfigured by an ugly birthmark, a purple welt that curled from his right upper lip across his cheek. From his early years he knew what it meant to be different. Later, he confided to a friend that at the age of ten he had vowed to himself that he would not let this disfigurement ruin his life. However, certain aspects of his personality were attributable in part of this facial blemish—his highly dignified, formal bearing, which many interpreted as coldness, his driving ambition to achieve success in his career, and his sympathy for the underdog.

Eliot's career could hardly have been a greater success, unless perhaps he had become President of the United States, an office for which many believed him well fitted. Resisting his father's advocacy of the life of a businessman, Charles chose to become a student and teacher of science at a time when the name "scientist" was scarcely known. He was fascinated by chemistry, especially its applied forms. Harvard College, from which he graduated in 1853, called him back a year later as a tutor. He was an imaginative teacher of mathematics and chemistry and was among the first to introduce both field and laboratory work in American higher education. He pursued enough researches to understand how passionately a scientist might dedicate himself to the search for truth, seeing it as good in itself, whether it was "useful" or not. But Eliot displayed such genius in another area of university life, administration, that in time he put both teaching and research behind him. He became the righthand man of Harvard's President James Walker and took over the duties of dean of the scientific school. With unrivaled ease and aptness, he could draw up an agenda, frame a motion, spot needless waste, suggest reforms in teaching method and curricular organization, and identify talent in others.

In 1869, after a period of study in Germany and teaching at the new Massachusetts Institute of Technology, Eliot became President of Harvard. At 35 he was the youngest man ever to hold that office, and he remained in it for 40 years. From the start, he pushed for higher standards and clearer organization (most dramatically in the medical school), but for all his administrative genius, it was dedication to individual freedom that dominated the educational work that made him famous. He unrelentingly advanced the free elective system and did more than any other single person to undermine the rigid curriculum of classics and mathematics characteristic of America's colleges. He had an almost romantic faith in the ability of young people to know what they liked and needed and accordingly to choose courses wisely. In harmony with this view of individual freedom, Eliot supported the abolition of required religious services and brought in a variety of religious leaders to conduct voluntary worship and to counsel students. Catholics, Jews, and blacks found the doors to Eliot's cosmopolitan Harvard open. At the same time Eliot, in the name of freedom, tolerated the exclusiveness of Harvard clubs and private dormitories, which set limits to this welcome.

Eliot's open university was consonant with his faith in unrestricted immigration. His views were particularly important because he gradually became more than a respected educational leader: he emerged as a respected publicist and in time was regarded as a national sage. He contended that being a university president did not compel him to limit his activities as a citizen. In 1884 he helped launch the Mugwump movement, which resisted the Republican presidential nomination of James G. Blaine, a legislator with a dubious reputation for honesty. Like other Mugwumps, Eliot argued for free trade, "sound money," and merit civil service. His study of economics during his college years had left an indelible effect, and he began his public life as a quintessential 19th-century Liberal. Certain economic laws set things right automatically and government should not try to do for people what they ought to do for themselves. To Eliot this belief in laissez-faire economics was widely applicable. For example, it even accounted for his (temporary) opposition to publicly supported high schools and state universities. Gradually, however, Eliot modified his advocacy of laissez faire. He began to call for public health measures, regulation of monopolistic industry, and conservation. As he put it in 1905, "The first half of the 19th century saw the development of individualism, the last half of collectivism. The generation to which I have belonged has had experience with both principles, and has found each wanting without the other."

Eliot spoke and wrote forcefully and simply in an era given to flowery and long-winded prose. He was among the first university presidents to travel widely on public relations junkets, and huge audiences came to hear him. Increasing during the 1890s, his popularity crested toward the end of his administration. Even after his retirement in 1909, he continued to make public addresses and to write for popular magazines. The *Harvard Classics*, which he edited, sold phenomenally well. Among the complimentary labels given him was "America's first private citizen," and when he wrote a letter to the editor, newspaper readers took notice. If what he said often reflected conventional wisdom or the skimmings from some one else's scholarship, it was put with memorable succinctness. The spirit in which he wrote was hard to resist. He had faith in democracy and in people. His optimism was boundless.

In that laissez-faire spirit which Eliot approved, the federal government long refrained from taking action regarding immigration. The first 19th-century immigration law came in 1882 when Congress, in response to West Coast agitation, excluded Chinese. In drawing up a platform for a proposed new national political party two years later, Eliot made one of its major tenets the proposition that immigration should be "without distinction of race, nationality, or religion." (Blaine, the standard-bearer of the Republican Party Eliot had just left, strongly supported Chinese exclusion.) In an article published in 1896, Eliot included free immigration as one of "Five American Contributions to Civilization." He ranked it in importance with peace-keeping, freedom of religion, manhood suffrage, and high standard of living.

Eliot apparently did not oppose the provisions of the 1882 act that made immigration somewhat selective by barring convicts, lunatics, idiots, and persons likely to become a public charge. He was willing to have the federal government assert such control. But when in the 1890s a movement developed that sought in impose a literacy test as a requirement for entrance, he was among those most strongly opposed. Literacy, he maintained, proved "neither health nor character."

In responding to restrictionists over the years, Eliot placed fundamental emphasis on the economic argument for immigration. In the baldest sense—and he could put things baldly—the United States needed laborers. The country had enormous potential, given its natural resources, rapidly improving technology, and entrepreneurial spirit. With labor in short supply, it was only common sense to welcome newcomers.

Immigrants were willing to do the rougher forms of labor, Eliot rather coldbloodedly pointed out, because they were used to hard work, and America's wage rates were high by European standards. Those already here could accordingly move up the economic ladder as new waves of immigrants arrived. Immigrant labor, Eliot also noted, tended to come in boom periods and to decline during depressions. In fact, many immigrants returned home in hard times. Did this make them bad Americans, mere birds of passage? Not at all, Eliot responded: they must have made some contribution, if they had saved enough to get home. Moreover, the elasticity they provided was part of an economically rational process. After the American Federation of Labor in 1897 officially urged a literacy barrier for immigrants, Eliot found it even more agreeable to expose the weaknesses of the economic case for restriction. He had always suspected that labor unions did harm by limiting the freedom of individual workers.

Eliot's arguments were sometimes dubious. When others announced that immigrants must now crowd into urban slums since America's free land was exhausted, Eliot branded this notion as nonsense. "Immense areas in the United States," he wrote in 1911, "are not settled at all, or are very sparsely inhabited. From New England to California the crops are not thoroughly gathered and marketed, because there are not hands enough to do the work." He overlooked, of course, the resistance of both immigrants and native Americans to settling in the often inferior lands passed over by earlier settlers. Reference to the peak needs for labor at harvest time left unanswered the question of what additional farm laborers would do during the rest of the year.

Eliot put with particular forcefulness the argument for America as a place of refuge, a view as old as the nation itself. "People who exile themselves and encounter all the risks of a new start in life in a strange land must have some strong motive for such extraordinary conduct. At any rate, the decision on the question whether America is still needed as a refuge may best be left to the decision of the people most interested, to the people who, being poor or hopeless at home, think they see brighter prospects and an animating hope in the New World." Immigrants were the "good Americans" of the future, Eliot insisted. Refugees from political and religious oppression had demonstrated their love of freedom. Those who fled poverty had shown themselves to be more "enterprising" than their countrymen who stayed behind. They also had been sturdy enough to undertake and survive the voyage.

This faith in assimilation rested not only on Eliot's view of the quality of the immigrants but also on his positive appraisal of American society. Besides the nation's physical environment, he stressed the openness which characterized American social institutions. America's "free institutions"—so different, he believed, from those of hidebound Europe—would transform the immigrant. How could any one resist the beneficial influences of democracy, religious freedom, and public education? The ballot he saw as a means of political education, and although people might vote wrong, they learned from their mistakes. Under religious liberty, men were more likely to develop a sincere religion and to respect those of a different faith. As to the common school, it taught not just information and skills but built the character needed for good citizens.

Perhaps of greatest importance in Eliot's belief in assimilation was his deep-running individualism: he hated to see people put into classifications that let them be treated routinely or mechanically. Although as a young man Eliot had shared his family's suspicion of Emerson's radical individualism, in time he incorporated much of Emerson's thought into his own. "Self-reliance," a central tenet of the Concord Sage, was persistently recommended by Eliot. In his opinion, this quality had brought the immigrant to the New World, and because American institutions stimulated even more self-reliance, the immigrant would thrive and come to share the social faith of his new homeland.

Eliot observed that even in the same family wide diversities could exist among individuals. He believed in family tradition and in the contribution of "durable families" to the nation, but he also was confident that a "natural aristocracy" would be drawn in part from members of hitherto undistinguished families. Following Darwin's emphasis on chance variations in nature, Eliot argued that new abilities could crop up anywhere. He was offended by one Harvard professor who held that all the nation's good literature came from "old American stock."

Although Eliot's pro-immigration attitude was clearly on record in the late 19th century, he rarely dwelt on the subject in that period. As advocates of restriction increasingly organized themselves into propaganda and lobbying groups, counter-organizations were formed, often led by immigrants. When such groups as the National Liberal Immigration League or the Society for Italian Immigration turned to Eliot for support, he was quick to respond. Not burdened by self-doubt, he could be counted on for emphatic statements, such as "The more Italian immigrants that come to the United States the better." He showed no sympathy for the Immigration Restriction League (IRL), which was formed by a small group of Harvard alumni in 1894 and gradually gained considerable influence. On one occasion, when an IRL leader sent him a copy of his latest restrictionist article, Eliot peppered the margins with negative comments. To the complaint, for instance, that "sentiment" and "humanity" were hampering the precise application of immigration laws, Eliot shot back, "Who would have it otherwise?"

It would be poor history, however, to imply that Eliot was not influenced by the same forces that triggered restrictionism. While pointing out that immigrants were often blamed for social problems that should be attributed to industrialization and urbanization, he worried about the political effects of large numbers of recently-arrived voters in eastern cities. By 1904 he favored the imposition of both educational and property tests for voting. When he toured the South in 1909, his eagerness to build rapport with white Southerners carried him away. He declared that Massachusetts could readily sympathize with the South's racial problem, since the State had large infusions of Irish, Italian, and Portuguese newcomers who lacked experience in self-government.

But Eliot never let this view make him an advocate of exclusionist measures. Indeed the increasing frequency with which Eliot wrote and spoke in favor of traditional unrestricted immigration suggests the rising opposition to that policy. His espousal of free immigration in 1884 was doubtless attuned to the feelings of most Americans, except in California, where agitation against admitting Chinese had recently succeeded. Soon, however, the national mood began to change.

The term "nativism" was coined in the United States about 1840 to identify the belief that the presence of foreigners was a major threat to the nation. Native-born Americans had earlier found many immigrants personally uncongenial, but this repugnance was not an ism. It usually was unconnected with any theory that immigrants as a group menaced the country.

Such pre-Civil War nativism had been strongly anti-Catholic. Eliot, who could recall events of that period, often mentioned that his father as Mayor of Boston had helped put down one of the anti-Irish riots. This early wave of nativism, sometimes labeled the "Protestant Crusade," had crested in the mid-1850s, when the Native American, or Know-Nothing, Party won elections in several states. But after the Civil War, nativism was in eclipse. The North recalled the contribution of foreign-born soldiers to the Union army, and white Southerners tried hard to attract European immigrants because they feared black labor would prove undependable.

One can usefully analyze nativism, as historian John Higham has done, by dividing it into the three categories of anti-Catholicism, anti-radicalism, and racism. The anti-radical form, which had played a major role in the anti-foreign legislation adopted under President John Adams shortly after the French Revolution, revived dramatically during the 1880s. A general uneasiness over the conspicuous gulf between rich and poor in the growing cities, the frequency of strikes, and the foreign origin of many labor leaders increased fears among those who had been eagerly welcoming newcomers.

The Haymarket Affair of 1886 catalyzed these feelings and led to the first widespread outburst of nativism since the 1850s. References to immigrants began to identify them less with the strong back than with socialism and anarchism. It became easy to blame labor troubles on foreign agitators.

Nativism further intensified in the late 1880s as anti-Catholicism showed renewed life. In Massachusetts, Illinois, and Wisconsin there were strong movements to bring parochial schools under public supervision. (Eliot testified against one bill with such a goal.) Old tales about Protestant girls held captive in nunneries began to circulate, as well as stories that the Pope was instructing his minions to migrate to the United States in order to seize control of the government. This wave of anti-Catholicism brought with it several new organizations, the most important being the American Protective Association, which had perhaps a half million members by 1894.

Then there was racism, which would show the greatest staying power as a force generating anti-immigration feeling. Racism was essentially the belief that inherited physical traits of identifiable population groups called races significantly shape the mental, moral, emotional, and social quality of individuals in that group, accompanied by the belief that some races are superior to others. The more self-conscious and rationalized a race-oriented social program is, and the more importance given it by its supporters, the more fittingly it is called an ideology.

The term "ethnic group" lets us speak of those who are significantly unified, whether by ancestry, religion, language, national background, or some combination of these. Blacks, Jews, and Italian-Americans are by such a definition ethnic groups. In the early 1900s, however, all three were called races, with little attention to a precise definition. Significantly, this was done by scholars who considered themselves experts on race.

American thought on the question of race was moderated first by a religion that pictured God as willing to intervene to affect the fate of any individual soul, and then by a strong belief in the power of the environment, a view developed as part of the Enlightenment. Environmentalism was often naive and exaggerated. Some shift away from it was almost inevitable. But if heredity had to be given its due, there was no pre-ordained reason that Americans should think increasingly of human beings as divided into races or should focus attention upon what was physiologically given at the time of birth as a measure of superiority and inferiority. Nor should they insist that heredity was vastly more influential than environment in determining an individual's characteristics. Yet such views became widely held in the United States after 1900.

Developments in the science of biology played a major role in this shift. Darwin had hypothesized a process of natural selection so that forms better adapted to the environment survived and reproduced, and this interpretation was generally accepted among educated Americans by the 1880s. While not inevitably racist, this view could be used to strengthen a belief in race. The focus on struggle could be applied to groups as well as individuals, and the revolutionary idea that species were not fixed for all time suggested disquieting possibilities of modification or disappearance of human types.

Among historians and social scientists, a naturalistic world view was spreading, and they gave the idea of race increased attention after Darwin's work appeared. Racist interpretations of America's greatness emerged conspicuously after the Civil War. Terminology revealed the chaotic condition of ethnology (the study of races) at the time. The favorite identification of the ancestral group was "the Anglo-Saxons," but some preferred to speak of "Teutons," and others chose the broader term "Aryans." Racial theories raised the question of whether immigrants were in fact as readily assimilable as had been believed, and even whether continued immigration was desirable. Some felt that Anglo-Saxon "blood" was powerful, consistent, and absorbent; others were not so sure.

Another article in the traditional American support for immigration, the belief that newcomers were an economic benefit to the country, came under challenge. It was charged that immigrants were being brought over to benefit, not the nation as a whole, but steamship companies that profited from cramming their vessels with human cargo, labor-exploiting industrialists, families wanting servile housemaids, liquor interests, and municipal bosses. Aliens allegedly took jobs away from natives and lowered the standard of living for all workers.

From a variety of motives, then, Americans began to raise doubts about the long-standing assumption that newcomers were a blessing. The way the wind was blowing was suggested by an essay contest sponsored by the American Economic Association in 1888. The topic was not "Immigration," but "The Evil Effects of Unrestricted Immigration."

*   *   *

Henry Cabot Lodge is best remembered as the Senator who led the struggle against Woodrow Wilson's plan for a League of Nations. Less dramatic and generally forgotten were his efforts to restrict immigration, which may be greater than those of any other single individual.

A superficial glance suggests that Lodge had much in common with Eliot. As children they shared some of the most intimate domestic memories, for when Eliot's father was wiped out by the 1857 Panic, the Lodges purchased his Beacon Street mansion and made it their home. Both Eliot and Lodge are properly classified as Boston Brahmins, a class that felt wealth obliged them to achieve personal distinction and social usefulness. Lodge was born in Boston in 1850, into a family whose inherited wealth was still growing through vigorous activity in the import business. His father owned some of the clipper ships that sailed in the China trade before the Civil War. By Yankee standards, the Lodges were latecomers; Henry Cabot Lodge's grandfather migrated to the United States only after the Revolution. But on his mother's side, he was descended from some of the earliest Puritans. His great-grandfather, George Cabot, had been a leader of the Federalist Party and a confidant of George Washington.

With his father's death, 12-year-old Henry Cabot Lodge was left as the only son of a devoted, over-indulgent mother. Short in stature, though physically vigorous, the curly-haired Lodge possessed youthful good looks that bordered on prettiness. As an older man, with the mustache and goatee that became his hallmark, he had an imposing, even commanding appearance.

Lodge had a good mind, but graduated from Harvard in 1871 with an undistinguished record. Lacking a fixed career goal, he married, travelled to Europe, and then took a Harvard law degree. His intellectual awakening in the mid-1870s seems largely attributable to his relationship with Henry Adams, one of America's greatest teachers of history and a brilliant social critic. Lodge enrolled as a graduate student in history at Harvard and also assisted in editing the highly-respected *North American Review*. At the same time, he began to write book reviews as well as articles on history and current affairs. In 1876 he received Harvard's first Ph.D. in political science and stayed on to teach history for three years. Lodge's thesis on Anglo-Saxon land law was shortly followed by a biography of his great-grandfather, George Cabot. He rapidly produced other biographies and a textbook on American colonial history. His flair for writing and his position on the Harvard faculty could easily have led to an academic future if politics had not begun to claim him. Making a gradual transition from one career to the other, he earned the label "scholar in politics."

If Lodge had had a remarkably favored existence, his political career was hardly handed to him without effort. Although he won a seat in the Massachusetts lower House in 1879 on his first try, he lost in his original bids for the State Senate and Congress. Opponents sought to brand him as the "silver spoon young man" and noted that he parted his name as well as his hair in the middle. Defeat taught him the ways of "practical politics." That he had learned well was clearly shown in 1884, when—although opposing James G. Blaine at the Republican convention—he refused to bolt after Blaine won the nomination. This stand brought him the scorn of the Mugwumps, who followed men like Eliot out of the Party, but more important, it gained the lasting gratitude of professional politicians and the Republican rank and file. Some of the Mugwumps got their revenge in 1890 by defeating the "opportunistic" Lodge for re-election to the Harvard Board of Overseers. Party loyalists, on the other hand, sent him to Congress in 1886. Elevated to the Senate in 1893, he remained there for the rest of his life.

The causes for which Lodge labored in Congress included legislation to establish federal supervision of polling places (in order to restore the free ballot to Southern Blacks), stronger merit civil service, protective tariffs, and opposition to free silver coinage. His friendship with Theodore Roosevelt was particularly important in advancing the political fortunes of both men. Together they fought to expand the navy, challenge Spanish rule in Cuba, and retain the Philippines as an American possession. While Roosevelt occupied the White House, Lodge was one of his closest advisers, especially on questions of party politics and international affairs.

Lodge's role in promoting immigration restriction in Congress reveals a fascinating mix of bookish ideas on race and a shifting assessment of political possibilities. Early in the 1880s he had spoken favorably of immigrants, as most Americans were then inclined to do. He hoped more were on the way because America was getting "the best elements, both mentally and physically of the laboring population." But during Lodge's first term in Washington he noted social disturbances in the cities and the scarcity of land for new farmers and concluded that immigration ought to be "judiciously checked." At that time there was no implication that his concern was connected with the racial characteristics of immigrants. Americans, according to Lodge, should ask themselves if the country were not getting too crowded. But he also was among the first to draw attention to the changing sources of European immigration.

The distinction between the "old immigration" and the "new immigration" has become a textbook cliché in American history. Statistically, the number of immigrants coming from southern and eastern Europe in the 1880s did begin to rise, both absolutely and relative to those from the rest of Europe. By 1896 the former had surpassed the latter. But without conceptualizations statistics mean nothing. Native Americans might laugh at the long black frockcoat and whiskers of a Russian-born Jew or turn up their noses at the garlic-rich odors of Sicilian cooking, but they did not automatically think of "new immigrants" as an entity or as posing peculiar dangers to the United States. Probably a large majority of Americans did think that way by 1920. Over the years they had been so conditioned by the writings of intellectuals like Henry Cabot Lodge.

That there were differences between old and new immigrants was undeniable. Italians, Poles and other Slavs, and Jews from Slavic lands were the most numerous groups within the new immigration. If one agreed to make the distinction between old and new immigration, then as generalizations, it was correct to say that the new had less education than the old, were less likely to come with industrial skills, were more likely to have dark complexions and were almost never Protestants. One of the easiest ways to generalize about the new immigrants, who differed immensely among themselves, was to note the indisputable truth that they were not Anglo-Saxons. But only if one held to some theory of Anglo-Saxon uniqueness or superiority was this "truth" an important one.

Once his interest was stirred, Lodge began to study the immigration question. In 1891 he published three significant articles. "The Restriction of Immigration" declared that the good character of the "older" immigration could be virtually taken for granted, but that in the 1880s "new and wholly different elements" had appeared. The greatest relative increase in immigration, Lodge claimed, was coming "from races most alien to the body of the American people." His racial concern was accompanied by fears about the rise in the number of immigrants and the higher proportion coming from "the lowest and most illiterate classes." It was these classes, he argued in "Lynch Law and Unrestricted Immigration," that aggravated lynchings. And his study of the national background of leading Americans, "The Distribution of Ability in the United States," established the superiority of those of English ancestry. Lodge's scholarly technique left much to be desired. In the last article, for instance, he uncritically identified leading Americans as those represented in a recent biographical encyclopedia, and he determined each subject's race in a slapdash manner. His conclusion was precisely what he had expected and what his approach guaranteed: the great majority of distinguished Americans were, like him, of English ancestry.

In 1895–96, when national psychic tensions were at a high point, Lodge turned with full vigor to immigration restriction. In the meantime, he had read the work of Gustave Le Bon, a French sociologist who confused nationality with race and predicted historical disaster for races that interbred. In a major Senate speech of 1896 Lodge cited Le Bon's theories in arguing that if the new immigration was not restrained, the national character would be "bred out." While to some extent mixture of a superior and inferior race might elevate the latter, the practice posed a long-run threat that the inferior would prevail. The nation's foundations were involved, since race determined moral and intellectual characteristics. Americans were a morally advanced, homogeneous people, Lodge said. It was folly to gamble with their proven high quality.

The vehicle for Lodge's program was a literacy bill, which he brought up in the Senate and his son-in-law, Augustus Gardner, introduced in the House of Representatives. It would bar those over 14 years of age who could not read and write some language. Lodge thought this issue more important than either tariff protection or monetary standards. While not racist on its face, the Lodge bill was clearly devised to keep out groups he considered inherently inferior and menacing, less because of their "backward" culture than because of the hereditary traits they would pass on to their descendants.

The measure failed to pass, but Lodge was undeterred, repeatedly returning to the issue. His literacy test bill faced hard going in the 1897–98 Congressional session. It passed the Senate, but not the House. Immigrants themselves had begun to bring pressure against restrictionism, and the mood of the nation changed even more as the economy picked up. The Spanish-American War diverted attention from old discontents and sharply lessened nativist pressures. The country came out of its "splendid little war" into a period of unity and confidence.

The indignation that followed the assassination of President McKinley by an anarchist renewed interest in restrictionism. (The assassin, Leon F. Czolgosz, was born in the United States but had a "foreign sounding" name.) The 1903 measure, however, excluded only alien anarchists and prostitutes and represented less the racist than the anti-radical form of nativism.

Lodge was a good politician who came from a state with a large bloc of immigrant voters and strong business interests that wanted more immigrant labor. How could he afford to support the cause so openly? It would merely be cynical to deny Lodge's deep convictions on the issue. He was morally certain that the country ought to be more selective in admitting immigrants. Aware of the political risks, however, he took steps to protect himself. Some of his political speeches contradicted the negative judgments he had made about certain groups in his formal writings. He praised the Irish as having been long associated with English-speaking people. The French Canadians were "a strong and most valuable element." And, as for the recently arrived Italians, he associated them with the glories of ancient Rome. An effective political orator, Lodge shaded his message about immigration according to his audience.

Probably because he recognized the danger to his political career in the issue, Lodge showed more circumspection about the 1907 immigration act, though he still pressed for inclusion of a literacy test. A majority of Congressmen probably agreed with him, but through a complex series of maneuvers, the bill reached final form without barring illiterates.

This measure was nevertheless important in the advance of restrictionism. The head tax on incoming aliens was doubled, and the four dollars each immigrant must now provide served as a mild exclusionary device. The act showed the Progressive trust in organized knowledge and scientific solutions to social problems by establishing an Immigration Commission to gather data and make recommendations. The Commission included three experts appointed by the President, three Representatives, and three Senators, one of whom was Lodge.

*   *   *

Of all the scholars who wrote on immigration in the Progressive Era, probably none reached the general public as effectively as Edward A. Ross. He himself took satisfaction in the belief that his writings had helped bring about the restrictionist laws of 1921 and 1924. Ross's early life contrasted sharply with that of Eliot and Lodge. For them education was important, but largely as a way of proving worthy of a prestigious family and inherited wealth. For Ross, it was a way to climb the social and economic ladder.

Describing his boyhood, Ross recalled himself as part of "an element that was *looked down on*." His father was a dirt farmer, his mother a schoolteacher. Both were descended from Scots-Irish immigrants. Beset by economic problems, the family moved often. Ross was born in Illinois, grew up in rural Iowa. An orphan at the age of ten, he lived in a succession of foster homes.

Ross was sometimes jokingly called a "giant" or a "Neanderthal man." Six and one-half feet tall, and capable of sustained hard farm labor, he also had a quick mind and a voracious appetite for reading. He won the spell-downs at his school and impressed teachers with his poems. Helped out financially by teaching school, Ross graduated from Coe College in 1886. Then, like many ambitious young scholars of that day, he studied in Germany and at the German-oriented Johns Hopkins University. His interests shifted from literature to economics (the field in which he took his Ph.D. in 1891), and then to sociology, where he did most of his scholarly writing.

Known as a capable young scholar and as a gifted teacher, Ross was also able to reach the general community with his ideas and seemed on the way to a lifelong career at Stanford University. But in 1900 he was forced to resign by its President, David Starr Jordan, acting at the behest of Mrs. Leland Stanford, the University's benefactress. Other professors had been fired under not too different circumstances, but the "Ross case" became a landmark in the history of American higher education. It was not so much that the injustice was flagrant (though it clearly was) as the fact that Ross fought back. He issued a statement to the press and appealed to fellow scholars for help. Seven other faculty members who supported him resigned from Stanford under pressure. The American Economic Association launched an investigation of the case, marking the first time that a professional organization sought formally to judge standards of academic freedom at any university. President Eliot played a small role in the affair by inviting the unemployed Ross to give a series of lectures at Harvard on "Recent Trends in Sociology."

Mrs. Stanford objected to Ross on several grounds. For one thing, he had supported the Populist Party, having known from personal experience the sufferings that accompanied agricultural depression, and his free-silver pamphlet *Honest Dollars* was widely circulated. Eliot, who felt quite otherwise on the issue, could fair-mindedly judge it "a very clear and vigorous presentation of the silver side of the controversy." Ross was, moreover, friendly toward organized labor. In 1894 he had supported Eugene Debs in the Pullman boycott, and he shared the powerful antagonism of West Coast labor toward Oriental immigrants. The dominant argument among white workingmen, repeated by Ross, was that Japanese, like the Chinese before them, were accustomed to such a miserable standard of living that they accepted lower wages and thereby replaced other workers.

Ross bluntly advanced these ideas about the Japanese in May 1900, before a mass protest meeting. The address was the last straw for Mrs. Stanford, whose late husband had used Chinese labor to build the Central Pacific Railroad. According to the newspaper account she read, Ross had declared, "Should the worst come to the worst it would be better for us to train our guns on every vessel bringing Japanese to our shores rather than to permit them to land." Ross denied having said that, but it was clear he had made a passionate address of the sort that endeared him to audiences of white workers. His opposition was economic, not racial, Ross claimed, yet he had made the charge that immigrant Orientals, because of their fecundity, were a threat to the Anglo-Saxon character of the United States.

History does not tidily deliver up heroes and villains. While Mrs. Stanford appeared to have a stunted idea of freedom of speech, she considered Ross's anti-Japanese comments inhumane and demagogic. She complained that he had stirred "evil passions" in people by drawing distinctions among men, who were all equal in the sight of God.

The "case" had a happy ending for its principal victim. Ross did some of his best scholarly writing during the crisis and went on to professorships at the University of Nebraska and the University of Wisconsin. Moreover, at the very time that Ross's professional career seemed threatened at Stanford, he was contributing major new concepts and techniques to the emerging discipline of sociology. His most important book, *Social Control* (1901), dealt with the maintenance of public order. He explored the problem both in the simple, highly personal community and in the impersonal urban, industrialized society. Having experienced this wrenching shift himself, Ross's treatment of the changes that came as "community" gave way to "society" combined scholarly detachment and concern for social betterment. Although his *Social Psychology* (1908) was designed as a textbook, it developed such concepts as "mass society" and "the mob mind" in important new ways and helped make social psychology a promising field for investigation. And in *Sin and Society* (1907), for which Theodore Roosevelt wrote the introduction, Ross observed that "latter-day sin"—sin in a complex, industrial society—was easy, refined, and indirect, especially when done through such instrumentalities as the impersonal corporation.

Ross could hardly have avoided discussion of immigration after the turn of the century. His 1902 lectures at Harvard criticized the simple-mindedness of those who believed in hereditarian determinism, and although *Social Control* revealed some stereotyped thinking about Anglo-Saxons, it argued against purely racial theories of behavior. Sharing the old view that America was a powerfully assimilating society, Ross could glory in the speed and effectiveness with which the United States stimulated "the dull, fat-witted immigrant."

Besides winning a high reputation among scholars, Ross effectively reached a general audience as lecturer and magazine writer. In 1911 the editors of *Century* magazine asked him to do a series of articles on immigration. He took three months to tour the country, interviewing both spokesmen for the foreign-born and native Americans who dealt with immigrants as employers, social workers, or teachers. He also turned to the report of the Immigration Commission and extracted statistics and quotations from its ponderous volumes. Ross's position, from which he never retreated, was that America should revise its immigration policy by erecting new restrictive barriers. In 1914 the articles appeared in expanded form as *The Old World in the New: The Significance of Past and Present Immigration to the American People,* a book that finds Ross simultaneously at his most intemperate and most influential.

Economics played a major part in Ross's increasing restrictionism. He listened sympathetically to laborers' complaints. Employers used raw newcomers to break strikes, the argument ran, and played immigrant groups off against each other, exploiting differences in language and mutual suspicions to prevent worker solidarity. There was, Ross admitted, a certain beneficial elasticity to immigrant labor. Foreigners stopped coming or went home in bad times and arrived in larger numbers during economic upswings. But there was always a time lag, he noted. The theory that immigrants performed the roughest work and "allowed" native workers to advance to more attractive jobs often fit the facts, but in areas without a "collateral growth of skill-demanding industries," those already here might be laid off or forced to take lower wages, and their industrial role could thus be treated with contempt. It was easy enough to demonstrate that in specific times and places laborers had suffered because of newly-arrived aliens.

Although the matter is complex, the general verdict of economists has been that immigration raised wage scales and improved the economy, especially that of an industrially developing nation. In the broadest sense, then, Ross was wrong in his economic arguments for restriction. Yet he effectively maintained that laborers felt the negative effects of immigration at once, whereas the comfortable classes were either unaffected or benefitted economically. Ross protested against the tendency of middle- and upper-class Americans to ignore the quality of life among working people. "The investor, landowner, or contractor profits by the coming in of bare-handed men. . . . The professional man, sitting secure above the arena of struggle, can nobly rebuke narrowness. . . ."

Not only economic problems alarmed Ross. His book, he believed, established "a causal connection" between the new immigration and a whole range of social ills, such as yellow journalism, prostitution, juvenile delinquency, and the inferior status of women. Some of these problems were undoubtedly intensified by continuing immigration, but he neglected evidence suggesting that such problems accompanied industrialization and urbanization per se. Ross's ambitions for America to have a high literacy rate, honest politics, and social insurance programs, ambitions that were admirable by most standards, contributed to his anti-immigrant stance. It was easy to make scapegoats of the newcomers.

Even though Ross poked fun at "humanitarian" advocates of unrestricted immigration, his own humanitarianism should not be ignored. It prompted him to urge an active role for government in the realm of social welfare. Ross was associated with those late 19th-century economists who tried to demonstrate the dangers of Americans' quasi-religious faith in laissez faire. This group, often called the "Historical School," was inspired by German economists who argued for government intervention in economic affairs. The government, Ross insisted, should no longer consider itself merely a policeman, leaving most matters to "the naked action of economic forces." Men need not rely on chance; they could apply their intelligence to the world about them.

Ross, then, was sympathetic toward labor, an advocate of humanitarian reform, and a proponent of the positive state. But he also revealed a deep-seated ethnic prejudice that colored almost all his writings on immigration. The combination of reformism, even radicalism, and racism in Ross, and in the novelist Jack London demonstrated that one need not be a reactionary, or a conservative like Lodge, to believe in the superiority of one's own race.

Ross probably did more than anyone else to popularize Francis A.

Walker's theory that immigrants affected the size of families of native Americans. Ross even coined the phrase "race suicide," which became one more way of glorifying motherhood. Women who found themselves with families larger than they wanted could rationalize that they were staving off race suicide. Ross kept restating the original Walker theory with powerful imagery: "Because he keeps them clean, neatly dressed, and in school, children are an economic burden to the American. Because he lets them run wild and puts them to work early, children are an asset to the low-standard foreigner."

In his ethnic arguments against unrestricted immigration, Ross also spoke of the dangers of "inter-breeding," and of social decay that followed from "mongrelism." Much like Herbert Spencer, he claimed that physical beauty, intelligence, and good character were all threatened by blending of the races. Ross also drew upon the discoveries of biologists about hybridism in plants and animals. Such influences, and Ross's generally increasing interest in heredity, allied him to the eugenics movement.

By 1910 eugenics was something of a fad among the better educated in the United States. Its theories seemed so favorable to immigration restriction that Prescott Hall of the IRL suggested changing its name to the "Eugenic Immigration League." "The same arguments," Hall calmly reasoned, "which induce us to segregate criminals and feebleminded and thus prevent their breeding, apply to excluding from our borders individuals whose multiplying here is likely to lower the average of our people." Barriers against individuals with hereditary weaknesses (assuming such could be known) would be a "eugenic" measure, but the broader application of eugenics to immigration had to draw on the notion that invidious genetic comparisons could be made among ethnic groups represented in the immigrant stream. In other words, it had to draw on racism.

Ross's most direct involvement with eugenics did not come until the 1920s, with the issue of birth control. But his pre-World War I restrictionist writings, which were a catch-all of ideas, included many that were shared by eugenists and some that drew directly on their theories. In 1901 Ross had branded the term "race" as "the watchword of the vulgar," but in 1914 in *The Old World in the New,* he referred to "that fundamental worth which does not depend on opportunity, and which may be transmitted to one's descendants," and he warned against the Mongolians who would "leave their race stamp" on the American people. "Thanks to our bland, syrupy way of appraising the naturalized foreign born," he complained, "the question of comparative brain power never comes up." That was the way eugenists were talking.

Eugenist theories about the primacy and power of hereditary traits enhanced the notion of an inferior "new immigration." Ross's *Old World in the New* includes the distinction between old and new immigrants, but to say that the racial inferiority of the latter was the main point would be unfair to the inclusiveness of his argument. The heart of his essentially negative view of immigration was the process of immigration itself —the motives moving Europeans from their homes, the cheap and oppressive sea voyage, the strain of arriving in a strange land, the psychic wrench of seeing old guiding values fail in a new social situation, and the confusion within families when children adapted more successfully than their parents. Ross found that this process led to an array of social evils that, though perhaps not the immigrants' fault, cumulatively threatened American society. He granted that there was probably a cycle of adjustment common to all immigrant groups, old as well as new, but he argued that the country could not safely go on suffering from social dislocations that accompanied the earlier stages. His book presents a complex description of immigration, but it was one nonetheless from which racists could take comfort.

Ross's book gained strength from its avoidance of a generalized treatment of the new immigration. It took up incoming groups one by one. It found at least some virtues in every group, an approach that later enabled Ross to defend himself against charges of bias. South Italians, for instance, had instinctive courtesy and warm sociability (and, of course, were musical). Yet his treatment of Italian immigrants ends with this racist passage: "As grinding rusty iron reveals the bright metal, so American competition brings to light the race stuff in poverty-crushed immigrants. But not all this stuff is of value in a democracy like ours." The United States would suffer a lessened democracy and a lowered efficiency, he claimed, by admitting "great numbers of wavering, excitable, impulsive persons who cannot organize themselves." These were, he implied, permanent hereditary traits.

In Ross's closing chapters on economic, social, political, and racial consequences of immigration, there is less stress on the virtues of various groups and on the differences among them. Rather, he emphasizes genetic consequences, thus giving his book a decidedly racist thrust. Even a casual reader, noting that the last chapter was entitled "American Blood and Immigrant Blood," with such subheadings as "Evading a degrading competition by race suicide" and "The triumph of the low-standard elements over the high-standard elements," was likely to conclude that Ross believed current immigrants were a racial threat.

Given the increasing racism in America, its function in discussions of immigration was inevitable. Even if there had been no shift in the flow of immigration from northern and western Europe to southern and eastern, the view that the "new immigration" was inferior to the "old" in its genetic potential would still have been important. Another hereditarian argument was available: the less able members of each national group were now coming. Ross described the Puritans as courageous and idealistic; the Germans as fleeing for their liberal ideas, and the Irish, who migrated because of famine, at least represented the entire spectrum of their nation. But, Ross maintained, most of those arriving now lacked those skills necessary to develop a stake in their old society. Might they not have genetic incapacity, Ross and others wondered, that marked them as "new" in the sense of being innately inferior to earlier migrants—even from the same area? The tendency of race ideas to strengthen class prejudice was not new. Henry Cabot Lodge could even call the struggle over socialism a "race struggle," implying that protesting workers were of a different genetic stock from supporters of capitalism.

The Old World in the New was persuasive in part because of its scientific patina. It abounds in figures and charts, many drawn from the report of the Immigration Commission. Sometimes Ross labelled as "facts" what were merely stereotypes or smoking-car gossip. He wrote (to cite a particularly flagrant example of this technique), "The fact that pleasure-loving Jewish business men spare Jewesses but pursue Gentile girls excites bitter comment." (The amusement that both Jews and Gentiles would find in *Portnoy's Complaint* lay far in the future.) Similarly, a negative estimate about southern Europeans could be attributed to "fair-minded observers." But *The Old World in the New* was an easy book to read. Ross had a lively style, and he knew how to use illustrative anecdotes to enliven generalizations. Since he granted the influence of environment and ideas as well as heredity, his account gave the impression of being balanced. He did not entirely forget his own judgment that "all lump condemnations are cruel" and even warned that inadequate knowledge made it risky to compare the ability of the old immigrants and the new: "Though backward, the latter may contain good stuff." But taken as a whole, the book was an unsubtle flattery of earlier immigrants and their descendants. It failed to meet the critical standards that should be upheld by a professional social scientist even when (or better yet, particularly when) he is trying to reach a general audience.

Unwilling to confine his ideas to the study or to the printed page, Ross expressed his restrictionist sympathies in political action. He allied himself with the IRL and lobbied for a law to exclude illiterates. A friend and former student of Woodrow Wilson, he sought to influence the President, partly by appeals to their shared Scots-Irish ancestry. But Wilson vetoed the 1915 literacy test restriction. His veto message cited the failure to provide exceptions for refugees from political oppression and condemned the idea that literacy was a proper distinction by which to evaluate human beings: "it excludes those to whom the opportunities of elementary education have been denied, without regard to their character, their purposes, or their natural capacity."

In spite of Wilson's ringing words, American attitudes were shifting in the direction of Ross's restrictionism. In February 1917, partly because of a nationalism heightened by the war in Europe, Congress passed the literacy test measure over Wilson's veto. By the time the majority at last had its way and the literacy bill became law, Ross had ceased to be active in the restrictionist movement. Perhaps frustrated by the defeat of 1915 and characteristically restless, he turned to other scholarly and reformist interests. He continued, however, to advise restrictionists who consulted him, and on occasion lent his name to one of their petitions.

*   *   *

Although IRL propaganda activities ceased after 1916, its concern for the weakening of the American fiber—by the admission of southern and eastern Europeans—spread more widely than ever. The writings of those who worked scientific theories of race into a comprehensive ideology was one important reason for this development. Of several such figures, the most influential was the New York socialite Madison Grant, author of *The Passing of the Great Race* (1916). The book's passionately expressed race-ideology was supported by "scientific" evidence.

Going back to William Z. Ripley's designation of three European "races," Nordic, Alpine, and Mediterranean, Grant linked this distinction to an assertion that the Nordic was distinctly superior ("the white man par excellence"). Culture, in his view, depended almost entirely on race, and he minimized environmentalist explanations of individual traits. He pessimistically described how native Americans (whom he equated with the Nordics) were allowing themselves to die out because they would not intermarry or compete with the newcomers. The power of Grant's book came from its inclusiveness, its boldness, and its theoretical consistency. Relatively moderate suggestions from the writings of Walker and Ripley were spliced together with eugenist ideas and generalizations of European anthropologists and made to support a racist philosophy of history.

The Passing of the Great Race merited no standing as science, but Grant's position as Secretary of the New York Zoological Society lent a scientific aura to the book, and certain ethnists hailed it as a "work of solid merit." Yet with all his fund of scientific information, Grant was blind to scientific method. He showed little willingness to reserve judgment or to distinguish between conjecture and demonstrable fact. But the reading public and reputable biologists were often taken in.

Much of the impact of Grant's book was delayed by the entry of the United States into World War I in 1917, which turned public attention to more immediate issues than race-ideology or immigration restriction. But many wartime developments heightened American nativism and ultimately strengthened exclusionism. The drive against the hyphenates led to a new phrase, "100% Americanism," which captured much of the wartime spirit. Americanization programs intensified during the war, despite conscientious participation by most immigrants. Yet many of them retained their "foreign ways," and frustrated Americanizers fell back on the idea that these outsiders were after all unassimilable. For those who felt this way, the literacy test passed in 1917 proved frustratingly weak. Basic education had been spreading in Europe and thereby lessened the impact of the statute. In any case, the law had watered down the requirement to a mere reading test and exempted both immediate families of a literate adult immigrant and those fleeing religious persecution.

The decade that marked the greatest change in the history of American immigration policy has been aptly labelled "the Tribal Twenties." In 1921 Vice President Calvin Coolidge published an article, "Whose Country Is This?" Although largely concerned about foreign-born radicals, he gave race a prominent place: "There are racial considerations too grave to be brushed aside for any sentimental reasons. Biological laws tell us that certain divergent people will not mix or blend." Increasingly, the public believed that so-called scientists like Madison Grant had established the truth about racial superiority and inferiority and that nonscientists had better give heed. For all his pessimism, Grant managed to strike one optimistic note in his preface to the 1921 fourth edition of his book. Americans, he maintained, were now aroused to the menace of un-restrained immigration and had stopped listening to sentimentalists. In his impression that things were moving his way, Grant was not mistaken.

The Congressional leader of the crucial restrictionist drive of the 1920s was Republican Representative Albert Johnson, who became chairman of the House Committee on Immigration and Naturalization in 1919. A small-town newspaper editor from the State of Washington, Johnson had appealed to voters with his verbal assaults on Japanese and on radical labor unions. Unpolished but energetic, he formed a strange alliance with the patrician intellectual racists of the East. Eugenist race theories impressed him, and in 1920 he appointed as "Expert Eugenics Agent" for his committee, Harry H. Laughlin, who had taken the lead in campaigns to sterilize the feeble-minded and the delinquent. Laughlin testified often and eagerly on the existence of inferior races and their threat to the American population.

While not recognized at the time, the immigration restriction law that was worked out in 1920–21 was to set the basic pattern of American immigration policy for over four decades. The bill began as a proposal from Johnson's committee to suspend immigration for two years. A one-year suspension passed by the House proved too extreme for the Senate. There an alternative was proposed: setting a numerical limit for annual immigration from Europe by establishing quotas for various (non-Asian) nationalities based on their proportion among America's foreign-born. Johnson and the House accepted this plan, but insisted that instead of 5%, the quota be 3% (of the number of those born in a given country who were resident in the United States in 1910). The bill was signed by President Harding in May 1921. Originally a one-year "emergency" measure, it was extended for two more years while Congress wrestled with plans for a more permanent law.

It is useful to note the control over immigrant volume apart from the quota system, even though the bill's authors considered them inter-related. In its original form the bill had set a ceiling of zero; the final figure was slightly over 350,000. For the first time, then, the United States placed a numerical maximum on the number of immigrants it would admit from Europe. This recognition of prudential limits to the number of newcomers that could be absorbed has remained American policy.

Both the ceiling and the quota system were applied more stringently in 1924 in the Johnson-Reed Act. Albert Johnson had been determined to lessen the number of "new immigrants" admitted. He insisted on lowering their quotas in two ways, by taking the 1890 census instead of that of 1910 as the base for each national group and by dropping the quotas from 3% to 2%. His plan was made law, but only for a limited period.

Even more restrictive were the rules of the Johnson-Reed Act sched-uled to go into effect in 1927 (later delayed until 1929). This plan was devised in part in response to the cry of new immigrants that they were being insulted and discriminated against by the quotas. It occurred to certain restrictionists that they could argue, with surface plausibility, that by basing the quotas on *foreign-born* residents, they had been discrim-inating not against new immigrants, but in their favor. For, it could be shown, the majority of Americans were not foreign-born, and this vast group, whose ancestors came principally from northwestern Europe, were not being counted at all. Accordingly, since the aim of the bill was to keep the pattern of immigration as close as possible to the national ancestry of the current American population, a fairer base for determining quotas would be the total American people, native as well as foreign-born. After all, why should Madison Grant not be "counted" as well as some newcomer with an unpronounceable name? Over the next few years an official study was made, based on demographically dubious but pre-dictably pro-Nordic calculations from the 1920 census. When this second part of the law took effect in 1929, the total of non-Western Hemisphere admissions was set at about 150,000. Roughly, 125,000 were allowed in from northern and western European nations, and 25,000 from southern and eastern Europe. Foes of the new immigration had good reason to feel satisfied.

In one important phase of designing the 1924 bill, the restrictionist career of the 74-year-old Henry Cabot Lodge and the most extreme form of racist exclusionism coalesced with devastating effectiveness. In the sweeping plan to preserve America's "racial integrity" through the new bill, Representative Johnson had included a proviso to bar all Japanese. The proposed action branded the Japanese as inferior to any European group, even the most despised of the new immigrants. The argument that exclusion was non-discriminatory since almost all other Asians were already excluded was no solace to the Japanese government, which properly considered any such step a unilateral violation of the "Gentlemen's Agreement." Under this agreement, worked out in an exchange of diplomatic notes in 1907–08, the Japanese government had agreed not to issue passports to laborers seeking entry to the United States, though it might issue such passports to immediate families of Japanese already there. Significantly, President Coolidge believed it would be unwise to adopt total exclusion of Japanese. Japan was an industrially advanced nation that had displayed considerable military prowess.

In the Senate, more sensitive than the House to international repercussions, the immigration committee dropped the anti-Japanese proviso, and there was a good chance that the upper house would follow this course. Then came a communication from Japan's ambassador. Though friendly in tone, it used the phrase "grave consequences" in referring to possible enactment of exclusion. At this juncture, Lodge demanded that the Senators go into secret session. Although Secretary of State Charles Evans Hughes disagreed, Lodge declared that such a phrase as "grave consequences" was "a veiled threat." Since the right to restrict immigration was among the "most fundamental rights of sovereignty," he urged his colleagues to uphold American self-respect by ignoring the Japanese protest. When the Senate emerged from its executive session, it voted overwhelmingly to retain Japanese exclusion in the bill. The vigorous restrictionist of the turn of the century had returned to his old issue and won a last victory. Six months later Henry Cabot Lodge was dead.

For all the rhetorical promises, the legal revisions of the 1920s failed to make immigration proportional to the "national origins" of the American population. Northern Europeans fell far short of filling the openings allotted them, and the exemption of the Western Hemisphere meant relatively open immigration from Canada and Latin America. But in another major aim, to decrease the volume of immigration, the new laws apparently succeeded. Immigration, which in the ten years before World War I six times exceeded one million persons, never reached a quarter of that figure from 1929 to 1949, and was usually under 100,000 during that period.

Even the European nations most strongly discriminated against by the new system usually did not fill their quotas. New visa requirements, the decline in the growth rate of European population, a decade of depression, and World War II were among the factors bringing this reduction.

But during the 1920s European laborers had stopped thinking of America as a land with an open door. For all its loopholes, the new policy had been intended to convey that message, and it generally succeeded. In his autobiography of 1936 Edward A. Ross proudly recalled that *The Old World in the New* had "helped build up the public sentiment which resulted in the quota laws of 1921 and 1924." The restriction should have come in the 1880s, he argued, to have stopped "the vast human inflow from sources ever more alien and backward."

The tight restrictions had particularly cruel effects when Europe became a continent overflowing with refugees. First Jews and others fleeing Nazi persecution and then political refugees and other dislocated persons in the aftermath of World War II found America's doors hard to open. There were stop-gap measures to admit a limited number of refugees apart from the quotas, but America did far less than its postwar prosperity or its relative size suggested as its fair share of population redistribution. Debates over exemptions for refugees saw old warnings of racial dangers repeated, though after the ghastly example of Nazi racism, far less often.

In passing the McCarran Immigration Act in 1952, Congressmen congratulated themselves that they had removed the racial bias from the system of the 1920s. How? By applying the quota system to the nations of Asia, where total exclusion had formerly applied. The essential racism of assuming the ethnic status quo to be the ideal remained built into the system.

In the middle of the 1960s, that memorable decade in which Americans came to see themselves and the world in a new light, immigration policy underwent major reform. The notion that some national origins made immigrants more attractive than others played no part in the bill signed into law by President Johnson on October 3, 1965, in ceremonies at the Statue of Liberty. A quantitative limit was set of 120,000 from the Western Hemisphere, 170,000 from elsewhere, but numerous exceptions admitted individuals without regard to these ceilings. Each nation outside the Western Hemisphere had an annual ceiling of 20,000, and "unused" openings were made available to nations that had additional applicants for admission. The preference system in admitting immigrants had nothing to do with race or national origin, but used humanitarian and economic criteria, such as uniting families, bringing in needed skills, and helping refugees from persecution.

Other evidence besides the 1965 law indicated that the thinking of the restrictionist leaders of the 1920s had finally lost its hold on most politicians and most of the American public. A great-grandson of Henry Cabot Lodge married a descendant of Italian immigrants. A Japanese-American Senator gave the keynote address at the 1968 Democratic convention. In 1974, largely out of respect for the achievements of an immigrant Secretary of State, a constitutional amendment was proposed to remove the bar to a naturalized citizen's becoming President of the United States.

Although the 1960s was not a period characterized by national self-congratulation, it is hard not to look back on the immigration law of 1965 as progress. While far from perfect (the limit on Western Hemisphere immigration soon proved frustratingly tight), it made the country's policy toward foreigners who wished to enter both more rational and more humane. There is another way to view the matter, however. The old policy had been so irrational and so inhumane and had been persisted in for so long that even when ending it Americans should wonder at their capacity for vanity and self-delusion.

Eliot, Lodge, and Ross, when they spoke about ethnic groups, thought of themselves as "the Americans" or "the native Americans." Now they would find themselves called WASPs and could not so readily assume that their genetic make-up or their cultural norms should serve as ideals for the nation. They would have to reflect further on the national motto "E Pluribus Unum." That phrase suggests a unity in diversity more complex than they or the Founding Fathers realized.

6

Alternative Roads for the Black Man

BOOKER T. WASHINGTON
WILLIAM E. B. DU BOIS
MARCUS GARVEY

by Saunders Redding
Cornell University

Sitting at the end of the row of other speakers on the platform of the huge auditorium, Booker T. Washington looked out on a larger audience of white people than he had ever seen; he was thrilled to think that he had been especially chosen to address them. When it came his time to speak, having been introduced by the Honorable Rufus Bullock, ex-Governor of Georgia, Washington smiled apologetically as he crossed in front of the men and women with whom he shared the platform. For an exhilarating month, while he scrupulously prepared himself, he had looked forward to this moment, and he meant to make the most of it. All that he valued was at the hazard of this moment: Tuskegee Institute and the funds to keep it going; his spreading reputation as a "sensible" and "prudent" Negro; and, not least, the power and influence once held by Frederick Douglass. But Douglass, now seven months dead, had been an irritant, forcing advances—if, Washington once said, advances they could be called—as an impatient rider forces a balky horse, with whip and spurs. There were other, better ways; and Washington, as he stood there in the westering sun of that September day in 1895, was confident that he had found them. What better proof than the cooperation he had from the white people of Alabama, his relations with the Superintendent of Alabama Schools, and with the Governor, Edward O'Neal, and with

110

William H. Baldwin, General Manager of the Southern Railroad. What better evidence, indeed, than his standing now on this Southern white platform as spokesman for his people!

"Mr. President, and Gentlemen of the Board of Directors and citizens," he began, reciting his speech from memory. His voice firmed noticeably as he continued and, approaching the thesis of his discourse, it rang with authority, even with a kind of defiance of those who would dispute him, and yet it did not lose a quality of suppliance. "To those of the white race ... were I permitted I would repeat what I say to my own race. 'Cast down your bucket where you are.' Cast it down among the eight millions of Negroes whose habits you know, whose fidelity and love you have tested in days when to have proved treacherous meant the ruin of your firesides. Cast down your bucket among these people who have, without strikes and labor wars, tilled your fields, cleared your forests, builded your railroads and cities ... While doing this, you can be sure in the future, as in the past, that you and your families will be surrounded by the most patient, faithful, law-abiding and unresentful people that the world has seen ... We shall stand by you with a devotion that no foreigner can approach, ready to lay down our lives, if need be, in defense of yours, interlacing our industrial, commercial, civil and religious life with yours in a way that shall make the interests of both races one. In all things that are purely social we can be as separate as the fingers, yet one as the hand in all things essential to mutual progress." The hand he had raised, fingers widespread, clenched into a fist.

The audience went wild, and so did the press the next day. The Boston *Transcript* noted, "The sensation it [the speech] has caused in the press has never been equaled." Clark Howell, editor of the Atlanta *Constitution* and successor to Henry Grady as the spokesman for the "new South," commented that "the whole speech is a platform upon which blacks and whites can stand with full justice to each other ... The speech stamps Booker T. Washington as a wise counselor and a safe leader." The President of the United States, Grover Cleveland, sent Washington a personal message: "Your words cannot fail to delight and encourage all who wish well for your race; and if our colored fellow-citizens do not from your utterances gather new hope and form new determinations to gain every valuable advantage offered them by their citizenship, it will be strange indeed."

Booker Washington had come a long way to this high eminence. Applying what he had learned in the "school of slavery," he would go higher. He had been an apt pupil in that school for eight, nine, or ten years (he never knew the exact year of his birth) and the first lesson he had learned through precept and example was the methods and the rationale for pleasing white folks. The methods were various; the rationale precise. Plunged into the threatening seas of freedom just as he reached his teens, he learned to warp and tack to take advantage of whatever wind that blew, and in 1871, the prevailing wind landed him in Hampton, Virginia. Just five years earlier an ex-general of the Union Army had been put in charge of the Virginia Peninsula sector of the federal Bureau of Refugees, Freedmen and Abandoned Lands with a mandate to succor and "administer the affairs" of Negroes. Samuel Chapman Armstrong could not tolerate idleness. The refugee camp he established was promptly functioning as a timber-cutting, land-clearing, crop-planting, hog-raising work camp, which he called a school. In 1869, with funds principally supplied by the American Missionary Association, the school became Hampton Institute.

General Armstrong was a benevolent man of fixed convictions. Brought up in Hawaii, where his missionary father became Minister of Education, he was convinced, he once wrote his mother, that "the differentia of races goes deeper than skin." He believed—and many "liberal" men shared his beliefs—that "not mere ignorance, but deficiency of character is the chief difficulty" with Negroes, Polynesians, and Indians. He believed that physical labor was a "spiritual force" and that salvation for Negroes lay in work, by doing which they would command the respect of whites. Having such respect, Negroes would then be admitted into the social order at the level on which they could best serve mankind. Month after month, as the Reconstruction period faltered toward its close, Hampton Institute's publication, the *Southern Workman,* over which Armstrong assumed complete control (since, as he said, he "comprehended the deep philosophy of one man power") inveighed against Negro political participation and agitation for civil rights. Day after day from the chapel rostrum General Armstrong hammered his lessons home: "Be thrifty and industrious"; "Make the best of your difficulties"; "Be patient"; "Patience is better than politics."

Booker Washington was a model student. While it took most students four or five years to complete the course of study, Booker finished in three. Eager, ingratiating, ambitious—and these qualities controlled by an ingenious mind—he quickly won the favor of the faculty and the personal approbation of the principal. All students, male and female, worked, but Booker was assigned the easiest, cleanest jobs. By the end of his first year he was the envy of his fellows. His training in the manual arts was hit and miss, but he was a diligent student of the art of oratory in which he was privileged to be personally tutored by a Miss Natalie Lord, who told him that competence in public speaking unlocked the door to success. From the middle of his second year he was regularly called upon to practice his art on chapel audiences. He had a gift for enlivening what he was told to say with jokes, anecdotes, and homilies, some of them quite original. He burned with ambition. No brickyard or blacksmith shop, no carpenter's tools or shoemaker's last for him. Rather, General Armstrong counseled him, teaching, the ministry, or the law.

Presumably his education at Hampton was preparing him to teach, but he would need further training for either of the other professions, and for the present a lack of money ruled them out. After graduating in 1874, Booker spent some months as a hotel waiter in the North, but when he was offered the one-room Negro schoolhouse in Malden, West Virginia, General Armstrong advised him to take it. Wash Ferguson, Booker's stepfather, had settled Janie Washington and her two illegitimate, slave-born children in Malden in 1866, and Malden was home. And it was good to go back home an educated man. He stayed two years.

Next to the minister of the Baptist church, the schoolteacher was the man black folk looked to and white folk went to when, in the stumbling course of race relations, contact and community seemed desirable or necessary. And toward the end of Booker's second term, community was desirable. The white people of southern West Virginia wanted Charleston named as the capital of the State, rather than Clarksburg or Martinsburg, which were also in the running. The issue was to come to a vote and, thought Charleston backers, the Negro vote was necessary. When some of the most influential white men of the area asked Booker Washington to campaign among his people, he consented gladly, and spent the summer of 1877 making speeches in the southern part of the State. This activity rekindled his "slumbering ambition to study law" and beginning in the fall, using books borrowed from a friendly white attorney, he read law at night and taught school by day. After almost a year, he abruptly relinquished both, left Malden in the fall of 1878, and enrolled in the Wayland (Baptist) Seminary in Washington, D.C.

The national capital and the seminary humbled him. In a city to which hundreds of the most ambitious Negroes had been attracted by political patronage during early Reconstruction, and by opportunities for education in the best Negro institutions; and in a city where Negro lawyers, doctors, schoolteachers, civil servants, and public figures—including Frederick Douglass, who was still the esteemed spokesman for the race—Booker T. Washington, aged 22, 23, or 24, was nobody. Moreover, his fellow seminarians had "more money, were better dressed and," he grudgingly admitted years later, "in some cases were more brilliant mentally" than he. Washington had made up his mind to withdraw after less than a year, when General Armstrong invited him to return to Hampton Institute in the anomalous, non-faculty (the regular faculty was all-white) position of "graduate." Under the benevolent eye of the principal, he taught a night class of backward students and was "house father to a hundred wild Indians." He was to boast afterward that he developed the night class "into one of the most important features of the institution," and it is recorded elsewhere that he conditioned the Indians to wear shoes, to march in step to the white man's tunes—played, of course, by the all-Negro student band—and to bathe once a week.

When the carpetbag Reconstructionists of Alabama, in a last effort, bulled through the legislature an act "to establish a normal school for colored teachers at Tuskegee," they could induce no white man to take charge. Samuel C. Armstrong was asked to advise. He recommended a "clear headed, modest, sensible, polite" mulatto—Booker Taliaferro Washington.

The hard facts of Negro life and the sorry state of race relations belied the optimism and burlesqued the compromise proposed in Booker Washington's Atlanta Exposition speech even as he made it. In that very hour, South Carolina's state political convention approved disfranchising Negroes. On that very day, law enforcement officials in Tallahassee, Florida, assured "a mob at the outset of the trial that an accused Negro would be hanged," and a North Carolina court declared not guilty a white farmer who had shot to death one of his "lazy" and "abusive" Negro tenants. Headlining its front-page account "An Eye For An Eye," the Memphis *Commercial Appeal* described how, with police standing by, a mob had mutilated and lynched a Negro prisoner. In Booker ·Washington's own State of Alabama, two days after the Atlanta speech, Wilson County published its education budget for the next year—Item: $28,108 for the teachers of 2,285 white children; $3,940 for the colored teachers of 10,745 black children. And within that same week, Tennessee Coal, Iron and Railroad announced the replacement of "87 negro laborers by others, mostly Chinese."

Nevertheless, before the end of September 1895, Washington had become—had, indeed, been made—*the* national leader of the Negro people: a "safe leader," the Atlanta *Constitution* said, confidently speaking for the majority. And safe he was. He knew and would follow the guidelines laid down by the whites who made him, and he would exhort his people to do the same. The guidelines were very clear. The patriots and politicians, the editors and educators, and the industrialists who laid the guidelines were never as blunt as Ben Tillman, the United States Senator from South Carolina, who campaigned on the slogan "Keep the nigger down," nor as forthright as William C. Oates, the Governor of Alabama who, speaking at the Tuskegee Institute commencement in 1896, told his listeners, "I want to give you niggers a few words of plain talk and advice . . . you might as well understand that this is a white man's country, as far as the South is concerned, and we're going to make you keep your place." But the industrialists and educators and editors meant the same thing, and it is precisely what Booker Washington implied when he urged his people to "learn to do a common thing"—plow and plane, cook and clean, mend and mind—"in an uncommon manner"; and when he wrote to the editor of the Tuskegee *News,* the local white paper, "It has always been and is now the policy of the [Tuskegee] Normal School to remain free from politics and the discussion of race questions that tend to stir up strife between the races."

Of course, there was no question as to what the Negro's place was: he was in it—and he was in the South and on the land. But in 1900, of 4 million Negroes only 120,000 owned the land on which they lived and worked. The rest were either sharecroppers under a system of peonage that kept them legally bound so long as they owed the landlord so much as a penny, or they were convicts whom the state—any Southern state— "employed" to clean ditches and maintain roads or hired out to farmers to work out their fines or until their prison terms expired. Another 2 million Negroes lived in towns and cities North and South. The more fortunate of these were cooks, waiters, barbers, porters, janitors, and bootblacks. The rest were "an industrial superfluity," whose very presence as potential strikebreakers had a stifling effect on labor unionist activities.

But if there was no question as to the Negro's place, there was some question as to how to keep him in it without arousing foolish aspirations for better places, better things. Booker Washington had some answers. Those derived from well-learned lessons and experience were recited in his Atlanta Exposition speech; others he would devise and recite—or get followers to recite—as necessity and/or circumstances might demand. In 1896, his loud silence on the outcome of *Plessy* vs. *Ferguson,* which established the ingenious doctrine of "separate but equal," was meant to be interpreted as it was—as tacit approval of legalized segregation. Washington believed that segregation not only kept down interracial strife and competition, but was positively good for Negroes. It compelled them to do and have things for themselves: their own schools, for instance, where they would be taught the manual arts; their own places of public accommodation; their own businesses. In 1900, Washington founded the National Negro Business League and remained its president until he died.

Politics was bad for his people, Washington believed, and where and while they were permitted to vote, he cautioned them to go to "Southern white people ... for advice concerning the casting of their ballots." His was the only Negro voice the white majority listened to. Those who dominated American institutions and helped to determine the American environment were his patrons and supporters. Through Booker Washington and at his word private philanthropy flowed, or did not flow, to Negro programs and causes. Negro candidates for even such low level public jobs as they might be given required his recommendation. Mary White Ovington, an independently wealthy white volunteer social worker in New York, who had reason to know, wrote, "He [Booker Washington] was appealed to on any and every subject: how many bathrooms to put in a YMCA, whether or not to start a day nursery in some town, and so on." After the publication of his second autobiographical work, *Up From Slavery,* editors and publishers called on him to advise them as to what they should and should not publish from the pens of Negroes. Thanks to the generosity of millionaires such as William Baldwin, president of the Long Island Railroad, Collis Huntington, president of the Southern Pacific, George F. Peabody, who had founded the museum bearing his name at Harvard, Andrew Carnegie, and John D. Rockefeller, Washington by 1901–02 was relieved of concern for Tuskegee Institute's financial support. And he went single-mindedly about the business of increasing and protecting his power and his influence.

In the early years of the new century Booker Washington could no longer ignore the opposition of forward-looking members of his own race. They said, in effect, that Washington's thinking was behind the times, that it had no future in it—only the present and the past. They rejected his postulates. Private philanthropy was *not* the equivalent of social justice and civil equality. Patience was *not* more effective than protest in surmounting the obstacles to Negro advancement. Early on, the Cleveland *Gazette,* a Negro paper, had lambasted him as "Prof. B(ad) T(aste) Washington the new Negro, but if there is anything in him except the most servile type of the old Negro we fail to find it. . . . So let the race labor and pray that no more new Negroes such as Prof. Bad Taste will bob up." In 1908, Monroe Trotter, a Negro graduate of Harvard and editor of the Boston *Guardian,* was even more caustic: "As another mark of the treacherous character of Booker Washington in matters concerning the race, comes his discordant note in support of Secretary Taft [for President] . . . Booker Washington, ever concerned with his own selfish ambitions, indifferent to the cries of the race so long as he wins the approval of white men who do not believe in the Negro . . . leader of the self-seekers, he has persistently . . . sought to entangle the whole race in the meshes of subordination. Knowing the race could only be saved by fighting cowardice, we have just as persistently resisted every attempt he has made to plant his white flag on the domains of equal manhood rights. . . ."

Washington grumbled that "those Negroes up North are hammering at me." But so were growing numbers of Negroes in the South. He tried, with some success, to silence the hammers. He managed to throttle one or two of the weaker Negro papers, to buy out and put trusted friends in control of the Chicago *Conservator* and, mixing threats with cajolery, to swing the Chicago *Bee* to his side. Seductive promises won the support of T. Thomas Fortune, editor of the New York *Age,* then the largest and most influential Negro newspaper. But there were others he could not silence, buy, cajole, or flatter. A teacher at Atlanta University named W. E. B. Du Bois was one of these.

As early as 1903, a collection of Du Bois's essays, *The Souls of Black Folk,* had alerted Washington to the dangerous potential of this young man's opposition, and Washington tried then to neutralize it. But Du Bois rejected his offer of the editorial control of the *Southern Workman,* a journal over which Washington had absolute power, although it was still published by Hampton Institute; and he was deaf to repeated invitations —conveyed through Baldwin, Peabody, and Carnegie—to transfer to Tuskegee Institute at any salary he cared to name. In 1906, when Du Bois issued a call for "aggressive action on the part of men who believe in Negro freedom and equality" and subsequently founded the Niagara Movement, Washington set out to destroy both the movement and the man. Those elements of the Negro press Washington controlled charged that Du Bois was "envious," "ashamed of his race," "wanted to be white." Through the General Education Board, a private philanthropy funded by Rockefeller, which contributed substantially to Atlanta University, Washington tried to have Du Bois dismissed. The United States Commissioner of Labor, having got the word from President Roosevelt who had it from Booker Washington, refused to publish a study Du Bois had been asked to prepare. Publication of the paper, he said, would not be in the interest of the American people.

But Du Bois was not to be silenced or bought. Speaking for a small but steadily increasing number of Negroes, he declared, "We will not be satisfied to take one jot or tittle less than our full manhood rights. We claim for ourselves every single right that belongs to a freeborn American, political, civil, and social; and until we get these rights we will never cease to protest and assail the ears of America." Some liberal whites joined the small chorus of cheering blacks; and in 1910, when a handful of these—including Jane Addams, John Dewey, Dr. Henry Moskowitz, Oswald G. Villard, Rabbi Stephen Wise, Ida Barnett, and W. E. B. Du Bois—organized the National Association for the Advancement of Colored People, it was not expected that Booker Washington would be among them. The day Monroe Trotter anticipated had come: Booker Washington's "utter elimination as a ... leader of his race."

Washington lived five more years, and when he died in 1915, the white South eulogized him. The *New York Times*, however, said that Washington "was far from being [the Negroes'] acknowledged leader ... There was a multitude who thought him timid and even treacherous." In his editorial in the *Crisis*, the official organ of the NAACP, Du Bois wrote, "In stern justice, we must lay on the soul of this man a heavy responsibility for the consummation of Negro disfranchisement, the decline of the Negro college and public school and the firmer establishment of color caste in this land."

*   *   *

William Edward Burghardt Du Bois had once held a much different opinion of Booker T. Washington. Shortly after the Atlanta Exposition speech in 1895, Du Bois, then a professor of Greek and Latin at Wilberforce University, had written the Tuskegee principal congratulating him on his "phenomenal success" and for "a word fitly spoke." But Du Bois had changed his mind before, and certainly would again.

Born in Great Barrington, Massachusetts, in 1868, of parents who, like their parents before them, had never known slavery, Willie Du Bois was part Dutch, part French Huguenot and, for all the Aryan cast of his features, wholly Negro. His yellow-brown complexion was no real problem for him in his hometown, and his family heritage of race pride was proof against emotional shock when he learned that the parents of some of his schoolmates considered the color of his skin a misfortune. Du Bois determined to prove that it was not. He excelled in his studies. His high school companions counted on his initiative and daring as a leader in their games and sports. Although Du Bois would soon learn that there was a color line dividing black from white, he did not think of it as running through the Great Barrington of his boyhood. And if it did, it was not defined by his experiences, not even the experience of serving as the local correspondent for a Negro newspaper, the New York City *Globe,* in which he urged his hometown readers—all ten or twelve of them certainly Negro—to attend town meetings, to join the local prohibition movement, and to vote in local, state, and national elections. As far as Willie Du Bois was concerned, the color line was nonexistent until he graduated from high school and went off to college.

Fisk, a college for Negroes in Nashville, Tennessee, was not his first choice: Harvard was, followed by Williams. But his high school principal demurred. The principal doubted that the donors of the scholarship he could arrange would approve. But Fisk? Willie Du Bois had never heard of it. It was a good college, however, and Mr. Hosmer was sure he would be happy among his own people. And Du Bois was. Fisk was his first real experience of the Negro world, and he reveled in it and in his own Negroness. "I am a Negro," he declaimed before a Fisk audience some months after his arrival, "and I glory in the name! I am proud of the black blood that flows in my veins. From all the recollections dear to my boyhood have I come . . . to join hands with this, my people." And join hands he did—literally at college "sociables," where the "gorgeous color gamut" of his race excited him nearly to delirium; and in summer recesses when he went into backwoods Tennessee and taught at a Negro school for the three months annually that state authorities permitted it to run. The backwoods experience confirmed the reality of the color line and exposed him to the "senseless cruelty" and "injustice" of a social and economic system that was completely controlled by "ignorant white men." Du Bois was already beginning to postulate that "knowledge . . . truth . . . as a matter of scientific procedure" was a cure for the ills of society.

Graduating from Fisk in 1888, Du Bois was awarded a scholarship to

Harvard, where he enrolled as a college junior. For three and a half years he studied under its most renowned teachers—Albert Bushnell Hart in history, William James in psychology, George Santayana in philosophy, and George Palmer in social problems. Under their tutelage, Du Bois earned a master's degree and their recommendations—ample testimony to his scholarship. They also supported his application for a fellowship "to study abroad for at least a year under the direction of the graduate department of Harvard." He studied for two years at the University of Berlin, where sociology, a new academic discipline, had already attained intellectual respectability. Convinced that Berlin had "saved scientific accuracy and the search for truth," Du Bois returned to Harvard in 1894, finished his dissertation, and in 1895 became the first Negro to whom Harvard awarded the Ph.D. His dissertation, *The Suppression of the African Slave Trade, 1638–1870,* was the initial volume in the Harvard Historical Studies series.

If most upward-striving Negroes thought that the attainment of a Harvard doctorate and the publication of a scholarly work marked a new height of accomplishment for the Negro race, there were those among them who also believed that it was a height from which Dr. Du Bois looked down upon them. Few liked the man, and fewer still seemed to understand what he was about: the accumulation and the systematic study of historical and scientific information upon which to base ethical behavior: "first the What, then the Why—underneath the everlasting Ought." They thought his allusions to "the talented tenth of Negroes" was exclusionism. He condescended to them, people said; he was irascible, tactless, dangerously outspoken, and "above the struggle." They cited as proof Du Bois's resigning a professorship at Wilberforce University, which was Negro, to take a mere assistant instructorship at the University of Pennsylvania, which was white. They cited his lengthening list of publications, including his second book, *The Philadelphia Negro: A Social Study,* and articles in the *Annals of the American Academy of Political and Social Science,* the *Atlantic Monthly, The Dial, The Independent,* the *New York Times Magazine Supplement,* and *World's Work,* which, by and large, were so objective and free of personal bias that they might have been the work of a foreign academician who had no stake in the meaning of the facts adduced. They pointed to Du Bois's membership in the rigidly selective American Negro Academy; and those—and they were by far the great number—still under the spell of Booker Washington in the early 1900s pointed to Du Bois's association with such self-confessed radical opponents of Washingtonian thinking as Monroe Trotter, editor of the Boston *Guardian,* as angry a weekly as was ever offered to Negro readers; Ida Wells Barnett, whose bright mind and sharp tongue got her driven into Illinois from her native Tennessee; and John Hope, a young reformist on the faculty of Atlanta Baptist College, which was only two city blocks from Atlanta University, where Du Bois had become Professor of Economics, History and Sociology in 1897.

But these proofs of Dr. Du Bois's pernicious thought and character—the citing of which testified to a troubling uneasiness in the consciousness of thoughtful Negroes—was topped with the publication of *The Souls of Black Folk* in 1903. In one way or another, Du Bois was critical of Booker Washington in practically all 14 of the essays, and four of them were point by point refutations of Washington's program of Negro vocational education, of political passivism, and of white-benefactor black-beggar relations. And Du Bois made no pretense of being simply the temperate scholar. "To have the Negro helpless . . . today," he wrote, "is to leave him, not to the guidance of the best, but rather to the exploitation and debauchment of the worst." Du Bois wrote, "So far as Mr. Washington apologizes for injustice . . . does not rightly value the privilege and duty of voting, belittles the emasculating effects of caste distinctions, and opposes the higher training and ambitions of our brighter minds—so far as he does this, we must, and firmly, oppose [him]. . . . We must strive for the rights which the world accords to men." He wrote, "The problem of the 20th century is the problem of the color line."

The Atlanta *Constitution*'s disapproving three-column review concluded that *The Souls of Black Folk* "is the thought of a Negro of northern education who has lived among his brethren of the South, yet who cannot fully feel the meaning of some things which these brethren know by instinct—and which the southern-bred white knows by a similar instinct—certain things which are by both accepted as facts." The Nashville *Banner* was less delicate: "This book is dangerous for the Negro to read, for it will only excite discontentment and fill his imagination with things that do not exist, or things that should not bear upon his mind."

But dangerous or not, many thoughtful Negroes read it, and when Du Bois invited three score of the best known and most influential of these to meet in Niagara Falls, Ontario, the so-called Niagara Movement was born. Its stated object was to voice complaints about the injustices under which Negroes suffered and, unstated but clearly implied, to organize opposition to Booker Washington's policy of obsequious appeasement. "The battle we wage is not for ourselves alone, but for all true Americans. It is a fight for ideals, lest this, our common fatherland, false to its founding, become in truth the land of the Thief and the home of the Slave. . . . We want full manhood suffrage, and we want it now. . . . We want discrimination in public accommodation to cease. . . . We want our children educated. . . . We mean real education. . . . We want our children trained as intelligent human beings should be, and we will fight for all time against any proposal to educate black boys and girls simply as servants and underlings, or simply for the use of other people."

This was a declaration of principles and the fixing of goals to which Du Bois was committed throughout the rest of his long life. Although the means by which he sought fulfillment would change as circumstances and strategic expedience seemed to require, his pursuit of these goals would never falter. The threats and hostility of others, and from the beginning there was plenty of both, could not turn him off. The New York *Age*, whose editor Booker Washington had in his pocket, characterized the men of Niagara as "senseless radicals," whose "pessimistic folly... does not reflect the sentiment of Negro brains." *Outlook*, the widely read national periodical that had serialized *Up From Slavery* a few years earlier, ridiculed Du Bois for being "ashamed of his race." Even as Booker Washington wrote disparagingly of Du Bois to one of his henchmen, he delegated another to "get right into the inner circle of the Niagara Movement... and keep us informed as [to] their operations and plans."

But to tell the truth, the Movement had no concrete plans; and it had no funds. Spirit alone sustained it for three years, and in 1909 that spirit, which did not exclusively haunt the men of Niagara, pervaded a series of articles by William English Walling, a distinguished Socialist journalist (in *The Independent*), the news and investigative reports of Mary White Ovington, and many of the public utterances of Dr. Henry Moskowitz. Although these three had other things in common, they were sharply exercised by what they saw as a steady erosion of democratic morality and a steady build-up of race-hatred—especially marked by a series of race riots in 1906, 1907, and 1908. So, in 1909, they issued a call "to all believers in democracy to join in a National conference for the discussion of present evils, the voicing of protests, and the renewal of the struggle for civil and political liberty." Du Bois and other members of the Niagara Movement, together with a score of distinguished white men and women—including Jane Addams, John Dewey, William Dean Howells, Lincoln Steffens, and Rabbi Stephen S. Wise—joined the initiators to organize the National Association for the Advancement of Colored People. Under the aegis of the Association, in which he accepted appointment as director of publicity and research, Du Bois founded and edited the *Crisis*.

In the first two issues (November and December 1910) Du Bois left no room for doubt as to what he and the NAACP stood for, and by the third issue he had established the personal tone that was to characterize the *Crisis* during the 24 years of his editorship. The NAACP, he wrote, "is a union of those who believe that earnest, active opposition is the only effective way of meeting the forces of evil. They believe that the growth of race prejudice in the United States is evil.... Much of it is born of ignorance and misapprehension, honest mistake and misguided zeal. However caused, it is none the less evil, wrong, dangerous, fertile of harm.... Fight the wrong with every civilized weapon in every civilized way." "I am resolved to be satisfied with no treatment which ignores my manhood and my right to be counted as one among men. . . . I am resolved to defend and assert the absolute equality of the Negro race with any and all other human races and its divine right to equal and just treatment. I am resolved to be ready at all times and in all places to bear witness with pen, voice, money, and deed against the horrible crime of lynching, the shame of Jim Crow legislation, the injustice of all color discrimination, the wrong of disfranchisement for race or sex, the iniquity of war under any circumstances, and the deep damnation of present methods of distributing the world's work and wealth." "We have crawled and pleaded for justice and we have been cheerfully spit upon and murdered and burned. We will not endure it forever. If we are to die, in God's name let us perish like men and not like bales of hay."

Although Du Bois frequently gave way to anger and pessimism, he never completely relinquished his belief that race prejudice and discrimination would yield to information and knowledge, and that "catholicity and tolerance, reason and forbearance can today make the world-old dream of brotherhood approach realization."

NAACP policy and programs and the often swollen rhetoric of the *Crisis* attracted a great many middle-class Negroes and not a few whites. The Association's local chapters increased from one to 165 in five years, and *Crisis* circulation peaked at 100,000 by 1917. But as prodigious as this growth appeared to be, it was exceeded by the growth of the come-lately Universal Negro Improvement Association (UNIA) and its official publication, the *Negro World*. In 1918, only about two years after the UNIA was transplanted from Jamaica, BWI, to Harlem, its founder and leader claimed, perhaps dubiously, a membership of more than a million in thirty branches and, after less than a year, a weekly circulation of 30,000 for *Negro World*. Beneath its sphinx-like symbol bearing the inscription *One God, One Aim, One Destiny,* "A Newspaper Devoted Solely to the Interests of the Negro Race," the *World* bannered week after week "Up You Mighty Race. You Can Accomplish What You Will!" and "Back To Africa!" And black people read it in English, French, and Spanish, and many were indeed uplifted by a new surge of pride.

*   *   *

The man principally responsible for this was named Marcus Garvey. Born in St. Ann's Bay, Jamaica, Garvey boasted of his African ancestry and a fierce pride in his "pure black blood." His formal education seems to have been sketchy, but he learned the printer's trade and practiced it for several years in Central and South America. In Limón, Costa Rico, already sick at heart because "no white person would ever regard the life of a black man equal to that of a white," he started a newspaper, *La Nacionale*. It failed. In Colón he started another, *La Prensa,* and it failed.

In 1910, age 23, he went to London, where he studied off and on at Birbeck College, and joined the nationalist clique of African, West Indian, East Indian, and Egyptian students and workers. He became an intimate associate of Duse Mohammed Ali, a Nubian and an extreme race nationalist. Garvey was deeply influenced by this radical and, somewhat paradoxically, by the conservative thought of Booker Washington at about the same time. He may have heard Washington speak when the latter visited London in 1910. But when he read *Up From Slavery*, his "doom— if I may so call it," he testified later, "of being a race leader dawned upon me." He wrote to Washington twice, the second time in April 1915, expressing a desire to come to the States, and the reply was politely encouraging: Garvey should come when ready. It was 1916 before he was ready, and by then Booker Washington had been a year in the grave.

Meanwhile, though, as war clouds gathered over Europe, Garvey returned to Jamaica. His heart was in tumult but his mind, he said, was clear. In the summer of 1914, he organized the Universal Negro Improvement and Conservation Association and African Communities League (abbreviated as UNIA). He issued a manifesto—two parts Duse Mohammed Ali, one part Booker Washington, and one part Garvey:

> To establish a universal confraternity among the race; to promote the spirit of race pride and love; to redeem the fallen of the race; to administer to and assist the needy; to assist in civilizing the backward tribes of Africa; to strengthen the imperialism of independent African States; to establish Commissionaries or Agencies in the principal countries of the world for the protection of all Negroes irrespective of nationality; to promote a conscientious Christian worship among the native tribes of Africa; to establish Universities, Colleges and Secondary Schools for the further education and culture of the boys and girls of the race.

Jamaica and its Negro population were not large enough to support these undertakings, so Garvey pocketed his organization and his manifesto and moved to New York. He drew immediate favorable attention from the unschooled black masses, and skeptical laughter from the middle classes. He knew what the world of common blacks wanted. They wanted a sense of security. Finding it difficult even to provide themselves a day-by-day living, they wanted protection against the financial emergencies brought on by sickness and death, so Garvey promised that UNIA would pay sick and death benefits from their monthly dues of 35 cents. They wanted opportunities in business and commerce, and Garvey established the Negro Factories Cooperation, which in a matter of months was operating a chain of grocery stores, a restaurant, a laundry, and a print shop. They wanted race solidarity and to be independent of the oversight and council of whites; so, unlike the NAACP, the National Urban League and the Amenia Conference, the UNIA was black from top to bottom. They wanted a place of their own, and Garvey's fertile mind conceived the Back to Africa movement and the African Legion, the African Motor Corps, the Black Eagle Flying Corps, and the Black Cross Nurses—all recruited from the dues-paying membership of UNIA, and all gaudily uniformed at the volunteers' expense.

Garvey traveled in 38 states, lecturing to black audiences. "Race is greater than law!" he told them. "We have died for 500 years for an alien race. The time has come for the Negro to die for himself." "Wake up Africa! Let us work toward the one glorious end of a free, redeemed and mighty nation." His message was printed in circulars that were distributed to Negro communities throughout the Western world; it was painted on billboards in Harlem, and stitched on the bunting that draped the platform in UNIA headquarters called "Liberty Hall."

But Garvey was not all rhetoric and bombast. In 1919, he founded the Black Star Line, which was incorporated by the State of Delaware and which would "own, operate and navigate ships." He even purchased a rusty freighter. He told his four million followers, "We will come into trade relations with our brethren on the West Coast of Africa, and transport to Liberia and other African countries those Negroes who desire to possess and enjoy the fruits of the richest country on God's green Earth." The Black Star Line issued stock and used the proceeds to buy a second ship and then a third.

Going back to Africa and colonizing American Negroes there had become an obsession with Marcus Garvey by 1920, and it was to be his undoing. It brought him into conflict with the policies and programs of the older, more traditional race uplift organizations, whose middle-class Negro sympathizers Garvey charged with "time-serving, boot-licking . . . subserviency to whites. . . . They want to intermarry with the [white] women of this country." "I believe in a pure black race," he declared, and he scathingly disparaged "the vile efforts of the miscegenationists of the white race and their associates, the hybrids of the Negro race."

The expression of these sentiments and the stated aims of the Back to Africa movement brought Garvey the support of some of the most reactionary white organizations. And Garvey seemed to welcome it. Representatives of the Anglo-Saxon Clubs of America and of White American Society accepted invitations to speak in Liberty Hall. *Black World* publicized a meeting between Garvey and Edward Y. Clarke, the Imperial Giant of the Ku Klux Klan, and in 1922 a rumor spread—never officially denied—that the KKK was contributing money to UNIA, which was then in financial difficulty.

Up to this time, as a matter of policy the old-line Negro organizations had avoided open confrontation with UNIA and tried to keep silent about Garvey's aims and his character. But now they broke their silence. He was their *bête noire,* threatening the fulfillment of all they stood for:

racial integration and, as W. E. B. Du Bois had said long before, "full manhood rights"; that is the implementation of the American democratic creed. A. Philip Randolph, the Negro labor leader, sloganized in his magazine, the *Messenger,* "Garvey Must Go!" and sponsored anti-Garvey meetings across the country. The Rev. Dr. Robert Bagnall, one of the most highly respected of black churchmen, speaking as a member of the NAACP, excoriated Garvey as a "sheer opportunist . . . egotistic, tyrannical, intolerant, cunning." Assuming a more moderate tone, Du Bois cautioned *Crisis* readers, "Do not invest in the conquest of Africa. Do not take desperate chances in flighty dreams."

If Garvey was scornful of these attacks and undeterred by the New York district attorney's investigation of the Black Star Line, he was deeply embarrassed by the charges that United States Postal Authorities brought against him. In February 1922 Garvey and three associates in UNIA-BSL were indicted for using the mails to defraud. Brought to trial 18 months later, his associates were acquitted, but Garvey, acting as his own attorney, was convicted and sentenced to five years in federal prison. An appeal was disallowed. From his cell in Atlanta, he tried to keep his following together and UNIA alive, but the effort was hopeless. His sentence was commuted in 1927, and he was immediately deported as an undesirable alien. He tried to make a comeback in Jamaica, but this effort too proved fruitless, and after a few months he went on to London where in 1940 he died, too senile to remember how profoundly he had stirred the race consciousness of Negro peoples throughout the world.

*   *   *

Although Marcus Garvey had counted W. E. B. Du Bois an implacable enemy and had made him the principal target of his attacks on the "old line" Negro improvement organizations, Du Bois was in fact entirely sympathetic to the *spirit* of Garveyism. He deplored the Back to Africa Movement on the grounds first that it was politically impractical, and second that it promoted race nationalism, was destructive of the effort to attain racial equality in a democratic, pluralistic social order. Moreover, Du Bois preferred to think of himself as an American first and as a Negro second. This is not to say that he wished to repudiate his African heritage, as Garvey charged. Quite the contrary—"a deep racial kinship bound him to the dark continent." He organized the first Pan-African Congress in Paris in 1919, the second in London in 1921, and two subsequent congresses, the last being in New York in 1927. Negroes of his own class and the Board of Directors of the NAACP expressed serious misgivings about this activity, and Du Bois felt constrained to explain that "this [the Pan-African Congress] is not a separatist movement. There is no need to think that those who advocate the opening up of

Africa for Africans and those of African descent desire to deport any large number of colored Americans to a foreign and, in some respect, inhospitable land. Once for all, let us realize that we are Americans. . . . There is nothing so indigenous, so completely 'made in America' as we. It is as absurd to talk of a return to Africa, merely because that was our home 300 years ago, as it would be to expect members of the Caucasian race to return to the fastnesses of the Caucasus Mountains from which, it is reputed, they sprang. . . . The African movement means to us what the zionist movement must mean to the Jews, the centralization of race effort and the recognition of a racial fount. To help bear the burden of Africa does not mean any lessening of effort in our own problem at home."

Although this statement was calculated to set minds at rest, certain officers of the Association continued to complain; and not only of Du Bois's advocacy of Pan-Africanism as running counter to, or at least non-supportive of, the aims of the NAACP, but of other things as well. Du Bois, they said, seemed to think the *Crisis* was his personal forum; and his editorials did not always reflect the thinking of the NAACP. And there was more than just a little truth in these charges. Indeed, considering Du Bois's far-ranging interests, his intellectual integrity and his commitment to freedom of thought and expression, it is rather remarkable that for almost two decades he was in general agreement with Association policies and thought.

But in 1924, disagreement was manifest. Du Bois urged readers of the *Crisis* to vote for Robert La Follette and Progressivism, while the NAACP officially backed Calvin Coolidge. Four years later, the Association plumped for Herbert Hoover while Du Bois, charging the Republican candidate with "lily-whitism," declared for Norman Thomas and the Socialist Party. Differences of opinion and outlook between Du Bois and the policy-makers of the NAACP gradually widened over the years, and in 1933 Du Bois wrote: "There seems no hope that America in our day will yield in its color or race hatred any substantial ground, and we have no physical or economic power, nor any alliance with other social or economic classes that will force compliance with decent civilized ideals in Church, State, industry, or art." His inference was clear. The NAACP was fighting a hopeless battle. Its policy of racial equality and its program of racial integration were failures.

Du Bois had come to this opinion by slow and painful degrees, slowly but compulsively changing his mind and modifying his direction as his reading of new facts and his assessment of new circumstances seemed to dictate. Gradually he came about-face. He began to advocate "voluntary segregation" and to envision a self-sufficient Negro community and a "new and great Negro ethos." Ideologically he now stood shoulder to shoulder with Marcus Garvey. This development, combined with the fact that the *Crisis* was now entirely dependent upon NAACP financial support, convinced Du Bois that his position as editor was untenable. He resigned and refused to consider the compromise suggested by the Board of Directors. In August 1934, he accepted a long-standing invitation to become chairman of the department of sociology at Atlanta University. He was 66 years old.

This return to academic life gave Du Bois time for the research he had neglected and the kind of writing he wanted to do—the scholarly writing that characterized his doctoral dissertation and his study of the Philadelphia Negro. But put off nearly 40 years ago, the scholar's mantle fit Du Bois poorly in the 1930s. His objectivity was all but gone, and his disputatious style was an ingrained habit. *Black Reconstruction in America*, published a year after his return to Atlanta, was a masterly recording of historical facts and sources, but its tone is polemical and an anagogic bias shows. Published four years later, in 1939, *Black Folk Then and Now* affirms only that "the truth of history lies not in the mouth of partisans but rather in the calm Science that sits between. Her cause I seek to serve, and whenever I fail, I am at least paying the Truth the respect of earnest effort." *Phylon*, the Atlanta University quarterly review of "race and culture," which he founded as a scholarly journal in 1940, was rather more declamatory than scholarly for the four years he remained its editor. *Dusk of Dawn: An Essay Toward an Autobiography of a Race Concept*, which came in 1940, was an anecdotal essay on his intellectual and emotional development.

Meantime, Du Bois had projected an encyclopedia of the Negro, and in 1936 he spent several months in Western Europe, Russia, China, and Japan "interviewing," he wrote in *Dusk of Dawn*, "scholars on the project." Perhaps it was this period of foreign travel that put him out of sympathetic touch with Negro thought at home and altered his perspective. What Du Bois saw of the working of Communism fascinated him. He turned more and more toward the political left, and it puts no strain on logic to speculate (since the facts have never been made public) that it was this leftward turning that prompted the abrupt cancellation of his contract with Atlanta University. But what is one to say when immediately upon the heels of this event the NAACP invited him to take over as chairman of a committee on special research? He stayed with the Association four years, and was one of its representatives at the UN's organizational meeting.

Du Bois was 80 years old when he accepted the Vice-Chairmanship of the American Council on African Affairs, and 82 when he was defeated as the Progressive Party candidate for the United States Senate from New York. In 1951, while serving as Chairman of the Peace Information Center, he was indicted for failing to register as an agent for a "foreign prinicpal," namely, the U.S.S.R. The Department of Justice failed to prove the charge, but the trial left him bitter and discouraged. Gorden

B. Hancock, a staunch supporter, testified to one reason for his unhappiness: "the important Negroes ... the headliners, the highly positioned, the degreed Negroes ... who claim to be race champions and crusaders and fighters and leaders and uncompromisers to the last ditch actually deserted Dr. Du Bois in the hour of his greatest trial."

How bitterly Du Bois felt this apostasy and isolation was made clear in the autobiographical *In Battle For Peace* (1952). It also made abundantly clear his conviction that Russia and the Communist ideology represented the forces that would bring about human equality and universal peace. Another trip to Russia and China (1958), where he was received with great honor and where he remained for almost a year, deepened this conviction. In 1961, he applied for membership in the American Communist Party, and later that year he accepted an invitation from President Kwame Nkrumah to live in Ghana, of which country he became a citizen just prior to his death on August 27, 1963.

* * *

Booker T. Washington was a realist, Marcus Garvey a racial chauvinist, and W. E. B. Du Bois an idealist, and each remained what he was until his dying day. Washington's perception of the reality of Negro life, which he did not think of as depressing, and of the flow of the national mind and mood, unruffled by cross currents of liberalism, convinced him that the Negro's place in the American social order was inferior and would remain inferior. Blacks stood in relation to whites as menials to masters or, at the very best, as protegés to patrons. As Booker T. Washington saw it, they were entirely dependent upon the good will of the white majority, and to gain and retain that good will, they must do as they were bid and do it better than was expected. He believed that generally speaking—for he admitted exceptions and counted himself among them—blacks were inferior to whites in all the indices by which human worth is measured. His Atlanta Exposition speech was a positive expression of his belief.

Marcus Garvey believed no such thing: Negroes were certainly the equals of whites, if indeed they were not superior to them. He said so on every possible occasion: "Up you mighty race. You can accomplish what you will!" What he urged his race to accomplish was independence and separation from the white race, which would follow upon a return to Africa. "Race is greater than law! ... Let us work toward the one glorious end of a free, redeemed and mighty nation." At the high point of his brief career in the United States, Marcus Garvey inspired and persuaded four million Negroes to believe in his dream. But reality defeated the dreamer, and the dream faded.

W. E. B. Du Bois was haunted by another dream commonly described as the "American Dream," and for the greater part of his long career he

believed that the elimination of the color line was requisite to its fulfillment. He believed that the day would come when Negroes would be
equal before the law, in the exercise of those rights that the 13th, 14th,
and 15th constitutional amendments were designed to guarantee them,
and in access to opportunities to pursue the "good life" that is comprehended in the term "democracy." He worked for this by every means he
could discover or create. He used education, propaganda, and agitation,
politics and personalities, and he often used them in ways often defined
as radical. When they all failed, when the American color line remained
seemingly as impregnable as ever, he renounced his American citizenship
and went to Ghana.

7

Breaking through the Male Barrier

ELIZABETH CADY STANTON
EMILY JAMES PUTNAM
CHARLOTTE PERKINS GILMAN

by Annette K. Baxter
Barnard College

In the lifetime of three remarkable women, the feminist movement in the United States grew from faint stirrings of awareness to a full expression of collective consciousness. Different as were their lives and personalities, Elizabeth Cady Stanton, Emily James Putnam, and Charlotte Perkins Gilman together symbolize the persistence and the resolve that were to be required of countless American women in their struggle for equal rights, educational advancement, and greater self-realization.

Since colonial days the American woman has been an active contributor to social order. While her participation in domestic industry helped establish the early settlements on a firm economic base, her major role, then as now, was as homemaker and helpmeet. In the conquest of the West women bore burdens of physical hardship, social isolation, precarious childbirth, and the rootlessness that attended constant mobility. Despite their perseverance, opportunities for individual self-expression were few. In fact, one historian observed that if we accept Frederick Jackson Turner's view that the frontier was the crucial setting for America's economic growth, we must concede that "for American women, as individuals, opportunity began pretty much where the frontier left off."

Even where the frontier left off, however, women's status for a long time remained unchanged. Indeed in 18th-century cities like New York and Philadelphia, where the appearance of a developed social life occasionally made it possible for a few women to gain access to the male world of politics and power, little change resulted in women's position in the community. Abigail Adams, writing to her husband, John, while he was attending the Continental Congress in 1776, was among the earliest to assert that women's inferiority was a direct consequence of the male drive for dominance: "That your sex are naturally tyrannical is a truth so thoroughly established as to admit of no dispute." Tyranny had its consequences: married women were deprived of the elementary rights of owning property, retaining possession of their earnings, and sharing legal control over their children. And all women were without certain basic legal rights, including the franchise, the essential instrument for correcting these wrongs. Thus, they had minimal influence upon the law-making process. Beyond this, they were almost universally deprived of the educational opportunities that would equip them to understand the historical origins of their predicament, and to embark upon a campaign of forceful persuasion and self-development. Most critically, they lacked a grasp of the broad social context in which women's interaction with men took place. As a consequence, they inclined to see the nature and role of women as fixed rather than as subject to evolutionary change.

Publication in 1792 of the Englishwoman Mary Wollstonecraft's *Vindication of the Rights of Women*, which called for thoroughgoing changes in the status quo, would not be followed by immediate feminist uprisings on either side of the Atlantic. Nonetheless, the ideas of this determined lady gradually seeped through the layers of indifference that theretofore confronted even the most benign feminist initiatives. Fundamental to her thinking was the conviction that the education of women had been essentially perverted. By stressing the young girl's need to please men rather than to develop her own identity, educators perpetuated those values that transformed potentially useful and creative members of society into superficial creatures whose minds were eternally bent on a search for pleasure.

The education of young women in America corresponded in general outline to Mary Wollstonecraft's diagnosis. Whether in the colonial dame school or in the academies and seminaries that were flourishing at the start of the 19th century, an education equal to that offered men was simply unavailable. However, in 1821 a pioneering New York educator, Emma Willard, determined to provide such a course of study for young women in her Troy Female Seminary. The school soon gained a reputation for academic excellence that approached that of some of the men's colleges. In fact, Elizabeth Cady Stanton, a member of the Troy Seminary's graduating class of 1832, was to offer the first serious challenge to the male barrier itself.

*   *   *

Like Margaret Fuller, who was born five years earlier, and whose mind came to be acknowledged as among the most brilliant of her time, Elizabeth Cady Stanton was raised in an atmosphere of intellectual cultivation and strong paternal influence. Judge Cady did not hesitate to express his deep disappointment that his daughter Elizabeth was the wrong gender. Having lost his only son in the flower of his youth, the Judge was not easily comforted by his daughter's independent academic achievements. With compensatory zeal, the 11-year-old Elizabeth had sought out a neighboring minister who responded to her plea to teach her Greek so that she could match her brother in every possible respect. Psychohistorians might claim that Elizabeth Cady's life-long need to propitiate an ultimately irreconcilable father accounted for the obduracy of her impulse to demonstrate women's equality with men in every arena. Whatever the explanation, her seemingly instinctive feminism unquestionably became focused in early young womanhood, when she learned in her father's law office of the legal injustices suffered by women.

During her youth in Johnstown, New York, she had enjoyed an active social life, healthy recreation, and relative economic security. Despite the repressiveness of early religious influences, she developed into a young woman increasingly confident of her powers. After her return from Troy Seminary, she joined the circle of her antislavery cousin Gerrit Smith. There she encountered a number of reformist minds. There too she eventually met her future husband, the eloquent abolitionist, Henry Stanton.

The fateful moment of Elizabeth Stanton's life was yet before her; in 1840 she and her husband attended the World's Anti-Slavery Convention in London where, much to her indignation, women were barred from participation simply on the grounds of sex. Her indignation fulminated into anger when she observed that delegates presumably in the fore of enlightened thinking supported this policy. "It struck me as very remarkable," she later recalled, "that abolitionists, who felt so keenly the wrongs of the slave, should be so oblivious to the equal wrongs of their own mothers, wives, and sisters. . . ." The convention triggered all of the muffled feminist sentiments she had harbored since girlhood, and her response, fanning out in several directions, would reverberate through assembly halls, legislatures, and law courts for the next 80 years.

The groundwork for action had been laid in the preceding two decades. With little conscious planning, women had begun shaping the life of their communities in an unprecedented way. The religious revivals of the early 19th century, particularly in the "Burned-Over District" of Western

New York, encouraged women to express emotions with unaccustomed daring. The search for moral perfectionism that characterized the religious-evangelical revivals was linked both to a new estimate of human possibilities and to a rejection of the dour Calvinism in which most Protestant Americans had been reared. A host of humanitarian movements emerged from this reconstructed world view—some of them, like hydropathy and animal magnetism, verging on the ridiculous, some of them, like the second-coming theories of the Millerites, verging on the ridiculously sublime. But at the heart of most of these reform movements was anti-slavery, a cause that had been gathering strength in New England and New York and was serving as an initiation into public life for many women who had previously led sheltered existences.

Out of the anti-slavery ferment several women emerged as especially persuasive oracles of change, among them Lydia Maria Child, Sarah Grimké and Lucretia Mott. Mrs. Child's sympathy with the oppressed of whatever class led her naturally into abolitionism and the publication in 1833 of her *Appeal in Favor of That Class of Americans Called Africans,* a work whose premonitory seriousness heralded the appearance of women as a force in the practical realization of humanitarian aims. Like the New Englander Mrs. Child, Sarah Grimké was absorbed in abolitionism, but her Charleston, South Carolina, upbringing gave her the additional authority of an intimate familiarity with slavery itself. She also held forth thoughtfully on a number of feminist themes, including two that made a strong impression on Elizabeth Cady Stanton: the legal disabilities suffered by women and the Biblical injunctions against women. Lucretia Mott, a wise and self-effacing Quaker abolitionist, had joined Mrs. Stanton at the World's Anti-Slavery Convention in London in 1840 in her resolve to call a convention at some future date in behalf of women's rights.

Eight years after their meeting in London Mrs. Stanton and Mrs. Mott were sufficiently free of other distractions and responsibilities to regain touch with each other. In that interim as wife and mother, Mrs. Stanton had experienced at first-hand the burden of women's many roles and had observed "the chaotic conditions into which everything fell without her constant supervision." Though herself robust and energetic, with sprightly blue eyes reflecting a perpetual interest in what took place around her, she was struck by the "wearied, anxious look of the majority of women." With Mrs. Mott's collaboration she arranged to call a woman's rights convention in Seneca Falls, New York, where she and her husband had settled after an instructive five-year period among the reformers in Boston.

The Seneca Falls Convention of 1848 marked the official opening of the women's rights movement in the United States. Its Declaration of

Sentiments, modeled on the American Declaration of Independence, asserted the case for women's oppression by men. It struck hard at the legal inequities inflicted upon the entire female sex, while listing the special hardships suffered by married women. It pointedly accused men of closing off opportunities in employment, education, the professions, and the church. Perhaps most damning was its attack on the double standard of morality: "moral delinquencies which exclude women from society, are not only tolerated, but deemed of little account in man." At the conclusion of the Declaration the convention proclaimed its intention to embark upon a campaign to invest women with the dignity and self-determination to which they were entitled by birth.

Not all women, and fewer men, were convinced that demands for the suffrage were politically wise at a time when more pressing injustices needed attention, but many women's rights advocates soon recognized the consistency of Mrs. Stanton's position. For her, the pursuit of thoroughgoing equality in all areas would establish for once and all the falsity of the familiar argument that women's aspirations should be confined to "women's sphere." In opting for this bold course, she confronted head-on the prevailing pieties of the day, thereby threatening the complacency of most women while arousing the ire of their husbands. If Mrs. Stanton triumphed, the whole interlocking system of beliefs involving the sacredness of motherhood and the home, in which 19th-century American society had so great a stake, stood to collapse. For each sympathetic male feminist like the radical reformer Parker Pillsbury, there were many articulate male opponents of women's rights like the influential minister Horace Bushnell, who warned that women's suffrage was a "reform against nature."

The Seneca Falls Convention was soon followed by another in Rochester, New York, and before long regular state and national conventions were held in which women from a variety of backgrounds became immersed in the cause. The movement spread to the West, where eventually Mrs. Stanton would go on speaking tours that would sorely try her mettle. But in the 1850s she was confined to her home by childbearing and domestic cares. Providentially for the cause, Mrs. Stanton met in 1851 the one person who could assist her in making the most of her available energies, a Quaker spinster of exceptionally strong conscience named Susan Brownell Anthony. Together they would become the standard-bearers of the battle for women's rights.

A faithful worker for temperance reform, Susan B. Anthony had not encountered serious prejudice against women until men rebuked her for speaking out at a state convention of the Sons of Temperance at Albany, New York. This incident could hardly have been better timed, for her new-found friend Mrs. Stanton quickly underscored the moral and unhesitatingly advised her on her response. In launching a Woman's State

Temperance Society, they advanced the radical notion that women had the right to obtain divorces from drunken husbands. At the Syracuse Women's Rights Convention of 1852 Miss Anthony felt confirmed in her growing radicalism and soon injected women's rights into temperance, all the while staying in touch with Mrs. Stanton in her home in Seneca Falls. It was the next meeting of the Woman's State Temperance Society, however, where her priorities were permanently joined to Mrs. Stanton's. There she stood by helplessly while men brought an end to the discussion of women's rights and engineered an amendment to permit themselves to become officers. They did both with the ignominious acquiescence of the women delegates.

In answer to such indignities Elizabeth Cady Stanton and Susan B. Anthony forged themselves into an unprecedented working team. Miss Anthony became the organizer in the field, while Mrs. Stanton hammered out policies at home. There was a remarkable emotional compatibility between the two, based upon a candid acknowledgment of their practical dependence on one another as well as upon their unqualified mutual respect. Miss Anthony even substituted as mother and housekeeper for Mrs. Stanton whenever the latter needed relief from her domestic responsibilities.

The alliance produced results. Coming to see that lack of funds would vitiate any reform movement, Miss Anthony shrewdly concluded that to receive support from their natural constituency of women, she and Mrs. Stanton must first concentrate on securing a legal basis for women's financial independence. Accordingly, she zealously collected signatures on a petition calling for a bill by the New York legislature to give women control over their earnings. In addition she agitated for the mother's right of guardianship in divorce cases. Last and most threatening to the male establishment in Albany, she demanded the vote. Elizabeth Cady Stanton, meanwhile, spoke before the legislature in support of these reforms. The lawmakers were highly impressed by the aplomb and skill of her address but remained intransigent. It was finally in 1860 when, together with a broadened property law and more equitable guardianship rights, New York women secured title to their own wages and income. Meanwhile the reformers had had a degree of influence in other states, where similar changes were under way.

Mrs. Stanton next turned to divorce, a question that in some ways was the most sensitive of all. From the first, divorce had been linked in their discussions to temperance, and Mrs. Stanton went so far as to address the New York State legislature in support of a bill that would make drunkenness grounds for divorce. With her unsparing view of men, she could imagine circumstances besides habitual intoxication that might warrant the dissolution of a marriage. Portraying women as too often the victims of their own timidity, she saw no point in their tolerating abuse for the sake of honoring convention. Legal authorities were cited to bolster her claim that the laws on divorce permitted guilty husbands to keep most of the community property while innocent wives were left paupers. And she noted that in most states women were compelled to sue for divorce under someone else's name because of their own financial powerlessness. When Mrs. Stanton raised the divorce issue at the woman's rights convention of 1860, it met with widespread opposition. Undaunted, she persisted in fighting for liberalized divorce laws in the years ahead.

Perhaps the greatest test of Mrs. Stanton's devotion to women's rights came after the Civil War. During the war, in keeping with her abolitionist beliefs, she had helped lead a movement to secure a constitutional amendment to end slavery. But when the war was over, she faced a new and anguishing reality confronting many reformers: the fight for a clear recognition of the Negro's civil and voting rights was taking precedence over the women's issue. For Elizabeth Cady Stanton and Susan B. Anthony there could be no lapse in priorities: they sought to use the opportunity afforded by the passage of new amendments protecting Negro rights as a means of securing woman suffrage at the same time. In this connection their effort to have the restrictive word "male" removed from the constitution came to nothing. In several speaking engagements Mrs. Stanton promoted the alternative solution of a separate woman's suffrage amendment. But audiences were frequently hostile. A rift developed between those women who followed Elizabeth Cady Stanton and Susan Anthony in opposing the 15th Amendment so long as it failed to enfranchise women as well as Negroes and those who regarded Negro rights as the paramount consideration. This split in the women's movement would not be healed until 1890.

Mrs. Stanton assumed the leadership of the National Woman Suffrage Association, the more radically feminist of the two organizations that emerged as products of this ideological battle. She now had an official platform from which to make numerous appeals to legislatures. The Association also served as a focus for debate on various ideas and proposals concerning the woman question. Despite the NWSA's association with the shady Victoria Woodhull, notorious advocate of free love and protegée of Commodore Cornelius Vanderbilt, it achieved growing authority as the conscience of the woman's movement. Mrs. Stanton was admiringly described in Victoria's *Woodhull and Claflin's Weekly* as a lecturer with a "fine sonorous voice" who used "weighty, well-chosen language" and who produced her effect "by her stately, impressive manner." Moreover she possessed a talent for verbal sparring that put insolent men in their place while disarming them with her good humor and her "mellow and agreeable" voice. Her ability to remain calm, whatever the momentary circumstances, and to avoid personal invective commanded the respect of radicals and conservatives alike.

Throughout her travels in behalf of the woman suffrage amendment, Mrs. Stanton came to mingle with people of different religious persuasions and different walks of life. Her conservative appearance and prematurely gray hair belied her openness to change. Her belief in cultivating the self without fear of restraining social customs was expressed in several of her widely known talks. Among the most famous were "Our Girls" and "The Solitude of Self," which emphasized that each woman was a unique human entitled to seek out her fullest measure of personal identity and freedom.

Perhaps the most controversial phase of Mrs. Stanton's career came at its close, when she encouraged women to reexamine the Bible in the light of the connection between canon and civil law, Biblical criticism, and woman's traditional role. Mrs. Stanton pointed to the contradiction between clerical exhortations to women to find sanction for their spiritual freedom in the Bible and the church's refusal to grant women a meaningful role in its institutional life. A systematic investigation of the treatment of women in the Bible, she suggested, would jolt the hierarchy into revising its outworn patriarchal attitudes and provoke a more enlightened view of women's status. She labelled as cowards those who feared the upheaval that such an undertaking would inspire. In characteristic fashion she asserted that the search for truth could not be compromised—since "all reforms are interdependent" and "whatever is done to establish one principle on a solid base, strengthens all." In keeping with her lifelong battle for the recognition of women's rights as part of a larger human quest for freedom and fulfillment, she reminded her critics that "the object of an individual life is not to carry one fragmentary measure in human progress, but to utter the highest truth clearly seen in all directions."

By the time Mrs. Stanton presented this issue to her feminist following for a vote in 1896, the suffrage organizations had reunited. In their ranks were younger and conservative women whose influence worked against its passage. At one point in the debate Susan B. Anthony admonished them for their narrowmindedness. In a moving defense of Mrs. Stanton she described her as "a woman who is without peer in intellectual and statesmanlike ability; one who has stood for half a century the acknowledged leader of progressive thought and demand in regard to all matters pertaining to the absolute freedom of women."

The Woman's Bible, prepared by Mrs. Stanton and designed to counteract anti-feminist uses to which the Scriptures had been put, failed of official endorsement, and it would take another quarter century before even the suffrage was won. But Mrs. Stanton's life, which ended in 1902 when she was 87, offered convincing proof of the breadth and vitality of the woman's cause. Thereafter it would be difficult to dismiss women's rights as the concern of only a small minority of fanatics. It would be equally difficult to deny that women who possessed the ability to recruit, organize, and agitate intelligently in their own behalf could also handle their property and earnings, assume guardianship of their children, serve on juries, and exercise the vote.

But before the male barrier could effectively be overturned, women themselves would have to be convinced of their capacity over the long haul to sustain the more demanding roles envisioned by feminist leaders. They needed the assurance coming from repeated demonstrations of women's ability to compete with men. In American society education had traditionally been the avenue to status and self-fulfillment for men. Women were deprived of that opportunity partly because their roles in life seemed not to require more than a limited education, but primarily because they were not thought equal to the mental requisites and physical strains that higher education demanded. Feminist leaders had often proclaimed the importance of disabusing men of these prejudices, and Mrs. Stanton herself had strong views on the subject. "To throw obstacles in the way of a complete education," she said, "is like putting out the eyes."

*   *   *

Not long after Mrs. Stanton had received her own superior training at Emma Willard's Troy Seminary others had begun working to improve the quality of education available to women. Among the most prominent of these early educators was Mary Lyon, a young teacher of modest circumstances from the back country of western Massachusetts. Through her own educational experience she knew that young women needed the intellectual incentives that were wanting in the conventional schools and academies. With characteristic resourcefulness, she had managed to acquire a sound classical education in between various teaching chores, but it was her attendance in 1821 at the local Byfield Seminary that proved to be the crucial episode in the development of her academic self-confidence. There she studied with an enthusiastic advocate of education for women, the Reverend Joseph Emerson, who considered hers the best mind he had ever encountered among his students. Another significant association there was with Zilpah Grant, who as Emerson's assistant pioneered the system of "self-reporting."

By the 1830s Mary Lyon was determined to found a permanent institution for the higher education of women. Academies and seminaries of that period were usually short-lived because of financial dependence on unreliable patrons. In addition they usually failed to take the long view toward academic survival. By seeking support among local farmers as well as among prominent businessmen, she widened the base of her school's support. Working "by persuasion, by insinuation, by tact and sympathy" and employing her "golden faculty of making others feel that her will was their own," she raised the funds for the new seminary that opened its doors at South Hadley, Massachusetts, in 1837. Adding a year to the customary two-year course, it combined a rigorous curriculum with a domestic work requirement that utilized student labor. This arrangement simultaneously strengthened character and cut maintenance costs; above all, it inspired students to serve others, and large numbers of them entered the missionary field.

Mount Holyoke's ongoing reputation as a fully respectable seat of learning helped to lend credibility to the idea that the nation had seriously underestimated its young women by having deprived them of opportunities to demonstrate their intelligence and usefulness to a fast-growing society. Beginning in 1841 Oberlin College in Ohio and then a succession of state universities granted the A.B. degree to women, but increasingly it was the women's institutions—Mount Holyoke and its successors, Vassar, Smith, Wellesley, and Bryn Mawr—that would lead women toward the highest academic standards. Furthermore, these institutions provided female role models from their faculties, who endowed young women with faith in their intellectual powers and the desire for fulfillment outside the home.

As the impact of these colleges began to be felt, each passing year saw fewer attacks of the kind levelled in the 1860s by the Reverend John Todd, who argued that "the female has mind enough, talent enough, to go through a complete college course, but her physical organization, as a general thing, will never admit of it." Similarly, in the 1870s Dr. Edward Clarke's celebrated book, *Sex and Education,* expressed even stronger doubts about women's ability to cope with the demands of higher education. The emergence of scholar-presidents like Alice Freeman Palmer of Wellesley and M. Carey Thomas of Bryn Mawr and the impressive percentage of degree-holders being turned out by the women's colleges during the last quarter of the century, indicated that male skeptics could be strikingly wrong.

In this atmosphere of mounting confidence in women's intellect, there were those who suggested that women could go beyond simply matching the curricula of the best Eastern men's colleges: they could invade those institutions themselves. Two embryonic women's colleges took this further step in their battle for equality: the first was the "Harvard Annex," later to be known as Radcliffe College, and the second was the "Collegiate Course" for women at Columbia University, later to be transformed into Barnard College. Harvard in 1875 allowed itself to be persuaded that the institution would suffer no harm in providing rigorous examinations to those women who wished to take them. Moreover, it later permitted its professors to repeat their lectures for the benefit of these women. These were important concessions, but for almost 20 years thereafter Harvard steadfastly declined to confer the A.B. degree upon women. The earliest genuine victory for women was won in New York City, where there had been intermittent dissatisfaction expressed at the absence of equal educational opportunities for women at Columbia University. The fruits of that victory would be the incorporation of an institution named after a noted male champion of women's education, Columbia's President Frederick A. P. Barnard.

Frederick Barnard's willingness to consider co-education at the University had not been matched by a similar receptivity on the part of his trustees, and it became apparent that some form of compromise would have to be sought. Barnard wished to insure that women would have the opportunity to meet the stringent requirements of the Columbia degree. After a brief experiment with the system of offering the same examinations to women as to men and even granting them the degree, the "Collegiate Course" was discontinued on the grounds that women, who were not permitted to attend lectures, could not be expected to pass the examinations based on them. Fortunately at this point the cry for equal opportunity at Columbia went beyond the right to hear lectures and became a demand that Columbia oversee the requirements and grant the degree to women students, whose interests would be represented in a separate sister college. In 1889 Barnard College was established and the new institution's acceptance of Columbia's academic supervision in return for the University's willingness to approve its degree marked the clearest capitulation to women up to that point by the male academic establishment.

*   *   *

After an initial period of adjustment during which its first class graduated with the precious degree in hand, Barnard in 1894 acquired its first official dean. She was Emily James Smith, a brilliant and beautiful scholar of Greek, with blond hair, sparkling eyes and a forceful personality. She had graduated from Bryn Mawr and her subsequent stay at Girton College of Cambridge University had been financed by admiring fellow students. Study abroad was followed by some years of teaching Greek at the Packer Collegiate Institute in Brooklyn and then by a year as a Fellow at the University of Chicago. Like Elizabeth Cady Stanton, Miss Smith had grown up in the invigorating atmosphere of upstate New York, she had been exposed to the thoughts of a father who was a state supreme court judge, and she had been tutored by a male neighbor who sympathized with her desire to learn. In Johnstown the Reverend Simon Hosack had taken the young Miss Cady under his scholarly wing; in Canandaigua a Mr. Lee, who taught Greek as a hobby, became the academic mentor of Emily Smith. Different as were the personalities of Elizabeth Cady and Emily Smith, the similarity of these early influences suggests their importance in giving them the confidence to lead unorthodox lives.

Miss Smith's appearance at Barnard was well-timed, for the college was facing problems new to the American educational scene. It was easy enough for Barnard to ask for Columbia's supervision; it was more difficult to insure that such supervision was not at the expense of Barnard's independence. From the first, Dean Smith recognized that the coordinate arrangement between a small women's college and a large men's university could offer a uniquely valuable experience. Women would best develop intellectually, she believed, in an environment that combined the stimulating challenges of a major educational center with the protective encouragement of an administration, and increasingly of a faculty, devoted exclusively to their needs. And so Miss Smith steered a prudent course in the negotiations that were to clarify and eventually codify Barnard's relationship with Columbia. Her diplomatic talents were undergirded by the respect in which she was held as a scholar and by her combination of delicacy and firmness.

Happily for the future of the two affiliated institutions Seth Low, President of Columbia, entertained a high regard for Miss Smith. Since he felt no condescension toward her, he unhesitatingly applied Columbia's rigorous academic standards to Barnard College. Miss Smith, for her part, studiously encouraged him in this effort. As their correspondence indicates, President Low understood the need for a "separate college course for women equally deserving of the same degree as a different course for men." Out of this working relationship between potential adversaries and, perhaps most importantly, out of Emily Smith's meticulous attention to the day-to-day details of Barnard's academic and administrative affairs, a highly successful educational arrangement emerged. Beginning with the "borrowing" of Columbia faculty, Barnard moved toward acquiring a faculty of its own. By appointing first-rate scholars who could be "borrowed" in turn by Columbia, Dean Smith ultimately inspired enough confidence to be able to negotiate an unprecedented agreement in 1900 that put a new seal on the dignity and importance of women's education. By giving Barnard's dean a place on the University Council equal to that of the deans of the other branches of the University and by allowing the College to be independent in its finances and governance while enjoying Columbia's academic approval and the prestige of its degree, a major American university conceded the intellectual equality of women. A new era in women's education had begun.

Emily Smith did not remain in office long enough to administer this new arrangement. The year previously she had married the prominent publisher, George Haven Putnam. And at the very point when she was assuring Barnard a full-fledged partnership with Columbia, she found herself in a familiar dilemma: she had become pregnant. Unwilling to admit her condition to trustees who disapproved of deans with divided responsibilities, she reluctantly surrendered the deanship. Following the birth of a son, she resumed her connection with Barnard in the new role of a trustee herself and later as member of the faculty.

During the years of the new century Mrs. Putnam broadened her activities in New York City to include civic and labor reform. But she also persisted in furthering educational experiment. Her intervention was crucial in the reorganization of the New School for Social Research when it was foundering. Partly because of her urging the New School was transformed into an institution dedicated to the education of adults. Alvin Johnson, its pioneering head, speculated that her enthusiasm for adult education might be attributed to her husband's ideas, for George Putnam believed that college-age youth would always need to be directed as well as educated. And no doubt Emily Putnam, as former dean of a woman's college, agreed that college faculties could not escape their responsibility to act *in loco parentis.* Only among adults could professors freely air their thoughts; hence only in a school devoted to adult education would there exist an atmosphere of unfettered intellectual freedom. Mrs. Putnam translated her support of the New School into concrete action, lecturing there in the 1920s and serving as Johnson's valued counsellor for many years.

The breadth of Mrs. Putnam's interests together with her busy life as the wife of a public figure suggest the strides educated women were making during the Progressive Era and into the 1920s. Few were more aware than Mrs. Putnam of the long history of women's struggle for status. In a witty and learned study entitled *The Lady,* and published a decade after her departure as dean, Mrs. Putnam considered women's roles through the ages. The lady of ancient Greece was reconciled to being the mere property of her husband; the medieval lady's secret weapon was "her power to please"; and the Frenchwoman of the salon needed a lifelong mastery of the art of *politesse* to overcome the male preference for younger women. In writing of the constraints on the British blue-stocking, Mrs. Putnam may have been speaking at first-hand and not without a trace of sarcasm. "She perceived that an individual here and there might study Greek or anything else, so long as she did not propose . . . to found a college for girls on the assumption that they were as well worth teaching as boys." Emily Putnam's grasp of the varying pressures upon women throughout history confirmed her belief that only an education fully equal to men's could invest women with honest self-regard and lead ultimately to their independence.

As a widow in the 1930s Mrs. Putnam lived abroad, braving machine-gun fire during the Spanish Revolution and finally settling in Jamaica where she died in 1944 at the age of 79. But her forceful presence in the early years of Barnard's growth and the impress of her striking personality continued to be felt among its graduates, including the youthful Virginia Gildersleeve, destined to serve as Barnard's dean for most of its first half century. Emily Putnam had helped define a style that college women would thereafter seek to emulate. Once the battle for suffrage was won in 1920, women of education and accomplishment no longer felt a need to storm the male barricades; instead, they quietly applied their intelligence and scholarship to the serious inequities that still remained in many areas of American life.

As the new century progressed and more women equipped themselves with the college training required for civic leadership, they quickly made their influence felt. In the Progressive Era they labored to cleanse cities from the corruption of political machines; they promoted public health, nursing care, and education for maternity among thousands of women living in rural backwaters and city slums; they fought to end the double standard and to promote enlightened policies of population control; and they encouraged support for schools, museums, and libraries.

The 1920s was a decade of business prosperity and diminished social consciousness. Because of this climate of political conservatism, the trailing banner of Progressivism was held aloft more often than not by educated middle-class women. In the assurance of their presence upon the American scene, in the skill they employed in their dealings with men, and in the realism of their approach to the myriad problems facing a nation whose promises were often far removed from its deeds, they constituted the type of active, educated women brought to full expression by Emily Putnam. Like her, they usually exercised power long enough to make a significant difference in the course of events.

Similar as were their backgrounds and as closely related as were their respective efforts at eliminating broad political, social, legal, and educational inequalities, Elizabeth Cady Stanton and Emily James Putnam differed to some degree in their predictions concerning women's fate. Mrs. Stanton spoke as though the removal of the final male barrier to women's fulfillment would suffice to liberate them from the shackles of the past and insure their full participation in the future. Mrs. Putnam's more skeptical analysis held that women's traditional domestic specialization had planted in them a dangerously "unsocial" tendency, an enduring inclination to concentrate their thoughts on the family instead of the larger world. This condition, of course, did not apply to all women: whether married or single, the educated women for whom Emily Putnam spoke could presumably look beyond their own immediate concerns. Even laboring women, according to Mrs. Putnam, had found not only an escape from the nursery but a kind of psychological salvation in the broadened outlook of the world of work. Yet the vast majority of women around the turn of the century had neither the education nor the working experience to widen their social horizons. They were inheritors of Catharine Beecher's philosophy of domesticity, with its twin principles of maternal sanctity and allegiance to the hearth. And paradoxically, because of the growing support given the women's movement in Elizabeth Cady Stanton's lifetime, conservative forces had come to dominate it. Nor did the new willingness to grant women the right to compete intellectually with men counteract the status quo. Still holding them back was the prevailing shallowness and insularity of most women's institutions of learning. The sense of social responsibility and cosmopolitan awareness cultivated at the more prestigious women's colleges was rarely duplicated elsewhere. Thus while Elizabeth Cady Stanton's optimism about the long future had served to inspire the advance guard among feminists, Emily Putnam's cautious view of the prospects for change corresponded more accurately with realities.

Emily Putnam's realism found an unlikely admirer over 60 years later. When early in the 1970s the American novelist Norman Mailer confronted the unbridled fury of women's liberationists who attacked his literary treatment of women, he reminded them of Mrs. Putnam's ironic formulation of a "natural law": "A girl should not be too intelligent or too good or too highly differentiated in any direction. Like a ready-made garment she should be designed to fit the average man." Those who defied that law, according to Mrs. Putnam, had to be "willing to eliminate from their lives the whole question of marriage and motherhood, for the sake of a free development irrespective of its bearing on the other sex."

But could educated feminists exist in such a selectively enlightened void? And even if they could, would they be wise to ignore the condition of the rest of womankind? Mrs. Putnam did not seriously address herself to the question of how the widespread influence of restrictive social customs as well as the limited aspirations of the average woman would affect the future of the race. In fact, only one figure at this time fearlessly faced up to the long-range implications of feminism. She was Charlotte Perkins Stetson Gilman, poet, novelist, essayist, and social thinker.

*   *   *

An impoverished descendant of New England Beechers, Mrs. Gilman was regularly subject to periods of depression and near immobilization. Dr. S. Weir Mitchell, the noted physician who once treated her, attributed her emotional disorder to the hereditary taint of "the Beecher women." Nonetheless, for one who functioned under such a lifetime disadvantage, Mrs. Gilman not only produced an impressive body of work but also achieved an international reputation. Indeed, her career suggests that the very conditions of domestic life others regarded as normal may have contributed to her own spells of abnormality. Although her child-hood was warped by a determinedly undemonstrative mother and a bibliophile father who retreated at an early stage from all family obliga-tions, she possessed the courage to make something significant of her life. What she ultimately succeeded in doing was to offer hope to women burdened by the sterility of their own lives.

A critical experience for Charlotte Perkins Gilman was her first mar-riage in 1884 at the age of 24 to a promising young painter from Provi-dence, Rhode Island, Charles Walter Stetson, who shared her own early interest in the visual arts. With every reason to expect a happy life, en-dowed with abundant good looks and a body consciously disciplined by frequent exercise, the young Mrs. Stetson inexplicably sank into a melan-choly state later described with moving candor both in her autobiography and in "The Yellow Wallpaper," a short story based on this episode. It is impossible to assess how much of her mental breakdown should be attributed to constitutional factors and how much of it was related to the feelings of enclosure she experienced at the prospect of her domestic routine and the responsibilities attending the birth of a daughter in her first year of marriage. What did become evident, however, was that absence from her home and family invariably brought relief from her symptoms and an almost instantaneous restoration of sound spirits. Her realization of the connection between her state of mind and the circum-stances of her life eventually led her to move to California and to an amicable divorce. In fact not long thereafter Charles Stetson married a close mutual friend and the three remained highly affectionate toward one another. The daughter, Katharine Stetson, cheerfully took turns liv-ing with her father and stepmother and then with her mother. An unusual arrangement for its time, it was not without its critics; but it signalled the start of the independent life that permitted Charlotte Stetson to become in effect her own person.

From the moment Charlotte Stetson embarked on her struggle to be self-supporting, she experienced the predictable disadvantages of single womanhood. Scraping together a meager livelihood by taking in boarders and reluctantly incurring debts that she always scrupulously repaid, she tried contributing occasional pieces to journals and magazines. In 1890 she was greatly encouraged by a letter from the novelist and editor, William Dean Howells, praising one of her poems and commenting favorably on her essay "Women of Today," which she had contributed to *The Woman's Journal*. She soon discovered, however, that her best efforts lay in public speaking. Her thoughts on socialism, women's rights, ethics, motherhood, and a host of related subjects seemed to crystallize most effectively when she took the speaker's platform.

Eventually a combination of people and events rescued her intellectual talents from what could easily have been obscurity: the success in England of her book of poems, *In This Our World;* her friendship with Helen Campbell, eminent home economist and author of *Women Wage-Earners,* an early study of women in industry; her acquaintance with Jane Addams, founder of the settlement house; her growing involvement with the organized women's movement in California; her discussions with the Fabians while serving as a delegate to an International Socialist and Labor Congress in London. Possibly most memorable among the multitude of personalities to whom she was exposed were the two pioneering figures of the fight for women's rights, and her comments on them suggest the strength of the spiritual affinities that they shared. "Of the many people I met during these years," Mrs. Stetson wrote, "I was particularly impressed by Elizabeth Cady Stanton. To have been with her and 'Aunt Susan,' as we called the great Susan B. Anthony, seemed to establish connection with a splendid period of real heroism." To an extent she could hardly have imagined, Charlotte Stetson was to further their work by becoming the leading theorist of the women's movement.

For some time Mrs. Stetson had been considering the relation between women's rights and human needs, and late in 1897 she set to work on a book that she tentatively entitled "The Economic Relation of the Sexes as a Factor in Social Development." Writing at a feverish pace and driven by a growing realization of the almost total ignorance of most women about the fundamental economic realities of their daily lives, she completed the first draft of the manuscript in 17 days. The book was published in 1898 under the title of *Women and Economics.*

In subsequent years this book was recognized as probably the most influential American work in the entire canon of feminist theory. What did Mrs. Stetson have in mind as she undertook the project? In her autobiography she expressed the motivating insight: "The political equality demanded by the suffragists was not enough to give real freedom. Women whose industrial position is that of a house-servant, or who do no work at all, who are fed, clothed, and given pocket-money by men, do not reach freedom and equality by the use of the ballot."

The inadequacy of the limited approaches of previous feminists was underscored by Mrs. Stetson's use of the evolutionary theories of Lester Frank Ward, a pioneer sociologist who advocated conscious control of man's environment in the interests of establishing a more cooperative society. Ward's broad perspective helped her understand that many of the solutions being advanced for the elimination of women's subordinate status overlooked the historically-induced difference between the sexes, which neither the ballot nor a college degree could eradicate. That difference, she suggested in *Women and Economics,* lay in an excessive sex-development in the female; that is, the distinctively feminine traits in women were unhealthily exaggerated. By depriving women of the ability to meet their own needs independently, men were conversely encouraging the cultivation of those personality traits that transformed women into creatures whose "power of production is checked" while their "power of consumption is inordinately increased" by the favors men bestowed on them. Furthermore, women's absence from the competitive arena intensified their concentration upon themselves and their families, thereby creating the kind of false and frenzied consumer demand that squandered the nation's economic energies.

Even in their natural role as mothers women were at a disadvantage because of their isolation and lack of training. For generations women had been told that their maternal instinct was sufficient to endow them with the wisdom to raise children properly. Perhaps drawing upon her own painful experiences, Mrs. Stetson called for professional nurses and teachers to care for young children; in any case, she convincingly demonstrated that motherhood was a highly specialized vocation. In the home she recommended the elimination of the kitchen, the establishment of communal dining halls and the rationalization of all domestic functions. She herself was an excellent cook, but she pointed out that "a good cook is not necessarily a good manager, nor a good manager an accurate and thorough cleaner, nor a good cleaner a wise purchaser." Her vision of the liberated household looked toward the division of household labor as a means of making the best use of human resources and thereby saving time and energy.

Such technical advances were not intended to detract from the importance of the home. On the contrary, Mrs. Stetson believed the home could better serve its function of uniting the family and offering respite from the world outside if the attempts of well-intentioned people to cope with their own varying inadequacies were eliminated from it. Mrs. Stetson's strictures were directed not against the home but at the inefficiencies that kept it from functioning at its ideal. Properly managed and used as a setting for the rewarding companionship that more leisure time would now allow, the home could serve as a restorative for the whole family rather than stifling its full-time female occupant.

Mrs. Stetson did not believe, however, that the well-ordered home represented the pinnacle of human achievement. She warned that the advance of human beings toward more cooperative forms of social organization entailed a recognition that the existing "economic basis of family life holds our friendly and familiar intercourse in narrow grooves." There "is a world of persons as well as of families." She submitted that "in our besotted exaggeration of the sex relation, we have crudely supposed that a wish for wider human relationship was a wish for wider sex relationship, and was therefore to be discouraged." She called for easy friendships among persons of the opposite sex, allowing those with common interests and needs to meet outside the family circle and establish a network of associations that would strengthen society as a whole. And she saw this as possible only when the economic independence of women enabled them to meet men on terms of equality in the labor force, in society, and eventually in the home.

The faith in human progress underpinning *Women and Economics* did not prevent Mrs. Stetson from taking a measured view of the prospects for social transformation. Three generations would be needed, she calculated, before her ideas began to be felt—and indeed it *has* taken that long for the broad implications of the women's movement to have any significant influence upon the thinking of the average American woman. Furthermore, Mrs. Stetson was reluctant to translate her ideas into radical communitarian experiments. Far from resembling those utopian visionaries who called into question the basic institutions of marriage and the family, she was a Fabian-style socialist who believed in the conscious but gradual accommodation of the present to the inevitable shape of the future.

Her grip on the outlines of that future became even firmer after a second marriage in 1900 to her cousin, George Houghton Gilman. His consistent support and their informed exchange of ideas were central and steadying forces in her life from 1897, when she resumed an earlier friendship with him, to his death 37 years later. Their personal correspondence testifies to the strength of Mrs. Gilman's belief in the reciprocity possible between the emotional and intellectual natures of enlightened men and women. And her faith was rewarded by the quality of their life together: Gilman was an extremely helpful husband, encouraging his wife's incessant writing and willingly tolerating the far-flung lecturing and unorthodox domestic arrangements attendant upon her busy career. Mrs. Gilman's life was thereafter punctuated by occasional lapses into her old emotional disorder, but hei continuing public activity, her single-handed virtuoso production of her own magazine, *The Forerunner,* which was published every month for seven years, and the increasing recognition accorded her ideas established her as among the movers and shakers of American feminism.

After *Women and Economics* Mrs. Gilman further documented her views on domesticity in *The Home,* published in 1903. Declaring that her criticism of existing arrangements was intended to "maintain and improve the home," she launched into an impassioned examination of every aspect of her subject, from chapters on the evolution and mythology of the home to the influence of the home on social progress. Her most magisterial book, *Human Work,* appeared a year later. Here was the crux of her argument: the differentiation between those "erroneous ideas and feelings" that had brought on the economic problems plaguing society and the "essential traits of human nature" and "essential conditions of human life" that should govern efforts to effect healthy change. Cautioning against the tyranny of inherited "concepts and habits," Mrs. Gilman called for the surrender of outdated notions of individualism and a shift to collective action to make possible the greatest "fulfillment and achievement." The essentially social nature of humanity could be expressed most fundamentally through work that was both needed and honored by one's fellow creatures. According to Mrs. Gilman, the increasing specialization brought about by industrialism confirmed her theories, for it made possible a more precise matching of individual talents and social needs. Even artistic labor would partake of this social purpose. Women, who may have regarded such labor as essentially selfish, would come to assess "self-expression" as "social expression."

Thus Mrs. Gilman expanded the ideological source from which many of her later writings and speeches were to issue. She steadily moved toward a philosophy that distinctly attributed to women qualities of co-operation and dedication to life; these contrasted with the competitive and destructive nature she assigned to men. Not surprisingly she was critical of Sigmund Freud. Her fear that his ideas would encourage further masculine dominance was a logical outcome of her belief in the dangerous consequences of stressing sexuality. But if the reproductive drive were adequately contained, she maintained, it could take its proper place within the context of a rationally directed society. With greater economic independence and with diminished maternal and domestic responsibilities, women would ultimately be able to exert a positive influence upon the course of evolution.

Mrs. Gilman's defiant feminism characterized her to the end. Rather than accept the slow deterioration of breast cancer, she took her life with chloroform in 1935. Her husband had died the previous year, and she had spent her remaining months with her daughter in California. The courage of her final gesture was in keeping with the independence she displayed throughout a tumultuous but incessantly re-examined lifetime.

*   *   *

It would be difficult to imagine personalities more divergent than Elizabeth Cady Stanton, Emily James Putnam, and Charlotte Perkins Gilman. Yet the qualities each possessed made possible contributions essential to the progress of women. Mrs. Stanton's inexhaustible energy and contagious confidence provided the initial impetus for the women's movement; Mrs. Putnam's scholarly attributes and uncompromising intelligence demonstrated what women could accomplish if afforded the opportunity; and Mrs. Gilman's adventurous mind and self-reliant style of life suggested frontiers of feminism yet to be explored.

Reaching toward an unclear future, they all had the urgent sense of reality to work for change in the present. And they also had the keenness of imagination to recognize that the male barrier to women's fulfillment would come to be as formidable an obstacle for men as for women. So long as dominance and submission were built into the roles of the sexes, the promises of American democracy could never be fully realized.

8

Variations on the Progressive Theme

JANE ADDAMS
ROBERT M. LA FOLLETTE
THEODORE ROOSEVELT

by Daniel Levine
Bowdoin College

The very act of giving a designation, "The Progressive Movement," constitutes an historical interpretation, for as the term implies, something very fundamental was happening in the United States from a few years before the turn of the century until about World War I. And whatever was happening was quite different from what transpired in the decades that both immediately preceded and followed.

During these years Americans were aware, clearly or dimly as the case may be that their nation was undergoing a rapid transformation: economic institutions were changing, population was expanding, and cities growing. The old certainties of the 19th century, moreover, no longer seemed so certain, and as a consequence there was a quest for firmer foundations for what had suddenly become an unstable world. Some Progressives would strengthen what was familiar; others would alter the traditional to accommodate the new; and still others would look for new certainties. Thus although the fundamental anxiety may have been the same, the Progressive years saw a variety of approaches to social tensions. People coming from different directions and heading toward not necessarily similar goals seemed to be traveling the same road. To cite both the title and the thesis of a study by Professor Robert Wiebe, they were engaged in a common "Search for Order."

The Progressive ferment ceased almost as suddenly as it began in the shattering experiences of World War I. In the 1920s there were a few feeble flickers of the progressive spirit, but a Progressive movement as such had literally vanished from the American scene. During those exhilarating pre-war years, however, those who thought of themselves as Progressives felt that they had stood at Armageddon and were battling for the Lord.

There were millions of Progressives, and it is a risky business to designate any one of them as "typical." Those presented here illustrate but three aspects, more or less taken at random, from among many that might be emphasized.

Jane Addams speaks of the human agony, as well as the opportunities, which could accompany urbanization. Robert M. La Follette presents an essentially rural version of the same language. Rather than confront social and economic problems with humanitarian and voluntary programs, he used political power against entrenched corporate power. While Theodore Roosevelt seemed more to gather together forces already in motion than to create new ones, yet only behind a dynamic leader like him could progressive pressures find national expression. These three then give no more than a partial glimpse into American attempts before World War I to come to terms with forces only dimly understood.

*   *   *

Jane Addams created the best known settlement house in the United States and became a symbol of charity and goodness throughout the world. Yet her importance does not lie in this institution, for there were other settlement houses that did about the same things as Hull House. Nor does it lie in her political activities, where she was generally ineffective. Nor was she important as a thinker, since most of her ideas were derivative. Jane Addams was notable because hers was the most persuasive voice in the United States asking the nation to confront its new industrial self, to give up the ideology of a rural age, and to develop institutions relevant to an urban society. Through a combination of genteel background and manner, an alertness to currents of thought around her, a willingness to learn from experience, and an almost mystical ability to communicate her sincerity, she became nationally known and respected. In the words of one magazine, she was "rousing the new conscience" to the social costs of industrialization.

Yet many of those who lionized Jane Addams failed to understand her message fully; if they had, they might well have opposed or scorned her. Through what seemed to be a series of mild humanitarian reforms, she was actually challenging basic American attitudes. Not listening to the fundamental points in her argument, people honored her for the mild reforms.

A more unlikely vessel for the voice of radicalism could scarcely be imagined. Born in 1860, she was a slightly frail, wide-eyed young girl, something of an invalid and family pet. Culture she received from her stepmother, money and social position from her father, a stern righteous businessman and a Republican leader of northern Illinois. Jenny worshipped him as the embodiment of virtue, wisdom, and manhood.

At her father's bidding, Jane attended Rockford (Illinois) Female Seminary, where he was a trustee, rather than the more prestigious Smith College, as she herself wished. She learned more of the sterner virtues at Rockford, an expatriate New England institution, where the spirit of 17th-century Puritanism struggled to hold fast in the 19th-century Midwest. Resisting repeated urgings from the Seminary, Jane Addams refused to become a missionary, or even to join any Christian denomination (she became a Presbyterian in 1885). She decided instead to take up medical studies in Philadelphia.

The shock of her father's sudden death from acute appendicitis, just before she was to go to Philadelphia, destroyed Jane Addams' resolution and undermined her health. After only one semester of medical school, she returned to Cedarville, Illinois, an invalid with a disabling and apparently psychosomatic back ailment.

The next eight years were a period of uncertainty and doubt for Jane Addams. While rejecting the traditional woman's role, she had been unable to begin a demanding medical career. In a sense, she was undergoing the pains of the first generation of liberated women. She had been unshackled from old stereotypes, and her inheritance had freed her from having to earn a living, but neither her own background nor society provided clear alternatives. On a trip to Europe in 1888, she began discussing a vague idea with her friend, Ellen Gates Starr. They had heard of college men in London settling in poor districts, and wasn't there something called Toynbee Hall? Perhaps college-educated young ladies might "settle" in a poor district of Chicago and have their bookish education modified by contact with "simple people" who in turn might derive great benefits from the young ladies' academic training. "The scheme" admittedly was vague, but it was better than endless indecision.

They returned to Chicago and with the help of well-placed relatives moved into the Hull mansion in a district where immigrants of a dozen nationalities crowded into old tenements. Ellen Starr and Jane Addams insisted that they were not setting up an institution, only their own home; but in an astonishingly short time they found themselves running a formidable institution indeed, with a nursery school, a day care center for infants, an art gallery, dormitories, boys clubs, girls clubs, literary discussion groups, courses in art, English language, telegraphy, and a veritable social club of intellectuals and reformers.

Such activities inevitably soon led Jane Addams to involvement in Chicago politics. To help keep the streets around Hull House minimally clean, she became a conscientious garbage inspector for the ward. She wanted clean politics as well as clean streets, and in 1894, 1896, and 1898 challenged the power of ward boss, Johnny Powers, a traditional politician who offered patronage and kindness in return for votes. She could only offer civic virtue and, consequently, her forces were beaten handily. She was also less than successful as a member of the Chicago Board of Education from 1905 to 1908. Although having clear ideas on education which were applied successfully at Hull House, she was politically maladroit, made all factions angry, and played what she herself described as an "inglorious role." She found, in fact, that politics was not her forte and that she was far more effective as a publicist and persuader, someone who roused the social conscience.

And the social conscience needed to be awakened. When Hull House first opened its doors, Benjamin Harrison was in the White House, the Horatio Alger myth was widely accepted, and government took only minimal responsibility for the needy. When Jane Addams died in May 1935, Franklin Roosevelt had completed two years as President (though Jane Addams had twice voted for her old progressive associate, Herbert Hoover), Congress had completed the highly dramatic emergency legislation of the New Deal's first 100 days, and the Wagner Labor Relations Act and the Social Security Act were well on their way to enactment. The ideology of the capitalist welfare state, though not universally accepted, was well ahead of its competitors.

Roosevelt's New Deal required changes in American political and economic institutions, but most of all, it required a new ideological orientation. Jane Addams became an effective vendor in hundreds of articles and 11 books for these new points of view. In addition she publicized these views on the lecture platform. She was very much in demand as a lecturer after 1900 and enjoyed being on the circuit. By then, all traces of the invalid had disappeared. Her physical presence reflected an emotional sense of security. She was a solid, mature woman, not yet too heavy as she would become, and equally persuasive whether talking to individuals, congressional committees, or lecture audiences.

In promoting her ideas, Jane Addams, in effect, also promot~d herself. The public was eager to hear this wealthy, educated lady who had settled among the poor; this invalid who became the champion of the downtrodden and their lobbyist in City Hall, the State House, and the national capital.

The starting point for Jane Addams' proposals was her view of children. She was convinced that children were uncontaminated by civilization and that their natural instincts were benign and constructive. Society suppressed these instincts at great cost to the child and to society itself. Of all the forces depriving society of "the divine fire of youth" poverty was the strongest, forcing children, for example to prematurely arduous work and destroying their chances later on in life.

In America more than in any European nation, poverty was taken as a sure sign of irresponsibility. Consequently, government had no ethical imperative to assume responsibility for those who took none for themselves. Beginning in the 1890s, Jane Addams was part of an army of social critics who insisted that poverty was due not to character defects in the poor but to a misconstructed society. If an American society of unlimited opportunity had ever existed, it clearly had vanished by the depression of 1893. Society, social critics insisted, did have a responsibility toward its least fortunate members, both by protecting them from exploitation and by giving them the power to protect themselves.

Jane Addams went further than most reformers; she was in fact a radical, though not a Marxist. Society, she maintained, had by no means fulfilled its responsibilities when it provided a crutch to a young man crippled in an industrial accident, or when it required fences around dangerous machinery, or even when it decreed that youths stay in school and out of factories altogether. Acting through government, society had the obligation to ensure that all of its members could meet their physical needs, and also the obligation to ensure that they could live productive and self-fulfilling lives. Every person, she insisted, must be allowed to "raise life to the highest."

Obviously this kind of social responsibility could not exist in a nation dominated by individual striving and conflict. Therefore while Jane Addams might vigorously support labor unions, and even refer to herself as a "sort of a socialist," her goal was not the triumph of the proletariat in a class war. She wanted a society in which tradition and institutions would minimize conflict. As early as 1895 she argued for a "social ethic" to replace the individual ethic. "To attain individual morality in an age demanding social morality," she said, "is utterly to fail to apprehend the situation." Unfortunately, the kind of society she envisioned, though it might have made sense for New Zealand or Scandinavia, was completely out of touch with the American reality.

Until World War I, Jane Addams was convinced that the new social ethic would find expression through government. She had a mystical and not very clearly thought out conception of the State as representing the will of all. While aware that special interest groups might wield excessive influence, she could not conceive of government itself as an interest group or of its misleading the people. For her, government was society manifest.

Yet while Jane Addams thus asked Americans to surrender their entire value system, she continued to address herself to more immediate concerns: discussion groups for working women, a milk fund for children of striking workers, and woman suffrage. These were all respectable and generally acceptable undertakings, and her work for them, made her, like Albert Schweitzer a generation later, a national, even international symbol for humanitarian reform. Persuaded that the way to a peaceable kingdom lay through social uplift, she sought to convince the nation of the necessity for reform, but not for Isaiah's heaven.

The coming of the new ethic might well be hastened, Jane Addams was sure, by the presence of women in government. Women, after all, were inherently kinder and less competitive than men. Besides, she argued, society had taken on many of what had traditionally been women's duties, such as insuring clean food. By 1911 she was deeply involved in the suffrage cause, both on the lecture platform and before national and state legislative committees. This led her back to politics and into Theodore Roosevelt's Progressive Party in 1912. She was a member of the resolutions committee, which forced the wavering Roosevelt to endorse woman suffrage as part of his efforts to win the "advanced progressives" to his standard.

Jane Addams worked hard for the Party, but neither the old Rough Rider's magnetism nor even a number of "Jane Addams Choruses" could overcome the results of a split party. Woodrow Wilson's victory, she thought, was no calamity. Though anti-woman suffrage, he seemed progressive in other ways; he became more so as his second election approached. But Jane Addams could not follow Woodrow Wilson into World War I. An anti-imperialist and pacifist, she argued that social reform could become, as William James put it, a moral equivalent to war. She had always spoken out for a society without conflict. As a natural consequence of her previous efforts, Jane Addams felt she could do nothing less than oppose war in all its forms. But unlike her domestic proposals, her pacifism had not been tested by any contact with daily reality. She came to pacifism, as it were, directly from Rockford Female Seminary.

As the nation that had seen Jane Addams merely as a symbol for goodness and human decency increasingly decided that the road to peace lay through defeat of the Central Powers, it could not understand how she could refuse to follow in this crusade for the final extirpation of evil from the world. Perhaps those who had called her naive or radical had been right after all! And she found herself part of an ever-dwindling bloc of pacifists. As one friend after another drifted away, her anguish was intense. She could tolerate being a leader of those who wanted change— she had been doing it for years—but she could not go against the stream as a rebel and outcast. Eventually she found her compromise by joining Herbert Hoover's food conservation effort. She could thus be both humanitarian and patriotic.

Jane Addams could not explain to herself how the horror of war had come to pass. Nationalism, which had seemed so constructive when Bismarck had created social insurance, had turned into a monster. She refused to consider that perhaps cruelty and destructiveness, like kindness and thirst for learning, were inherent human instincts.

Jane Addams' problems did not end with the coming of peace. Through the first half of the '20s, the "post war psychology," as she called it, pursued her, and she was frequently accused of Bolshevism or treason. By 1925 the "patriotic" mania had begun to subside, and by the time Jane Addams won the Nobel Peace Prize in 1931 (sharing it, ironically, with Nicholas Murray Butler, President of Columbia University who had vigorously supported America's war-time policies), she again was popular. Hers, however, was the popularity of an old and toothless lioness. Even her friends knew that Jane Addams, now in declining health, was from another era. A new generation of reformers, many of them former Hull House residents, would take up the struggle.

Jane Addams was a failure in her own terms. American self-seeking, the drive for success, the acquisitive society—all have, if anything, been strengthened by the prosperity of the periods following both World Wars. If a few of the younger generation reject these values, they are only a small eddy against the mainstream. But in working for a changed value system, Jane Addams gave strength to those partial reforms that made more humane even a society based on individual accumulation. She was realist enough to know that no one wins battles completely, and perhaps her compromising nature would have asked her to be satisfied with the partial victories she had helped to win.

*   *   *

Robert M. La Follette was a serious contender for the presidency in 1912. Born in a log cabin in 1855, he thereby fulfilled a major requirement for chief executives. He achieved power and influence through stubborn devotion to a few simple ideas about politics and society and through his capacity to play the political game of compromise when need be. La Follette pictured himself as the supreme anti-politician, as the people's champion against political bosses. Yet he created a political machine that was strong enough to control his home state of Wisconsin, not only for 25 years while he was alive, but for nearly as long after his death. He thought of himself as a rebel against the system, and in some ways he was. He fought "the interests" of the party regulars and his own party's President. But it was not until 1916 when he stood on principle against American armed involvement in World War I that he placed himself outside the mainstream of public opinion. It was a fateful decision politically, for he was never able to recover completely from it.

The public face La Follette chose to emphasize, that of "fighting Bob," was by no means a mask. He was indeed independent, stubborn, self-confident and often belligerent. But like any good politician he kept his ear to the ground. He knew where the possibilities were to be found within Wisconsin Republican politics. He cultivated, and in turn was supported by, the "comers" in the Party. He appreciated the value of political organization, and was clever enough to pick enemies who, while strong, did not have widespread public support—for example, Boss E. W. Keyes of the Madison Republicans and the railroad companies.

La Follette also realized that his constituents saw Wisconsin and the "west" of which it was a part as disproportionately excluded from national political and economic power. He knew that the section was consciously beginning to assert itself. Frederick Jackson Turner's paper on the significance of the frontier reflected that consciousness, and the very fact that 1893 saw a world's fair in what, only a few decades before had been a frontier village, was evidence of the same western thrust. La Follette could capitalize on this impulse and consequently capture support from many Populists or "Popocrats" even though he was a Republican. In picturing himself as a brave fighter against the interests, against eastern politicians and eastern trusts, he was also mirroring his constituents' sentiments. And that, after all, is a politician's job.

To many persons then and since, La Follette seemed to have had too simplistic a devotion to an economic world of small businesses competing vigorously with each other. The direction of history, these critics argue, was toward large corporations, large unions and large government. Yet this in turn is too unsophisticated an interpretation of La Follette. Having ourselves seen the difficulties and ambiguities of existing anti-trust regulations, it could well be that La Follette's more stringent regulations might have been far more effective in curbing the abuses of corporate power.

By 1917 La Follette was an outcast, except in his own state. Damned by Woodrow Wilson as one of that "little band of willful men" who resisted preparedness, damned by Theodore Roosevelt as a coward and traitor, he became an anti-interventionist or isolationist. As such, he was criticized by patriotic America in wartime. Later, in the 1920s, when isolationism became the majority sentiment, La Follette's views on United States involvement in Europe were eminently respectable. But by then he was no longer alive.

Bob La Follette was a country boy from the small town of Primrose, Wisconsin. He moved away from home at age 14 and took his first job as a barber in Argyl, a slightly larger nearby community. Working his way through the fledgling University of Wisconsin, he also helped support his mother and sister by buying the student newspaper and turning it into a profitable enterprise. He made a reputation for himself not as a student, but as an orator, winning contest after contest. In fact, as La

Follette recalled, he almost became an actor. Instead he "read" law, and in those casual days of legal preparation passed the bar after only seven months of study. Plunging immediately into politics, he demonstrated no driving desire to reform the State or the nation; nor did he have any political convictions. It was a career available to a young lawyer, and provided La Follette an opportunity to use his oratorical skills—almost all he had to offer when he ran for county attorney of Dane County. Although later picturing that contest as the beginning of his insurgency, he was in fact praised by the party newspapers and ran with their blessings.

After four years as county attorney, during which La Follette turned out to be the Republicans' best vote-getter, he began to eye the Congressional seat in his district. Again his own re-telling described himself as an insurgent running against the machine. Actually, La Follette was the spokesman for a younger group of men about to take over from an aging and declining political boss. Entering the State Republican nominating convention more as a compromise candidate than as a rebel, he won the nomination and ran in behalf of a reasonably united party.

La Follette was fortunate in having the kind of dramatic good looks that made him recognizable even to voters back in the crowd: strong clear features and high straight forehead, set off by a shock of long, wavy hair, which was white through much of his career. A political cartoonist's dream, he could have been mistaken for the male lead in a Broadway musical. La Follette's energy seemed to animate his speeches, virtually lifting up his audiences and carrying them along. He won the Congressional seat in 1884 and again in the 1886 and 1888 elections, serving as a conscientious and more or less liberal, but not insurgent, Republican congressman. In 1890 he was swept out of office in a Democratic landslide.

The next decade was La Follette's time of testing, his years in the political wilderness. During this period he found the direction that would give purpose to his life. His career to 1890 had been one long upswing, where success followed success in regular and ordered steps. Increasingly popular and apparently destined for greater successes, he was unceremoniously forced out of public life and back to the starting point of ten years earlier. It was during the next decade, in the course of three losing elections, that he found his issue, and it defined his position in the party. That issue would be the railroads, as it was for so many western and southern politicians, whether Democrat, Populist, or Republican. Railroads not only had the power of life and death over farmers, whose markets were hundreds of miles off, but they also controlled the political life of many states, being so intertwined with other interests (timber in the case of Wisconsin) that there seemed to be a controlling net of "interests" and politicians in which the rest of the population was caught.

La Follette concentrated his attack on the ridiculously low taxes railroads paid on their property—a simple and straightforward issue close to the hearts of everyone but particularly to those who owned real estate. In attacking the net of corporate and political interests that controlled Wisconsin, La Follette found himself an insurgent for the first time. Yet his insurgency was well within the political mainstream. Unlike the Populists, he did not advocate nationalization of the railroads. He and a group of friends fought the railroad and lumber interests in 1894, 1896, and 1898, only to lose in every election. Each loss pushed La Follette further toward reform, which was becoming politically fashionable. The last two of the three losing campaigns were for the governorship, and they made the insurgents well known throughout Wisconsin. By 1900 the GOP regulars were an aging bloc of politicians, and the rebels were becoming shrewder. La Follette moderated his rhetoric, smoothed over old antagonisms without creating new ones, and won the 1900 gubernatorial election in what was known as the Harmony Campaign.

La Follette had by no means forgotten the issue of railroad taxation. Nor had the memory of how an entrenched political organization had kept his group out of power faded away. When he introduced railroad legislation and a direct primary bill, that fragile political harmony of the campaign evaporated and La Follette realized that getting himself elected did not guarantee sympathetic state senators. However, he was no amateur "clean-government" reformer who would ride to victory on a wave of rhetoric and then disappear almost overnight. Thoroughly professional, La Follette knew how to build a political following. After four years of hard organizing work and open fights with the party's stalwarts, La Follette created his own state Republican machine that was virtually unchallengeable until the days of Senator Joseph McCarthy in the 1950s. He did not, of course, fight the battle alone. The complex of organizations, politicians, and publicists known as the Progressive movement, of which he was both a leader and a product, lent national backing to his proposals. Yet he had to persevere four years before railroad taxation and direct primary laws passed the legislature. By this time he also was seeking enactment of additional bills on banking, conservation, and lobbying.

By 1906, when La Follette went to the United States Senate, he was no longer a young man. His experiences in Wisconsin over 15 years of frustration, defeat, partial victory, and finally complete triumph shaped both him and his politics. He had had his immense self-confidence confirmed: the issues to which he was committed for a decade and a half had proved to be the right ones. By not yielding, by stubbornly clambering to his feet whenever knocked down, he had eventually won. La Follette's rather simple perception of the good guys versus the bad guys, us versus them, had led to many defeats, but also to ultimate victory. With enormous, indeed unchallenged, popularity at home, he came to Washington at the height of reform, in a party with a reform-minded, though essentially cautious political leader, Theodore Roosevelt, who was then in the White House. Indeed, so successful and so secure was La Follette at home, so battle-scarred and politically experienced, that, even though new in national politics, he could afford to appear stubborn to the point of mulishness, and in a sense, to seem even unpolitical. Having so much to offer politically, why ought he follow the President, whether Democrat or Republican?

Senator Robert La Follette again started from a minority position. By standing firm, holding to his ideals, often rejecting the half-a-loaf argument, he became the leader of a band of Republican rebels who eventually held the balance of power in the Senate. He became, within a few years, the undisputed spokesman for progressive Republicans in Congress and very nearly (with the exception of Theodore Roosevelt) their leading spokesman in the nation.

As a Senator who had ridden to power on two issues, railroad control and direct primary, it would be easy to dismiss La Follette as a midwestern farm senator, the GOP version of a Populist, a man whose horizons were limited to what he could see from Primrose, Wisconsin. His rhetoric may have been overly simple, but he knew that the age of the yeoman was gone for good. Although farmers were important, the problems of the factory and the city were no less public responsibilities. His wife, Belle Case La Follette, was an important influence in keeping him aware of urban issues. A co-worker in his political life and in the editorial offices of *La Follette's Magazine,* where she often wrote on women's affairs (and not only those of farm women), she was in close touch with Jane Addams, who informed her of the problems of the economically distressed family and of the workers injured in industrial accidents. La Follette, or his lieutenants, introduced a minimum-wage law for Wisconsin, passed a workman's compensation act, abrogated the doctrine of contributory negligence, and created an industrial commission to supervise and enforce the nation's most comprehensive program covering child labor, hours of work, and industrial safety. The only major piece of federal legislation to bear La Follette's name was probably the most unparochial legislation conceivable. The La Follette Seaman's Act concerned Americans from every part of the country and their conditions of employment throughout the world.

Far from endorsing a pre-industrial rural freehold society, Bob La Follette by 1909 was willing to go very far toward what would now be called a welfare state. He insisted that both rural and urban industrial poverty was not due to inability but to exploitation, and he hoped for a new day when "society would be formed in which common responsibility for the general welfare would be recognized." He approved the proposal of the English Fabian Socialist, Sidney Webb, for a "National Minimum," a standard of living set by the government, below which no one would be allowed to sink. Likewise, he applauded David Lloyd-George's budget of 1909, which was widely regarded by its enemies as the entering wedge for socialism in England. La Follette consistently supported the formation of unions and their exercise of economic power, and he favored a graduated federal income tax which would inquire into areas hitherto considered private.

Yet Bob La Follette cannot with justice be called a radical. Along with other advanced Progressives, he challenged the absolute dominance of the business ethic, and he was willing, at least rhetorically, to go further toward a welfare state than some. But because he gloried in the role of martyr and underdog, his rhetoric was often more radical than his intent. He was not radical in the socialist meaning of that term, as for example, Eugene V. Debs, or in the Quaker-ethical sense, like Jane Addams. His actual political proposals were an attempt to maintain democracy in an industrial age, to humanize corporate capitalism and to subject it to some degree of public regulation. But significantly in La Follette's scheme of things, private ownership, the corporation, and free-market competition would remain. In 1911, for instance, he introduced an anti-trust bill that would give to the Interstate Commerce Commission powers denied to it by Supreme Court decisions. It provided that any firm controlling 40% of the market in a commodity would be considered *prima facie* in violation of the Sherman Act. The bill was politically impossible that year —it died in committee—but La Follette knew that the politically impossible one year may be feasible a few years hence. The regulation was more stringent than Theodore Roosevelt wanted, and it might have been as difficult to administer as existing legislation; but radical it was not.

By 1912, both the progressive and conservative wings of the Republican party saw the Senator from Wisconsin as a serious presidential possibility. La Follette expected firm opposition from President Taft's conservative supporters, but thought he had a good chance at the nomination, provided Roosevelt kept his word and stayed out of the race. When the old Rough Rider announced that "his hat was in the ring," La Follette was bitter and felt betrayed; his own supporters melted away, only to reappear around the former President. He ended up by opposing Roosevelt whom he had once admired, as well as many former comrades, and quietly endorsed the Democrat, Woodrow Wilson. Over the next four years, in fact, La Follette worked more comfortably with Wilson than he had with the hero of San Juan Hill.

This comfortable cooperation could not survive the debate over American entry into World War I. Without any serious attempt to analyze what America's position in the world ought to be, or whether changing power relationships in other parts of the world imposed new strains on

American traditions, La Follette was sure (as was Secretary of State William Jennings Bryan) that Wilson's version of neutral rights was too legalistic. He was convinced, quite correctly as it turned out, that rather than continuing progressivism on a larger scale, the war would write finis to those reformist tendencies that were just beginning to bear fruit. He opposed preparedness, conscription, arming merchant ships, and along with only five other Senators, he voted against the Declaration of War in 1917. On each issue he lost, and on each issue he stood with a shrinking and increasingly isolated group. The President and the Senate were both against him; so, too, was the country. La Follette, who had seemed to be riding the crest of a popular wave a few years before, now stood nearly alone. He had been betrayed by old friends in 1912 and deserted by new ones in 1917. With all his old fervor he insisted that he was right, but few listened. "Fighting Bob," 62 years old, was alone in the ring. The rest of his life (he died only seven years later, in 1925) was an attempt to prove that he had been right both in 1917 and in 1912.

In a sense La Follette's run for the presidency in 1924 on his own third party ticket was testimony to the futility of that attempt. He won the electoral votes of only his own state. But across the whole nation his total was 4.8 million, nearly ⅛ of the votes cast and a quite remarkable showing for a new third party. Beneath the easy victories of Warren Harding, Calvin Coolidge, and Herbert Hoover, the kind of political liberalism he represented was regathering strength, and the La Follette political forces were to be a part of what came to be Franklin Roosevelt's coalition.

Robert M. La Follette was neither reactionary nor radical. He was abrasive and arrogant, but he wanted nothing more than step by step reform (though it must be a *whole* step, he insisted) within the Progressive–New Deal tradition. He was one of those who helped define what that tradition was, and is.

*   *   *

For many people, the Progressive Movement is symbolized by the dynamic, larger-than-life figure of Theodore Roosevelt. He seems to pull together the various movements in the often cacophonous clamor for reform and give them direction. And yet a man of more baffling contradictions would be hard to find. Was he truly the reformer who dragged a reluctant capitalist elite into grudging acceptance of public regulation, or was he the pseudo-reformer, who mouthed reform slogans only to contain reform and keep it from threatening those who already held power in the nation? That larger ambiguity is paralleled by many smaller ones. Was he, for example, the philistine who scornfully dismissed modern art, or the well-read patron of poet Edwin Arlington Robinson? Was he a social analyst who shared the ideas of critics like Walter Lippmann and Herbert Croly, or was he the supreme co-optor, who sucked intellectuals into his orbit only to exploit them? Was he a serious naturalist, or a dilettante? Was he a racist and colonialist, or the first American President to recognize the full humanity of the black man? Was he all bluff and bluster, or someone to be taken with the utmost seriousness? Roosevelt was all of these things and more. Like Winston Churchill a generation later, he was one of the truly remarkable men of his age.

Roosevelt's impact on what was in many ways "The Age of Roosevelt" was closely tied to his personality. He possessed enormous self-confidence, even arrogance. Once, when asked how he knew right had been done in a particular instance, his quite genuine response was, "because I did it." He had no hesitation in dealing with new problems or accepting new offices, confident always that he would quickly master the issues and be master of the forces pressing upon him. By example he convinced his countrymen that they could control rather than be controlled by the forces of history.

The mature Theodore Roosevelt presented a sharp contrast to his early years as the sickly child of a wealthy Dutch patroon family of New York. Until the age of 12, in 1870, he seemed destined for the life of an affluent semi-invalid, but at that point he determined to be frail no longer. "I will make my body," the lad asserted, and he did so. He was never again seriously ill until the age of 56. Then, an ex-President, he nearly died of malaria contracted on an expedition to the Brazilian jungle.

At the center of Roosevelt's drive and achievement, it is sometimes forgotten, was his superb intelligence. While still a boy he became an excellent field naturalist. As an undergraduate at Harvard, where he received only moderately good grades, he wrote *The Naval War of 1812*, which was well received on both sides of the Atlantic. Years later, simply in the course of conversation, he compared medieval to modern French rhyming patterns. This intellectual breadth, which seemed to include everything from Scandanavian sagas to fauna in the Amazon basin, was peripheral to his central concern: the art of politics.

This primary interest was first expressed when he ran in 1881 for a seat in the New York State Assembly. Outside of a general desire to be, as he said, "one of the governing classes," Roosevelt probably had very little in the way of a program when he first went to Albany. With surprising speed, he took a strong position in favor of honesty in government and against the influence of what he would later call "malefactors of great wealth." But he had nothing against wealth or even big business, and he never did believe that either was in itself malevolent. When wealth began to corrupt the political process, however, Roosevelt went on the war path.

It was in Albany during his second term, to which he was elected by a spectacular margin, that the young legislator began dimly to see some of the human problems which large industry created in industrializing America. As a member of a committee investigating cigar manufacture, he went with Samuel Gompers, head of the American Federation of Labor, on a tour of crowded filthy tenements where cigars were made. Having seen conditions at first hand, he became the leading spokesman for a law prohibiting such work in tenement houses. But the bill, enacted after great difficulty, was declared unconstitutional by the Supreme Court.

Yet Roosevelt did not conclude that the power that corrupted politics or exploited labor must be destroyed. Large organizations, he believed, were an inevitable and beneficent part of modern life. As the policeman must control evil impulses in individuals, so government must act as a policeman to control overweening economic power. This human sympathy with the exploited, and opposition to misused power (but not to power itself) became his central approach to political economy.

Another element entered into the formation of the complete Theodore Roosevelt when, on February 14, 1884, his young wife died in childbirth. Distraught, the young widower gave up politics and plunged into a different world, partly to forget the one he had left, partly to prove himself yet again. He became a rancher in the Dakota Territory, an experiment that was a financial disaster but a therapeutic miracle. Arriving in Dakota as an Eastern dude whose only virtue seemed to be the size of the check he could write, he ended up two years later an experienced cowhand, rancher and head of the stockbreeders association. TR became convinced that only "the strenuous life" made a man, or a nation, healthy, both physically and mentally.

Putting his ideas into practice, Roosevelt returned East, ground out five books, served as a United States Civil Service Commissioner, Police Commissioner for New York City and, in 1897, became Assistant Secretary of the Navy under William McKinley. In that office Roosevelt pleaded for war with Spain, some say even intrigued for it. And when war came, he quickly abandoned his desk job to seek personal glory on the field of battle.

In a sense, Roosevelt's life as a soldier was a continuation of the strenuous life in the Dakotas. The regiment he organized, the Rough Riders, included many friends from his ranching days, as well as eastern college football players. On the field he seemed to hunger for danger and actually exulted in seeing Spanish soldiers die. This assertive personal role in Cuba was for him simply an expression of his belief that the United States must play an assertive role in world politics. Along with honesty in government and limitations on human exploitation, this conviction would become the third element in all his later policies.

Roosevelt returned from Cuba a popular hero and was easily elected Governor of New York. There he continued along the lines already marked out as Assemblyman. While frightening some elements in the Republican party, he did not get too far ahead of the conservatives. For example, he vigorously condemned labor violence and he held fast to the gold standard and high tariff. Thus, he was an acceptable and electable candidate for the vice presidency under William McKinley in 1900. When the President was assassinated after serving only six months of his term, Theodore Roosevelt became the youngest head of state in the nation's history. He was then 43.

Roosevelt shaped the presidency to his own image of leadership and established therewith a new 20th-century chief executive, unenvisioned by even the strongest Presidents of the past. He acted as his own Prime Minister, shaping legislation through bargaining with various interest groups and then maneuvering measures through Congress. He was the party leader, taking the GOP away from the control of McKinley's lieutenants and making it a Roosevelt party. He shaped public opinion by formulating issues and answers. The office was, as he said, a "Bully pulpit" and he used it as such. In part, the Roosevelt presidency was simply an extension of his own desire for power, but it was also, as recognized, a new creation. The economic system, he realized, was powerful and national. Governmental institutions would fall under the power of corporate wealth unless government itself could operate independently of economic interests. Consequently, the federal government, vigorously led by the executive, would have to act where the states did not. Temporarily the executive was Theodore Roosevelt, but he knew he would become the measure of the office thereafter, and he meant all future Presidents to be strong leaders.

If in the simplest form one defines a leader as a man who has followers, Roosevelt was a glorious leader, a celebrity *par excellence*. Captain of the ship of state, he was tour guide, social director, and ship's chaplain as well. Men followed him because of his immense charm and self-confidence, but mostly because he took them where they were already going. He showed the citizenry more clearly than they themselves had known exactly what they wanted.

Theodore Roosevelt's pleasure was power, and his passion was order, yet both pleasure and passion were tempered. He loved public office and the power it brought. His whole adult life was spent exercising or seeking office. From private conferences with men who exercised private power, to speaking before public meetings crowded with ordinary voters, Roosevelt was enamored of politics—but always democratic politics. He was sure of his own judgment, his own ability, almost his own right to lead. A sensible and informed electorate would, he was sure, agree. If they did not, as they did not after 1908, they would be making a mistake, yet one he accepted with only the normal amount of bitterness—with never a thought of scorning the democratic process.

Likewise his passion for order. Men of breeding, character, and of Anglo-Saxon heritage, he believed, were natural leaders and always would be. The top would continue to be on top, unless the upper class destroyed itself. The upper strata must, however, remain in power not by resisting all change, but by recognizing emergent forces. They must avoid creating permanent groups outside the system, groups that might gather enough strength to challenge it. Labor unions, for example, could not be repressed but must be accommodated. Not only were many of their demands just, but ignoring these claims might lead them to challenge the social order itself. In short, order could only be maintained by the true broker state, not by repressing some groups in the service of others, but by responding to new interest groups in the service of a larger stability. And he expected the interest groups to fit into that scenario as well. Pressing for their own ends was legitimate. But if they threatened social order, if they declared, "the public be damned," they must be opposed.

President Roosevelt's first term in office was a cautious probing period, during which he captured the Republican party and took care not to offend, or not very much anyway, the forces of large corporate power. At the same time, he established good credentials with the reform wing of the party, by prosecuting the Northern Securities Company, a trust designed to insure cooperation rather than competition between the railroad interests of J. P. Morgan and E. H. Harriman in the Northwest. Reformers were further cheered when Roosevelt intervened in the 1902 coal miners' strike. He recognized, *de facto*, the miners' union and forced a settlement generally favorable to it. Although in both cases TR asserted the primacy of governmental power, he did not in fact use that power to challenge anything more than the extremes of other power centers. In the coal strike his aim was more to avoid disorder in coal-starved cities than to serve the cause of justice for the workers, and the Northern Securities prosecution left both Harriman and Morgan virtually unscathed. In fact he ran in 1904 under the ultimate conservative slogan "all is well with the Republic."

The one area in which Roosevelt went beyond the political necessities was conservation of natural resources. Though often using language couched in the rhetoric of keeping public wealth out of private hands, he was in truth more the naturalist and outdoorsman than the progressive. Previous presidents had begun the process of preserving some public lands, and pressure for conservation was relatively slight. Roosevelt could have continued in the paths of his predecessors without political cost. But, along with Chief Forester Gifford Pinchot, he took the Forest Service out of the patronage system, established millions of acres of forest reserves, and during his two terms created five national parks, 16 national monuments, and 51 wildlife refuges. The President made this issue his own and probably felt more deeply about it than any other single program. Later William Howard Taft's dismissal of Pinchot would mark the real beginning of the break between Theodore Roosevelt and his successor.

The "Colonel's" second term might be seen as belying his essential conservatism. He confronted "railroad" Senators and succeeded in passing a rate regulation bill, the Hepburn Act. He confronted the meat packers and had a meat inspection bill passed. However, progressive voices all over the country were louder in 1906 than they had been in 1902, and one could argue plausibly that once again the skilled leader was doing little more than finding where his followers were headed and then hurrying to lead them there. Moreover the legislation as finally passed only ended the extremes of corporate misuse of power, was not opposed by all railroad men or meat packers, and essentially left the reins in the same hands they had been in.

The limitations he felt in domestic policy did not apply overseas. In foreign affairs, the chief executive was the nation personified, and Roosevelt's nationalism, racism, and desire to take charge of things turned the United States irreversibly to world power. He also started the executive office on that long road of increasing power, which on some occasions has seemed essential to national survival and at other times the gravest of national dangers. Under his personal leadership, the United States asserted and maintained a proprietary interest in Latin America, especially the Caribbean and areas close to the Panama Canal. Roosevelt intervened in Asia, acting as a shrewd and not completely disinterested third party to settle the Russo-Japanese War. For this effort he received the Nobel Peace Prize. He even interfered in traditional European diplomacy. In sum, Theodore Roosevelt implemented what was symbolically begun when he took his Rough Riders to Cuba, and he now implicitly proclaimed that the United States had global interests that other nations would ignore at their peril.

Roosevelt was a racist and of that there can be no doubt. Along with virtually everyone else, he believed that man was to be found in several varieties and that some of these were better than others as well as being more endowed with capacity of leadership and more advanced toward "civilization." The Spaniards should be driven out of Cuba, and the Filipinos should be governed by white men. Yet his racism was of a limited sort, because his time frame was brief. Those not yet far along toward civilization could be improved. And Roosevelt did not mean centuries, but decades. American Negroes had only recently been "backward." Now many of them were "advanced," as illustrated by the accommodationist Booker T. Washington, whose dining at the White House outraged racist circles. His definition of "race" seemed to be only partly biological. It was also sociological because he seemed to be saying that by improving the level of "civilization"—which meant of course resemblance to England, Germany, and the United States—one could improve individuals.

Out of office and seeking a comeback, the Rough Rider's domestic program appeared to grow nearly as bold as his foreign policy. In 1912 he adopted nearly all the positions of what he had called "the extreme" progressives. By 1918, in his last public speech, he advocated river valley development, public housing, and social security. Perhaps the second President named Roosevelt did little more than realize proposals of the first. Yet Theodore Roosevelt out of office, looking for a constituency, was different from Theodore Roosevelt in power. In office he moved only enough to avoid frustrations that might encourage more dangerous social change, and he attacked only the extremes or "Romanovs of our social and industrial world." Under his stimulating but essentially moderate leadership much was begun, but he was not the man to do more than make the beginning.

*   *   *

There are historians who dismiss Progressivism as a sham, a conservative attempt to maintain the older order while only seeming to respond to new problems. Certainly an argument can be made that the demands of the new urban industrial society were far from met during the Progressive years. Yet all reform movements, whether in the United States or other countries, must be evaluated in their historical context. Although the decade and a half after the turn of the century found a new social democracy on the rise almost everywhere in the world, Progressivism was nonetheless an American phenomenon and dealt with very fundamental American assumptions about private property, the place of government in society, and the individual's responsibility for his own fate. Reformers might alter these ideas in significant ways, but could not challenge them at a basic level. Equally if not more importantly, Progressivism was also a first attempt in a country that had defined itself as rural to come to terms with its urban future. While only partially successful, it nonetheless set the tone and direction of future efforts from the New Deal to the New Frontier and the Great Society. The problems of the progressive years are still with us, and the terms in which we debate them were formulated at that time. If we criticize the progressives for not solving the problems, we should at least acknowledge that we have not solved them either.

9

From Sisterhood to Self: Women's Road to Advancement in the Early 20th Century

KATE RICHARDS O'HARE
ROSE SCHNEIDERMAN
MARGARET SANGER

by Mari Jo Buhle
Brown University

The founder of Sorosis, the first women's club in the United States, noted that among the remarkable achievements of the 19th century was one rarely or fully appreciated, namely, the emergence of a new woman. Jane Cunningham Croly, who helped organize Sorosis in 1868, described this phenomenon in terms of "the woman who works with other women; the woman in clubs, in societies; the woman who helps form a body of women; who finds fellowship with her own sex, outside of the church, outside of any ism, or hobby, but simply on the ground of kinship and humanity." By 1890 national women's organizations—the General Federation of Women's Clubs, the National Woman's Christian Temperance Union (WCTU), and the National-American Woman Suffrage Association—had penetrated every state in the union. Their membership consisted predominantly of native-born women. The associational impulse, however, transcended class and ethnic lines. Clubs for working women, for black women, for immigrant women were no less prolific, and all gave witness to Croly's claim that women were stepping forward in great numbers.

Many of Croly's contemporaries agreed with her assessment and were indeed optimistic about the fate of their sex. They, too, believed that the notion that the home is woman's sphere had been blown to the four winds. Some called the 19th century the great iconoclast because it had so successfully destroyed the time-worn ideal of woman as man's helpmeet. Great advances had been made; these were measured not only by the ubiquitous women's organizations but also by the colleges and professions that had opened their doors to women. The Twelfth Census of the United States recorded over 5 million women in gainful employment in 1900; thousands more labored in the marginal occupations that escaped the notice of the census taker. Compared to women's position in 1800, these changes marked significant progress.

Although hopeful, most perceptive women were not content with their lot. Every step forward into public life, they observed, carried with it new injustices and hardships. Vocational opportunities outside the home placed many young women in a quandary: could they combine a career with marriage? This question, now so familiar as to be accepted almost casually, proved challenging to the women who first phrased it shortly after the Civil War. In fact, the graduating classes of the newly opened women's colleges—Smith, Vassar, Bryn Mawr, and Wellesley—answered generally negatively. They were criticized as over-educated women, self-seeking spinsters who threatened the supremacy of the Anglo-Saxon race by forsaking their maternal duties. Many of these women did remain single or married comparatively late in life, thus contributing to the perceptibly declining birth rate among native-born white women. Their less fortunate and more numerous peers faced different but no less troubling problems. Gains in paid employment were offset by menial jobs, low wages, and unhealthy working conditions. The increase in prostitution could probably be traced to these factors; and marriage, even motherhood in many cases, brought no escape from them. The "new woman," indeed, had many questions to answer.

Women coming to maturity at the end of the 19th century constituted a transitional generation. Every generation, of course, marks the passing of an era. But perhaps never before had a generation of women been so acutely aware of the differences between themselves and their mothers. They carefully recorded the daily changes that seemed almost palpable, transforming the study of history from a mere academic pursuit into a way of ordering life experiences. Between 1870 and 1900 they produced a considerable body of literature "scientifically" documenting the various advances women had achieved in labor, education, religion, and the arts. Discussions of the Woman Question, queries about the nature of the "new woman" filled the pages of popular journals, both high- and low-brow. Many women across the country were caught up in this heady spirit and were determined to chart their own course.

Pioneering women found encouragement in the burgeoning feminism. As Jane Cunningham Croly had noted, women had left their homes for untested seas and had created societies based on "kinship and humanity." "Sisterhood" was no empty slogan, for the members of the many clubs and organizations formed since the Civil War professed a deep and sincere loyalty to their sex. Their various endeavors represented a self-conscious effort to advance women's roles in public life. The highly influential Frances Willard, then president of the WCTU, took pride in the massive army of women assembled under the temperance banner. In Willard's estimation, they were training and disciplining themselves for unfamiliar roles outside the home. In fighting the liquor traffic, Willard explained, women were learning "how to use the weapons with which the future is certain to equip them." Although no one strategy dictated the means toward this end, women engaged in the struggle for temperance, suffrage, or self-improvement found in sisterly solidarity the courage to strike down those old-fashioned notions of femininity still espoused by adamant defenders of True Womanhood.

It is hardly surprising, then, that many young women at the end of the 19th century did not differentiate between their own personal quest for fulfillment and a dedication to the uplift of their sex. They were missionaries, not martyrs, and there was much joy in this collective struggle.

*   *   *

Kate Richards O'Hare was the most prominent woman in the Socialist Party of America during its prime shortly before World War I. She was a close personal friend of its great leader, Eugene V. Debs, and along with him and her husband, Frank O'Hare, produced the *National Rip-Saw,* a popular Socialist weekly magazine published in St. Louis. Thousands knew her from the Socialist lecture circuit, for Kate Richards O'Hare, affectionately called the "red-haired beauty," was a gifted orator. She did, however, advance beyond her local constituency, serving on several national committees and becoming the party's first woman delegate to the prestigious Second (Socialist) International.

Editor, lecturer, propagandist, and international dignitary, Kate found a vocation in the Socialist movement. But in serving it she nevertheless kept before her those principles learned as a young activist in the late 19th-century woman's movement. Socialism might prove the definitive solution to the Woman Question but women, she noted, nonetheless required the support and dedication of others of their sex.

Born in Ottawa County, Kansas, in 1877, Kate Richards was a dyed-in-the-wool midwesterner. Her parents, homesteaders from Kentucky, had built a prosperous ranch on the Kansas frontier and there raised five children. Kate's earliest memories included the open prairies, cowpunchers, herds of cattle, and the pervasive friendliness of rugged rural life. In typical American fashion, she believed that frontier democracy had taught her the values of freedom and self-reliance.

In all likelihood the most traumatic event of her childhood played a determining role in shaping her future. The 1880s were hard for those living on the land. Railroad monopolies drove up prices, and most farmers had a difficult time paying for services while still keeping a margin of profit for themselves. Although Kate's family had managed fairly well in most years, a severe drought followed by a wide-spread financial panic in 1887 brought disaster. Kate remembered her father's face "gray and set," her mother's feigned smiles, shortly before the ranch was dismantled and sold. Andrew Richards left for Kansas City to find work, and after a bitter winter he was able to send for his wife and children. A once-proud and independent farmer, Kate's father had become a wage-earner. He supported his family, now housed in a poor section of town, on a weekly income of nine dollars.

Kansas City introduced Kate to urban poverty, "a picture of inferno," she recalled, "such as Dante never painted." It also provided a rich milieu for social activism. Kate spent one lonely winter teaching in a rural sod-house school before forsaking this customary avocation for women as well as her own frontier heritage. She gladly returned to Kansas City and in 1894 became an apprentice in her father's machine shop. Moreover, she flaunted tradition further by joining the International Association of Machinists, a union that did not normally admit women. Life in the city, despite its sordidness, had seduced this high-spirited young woman and it also supplied more opportunities than she would have found on her father's farm or in the small country towns. Deeply religious, Kate nurtured hopes of entering the ministry of the Disciples of Christ, but she slowly began to traverse a path away from, as she later described it, religious fanaticism to secular politics. In setting out on the road of urban reform to make the city clean and wholesome, she moved beyond the parameters of woman's traditional sphere.

Like so many other midwestern women, Kate took her first step in this direction by joining the temperance crusade. She still harbored vivid childhood memories of "a dear old preacher, tall and spare, with patriarchal beard and snowy hair," who used to stand in the pulpit of the country church and thunder forth "in awesome words his denunciation of 'Rum.' " Although nominally dry since the 1880s, Kansas was still a hot-bed of temperance agitation; it was the home of Carrie Nation who wielded her famous axe against illegal saloons. Although as a youth she "thrilled in terror" to such unleashed hatred of alcohol, the mature Kate chose a different, more practical approach to the wide-spread problem: she became a worker in the Florence Crittenton Mission in Kansas City.

The Florence Missions were part of a gigantic social purity campaign fostered primarily by the woman's movement and led in the midwest by the WCTU. They were a direct response to the rise of reported incidents of sexual abuse, a problem which had become especially acute in the late 1880s when numerous young women searching desperately for work migrated to the city. In Kansas, for example, it was not uncommon for a farm family facing disaster to try to salvage its homestead by sending its children to an urban area for employment. Usually traveling alone, virtually penniless, ignorant of the ways of city life, and unprepared for the brawling openness of Kansas City, young women were prey to all sorts of swindlers, as well as to those engaged in recruiting prostitutes. Responding to the dramatic rise in prostitution and illegitimacy, social purity reformers created an array of programs designed to spare young women the public shame and emotional suffering caused by rape or seduction. They set up travelers' aid bureaus at the railroad stations; these directed women new to the city to "respectable" boarding houses and hotels. They opened their own shelters for women searching for work and supplied job referrals for factory, retail, and domestic positions. They agitated for more stringent penalties for keeping houses of ill-repute and for changes in the legal age of consent. In many midwestern states, purity reformers succeeded in having the legal age of consent raised from 10 or 12 years to 16 or 18. They also instituted educational programs. The WCTU, for example, conducted meetings for mothers and also for boys and girls in whom they wished to inculcate the principles of social purity. The Florence Missions were similar evangelical operations, providing religious and other inspirational messages. Florence workers regularly toured Kansas City, trying to remove young women and inebriated men from the streets, for then as now the incidence of sexual abuse correlated highly with drunkenness. The Florence Missions also served any woman needing guidance or practical assistance.

These were formative years for Kate. As a Florence worker in Kansas City, she learned to deal with prostitution "in its most bestial forms." She dedicated herself to saving women from it and to advancing the cause of working women. An ardent devotee of woman's rights, as were most temperance activists, she was determined to hold her own; as a member of the mechanics union, she had ample opportunity to defend her position as a self-supporting woman. Most important, she grew to appreciate the supportive milieu of the woman's movement and came to understand her own struggle as part of a larger, collective advance of women into public life.

At the same time, Kate began to read popular political tracts, such as Henry George's *Progress and Poverty,* Ignatius Donnelly's *Caesar's Column,* and Henry Demarest Lloyd's *Wealth vs. Commonwealth.* These were radical books, to be sure, but an alliance between the People's party and the radical wing of the temperance and suffrage campaigns was quite strong in the Kansas City locale. Finally, while attending a ball given by the Cigar Makers' Union, Kate heard Mother Jones, the "angel" of the coalfields, and was almost instantly converted to Socialism. She had been unwilling to dampen her spirit by unquestionably following woman's calling from school room to vine-covered cottage; now she completed her journey.

Fired by a missionary zeal, she joined the Socialist party, attended its school for organizers in Girard, Kansas, and established herself as a prominent social reformer.

Once in the Socialist movement, Kate rose rapidly as a lecturer and agitator. In 1902, she married Francis Patrick O'Hare, a classmate at the organizers' school. Her honeymoon was combined with a lecture tour of Missouri towns. She told audiences that although she would rather be at home a sense of duty forced her "to do something to improve the conditions of women in the industrial struggle for existence." Over the years she embellished this picture of self-sacrifice, insisting that she had renounced the joys of domesticity for the great struggle for Socialism. Kate gave birth to four children between 1904 and 1908, but even the demands of motherhood did not keep her at home. Her offspring often traveled, sometimes unwillingly, with their energetic mother and compliant father. Whatever her domestic situation, Kate was continually on the road, working during the summer months in the Socialist encampments of Oklahoma and Texas, speaking day after day to crowds of up to 20,000 people; in the winter she concentrated on towns and cities.

Within the Socialist movement, O'Hare found political and spiritual nourishment. Like Kate, thousands of midwestern women had gone over from the temperance and suffrage causes to Socialism and recreated within the Socialist movement the organizational forms that had served as the basis of the woman's movement since the Civil War. Within a few years after the party's formation in 1901, almost every Socialist local had a women's club as well; by 1908 a genuine movement had emerged. At its national convention of that year the Socialist Party instituted a Woman's National Committee to coordinate activities among the numerous women's organizations.

Kate served on this Committee for several years and found her most loyal supporters among these socialist women; she needed them, especially after renewing her campaign for social purity reform. She sought more than simple economic or political demands for workers, and she was instrumental in shaping socialist agitation toward social ends as well. During its 40-year history in the United States, however, the socialist movement as a whole had not been very receptive to women's issues. Only in the 1890s did party leaders quietly accede the legitimacy of women's claim to the ballot and accept the permanency of their position in the paid labor force. But even after the turn of the century, few Socialists considered such issues to be of pressing concern. O'Hare nonetheless insisted that party leadership promote the campaigns pioneered by the woman's movement. If socialism promised the eradication of all injustices, O'Hare asked, how could its advocates ignore the often debilitating problems women faced as they moved beyond their traditional sphere? Socialists had to address their responsibilities squarely. She encouraged the party leadership to initiate campaigns for woman suffrage and to assist in the unionization of women workers. Moreover, she sought to demonstrate how the Socialist movement was the legitimate successor to the temperance crusade. O'Hare, who eventually became one of the party's most versatile propagandists, could not be swayed from her original course.

Kate concentrated her energies upon the social purity campaign because its issues spoke loudest to her grass-roots female following. In 1904 she produced her first major work, *Whatever Happened to Dan?*, revised in 1912 as *The Sorrows of Cupid*. Stressing the twin desires for conjugal joy and emancipation, she spelled out in the book the effect of capitalism upon woman's prospects. "Love, home and babies," she affirmed, were the "three graces that make the trial, struggles and suffering of life worthwhile." Women might save these ideals from destruction, purify and reconstruct them as the basis of a happy life—or see them further corrupted and destroyed by the economic beast. The choice, she argued, rested upon a fundamental change in society prompted by women as well as by men. As they defended their traditional prerogatives and fought off the intrusion of marketplace values into their private lives, women would help bring about that new world where Cupid's sorrows would be forgotten.

This curious but vital mixture of old claims for womanly virtue and the distinctively modern cry for emancipation gave Kate O'Hare a strong position among her prairie states supporters. She herself had bridged the apparent gulf between Christian piety and class-conscious Socialism without dissolving the bonds that united women activists. Her wing of the radical movement had provided a shelter and a school for women of various kinds and, above all, an arena for voicing common sympathies. In this era of brimming Socialist Party optimism, she gained there more than an occupation; she had found a calling.

O'Hare held tenaciously to her collective labors. Her *National Rip-Saw*, with a circulation of more than 50,000, remained firm in its drive for economic justice until federal war-time, anti-radical suppression destroyed the paper. She also served as a leader of the peace crusade, dear to the hearts of so many of her female constituency, until prosecuted for her statements and finally sent to federal prison. Following her release, she championed the cause of prison reform. Along with a handful of other women leaders, she had brought increasing respect for her sex if something less than total equality within the socialist movement. Kate's tragedy rested in the movement's ultimate failure and dissolution.

*   *   *

Rose Schneiderman's milieu of Jewish garment workers had a social depth and ethnic cohesion that no socialist political movement could hope to equal. And the formation of a trade union movement among women that emerged out of this milieu required equal courage or conviction. Moreover, it represented a more tangible goal than the inauguration of the Cooperative Commonwealth, and it touched the lives of its union members at a point where they could respond with all their energies. To some, like Rose Schneiderman, the resulting institutional network provided an arena for life-long dedication.

Prior to 1920, women's unionism in the United States had been repeatedly repressed by employer opposition, economic distress, and sheer apathy from the labor movement itself. Not until the advent of The Knights of Labor in the mid-1880s did significant numbers of women organize; not until the 1890s did their major sector, the needles trade, show signs of stable organization. But the constituency for a successful union drive was lacking until mass-scale Jewish immigration brought thousands of women into the rapidly expanding garment trades. The downtrodden daughter of the slums, the sentimental heroine of immigrant literature, led in the formation of the first permanent needle-trade unions.

During the first decade of the 20th century, activists in the garment trades began to establish scattered locals. They built more upon experience than institutional victories. As a case in point, the strike of the New York shirtwaist makers, from November 1909, to February 1910, enrolled more union members than all previous labor actions. The "Uprising of 20,000" shut down the garment industry by closing the doors of more than 500 shops and drew in thousands of young women previously thought impossible to organize. Heretofore scarcely a visible presence in the International Ladies' Garment Workers' Union (ILGWU), women sparked its major drive for the comprehensive organization of the trade. Triumphs did not follow easily, but a chain reaction of strikes in Philadelphia, Chicago, Cleveland, and other needle-trade centers raised prospects of ultimate success.

An immediate victor was the Women's Trade Union League (WTUL), which was pledged to assist the unionization of women. The League was as much an outgrowth of the late 19th-century woman's movement as a formal affiliate of the American Federation of Labor. In the 1880's for example, major organizational drives among women workers had been conducted in New York and Chicago by a cross-class alliance of women reformers and aspiring trade unionists. Formed in 1903 by a similar mixed assemblage, the WTUL continued this tradition. It promoted legislative bills to improve working conditions, conducted programs to educate women in trade union principles, and tried to organize a few trades wherein women constituted the majority of the work force. The League met with only marginal success until the great garment strikes of 1909–11. Many working women were suspicious of the WTUL because its cross-class cooperation clashed with the reality of growing cultural differences between WTUL officials and potential constituents. League leadership, mostly white Anglo-

Saxon Protestants, and its rank-and-file, mostly Jews and Italians, often interacted with great difficulty. But the WTUL finally got its opportunity during the shirtwaist makers' strike. It proved instrumental in organizing the ILGWU by raising funds, maintaining picket lines, providing welfare for the strikers, and rallying community support. It emerged from the strike as a major institution in the labor movement. From its headquarters in New York, a handful of trade union leaders, drawn mostly from the Jewish rank-and-file, shaped the potentialities of trade unionism. Here Rose Schneiderman found the sisterly solidarity that enabled her to rise to national fame as a trade unionist.

Rose Schneiderman had emigrated with her family from Saven, Poland in 1890. Although just eight years old at the time, she retained vivid memories of *shtetl* life. Her father was a master tailor; her mother made uniforms for Russian army officers and sewed for local families. In the old country the Schneidermans were not wealthy but neither were they poverty stricken. Rose began Hebrew School when she was four, which was unusual for girls of any age, and entered a Russian elementary school at age six. Shortly thereafter the family started its long trek to the United States—first to Khelm, where Rose learned to read and write in Russian, then to Lodz, where the family slipped across the border into Germany, and finally to Hamburg where they boarded the steamship headed for the promised land.

New York's Lower East Side did not live up to the promise. Samuel Schneiderman found a job for $6 a week and supported his family of five in a two-room apartment. Illness struck him down during the winter of 1892. Disoriented by unfamiliar customs and language, Rose's pregnant mother was unable to keep her family together. Two boys were sent to Hebrew orphanages, the living room rented out to a boarder, and, when the baby was finally weaned, Dora Schneiderman found a job in a fur factory while Rose stayed at home to care for her tiny sister. At ten, Rose spent a year in an orphanage with her brother; at thirteen, she was old enough to get a job.

Although encouraged by her father to value an education, Rose did not suffer emotionally upon leaving school at such a young age. Rather, she entered a friendly community of co-workers in a near-by department store where she worked primarily with other women. She enjoyed her job; the older employees treated her with affection, gave her presents, and introduced her to many young people. In making her first real friends among the department store workers, Rose also discovered ways to acquire knowledge outside of school. She joined the Lady Manchester Club, a literary society that met in a settlement house. The store clerks also exchanged books, which Rose supplemented with serialized novels printed in the *Abendblatt*, a Yiddish Socialist newspaper. Although Rose liked the work and its amenities, especially her fellow workers, she was discouraged by a salary of a mere $2.75 per week after three years of employment. She decided to move on. Her mother had saved enough money to buy a sewing machine, which Rose learned to operate in less than a month, and for her first week's work at the Fox and Lederer factory, she earned $6 making linings for men's caps.

Rose's new job not only brought better pay but also introduced her to the bustling world of Jewish trade unionism. Unaware that a union existed in her trade when she first entered the factory, or that women could become members, Rose was a quick learner. She and several other workers approached the secretary of the United Cloth Hat and Cap Makers' Union and told him that women in their shop wanted to be organized. After finding the twenty-five women required for the issuance of a charter, they established Local 23 of this Union. Rose worked all day in the shop, attended to union business at night, and still managed to find time for the new educational opportunities suggested by fellow union members. She began frequenting the meetings of the Manhattan Liberal Club and Sunday morning lectures at Bryant Hall. Elected to the General Executive Board of the Cap Makers' Union at the age of 22, she was the first woman to hold such a position in the entire American labor movement. Although her mother warned prophetically that if she kept so busy with union affairs she would never marry, Schneiderman remembered these years as a time of fulfillment: "All of a sudden I was not lonely anymore. A new life opened up for me."

Rose Schneiderman found an even greater sense of solidarity within the Women's Trade Union League. Initially skeptical of the commitment of middle-class women to the issues at hand, she was won over by the assistance that Mary Dreier, branch president of the New York WTUL, gave to the 1905 cap makers' strike. The following year, Rose ascended to vice-president of the WTUL and began to form those cosmopolitan contacts and enduring personal relationships that would shape the rest of her life. But she remained on the League sidelines until the great stirrings in the needle trades cast her as well as the WTUL into the public limelight. At this historic juncture the concept of women's unionism as a special phenomenon—better understood by many sympathetic women across class lines than by even the best male unionists—permanently altered her consciousness. She returned to the union movement full-time in the turbulent years of 1915–17, shifted back to the WTUL a year later, and served it faithfully until 1955, when the New York branch finally dissolved.

Schneiderman had become a socialist in those fervent days of union militance as a matter of course. It was almost inevitable then for a labor activist like her to be dedicated to "the ideal of Industrial Democracy," to a time when "every man and woman doing the world's work shall have a just share of the world's goods—a share that would enable him to live a full life, as he understands it." Nor was Schneiderman limited to WTUL and union activism. She was also one of the most prominent suffragists from labor's ranks, chairing the industrial section of the New York Woman Suffrage Party in 1917. But neither the industrial democracy nor suffrage commitments were as sustaining as the labor activity which remained her inspiration and her fate. Persisting in it after the other causes fell away, she was closely allied with Eleanor Roosevelt by the 1930s and reached the apogee of public respectability, maiden aunt to the CIO women's unionism of the New Deal era.

Rose Schneiderman reflected in her long and remarkable career the tenacity of a women's political culture more modern than O'Hare's semi-rural domesticity, but subject as well to the strains of modern social relations. She saw in the trade union movement the best means for women to achieve self-improvement, sisterly solidarity, and ultimate emancipation. At 83 Schneiderman remarked that working women in the 1950s had not "the faintest inkling" of the great labor struggles that had preceded them. She was undoubtedly right.

*   *   *

Margaret Sanger, leading figure in the national birth-control movement and for a time avant-garde enthusiast within the Socialist Party, travelled another path; namely, the single-minded crusade for women's sexual rights which she ultimately became identified with. She possessed the sophistication that O'Hare and Schneiderman lacked and more than the others she had to carve her own niche. However, she paid a price in a lifetime of emotional instability.

Born Margaret Higgins in 1883, in the small industrial town of Corning, New York, she had a radical father—a freethinker, single-taxer, and advocate of woman suffrage and of Socialism. But he barely managed to support his own household. Despite the responsibilities of caring for younger siblings, Margaret managed a limited private education in a Methodist co-educational institution and taught school in New Jersey until called home to care for her dying mother. She later worked as a practical nurse in White Plains and in Manhattan and shortly after her graduation fell in love with a young architect, William Sanger. Influenced by her father to believe in women's equality, Margaret was poorly placed to practice its tenets. Touched by tuberculosis, she gave birth to her first child while on leave from an Adirondack sanitarium where she suffered acutely. After her recovery and the birth of a second son, she nearly settled down to a wifely suburban existence. It was only when she saw her family home literally go up in flames that Margaret Sanger began to glimpse another life as possible and necessary.

Moving to Manhattan, Sanger soon became part of a remarkable bohemian-radical circle. This new cultural intelligensia, centered in Greenwich Village, broke through the walls of traditional mores, enjoyed fresh breezes of Continental thought and an open-ended life style. The Villagers included the "ash can" artists, poets and litterateurs, and colorful political activists. Their gifts were reflected in the pages of *The Masses,* the most sophisticated Left publication in memory, and in innumerable other radical and commercial ventures that carried the message of a cultural renewal. They emphasized self-development and sexual equality—in politics, art, friendship, and love—and helped create the archetype of the "free woman." Here, in this new environment, Margaret Sanger found the political, psychic, and erotic inspiration that was to change her life.

Sanger's bohemian friends were notably interested in the recent European research and theory on human sexuality. Popularizing the ideas of Freud, Ibsen, Havelock Ellis, and Ellen Key, the Greenwich Village radicals called for a rebellion against Victorian moral standards. One of their British prophets, Edward Carpenter, put it best: "Love is doubtless the last and most difficult lesson that humanity has to learn; in a sense it underlies all others. Perhaps the time has come for the modern nations when, ceasing to be children, they may even try to learn it." All true revolutionaries, Carpenter insisted, must struggle for sexual liberation. Contemporary changes in popular manners, permitting millions of women to smoke cigarettes, drink liquor, dance sensuously, and quest generally for self-emancipation, gave the radicals a sense of mass revolution already underway. Concurrent proletarian stirrings, led by the militant Industrial Workers of the World, seemed to project the sharpening of class conflict toward some explosive conclusion. This apparent conjunction of economic and cultural rebellion promoted an ardent romantic faith; a breakthrough for human freedom seemed imminent.

Sanger assimilated, as best she could, the swirling mass of economic, political, and sexual ideas, while locating a focus for her own energies in practical work. A maternity nurse in New York's Lowest East Side (she was not a Registered nurse), she mingled with blue-collar workers and treated wives of small shop-keepers and pushcart peddlers. The profound ignorance of immigrant women about their bodily functions and their desperate efforts to prevent too-frequent pregnancies gave Sanger an embracing purpose. She entered political agitation for her new-found cause by chance. Fitfully active in the Socialist party, the organizer of a local women's committee and secretary of its Socialist Suffrage Society, she was called upon one day to replace a public speaker who had taken ill. She agreed only upon the condition that she be allowed to speak practically—about sexual hygiene. The address was received so enthusiastically that she was pressed to deliver a series of lectures and the editor of the women's column of the New York Socialist daily, *The Call,* urged her to write a series of essays on the topic. Thus socialist women provided a supportive milieu, and Sanger stepped out on the road to fame and notoriety.

Beginning in 1912, Sanger instructed her Socialist audiences in the beauty and grandeur of the sex function and on woman's obligation to push aside fear and proclaim her creative instinct, the highest mission of sentient beings. Mixing philosophy with practical information, she stirred her socialist readers to great praise and (largely male) indignation. Despite Anthony Comstock's censorship of one of her columns—no doubt in part because of the notoriety it had received—Sanger made the subject of sexual hygiene part of internal socialist debate.

Traveling to Europe in 1913, Sanger collected traditional and modern contraceptive devices as well as theoretical and practical literature on the subject. She was primed for a public crusade that the once-timid housewife and visiting nurse could scarcely have imagined.

For several heady years, family limitation (or "birth control," as she and her associates renamed the practice) emerged only as a specialty, one of a number of Sanger's concerns. Before her European trip she had taken an important role in the logistical efforts conducted by Socialists and Wobblies to aid new-immigrant workers and their families during the Lawrence and Paterson strikes, and in the process had become highly critical of the Socialist party's cautious attitude toward radical labor policies. Upon her return she launched her own newspaper, the *Woman Rebel* (with the masthead, "No Gods, No Masters"); it was ultra-revolutionary in tone. Denied mailing privileges by post-office authorities for its statements on sexual matters, the *Woman Rebel* ended abruptly when Sanger herself was indicted, notably for publishing an article defending political assassination. Her career as a political prophet seemingly at an end, Sanger fled abroad to avoid arrest.

On this occasion she met several major figures in the European sexual reform movement. Sanger found in Havelock Ellis and others the comprehensive philosophy she had been seeking. She was also persuaded that birth control was not merely a matter of information but was primarily a medical procedure. Upon returning to the United States in 1915, Sanger was a tempered crusader. Not that she would avoid legal confrontations or hide her socialist banner, but she viewed her special mission as all-consuming.

The National Birth Control League, formed during Sanger's absence, now occupied her attention. Her pamphlet, *Family Limitation*, distributed in the tens of thousands, stirred enormous public interest and resulted in the arrest of her estranged husband for aiding its circulation. Radical intellectuals, a scattering of rank-and-file Wobblies and Socialists across the country, including Kate Richards O'Hare, joined in a two-pronged campaign of legal defense and agitation. After a much-publicized national tour, Sanger opened a birth-control clinic in the poverty-ridden Brownsville section of Brooklyn. Repeatedly arrested, she acquired celebrity status. In 1917, together with a few Socialists, she established the *Birth Control Review*, which served as a forum among her supporters and a bulletin board for local activities and legislative lobbying. Long in embryonic form, her leadership now assumed a definite institutional shape.

Sanger's radical alliance was on the verge of success when it precipitously disintegrated. The Greenwich Village milieu that had nurtured her initial development proved unstable, lacking the economic, social, or ethnic roots to sustain birth control initiatives. The First World War shattered American radicalism. It drove a prominent handful of her comrades to patriotism and others to silence and despair. Yesterday's free lovers and philosophical anarchists became today's solid family men and women, tomorrow's successful professionals. The very concepts of Bohemia were commercially retailed, shorn of their political edge and reduced to high-living nihilism among the youth of the 1920s. Like so many activists, Sanger found herself narrowed in strategic purpose. Her American Birth Control League, launched in 1921, was devoid of Socialist leanings and supported by middle-class respectables. Succeeding with her new orientation, Margaret Sanger would continue in this direction for the remainder of her life, for a long time on the fringes of Left movements but for all practical purposes dedicated single-mindedly to birth control.

*   *   *

Margaret Sanger's personal evolution mirrored the development of women's reform from its 19th-century origins to the full flush of the 20th century. The early demands for special protective measures for the female work force, and the assertion of an elemental economic unity among women and their right to full civil and political equality, had been superseded to a considerable extent by woman's desire to control her individual life. Not that the old crusades had wholly lost their meaning, but rather the search for subjectivity began to affect modern woman more and more.

Ironically, the social purity, trade union, and birth control foci of O'Hare, Schneiderman, and Sanger respectively also expressed the dissolution of that female solidarity that made women's advance possible. Women's forced march from the domestic sphere to the edge of the mainstream of American public life presents a paradox; namely, that the very individuality and greater access to a previously-defined male culture markedly diminished the perceived need for a militant sex-consciousness. O'Hare's rural followers had existed within a female culture and formulated their wishes accordingly; Schneiderman's genteel supporters and trade union sisters straddled the older reform traditions and newer prospects of economic integration; Sanger's bohemian milieu, encouraged physical love without the constant threat of conception. Nothing in the power of women's reform movement could reverse the progression toward heterosocial relations nor shed light upon the problems that remained for woman beyond her initial ascent. At its most radical, each reform tendency embraced a vision of wider social transformation in which woman would be completely free. The failure of political and trade union radicalism helped doom the ideal of woman's collective self-expression.

Nevertheless the women reformers had their day. For roughly half a century after 1870, many thousands of American women found a mission and source of self-realization in social movements. O'Hare, Schneiderman, and Sanger each rose from obscurity, from the poverty and agonies of their mothers' generation, to dignity and fame. They gained in the process something more valuable than individual renown; namely, a sense of shared responsibility and collective purpose through improving the prospects of uncounted, anonymous women, the ostensibly powerless and unconsulted. The movement itself was their real triumph, for the purposeful activity afforded a profound increase in personal strength and self-confidence. In the legacy of their experiences bequeathed to future women's movements, they had indeed bestowed a lasting message: the transformation of society went hand in hand with the emancipation of women. Any movement that sought to tap the dormant energies of ordinary women had to set itself to change the way the women viewed their lives and their most intimate relationships, or console itself with abstract slogans.

10

Race, Ideology, and World Order

ALBERT BEVERIDGE
WOODROW WILSON
WILLIAM E. BORAH

by Robert H. Ferrell
Indiana University

To observe the mistakes of individuals other than ourselves is a fascinating enterprise, and the more illustrious those individuals, the more pushing their efforts to make names for themselves, to write their qualities into the history books, the more piquant become their ultimate downfalls. And, actually, the more instructive, as their errors become sharply etched in our minds. Many mistakes have been made in the conduct of American foreign relations, especially during the era that began in the last decade of the 19th century when those relations took a turn not merely into importance but into complexity. Albert J. Beveridge, Woodrow Wilson, and William E. Borah were not least in mistakenness. One should add, of course, that their errors were shared by innumerable persons during the years from the 1893 Hawaiian revolution, which opened the new era of involvement in world affairs, down to the early 1940s when involvement became so omnipresent that no American could escape its consequences.

Albert J. Beveridge was a handsome young man from Indiana who, upon entering the Senate in 1899, seized upon what he considered a great personal and public opportunity to show Americans their destiny as members of the best race on earth, the Teutons. The march of events the inevitable movement of the American flag to the remote corners of the world, had forced this destiny upon his countrymen, he liked to tell them. Beveridge's error was racism. Woodrow Wilson, a professor of history and political science at Princeton University when the old century passed into the new, became president of his university in 1902, the first individual not a Presbyterian clergyman to achieve that honor. Lack of clerical status did not deter him from speaking about Princeton in the Nation's Service, to use the title of one of his best-known addresses, and a little more than a decade later he would undertake leadership of that nation, first with a grand series of domestic legislative enactments and then, reaching the pinnacle of his national service, involvement of the country in the World War. At the peace conference in Paris in 1919 he drew up the constitution for a League of Nations. When the League of Nations Covenant, firmly embedded in the Treaty of Versailles, then was presented to the Senate of the United States, it failed to obtain the consent of that legislative body. Wilson's error was an excess of idealism. The League's failure in the Senate was due in no small measure to the maneuvering of one of the few senators for whom Wilson would retain respect, William E. Borah of Idaho. Borah not merely helped prevent American membership in the League but became the single most important figure in the making of foreign policy during the 1920s and the leading isolationist of the 1930s. In Borah's case the error was neither racism nor idealism but an unending, nihilistic (at the time often convincing) legalism mixed with vague moralism, a combination stressing the ideas of the founding fathers and the great men of American law as well as the precepts of the Bible broadly construed. In the beginning was the Word, he seemed to be saying, but the Word itself never emerged from behind its curtain of legalism and moralism.

*   *   *

Never again will there be a decade quite like the 1890s when great, pulsating thoughts of national destiny, of mission—of Darwinian selection—all came together in what Rudyard Kipling described as the need to take up the white man's burden and young Albert Beveridge saw as the unfurling of the country's banner, the march of the flag. The early part of the decade had run along quietly enough under the guidance of a Hoosier president, Benjamin Harrison, grandson of the general-president of 1841. Beveridge hated Harrison for his coldness—as did many other people, and for much the same reason. (It was said that the President was such a cold man that when he entered any room the temperature immediately went down ten degrees.) Beveridge had asked the President some years earlier, when Harrison was a leading Indianapolis lawyer, to read law in the great man's office, and Harrison had turned him down rudely and coldly. But this frigid episode passed. And Harrison also passed, retiring back to Indianapolis from Washington in 1893. After a Democratic interlude, the second nonconsecutive presidential term of Grover Cleveland during which the economy plunged into the depths during the panic of 1893 and remained there for several subsequent years, the Republicans came back into power in 1897 and shortly thereafter a war blew up over Cuba. Without much forethought Commodore George Dewey sank a decrepit Spanish squadron in Manila Bay, and soon thereafter large parts of the Spanish empire including the Philippine Islands passed under the American flag. On maps of the time the new American possessions received the nation's imperial color, which (because the best colors—red, green, and orange—already were taken) happened to be an unconvincing yellow. But no matter. It had been a heady war, a splendid little war as Ambassador John Hay described it from London to his friend Lieutenant Colonel Theodore Roosevelt. It had been the sort of war in which Roosevelt could wave his saber at the bottom of San Juan ridge and tell his men that "Gentlemen, the Almighty God and the Just Cause are with you. Gentlemen, CHARGE!" The Rough Riders, without their horses, had charged up that hill toward certain death, and for the most part survived. A generation later Americans in France would charge up hills toward certain death and achieve it.

Perhaps it was the popular song of the era, "There'll Be a Hot Time in the Old Town Tonight," which gave the period a kind of wild nonchalance, in which an orator like Beveridge, handsome, eyes gleaming, metallic voice almost rasping as the words poured forth, hand ostentatiously (Beveridge for years had practiced his speeches before a mirror and knew the most effective gestures) buttoning the top of his coat, could say the most outrageous nonsense. America's duty was to annex whatever was annexable. "The present war," he declared, "has been one of the . . . great national blessings that God's watchful providence has given to his people. . . . No, not *a* Nation but THE *Nation. The Nation,* God's chosen people." Historians many years later, when God's chosen people lived in an era of atomic bombs and genocide, would put excerpts from Beveridge's speeches into anthologies, to be read by college students as examples of the worst of American racist oratory.

Just what inspired Beveridge's Senate oratory at the turn of the century, apart from the hallucinations of the time, is difficult to say, but there surely were factors in his youth that accounted for the shape of his public career. Albert Jeremiah Beveridge was born in an Ohio farmhouse during the Civil War when his father was a lieutenant in the Union army. His early days were passed in a succession of locales over which the cloud of poverty continually hovered. His father went bankrupt in 1866, and at his death years later in 1895 the family house had to be sold to pay his debts and back taxes. Young Beveridge, however, managed to put together 40 dollars, and borrow 50 more, and in 1881 entered Indiana Asbury

University (shortly thereafter renamed DePauw University in honor of a wealthy benefactor), at that time the leading Indiana institution of higher learning. The entering freshman came to college without ceremony; upon arrival in Greencastle he borrowed a wheelbarrow and trundled his trunk the two miles to the campus.

The work at Indiana Asbury called attention to the attractions and importance of oratory. The local literary societies, the Platonian and its rival the Philological, such organizations as would inspire a present-day college student not to tears but to drink or pot, proved attractive to him, for there he could practice orations. He was a very good student, so good in fact that in the autumn of 1884 the authorities allowed him a kind of leave to go out and speak for the Republican presidential candidate of that year, James G. Blaine. Indiana was a Republican stronghold and Beveridge's speeches may not have been necessary for Blaine to carry the state; but the Plumed Knight would lose New York anyway and thereby the election. Beveridge did his best, however, and become known to local Republicans; the experience helped turn him toward a legal career and toward politics.

As a lawyer Beveridge rose rapidly in prominence in Indianapolis, the state capital. After some initial debt collecting he received important corporation cases. All the while he was speaking on every political occasion and at every opportunity. Years later, to be sure, he was criticized by Washington's reporters at a Gridiron Club dinner for speaking not merely at every opportunity but sometimes when there was no opportunity. There may have been some of that in the 1880s and 1890s. But it was a time when Americans admired oratory more than any other single quality in a public man, and Beveridge was good at it and was constantly improving. By 1899 an opportunity opened to take advantage of a split within the Republican ranks in Indiana and obtain enough supporters in the State legislature to be chosen as Senator.

His first speech in the Senate, on January 9, 1900, turned out to be the greatest moment of his public career. Thereafter he delivered many more speeches, but never did his oratory possess quite the electrifying effect of that initial address. He had prepared himself by making a whirlwind trip to the Philippine Islands including stopovers in Hong Kong and Japan. In the Philippines he had gone about with a little red notebook, asking the American troops about their experiences putting down the Filipino Rebellion which had just broken out and would last until 1902 with flareups for several years thereafter. On the appointed day for his great speech, an hour and a half before the Senate met, the galleries had filled with people, and others were lining up to get in. A hush settled as the freshman senator, 37 years old, nervous and pale, began. God, he said, "has marked the American people as His chosen Nation" to lead "in the regeneration of the world." The divine mission of America was to uplift "savage and senile peoples." The Philippine archipelago was a treasure trove, and it lay next to the measureless markets of China, which could take up the surplus of American farms and factories. The nation had to keep the Philippines; if some of the local benighted inhabitants objected, that was too bad. It was necessary to hold this prize, to "hold it fast and hold it forever." The Declaration of Independence applied to civilized men, not "a barbarous race" like the Filipinos. The Constitution gave Congress authority to "make all needful rules and regulations respecting territory belonging to the United States." If the people of the United States listened to the anti-imperialists, the Little Americans of the day, and the nation withdrew from the islands, what would history say?

> Shall it say that we renounced that holy trust, left the savage to his base condition, the wilderness to the reign of waste, deserted duty, abandoned glory, forgot our sordid profit even, because we feared our strength and read the charter of our powers with the doubter's eye and the quibbler's mind? Shall it say that, called by events to captain and command the proudest, ablest, purest race of history in history's noblest work, we declined that great commission?

It was said of the Italian liberator Mazzini that he inflamed a generation he could not lead, and such was the case with Beveridge, for leadership of his crusade fell to a man five years older, Theodore Roosevelt, who occupied the presidency beginning in September 1901. The New Yorker, every bit as energetic as Beveridge, was better educated, much more tactful, far less obviously egotistical than the imperious Indiana senator. He was not as good an orator but nonetheless effective in his squeaky-voiced, fist-in-cupped-hand way. Despite intense presidential ambitions that lasted almost to the end of his life, Beveridge never was able to follow through with the promise of his speechmaking. In 1901 he made another trip to the Far East, and two years later published a book entitled *The Russian Advance,* shortly before the outbreak of the Russo-Japanese War. After two terms in the Senate he was defeated for reelection in 1911, and thereafter his political career passed into eclipse. Upon the outbreak of the World War he went to Europe and reported the military scene. He came to like the Germans, the premier Teutons, and discovered that the Kaiser was "hard as nails, extremely intelligent, and well-informed, and with a steadiness that was amazing." In the course of his European travels he watched "a real battle" between the Russians and Germans, replete with "shells tearing up the earth, men killed, the wounded, the prisoners, the earthquake of artillery, etc." "It was splendid!," he wrote his wife. His published observations appeared in 1915 under the title *What is Back of the War.* After the United States entered the conflict there was never any doubt about his patriotic sentiments. His admiration for the Germans ceased. At the end of the war he became a bitter opponent of President Wilson's proposed League of Nations, which he considered a part of the alien propaganda flooding the country and which would weaken and destroy the very foundations of American nationalism.

And yet there was a scholarly, deeply intellectual side to Beveridge which, if hardly in evidence at the turn of the century and in his attitudes toward the World War and the peace settlement, began to emerge after the failure of his political career in 1911 when he turned to the writing of a four-volume *Life of John Marshall* for which he received the Pulitzer Prize for biography in 1920. After an attempted political comeback two years later he commenced work on a multivolume life of Lincoln, perhaps a natural subject for one who had been born in Ohio, grew up in Illinois, and spent most of his adult life in Indiana. Death interrupted the writing of this biography in 1927, but the posthumously published two volumes showed a promise—"a noble fragment," as one reviewer put it—in some ways even more impressive than the life of Marshall.

Ironically, Beveridge's name probably will go down in history not as a leader of American foreign relations but as the writer of a great biography and the author of a partly finished biography. But it is a fortunate irony, for his invocation of racism in 1900 and later was hardly a fit foundation for American foreign policy in the 20th century.

*   *   *

History possesses its ironies, and as Beveridge would make his mark as a biographer of our greatest chief justice, so is it noteworthy that the advocate of idealism in American foreign relations, Woodrow Wilson, was a legal scholar by training, a political scientist and historian by profession, the author of a dozen books, and perhaps half a hundred articles including a five-volume *History of the American People*. Yet Wilson's reputation has come to rest not upon his writing on history and government but upon his political leadership—and not so much his leadership as his idealism. In the course of sponsoring the League of Nations he managed to break almost every rule in the political rule book!

Wilson was born in the manse of the Presbyterian church in Staunton, Virginia, in 1856. His father, a Presbyterian minister, moved about from church to church, and the young Wilson grew up in small towns and cities in the South during the era of the Civil War and Reconstruction. One of his earliest memories was of men running past his father's gate and shouting that Mr. Lincoln had been elected and there was going to be war. He was the first Southern-born and bred man to reach the presidency since the era of John Tyler and James K. Polk; the South had been removed from the national councils for more than 60 years after them, from 1849 until Wilson's inaugural in 1913. Wilson always was proud of his Southern heritage and liked to say that the South had nothing to apologize for in its history, absolutely nothing to apologize for.

Wilson's Southern traits had a way of appearing in his domestic politics and foreign policy once he reached the presidency. It is well known that the racial arrangements in the offices and bureaus of the federal government in Washington deteriorated sadly during Wilson's presidency. It is not so well known that he could take a racial view of foreign relations. He sometimes speculated about the international dangers of the colored races—that their sheer numbers might overwhelm the whites. In discussions within the cabinet during the hectic weeks before he went to Congress on April 2, 1917, and asked for a declaration of war against Imperial Germany, there was a cabinet colloquy on this subject, and the President related his intense concern that the white races should win out over the colored, that there should not be a kind of racial suicide of the whites on the western front in France; hence the need for American intervention in the war.

Wilson's boyhood appears to have been happy, and relations between his busy father and young Thomas Woodrow—known in youth as Tommy —were close, contrary to the sensational notions advanced in a book co-authored by the late Sigmund Freud and published in 1967, years after its composition. His father trained him carefully, in ambition and especially in use of words. Young Tommy gave evidence of being a good student, though not a precocious one.

Wilson's life until 1912 and election to the presidency is an oft-told tale and does not need retelling except perhaps to stress its academic, its idealistic, nature. For the future President was preeminently an academic man; he was the only professor of history and political science ever to head the government of the United States, and indeed the only professional academic man ever to achieve that high office. He began his undergraduate studies at Davidson College in 1873; after a year he left and subsequently enrolled in 1875 at the College of New Jersey, later known as Princeton, a good Presbyterian institution. Graduating in 1879 he studied law at the University of Virginia for a year or so, and practiced unsuccessfully in Atlanta in 1882–83. In disappointment he cast around for something better to do, and fixed upon the career of a college teacher. He chose the leading graduate school of its day, The Johns Hopkins University in Baltimore, and in 1886 received a Ph.D. His doctoral thesis had been published a year earlier under the title of *Congressional Government*, a study of the dominance of Congress in the federal government contrary to the injunction of Montesquieu that the ideal government consisted of a balance among the executive, legislative, and judicial. In subsequent years he taught at Bryn Mawr and Connecticut Wesleyan, and in 1890 returned to Princeton where he remained until 1910 and election to the governorship of New Jersey.

His 20 years on the Princeton campus were a formative period in which his subsequent actions in his presidency, in domestic and foreign affairs, were almost clearly foretold. Indeed it is possible to advance the thesis that the intense idealism of the man, his willingness to glorify the ideal rather than accept the real, came out of the Princeton experience. Year after year he was voted the most popular professor on the campus, and this adulation quite possibly went to his head. He rose to the presidency of this then rather small institution—Princeton in Wilson's time was no great "multiversity" of the sort so well known to Americans in the period after the Second World War, but a small college of a few hundred students and a few dozen professors. His administrative triumphs at Princeton persuaded him that the politics of the campus were akin to politics everywhere. All the politics he knew, he learned on the Princeton campus, he once remarked. This was a questionable boast, although Wilson had participated in some bitter campus political infighting. But politics as practiced in the cities and states and federal government of the United States at the turn of the 20th century was even less a game, and far different from the Princeton campus. Wilson was full of academic idealism, which he translated to the national scene, and which for a while took him very far in the legislative triumphs of the Progressive era (from 1913 to 1916), then in America's entry into the World War and finally in his wartime leadership—until at last he overreached himself.

Wilson's idealism in regard to the League of Nations, his willingness to fight for such an ideal and if necessary die for it, came very late in his public career. Not until the summer of 1918, and perhaps the early autumn, did he begin to think much about a League. Prior to that time he had occasionally given lip service to the idea of collective security. He had made some statements of modest interest in the cause of the League to Enforce Peace, an organization mostly of former Republican officeholders and of college presidents that was sponsoring a project for enforced mediation. According to the LEP, the nations after the World War should organize a concert of force that would use economic and military sanctions against any nation that went to war without first resorting to a process of mediation. Presumably after mediation the nation might freely go to war. Wilson at the outset did not like this idea. As late as March 1918 he remarked that "the United States would never ratify any treaty which put the force of the United States at the disposal of any such group or body." He was considerably suspicious of the men who had been working on projects for such a world organization, often against serious obstacles, and referred to them almost contemptuously as woolgatherers. He preferred the program of a British group of publicists and scholars and Labor Party members known as the Union of Democratic Control; the Union believed that moral force and public opinion would keep peace and that any plan without such a basis was bound to fail.

Throughout the period of United States participation in the overseas conflict, from April 1917 until November 1918, the President was too busy to think much about the future of the world, other than make a few statements about the need to ensure peace. Once the Armistice brought an end to the fighting, and preparation began for the peace conference, Wilson decided—contrary to the advice of his confidant Colonel Edward M. House and of Secretary of State Robert Lansing—to go in person to Europe as head of the American delegation; and his actively idealistic mind only then began to focus on the need for world organization. He quickly brought together the strands of a program.

At that point he made a serious mistake: he did not consult with any of those prominent Americans who had thought the most about problems of world organization, among them such intelligent students of international affairs—and leading Republicans—as former Secretary of State Elihu Root and former President William H. Taft, not to mention Senator Henry Cabot Lodge who became Chairman of the Foreign Relations Committee in the spring of 1919. He consulted largely with himself, and borrowed ideas from the British projects for a League of Nations championed by James Bryce and General Jan C. Smuts and Lord Robert Cecil. Colonel House had made some gingerly suggestions, which he largely ignored; House backed off, as he always did from ideas that might lead to a clash with his friend the President. Lansing was a skilled international lawyer who possessed a keen sense of what sort of world organization the Senate of the United States might find acceptable, but Wilson not once had discussed the grand problem of the organization of the peace with his own nominal leading adviser. Once he got to Paris he ignored Lansing, telling the Secretary of State that he did not intend to have lawyers drafting the treaty of peace.

When the peace conference opened in January 1919, he compounded this tactical error of failing to consult with experts in his own country by rushing the completion of the new world constitution. The President arranged to become chairman of the commission to draw up a constitution for the League of Nations, and delayed many projects of the conference until he could push the commission into finishing the Covenant. The work was completed in great haste, by mid-February, after which Wilson returned to the United States for a month to sign legislation passed by the session of Congress that ended early in March.

In the course of his quick work Wilson then made a strategic error, a mistake of large dimension. It was during the helter-skelter drawing up of the Covenant that Wilson's conversion to a League with economic and military sanctions first became evident. Herbert Hoover, at that time unsure of his true political affiliation but certain of his admiration for President Wilson, was astonished to discover that the President who had so carefully sidestepped the private proposals for a forceful organization of the peace was now himself in the vanguard of the enthusiasts for force.

Without much finesse Wilson had made a fateful choice, an academic, idealistic choice of the form for his world organization that ignored two much better forms, either one of which would have promised a better international order than in fact obtained after the World War. One admittedly would not have been politically feasible in the United States, however attractive and reasonable, namely the creation of a new Holy Alliance, or concert of the powers, similar to the arrangement for European peace after Napoleon's defeat in 1815. The American people could have joined with those of Britain and France and forced peace upon Europe and probably the world, if Americans had been so inclined. But they were not of such mind, nor were the people of Britain; the only ones willing to enforce the peace were the French, who twice in a half century had suffered at German hands.

The other possible form for the League's constitution in 1919 could have been an enlargement of the work of the peace movement of the quarter century that had preceded the World War. In the 1890s peace sentiment began to gather in the major Western countries—Britain, France, Germany, the United States. One result of this desire to organize international relations for peace was the Hague Conference of 1899, followed by a second conference in 1907; plans were being laid for a third meeting when the World War broke out. Meanwhile, commencing in 1897, the United States had proposed arbitration treaties. Secretaries of State Richard Olney, Hay, and Root had sought to engage the country in a network of bilateral treaties looking to the peaceful settlement of disputes. Secretary of State William Jennings Bryan in 1913–15 pushed an idea he long had held, that nations pledge themselves not to go to war until after a one-year "cooling off" period of conciliation by international commissions; Bryan concluded 30 bilateral treaties along this line, and if every nation in 1914 had been tied up by such engagements it is possible that World War I might not have broken out. During the years before the war many men of good will, and a considerable number of statesmen who sensed the usefulness of such moves as the arbitration and conciliation treaties, also had met in conference to codify the international law of war, in the hope that clear rules might restrain the violence of any war that did happen to break out. A League of Nations looking to the continuation of these tasks was entirely possible in 1919. It almost surely would have obtained the consent of the Senate of the United States, for it was in the American tradition in international relations.

In long retrospect one might contend that such measures as the pre-1914 peace movement had championed could not have worked after 1918, for the arbitration treaties had never been invoked in the pre-war years; nor have they—or the conciliation treaties—been invoked since then, despite the fact that most of them remain in force or at least on the law books. Still, there was a foundation here, and a tradition that was politically possible in the United States.

Instead Wilson chose, in Article X of the Covenant of the League, a guarantee of the borders of the League's member nations. It was, if one looked at it closely enough, a guarantee to which some strings were attached, but it was nonetheless a guarantee. If grouped with the other articles of the Covenant, it clearly implied the defense of political boundaries by economic and military means. League members undertook to "respect and preserve as against external aggression" each other's "territorial integrity and existing political independence." Wilson later wobbled on the meaning of this article. In Paris he seems to have seen it as a military guarantee. After he returned home and in August 1919 was questioned sharply by members of the Senate Committee on Foreign Relations he claimed that it was a moral guarantee, not a legal one, but in response to a question at the same meeting he declared that a moral guarantee was more binding than a legal one.

> It is binding in conscience only, not in law. . . . When I speak of a legal obligation I mean one that specifically binds you to do a particular thing under certain sanctions. That is a legal obligation. Now, a moral obligation is of course superior to a legal obligation, and, if I may say so, has a greater binding force; only there always remains in the moral obligation the right to exercise one's judgment as to whether it is indeed incumbent upon one in these circumstances to do that thing. In every moral obligation there is an element of judgment. In a legal obligation there is no element of judgment.

Article X, he publicly stated, was the heart of the Covenant and any American reservation of the article would be unacceptable. It was, he told some Democratic senators, "the king pin of the whole structure. . . . Without it, the Covenant would mean nothing. If the Senate will not accept that, it will have to reject the whole treaty."

The article was most injudiciously worded, contrary to the traditions of American foreign policy as set down by Presidents Washington, Jefferson, and Monroe, and as elaborated especially in the immediate pre-war years. The result was personal and public tragedy. Wilson not merely insisted upon Article X but virtually threw it in the face of the Senate. When he submitted the treaty and Covenant to the Senate in July 1919, he said in an impromptu peroration:

> The stage is set, the destiny disclosed. It has come about by no plan of our conceiving, but by the hand of God who led us into this way. We cannot turn back. We can only go forward, with lifted eyes and freshened spirit, to follow the vision. It was of this that we dreamed at our birth. America shall in truth show the way. The light streams upon the path ahead, and nowhere else.

When the senators began to prove reluctant, refused to go forward with lifted eyes and freshened spirit, spurned the hand of God, and wanted to turn back, Wilson left on a tour of the country to raise their constituencies against them. The tour was too much for a man 62 years of age, speaking in an era before microphones and amplification when it was necessary to shout to the rafters to carry one's voice to several thousand people in creaking wooden chairs packed into a great barn-like hall without soundproofing or air-conditioning. Wilson had suffered for years from cerebral thrombosis, the blocking of an artery in the brain with subsequent destruction of part of the brain, the first known instance having occurred in 1896, another in 1906 when he suddenly lost the sight of an eye and required weeks to recover. After a warning collapse following a speech in Pueblo, Colorado, he gave up his tour, returned to Washington, and in a few days suffered a major, permanent paralysis of his entire left side. Incapacitated, he was effectively removed from the day-to-day problems of the presidency and should have resigned. But Wilson did not. He remained in bed or in a wheel chair in the White House until the end of his term in March 1921. All the while he refused absolutely to compromise, and when the Senate minority leader proposed that he should hold out the olive branch his response, almost horrifying in its intransigent idealism, was that Lodge should hold out the olive branch. With this pitiful collapse of judgment the possibility of American participation in the collective security of Europe and the world went aglimmering. It was idealism pushed to the point of stupidity. There was very little that was admirable about it.

*   *   *

One might well argue that the idealism of Wilson was more noble than the racism of Beveridge, if equally impractical. But in the lexicon of American foreign relations during the years from the 1890s until the beginning of the Second World War there was yet another error—legalism-moralism, personified by Senator William E. Borah. The Lion of Idaho was a burly, jut-jawed, open-faced man with a thick mane of hair. Entering the Senate in 1907 he remained there until his death in 1940. He was one of the principal architects, perhaps even the chief architect, of the defeat of the Versailles Treaty, which included the League of Nations Covenant. The cement of his handiwork in that task was legalism and moralism. After this achievement, as he regarded the outcome of the League fight, the Senator became the leading figure in American foreign policy during the 1920s and the leading isolationist of the 1930s.

Borah's background resembled that of Beveridge and Wilson, in that his origins were humble if not obscure. Born on a farm in Illinois, the seventh child in a family that eventually included ten, he grew up there

and in rural Kansas. He entered the University of Kansas as a preparatory student, a sub-freshman, in 1886, and the university itself the following year. Because of a threat of tuberculosis, he did not finish this initial
school year and never returned. After a few months of reading law he
was admitted to the Kansas bar, where he practiced until the autumn of
1890. He then took a train in the direction of Seattle and got off at Boise
short of funds, with $15.75 in his pocket.

In the next decade and a half his career in Idaho developed rapidly.
He established himself as a lawyer, voted for Bryan in 1896, but drifted
back to the Republican Party in subsequent years. After the turn of the
century he became involved in a famous law case that took him into the
Senate. One day in December 1905, former Governor Frank Steunenberg
swung open the side gate of his house and was blown to pieces by a bomb
hidden in the snow under the gate. The ex-governor had used severe
measures against striking miners a few years earlier, and the immediate
presumption of the local people was that the miners union had arranged
the killing. Three union officials were kidnapped in Denver, brought to
Boise, and put on trial. Clarence Darrow was attorney for the defense.
Borah, the prosecutor, proved himself eminently fair. The jury voted
acquittal, and Borah went to the Senate.

In the pre-war years Borah was a nationalist and imperialist, but his
main concerns were domestic politics wherein he was a supporter—but
not all the way—of Theodore Roosevelt. He admired the ideas of Progressivism, but did not want conservation measures to hurt Idaho's development and consequently voted against legislation involving timberlands
or water rights. He favored the rights of individuals, but did not wish
those rights so protected that corporations would not feel free to develop
the American West or any other portion of the country that needed development. When Roosevelt began to move toward championing considerable federal legislation against corporations, in the hope of winning
the 1912 Republican presidential nomination, Borah remained personally
loyal. But when the ex-president took his supporters out of the Republican convention in Chicago and went down the street to organize the
Bull Moose Party, Borah was not seen in that great throng that paraded
around to the tune of "Onward Christian Soldiers."

Borah was, in a word, unpredictable, as Roosevelt discovered. There
was a kind of frontier independence and impulsiveness about him. He
regarded himself as a free agent elected by the people of Idaho, and
believed that if they did not support him, they could let him know in the
next election.

Borah's Senate seat was always secure: Idaho's voters never let their
Senator down. This had especial meaning at the very time of the Paris
peace conference when Borah's interests turned permanently toward foreign relations, an arcane business to most of his constituents. In the year

1931 a grand total of 17 citizens of Idaho applied for passports to travel abroad. Borah could say almost anything he wanted about American foreign policy and have the full support of the Idaho electorate.

Borah, incidentally, never managed to go abroad himself, perhaps in imitation of Idaho customs. Two or three times he applied for a passport, but something always came up to prevent his departure, even to the extent of visiting Canada or Mexico.

One of the Senator's biographers chose to characterize him as a negative statesman, and truer words were never written in regard to his positions on foreign policy. In the League fight of 1919–20 he was against any concrete organization of the nations of the world. Borah believed, he said, in moral force, not legal force, but if the former carried greater forcefulness than a treaty (as Wilson claimed) the power of Borah's morality was entirely ethereal. He took refuge in all the traditions of the 18th as well as the 19th centuries, and if his country had become independent earlier he would have appropriated the traditions of those times. The present as Borah saw it must always be touched by the hand of the past. His legalism was sustained by a moralism so intense that Wilson never took offense and always spoke kindly of him, even after the President had suffered physical collapse and had become a suspicious, vindictive invalid. Borah had a way of making his causes impersonal—he seldom spoke ill of anyone, and never engaged in the quips or barbs that enlisted Wilson's ire against such individuals as Lodge. (When once discussing the Covenant with a friend Lodge had said that "As an English production it does not rank high. It might get by at Princeton but certainly not at Harvard.") Lodge could be frustratingly specific about his public or private dislikes. Borah always took higher ground.

Having elevated his objections, Borah was not beyond petty maneuvers, and it was one of his confrontations with Lodge that may have prevented the Senate's acceptance of the treaty and Covenant in 1920. After the lawmakers had voted against the treaty in November 1919, some Democratic senators moved toward a break from Wilson's leadership and toward passage of the treaty with some reservations. Lodge, who had been proclaiming his reasonableness in regard to the treaty (his true attitude has remained something of a mystery, though one must presume that he was willing to see the treaty fail), commenced meeting with some of the Senate moderates, both Republicans and Democrats. Borah and his little group of "irreconcilables," a dozen or so men who wanted the treaty and League "twenty thousand leagues under the sea," took alarm and threatened an open revolt against the majority leader. Because the Senate had been organized by the Republicans on the basis of a single vote, Lodge was cornered. Borah knew it, and was unwilling to let any modicum of respect for the aging Massachusetts Senator affect his parliamentary tactics. Years after Lodge's death Borah told the historian Thomas A. Bailey of a meeting that he had forced between Lodge and the assembled and angry irreconcilables. The conversation had gone as follows:

> *Lodge:* "Can't I discuss this matter with my friends?"
> *Borah:* "No, Cabot, not without telling your other friends!"
> *Lodge:* [Visibly shaken; leaning against a wall for support] "Well, I suppose I'll have to resign as majority leader."
> *Borah:* "No, by God! You won't have a chance to resign! On Monday, I'll move for the election of a new majority leader and give the reasons for my action."

According to Borah, after a great deal of talk Lodge agreed to stand firm in favor of severe reservations to Article X and the threat to his leadership came to an end.

Borah's enmity toward the League was implacable, and he announced on the Senate floor that if Jesus Christ were to come down to earth Himself and plead for the Covenant, Borah would still oppose it. He constantly twitted Wilson's supporters by saying that either the League meant military sanctions and would be effective, or it had none and would be ineffective. "What will your League amount to," was his taunt, "if it does not contain powers that no one dreams of giving it?" The Wilsonians were attempting to straddle this issue, and his logic was unanswerable. When the beleaguered President went out on the trip to the West, speaking in support of the Covenant, Borah was one of several senators who followed Wilson's train after a few days as a self-appointed "truth squad" and gave rousing speeches in opposition. Against the League he was willing to invoke anything, including anti-British sentiment. The British government, he said, wanted the Covenant. "The League of Nations," he declared in Fort Wayne, Indiana, "makes it necessary for America to give back to George V what it took away from George III."

During the 1920s Borah kept constantly in the limelight. No spokesman of American foreign policy, including the three Secretaries of State of the period, Charles E. Hughes, Frank B. Kellogg, and Henry L. Stimson, was so well known. His fame spread to China, and according to one newspaper there any school child asked to name a famous American statesman would likely reply "Lin-Kun," and if asked to name a second statesman invariably responded "Bor-Ah." Upon the death of Lodge in 1924, Borah became Chairman of the Senate Foreign Relations Committee, and thereafter enjoyed a first-rate platform for his ideas. His easy accessibility to the press also had something to do with the currency of his opinions. He never refused an interview and could always come up with some kind of opinion, simple or complicated, that would make the papers. He expressed his views in the legal and moral phrases so attractive to post-war America, when disillusion with the war and the peace was accompanied by feelings of guilt but, even more, of legal rectitude (Americans had a government that "worked") and moral superiority (the American record in foreign policy was honest and principled, as compared to that of Europeans).

Borah's opinions appeared year after year, and never was he completely in support of anything. He usually was against it at the outset, would undergo a conversion, and would then have renewed doubts. At the time of a final committee or Senate vote he might be with the majority, but his tent would stand to the side, and until the vote itself no one could be sure if he was putting up the tent or taking it down. He favored naval disarmament in 1921–22 but was not altogether happy with the results of the Washington Conference. He was adamantly against the League-associated World Court and helped defeat American membership in it in 1926, though he favored some kind of world tribunal that would help codify international law. The next year, he seems to have suggested that Secretary Frank Kellogg extend to all nations Aristide Briand's original two-nation proposal for the outlawry and renunciation of war as an instrument of national policy. This suggestion, if not original with Borah, made the pact worthless, which was perhaps what he had in mind. Borah favored the recognition of Soviet Russia, a safe enough position since none of the Republican administrations of the 1920s was about to recognize it. In the latter 1920s he opposed American intervention in Nicaragua, the small police force of about six thousand marines that President Calvin Coolidge sent into that little country when its government dissolved. Borah made this petty incident into one of the major issues of American foreign policy, forgetting his advocacy of the invasion of Mexico during the first term of Wilson's administration.

In the 1930s, his last decade in the Senate, he supported many of the New Deal measures, but turned to bitter opposition over foreign policy, invoking every legalism and moralism he could muster against American involvement in the increasing troubles of Europe during the Hitler era. His last notable move in foreign policy involved a meeting of several leading senators with Vice President John N. Garner, Secretary of State Cordell Hull, and President Franklin D. Roosevelt in July 1939, in which the President showed deep concern for the deterioration of European peace and asked for Senate reconsideration of the neutrality laws. In the midst of the discussion Borah suddenly spoke up. Sources in his possession, he declared, indicated that there would be no fighting in Europe in the near future. His assertion broke up the meeting, and Roosevelt announced publicly that nothing further could be done until the next session of Congress. It later turned out that Borah's certainty rested on the reporting of a private British journal which had brought together a few surmises and asserted them as fact.

Borah died in 1940, when the world had changed very much from the Idaho he had known as a freshman Senator.

*   *   *

The setting out of American foreign policy, one might conclude, is necessarily a difficult task, in calm as well as in stormy periods, but at no time has it been more difficult than in the years since the 1890s—at no time have there been more changes in world affairs. The opinion of Henry Adams, ventured at the beginning of the period, has surely been correct; the world is moving ever faster and events have been multiplying almost by geometric ratio. Rapid change and mounting difficulty in the conduct of foreign policy has been matched by the growing complexity of international affairs.

Given this complexity, the principles of such men as Beveridge, Wilson, and Borah were, for the most part, less than realistic—for they were the results of hunches and quick extrapolations and seriously in error if only for that reason. None of the three was a close student of American foreign relations or international relations in general. They were all orators: Beveridge went to the Senate and stayed there largely because of his speeches; Wilson was one of the great spellbinders of his time; Borah was much in demand as a public speaker. They were loners in American politics, preferring to take their positions after consulting at best with a few friends, sometimes with no one at all. And they were preeminently ideologues—one-idea men, convinced that some special course confided to them would solve the complexities of their country whether at home or abroad, and if the latter then perhaps the troubles of foreigners too. Theirs were considerable convictions, large burdens for single individuals, and their public careers moved inexorably into failure.

11

Piety, Profits, and Play: The 1920s

BRUCE BARTON
HENRY FORD
BABE RUTH

by Warren Susman
Rutgers University

Few decades in American history have been so little analyzed and so thoroughly caricatured as the 1920s. With the mere mention of these years, who among us does not think back, almost as if by reflex, on "Scarface" Al Capone and his mobsters, John Held's shapeless flappers, Warren G. Harding's lives, loves, and scandals; Calvin Coolidge's notorious propensity for silence, Hiram Evans' legions of hooded Ku Klux Klanners, and Flo Ziegfeld's gorgeous and leggy follies girls? Those were the days, it seems, when life was still in tune with the rhythms of small-town America, when one could shoot off a week's salary (and sometimes one's fingers) on Fourth of July fireworks or feel slightly wicked meeting the local bootlegger under the cloak of night to purchase a bottle of forbidden booze.

But to approach the '20s in this essentially superficial vein is to ignore the really fundamental changes that were occurring simultaneously in American life. For it was in the '20s that the art of advertising was perfected as an indispensible component of the country's industrial economy and as a dictator of the public taste. It was in the '20s that the United States went through the automobile revolution which was to change the very nature of the American's society as well as its landscape. And it was in the '20s that the American infatuation with professional athletics began, giving a virtual coup de grace to religion as the non-economic and non-sexual preoccupation of millions of middle-class Americans. A convenient way of looking at these significant and lasting developments is to consider the careers of Bruce Barton in advertising, Henry Ford in automobile production, and George Herman "Babe" Ruth in baseball.

*   *   *

When Bruce Barton died at the age of 80 in 1967 it seemed almost inevitably and perfectly logical that at least one writer of his obituary should refer to his own life story as "legendary in the best Horatio Alger sense." Among the most prominent men of his time, Barton had come out of a small Tennessee town to become one of the most widely read and respected authors of his day. He would serve in the Congress of the United States, run for the Senate, and even be considered as a possible presidential candidate. He was to found one of the most important advertising agencies and to shape the development of the advertising business—so crucial itself in shaping the new mass society of the period—in significant ways. Barton's success in managing his agency can in part be measured by the fact that when he retired in 1961 the company could boast of billings in excess of $230 million. While Barton himself was known to millions of Americans through his writings and public service, his company could, in a special memorandum on the occasion of his death, point to the special meaning of his vast "contacts." "It meant contact with presidents of the United States, with senators, with cabinet members, with leaders of industry. . . . Bruce could call anyone in the United States and time would be found for him." But perhaps most significant, Barton's life recalls Horatio Alger because, in a sense, he rewrote the American primer on success in a special way that most effectively served the middle class of the 1920s. This revision provided a necessary kind of secular religion, a special vision of piety essential to the nation's transformation into a modern industrial mass society. His version of the success story helped ease the transition from an older, more producer-centered system with its traditional value structure to the newer, more consumer-centered system with its changed value structure. Barton's inspirational writings (and in a sense this includes his brilliant advertising copy) found a way of bridging the gap between the demands of a Calvinistic producer ethic with its emphasis on hard work, self-denial, savings and the new, increasing demands of a hedonistic consumer ethic: spend, enjoy, use up.

Barton once explained his own success in a tongue-in-cheek article he published in 1919:

> We preachers' sons have an unfair advantage over the rest of the world. Out of about 12,000 names in one of the editions of *Who's Who*, more

than 1,000 were names of us. In England's *Dictionary of National Bi-ography* we appear 1,270 times; while the sons of lawyers are there only to the number of 510, and the sons of doctors score only 350 times. In fact, we show up so well that any unprejudiced man will agree that all the money given to the church would have been well invested had it done nothing more than enable preachers to raise sons. . . . Not all of us make good, of course. A third of us go to the devil; another third float around in between; but another third rule the world.

A well-known authority on the American idea of success has provided a shrewd generalization: "Whenever Calvinism's stern demands bit deep, as in Woodrow Wilson, Henry Luce, Norman Thomas, Robert Hutchins, Adolf A. Berle, Jr., DeWitt Wallace, or John Foster Dulles [all sons of preachers], there was a moral earnestness, a mission—and often a destiny." William Eleazar Barton instilled this evangelical sense and moral purpose in his son. Bruce Barton, in his writings as in his life, provided convincing evidence of his deep dedication to and the profound influence of his Congregational minister-father.

William Barton, a descendant of a soldier in the American Revolution, was at the time of his son's birth in 1886, a circuit rider working out of a small church in Robbins, Tennessee. Bruce Barton was the eldest of five children. His father's missionary zeal led him to seek further education even after he had started his family. Moving on to Oberlin Theological Seminary, William Barton graduated at the top of his class when he was almost 30 years old. That same zeal plus a special flair for writing and preaching enabled him to move from one important church to another. At the same time, he lectured at seminaries, edited a magazine, wrote a series of books (significant among them detailed and scholarly studies of Abraham Lincoln and a biography of Clara Barton, no relative, the founder of the Red Cross). Eventually he became a famous preacher and at one time was Moderator of the National Council of Congregational Churches. In speaking of his childhood it pleased Bruce Barton to insist: "We were not poor; we just didn't have any money." The family's wealth included a library, with books coming before cakes in this intensely intellectual household. His mother, who was a school teacher, helped establish such priorities. Barton delighted in the memories of that en-vironment of books, simple living and countryside trips with the father he worshipped and whom he held onto as they both rode on the back of the family's white mare. Meanwhile, he was also being prepared for a more sophisticated life in commerce and journalism.

In the hallowed Alger tradition, Bruce Barton had a paper route by the time he was nine. The family eventually settled in a fairly com-fortable middle-class professional life with a ministry in the Chicago suburb of Oak Park, Illinois. He went to high school there, and received his initiation into the business world. Arranging with an Ohio uncle to sell maple syrup tapped from trees on his uncle's farm, young Barton netted some $600 a year. Simultaneously, he was also developing his skills as a journalist, serving as writer, editor, proofreader, and copy-runner on the high school newspaper. Barton also found work as a part-time reporter (at three dollars a week) on a community newspaper. His intellectual interests did not slacken; and as graduation approached, he determined to go to Amherst College.

While William Barton had no objections, he induced his son to take at least one year at Berea College in Kentucky where all students worked part-time to pay for tuition. Bruce Barton's own accounts make clear that his father's desire was not prompted by financial necessities or by loyalty to Berea, which had been his own alma mater. Reverend Barton's object was simple: to guarantee that his son remain sympathetic toward those who must work for what they want. At Berea, Barton chose the printing office, where he learned to set type, read proof, and handle a press—for eight cents an hour.

After his freshman year, Bruce Barton did transfer to Amherst. There he was elected to Phi Beta Kappa, headed the Student Council, served on the debating team in outstanding fashion, and even managed to play some football as a substitute lineman. Predictably, he worked his way through college (by selling pots and pans) and was elected the member of his class "most likely to succeed"—the whole pattern of his biography demands such things. Bruce Barton's post-graduation plans, however, were not consonant with this formula for worldly success. He had decided that being a professor of history would be a sufficient goal and was delighted at the prospect of a fellowship from the exciting department at the University of Wisconsin. But 1907 was a depression year and Bruce Barton felt the need to work. After weeks of job hunting in Chicago, one of his father's parishioners found a position for him—as timekeeper in a western Montana construction camp. Working ten hours a day, he earned $65 a month; he valued the experience because it taught him to get along with tough men in a tough job.

Bruce Barton returned to Chicago at the age of 21 to sell advertising space for three magazines. He was soon working as a public relations counselor and as editor of a small religious paper. His paper was nearing bankruptcy, but the crisis, Barton's biographers love to recall, led not to personal failure; rather it only served to heighten his "enterprising spirit." It also gave him his first opportunity to write an advertisement. He asked for, and received, permission to take back salary in advertising space and made arrangements with a friend who operated a travel agency. He would drum up customers for a Bavarian tour, this being the year of the Oberammergau Passion Play, and would receive a fee for every customer he secured. "Just a few dollars will take you to Europe to see the Passion Play" was typical ad copy, as salesmanship and religion united. The result: enough money to take Barton to New York City where he settled in at the YMCA, first to work at *Vogue* magazine and then as managing editor of another religious weekly that soon folded. P. J. Collier and Son soon hired him as assistant sales manager. His flair for promotion and sales led to increased self-confidence and a firm belief in the value of salesmanship. His copy for Collier's Five-Foot Shelf of Harvard Classics (sometimes known as Dr. Eliot's Five-Foot Shelf of Books) helped lift that work to fame and played a significant role in the popularization of knowledge and culture so characteristic of this age. It was Bruce Barton who successfully urged countless readers to "let Dr. Eliot of Harvard give you the essentials of a liberal education in only 15 minutes a day."

From 1914 to 1918 Barton served with the Collier company as editor of *Every Week*, a Sunday supplement with a format that presaged the modern picture magazine. His editorials and articles brought him a flourishing literary career, and one article in particular, about Billy Sunday, the evangelist, attracted the attention of an editor of the *American Magazine*. Invited to contribute to this journal, his articles, especially his interviews with famous people, stressed the inspirational and up-lift aspects of life and long remained popular. Indeed, these articles were so admired that they were reproduced in a series of volumes during the 1920s; their titles suggest the over-all theme: *More Power to You, It's a Good Old World, Better Days, On the Up and Up.*

During World War I, the federal government asked Barton to co-ordinate fund drives of the YWCA and YMCA, Knights of Columbus, Salvation Army, and Jewish Welfare Board. Out of this experience two significant developments emerged. First, Barton's effort to help publicize the Salvation Army inspired one of his most famous slogans—indeed one of the most famous in an era of sloganeering—"A man may be down but he is never out." Second, the fund-raising campaign itself led him to enlist the aid of two advertising men, Alex Osborn of Buffalo and Roy Durstine of New York. That this campaign did not begin until Armistice day, failed to discourage the trio, since the funds were still needed. Their determination was justified: They topped their goal of $150,000,000 by some $50,000,000 more. Out of their successful team effort came the creation of a new advertising agency, Barton, Durstine, and Osborn, in January 1919. In 1928 the company merged with another agency, the George Batten Company, to become the highly publicized BBD&O. Its fame was hardly limited to professional advertising men. The agency was well known to the general public and was very much the product of a transformed America, of a new era of the consumer-oriented mass society. Jokes, cartoons, and other popular references to its kind of activities made the agency's name a commonplace. By the time of Barton's retirement, it was the nation's fourth largest advertising firm. Its clients included many of the industrial giants—General Electric, General Motors, United States Steel. Founded on a $10,000 loan the company had become a multi-million dollar enterprise. Barton, who never seemed to seek money, attracted it with extraordinary ease. At the beginning, legend has it, he took a salary of only $5,000 a year from the agency, claiming that it was all anybody needed. He and his family obviously lived well (although never extravagantly) in later years, but it is probably true, as Barton delightedly used to insist, that "it would be a scandal if people knew how little I make as chairman of BBD&O. I think it's almost a disgrace for a man to die rich." He was always equally generous with his contributions to charity and his time to public service work.

Barton's original fame rested on his prolific and unsubtle contributions to inspirational literature. Some found his work sentimental, even cloying but there seemed to be a ceaseless public demand for it. Many of these qualities appeared in his most famous advertising copy. What Bruce Barton possessed was a special insight into human nature, especially into the character of the American middle-class in a period of transformation. He had a special sensitivity to its fears and hopes, yearnings and ideals. Richard M. Huber rightly finds him a man, "with a knack for retailing simple homilies"—very much like the poet Edgar Guest. It seemed both easy and natural when "this leading retailer of values poured most of his energies into retailing products." But perhaps Alistair Cooke was most perceptive of all in seeing the special meaning of Barton's career in advertising. Writing in his column for the *Manchester Guardian* on the occasion of Barton's death, Cooke stated: "He came as close as any one will to achieving a philosophy of advertising, because he saw the whole of human history as an exercise in persuasion."

Bruce Barton understood the power of communication in an era when new techniques of communications were remaking the social order. In a memorable piece immediately after World War I, "They Shall Beat Their Swords Into Electrotypes," he pleaded for a new effort in the cause of international understanding. Each nation, he said, should pledge itself to spend at least one percent of its war costs in international advertising, "explaining to the rest of the world its own achievements and ideals; and seeking to eradicate from the character of its own people those characteristics which are a source of irritation to their neighbors." In the same article he urged the international exchange of newspapermen, clergymen, professors—of every group that had "in its power the shaping of public opinion." And, he continued, "In all these ways—plus the regular use of the printed word and motion picture—I would make the people of the world to know each other, knowing that ultimately they would come to like each other." These are ideas very much in harmony with so-called advanced thinking in an era fascinated by the power of new agencies of communication and mass culture. In the early 1930s, Barton's article "Let's Advertise This Hell," proposed an entirely new series of ads that would be offered to any publication that could be persuaded to print them as a way of keeping the United States out of another war. Late in 1923 he was busy proposing to Calvin Coolidge's political advisors a publicity campaign for the President's 1924 bid.

Barton's famous "Creed of an Advertising Man," first delivered as an address in 1927, is even more characteristic of his thinking and greatly contributed to an understanding of his 1920s vision of the importance of advertising in the social order. He writes:

> I am in advertising because I believe in business and advertising is the voice of business. I recognize the waste and inefficiencies of business. I recognize the cruelties of competition, and the dishonesty that still stains too many business operations. Yet I believe that in the larger development of business and the gradual evolution of its ideals lies the best hope of the world.
>
> I am in advertising because advertising is the power which keeps business out in the open, which compels it to set up for itself public ideals of quality and service and to measure up to those ideals. Advertising is a creative force that has generated jobs, new ideas, has expanded our economy and has helped give us the highest standard of living in the world. Advertising is the spark plug on the cylinder of mass production, and essential to the continuance of the democratic process. Advertising sustains a system that has made us leaders of the free world: The American Way of Life.
>
> If advertising sometimes encourages men and women to live beyond their means, so sometimes does matrimony. If advertising is too often tedious, garrulous and redundant, so is the U.S. Senate.

Advertising, then, was persuasion and persuasion could and would change the world; but advertising at the moment was doing its greatest and most necessary service in its special relationship to business—by publicizing products and urging consumers to buy them. (His method of dealing with Communism, stated later in life, is characteristic: "Give every Russian a copy of the latest Sears-Roebuck Catalogue and the address of the nearest Sears-Roebuck outlet.") The special genius of Barton's own advertising copy was based on the assumption that the use of products advertised effectively contributed to growth and progress, sometimes of the nation but more often of the individual himself. The most successful ads would seek to employ the products of a business in the service of the sanctity or betterment of human life. Witness, for instance, one General Electric ad: "Any woman who is doing any household task that a little electric motor can do is working for three cents an hour. Human life is too precious to be sold at the price of three cents an hour." Or that ad for the Alexander Hamilton Institute (a two-year correspondence course): "A wonderful two years' trip at full pay. But only men with imagination can take it. Only one man in ten has imagination, and imagination rules the world." Or that for General Foods: the creation of Betty Crocker as "the kitchen familiar of every lonely American housewife." The ad shaped for each situation sought to provide everyone with a simple way to understand a rapidly standardizing and mechanizing way of life. In a world of increased complexities, mass technology, and fearful changes, such advertisements offered a chance to retain human dignity as well as individual meaning and development. Bruce Barton, the great master of the uplift essay, without doubt had put uplift at the service of American business enterprise; without doubt he did so largely because of that learning he had received as a young boy at his father's table.

Bruce Barton, it is clear, had been fascinated by ideas about salesmanship and religion many years before writing his 1925 best seller, *The Man Nobody Knows.* He had often commented, in writing and conversation, what a great textbook the Bible could be for an advertising man. Barton's own writings delighted in Biblical-like parables and even his advertising copy had a Biblical quality to its prose. But it was only in 1925, the year of the Scopes Trial and William Jennings Bryan's fundamentalist interpretation of the Old Testament, that the Republican business-oriented Barton finally provided his important and widely read interpretation of the New Testament, which especially emphasized the life of Jesus.

Ever since the 19th century had sought and found an historical Christ, it had become increasingly popular to see Him in ways that suited the historical needs of a given moment. Jesus had been recreated as a fairly respectable Christian Socialist or a not-so-respectable proletarian revolutionary. Now in the 1920s Barton claimed Him for yet another historical role. He set out specifically, we might argue today, to give Christ a new image. In the process he provided a new vision of Christianity. Such a vision was consistent both with the tough demands of a more difficult and rigorously ordered mass society and with a new religious glow destined, not as a simple justification of capitalism and the virtues necessary to sustain it, but as a means of sanctifying the new order of modern business—one organized through the instrumentality of salesmanship to service the newly emerging consumer-based mass society. In a society where the older ideal of the stewardship of wealth could no longer serve, a new idea evolved: business—all business—as service to others and something fundamental to the development of self. Barton, Richard Huber observed, "soaked the idea of success in the sanctity of the New Testament." He moved American Puritanism, in a profound sense, from a more traditional dependence on the God of the Old Testament, to a greater reliance on a carefully reexamined and reconstructed vision of the New Testament.

The initial task at hand was to develop a necessary new view of the personality of Jesus and the basic values that went with it. Barton took special aim at the Sunday School image of Jesus: a weakling, a kill-joy, a failure, a sissy, meek and full of grief. In its place there was a new Jesus: the physically strong carpenter, a healthy and vigorous outdoors man, a sociable companion, a strong and effective leader. "A kill-joy! He was the most popular dinner guest in Jerusalem! . . . A failure! He picked up twelve men from the bottom ranks of business and forged them into an organization that conquered the world." Barton insisted on Jesus' masculinity, suggesting his attractiveness to women and stressing his role as father figure and even emphasizing the role of Jesus' own "historical" father, Joseph. Jesus emerges, as it were, a consumer himself, enjoying life and parties, turning water into wine. His methods are those of advertising; He is the founder of "modern business" and modern entrepreneurial tactics. Barton's understanding of what Jesus meant by his "Father's business" is the key to his own analysis. God seeks, Barton tells us,

> to develop perfect human beings, superior to circumstance, victorious over Fate. No single kind of human talent or effort can be spared if the experiment is to succeed. The race must be fed and clothed and housed and transported, as well as preached to, and taught and healed. Thus *all* business is his Father's business. All work is worship; all useful service prayer. And whoever works wholeheartedly at any worthy calling is a co-worker with the Almighty in the great enterprise which He has initiated but which he can never finish without the help of men.

The Man Nobody Knows first appeared in serial form in the *Woman's Home Companion* and then for several years in the late 1920s continued to ride high on the best seller lists. Barton followed it in 1927 with *The Book Nobody Knows*, a study of the Bible. These works have never been without an audience since they were first published but they remain peculiarly documents of the 1920s and in a sense the high points of Barton's career.

Barton, of course, continued with his agency and his writing. He was elected to Congress from Manhattan's East Side "silk-stocking" district in 1937 and easily re-elected in 1938. Earning a considerable reputation, among reporters at least, for his ability and service in the House, he was a vigorous opponent of Franklin Roosevelt's New Deal. He lost a bid for the Senate in 1940 and retired from politics—only after the President borrowed something from Barton's book with a little sloganeering of his own. His jocular condemnation of three outstanding GOP House critics with the repeated phrase "Martin, Barton, and Fish," delighted his audience and gave Bruce Barton still another claim to national fame.

But it is fair to say that the major impact of Barton's life and ideas rests in the 1920s. Somehow his special vision of the world served these pre-Depression years in a special way. Barton's optimism, his defense of business, and especially his often profound sense of the importance of communications, of techniques of persuasion, of the significant role played by salesmanship and advertising in the new order of things served this period most particularly. Of no less service to the '20s was his basic and old-fashioned evangelicalism, which he carried with him from the 19th century and which was transformed in a way that coincided with the needs of millions of middle-class Americans living in a time of clashing values and sharp institutional change. Much of Barton, of course, today seems camp, unsophisticated, self-serving, unreal. We know that most of his ardent beliefs were being attacked or mocked even during the period in which he wrote. Yet Barton tried to accept the new order as well as redefine older values without abandoning what he deemed best in the latter—ideals of self-development and individual human dignity in an era of mass technology, mass organization, mass society. He tried to redefine Christianity and make it again a potent moral force.

Barton's salesman as hero replaced William Graham Sumner's savings-bank depositor as hero for the conservative sons of American puritan ministers—much like one age of social order was in effect replacing another. At a time in which the values of a producer society dominated, Sumner, the Yale sociologist, could claim that the man who saved his money and practiced self-denial was the hero of civilization; in an age of increasing consumer orientation stressing sales and spending and joy rather than self-denial, Barton, the advertising man, glorified the sales-man-businessman. The type, of course, was subject to Sinclair Lewis' bitter satire at almost the instant Barton was creating him. Later, by 1935, novelist Thorton Wilder would present his extraordinary study of both modern salesmanship and modern Protestantism in *Heaven's My Destination*. And during the 1940s and 1950s the images of the salesman that emerged from works like Eugene O'Neill's *The Iceman Cometh* and Arthur Miller's *Death of a Salesman* have the appearance of tragedy and perhaps even symbolize the whole tragedy of American life. Only in the mid-'60s, with the Maysles brothers' documentary film *Salesman*, does the salesman image evoke neither heroism nor tragedy; rather pathos and perhaps a touch of comedy. But these are other times.

To return to the 1920s, however, it is apparent that we will not understand this decade until we understand Bruce Barton's life and contribution to it—or better yet, why so many Americans responded to Barton's message in quite the way they did. A successful salesman best served the world, Barton firmly believed, and in the 1920s he was perhaps the best salesman of all. A secular piety and a new priesthood. Preacher's sons might indeed rule the world.

*   *   *

By the time of Henry Ford's death in 1947, at least one of the crucial ideas in Bruce Barton's life and work—the proposition that business was service—was firmly fixed in American thought. Notwithstanding depression and world war, the idea of business success had also become sharply identified with the business of being American. Maybe Calvin Coolidge had said it crudely in the 1920s, but the overwhelming majority of the public opinion makers in 1947 seemed to agree: the business of America *was* business. This identification was so complete that Ford himself as well as his achievements seemed, as the *New York Times* declared, the very "embodiment of America in an era of industrial revolution." Yet Ford's career had been made possible *because* of the American system itself; he was the product of our "free enterprise" way while also serving as the living symbol of its achievement and success.

This account of the relationship between Ford and America produced a series of complex intellectual problems. First, the portrait of Ford was that of a simple man who sought neither a vast fortune nor luxuries, whose constant concern was for "the great multitude," for the "common man." Second, his great accomplishments, possible "only in America," were ultimately based on a "single-minded devotion to fundamentals as he saw them: hard work, the simple virtues, self-reliance, the good earth. He profited by providing what was new, but he also treasured that which was bygone." None of this enables us to come to grips with the essentially radical if not revolutionary consequences of Ford's achievement. Nor do we necessarily understand why, even outside America and indeed in the very heart of socialist Europe, Ford and his system—*fordismus,* the Europeans often called it—was hailed in the 1920s as a major contribution to the 20th-century revolution by Marxists as imposing as Vladimir Lenin. Indeed, it was not at all unusual to find Ford's portrait hanging alongside that of Lenin in Soviet factories. (Nor was Ford himself unappreciative of the achievement of Soviet engineers and factories.) Ford's favorite authors may have been Horatio Alger and Ralph Waldo Emerson; he may have repeatedly quoted homilies from the McGuffy *Readers,* which appear to be his only source of formal education, but he was nonetheless considered a major architect of the new social order that came into being during the first two decades of the 20th century and must be understood if we are to grasp the nature of the 1920s.

Biography, then, includes both the subject's achievements and the way these provide for continuity and/or change in society. It also tells us, by the use some elements in society make of a man's life, something about that society as well. The Ford as Horatio Alger hero—simple mechanic to industrial giant; the Ford as living evidence of the success and meaning of the American way; the Ford as villainous autocrat, brutally exemplifying the worst features of class warfare; the Ford as genius whose wisdom gives him the right if not the responsibility to speak with authority on all human and social problems; the Ford as revolutionary who remade the modern world in his own vision—the "legends" of Henry Ford are in many

ways as significant to an understanding of history as is any study of the
"true" achievements of a life's work, properly assessed.

Ford was 57 years old in 1920 (Bruce Barton was 34, and Babe Ruth
25). The decade saw the culmination of his major work and witnessed
even the beginning of the decline of the system he had dreamed and
schemed to create. Like Barton, he was a man with a mission and the story
of that mission and what happened to it in the 1920s dominates this discussion. Roger Burlingame has insisted "It is hard to deny that Henry Ford
was ridden by two obsessions: mechanical perfection and the 'common
man.'" Those obsessions, the way they often conflicted and the attempts
to achieve some kind of effective balance between them, is important here.
They are explored not only because such an approach helps us to understand more fully the life of Ford himself but because in a profound sense
their story is the central theme of our century, a theme that reached a
peak of sorts in the 1920s.

Henry Ford did not worship his father. William Ford was a prosperous
farmer of pioneer Scots-Irish stock, well established on a largely self-
sufficient and profitable farm near Dearborn, Michigan, when Henry was
born in July 1863. The farm had its own saw mill and grist mill and machinery for making homespun of wool that was sheared from William
Ford's own sheep. There were, of course, many chores for a farm boy,
but Henry from earliest childhood seemed to loathe such work. From the
outset however, he seemed attracted to and useful in dealing with the machinery on the place. By all local accounts, he had a special mechanical
aptitude and a kind of intuitive mechanical logic. At an early age, for instance, he developed a passion for timepieces and spent considerable time
fixing things; that is, "tinkering"—a fine old Yankee tradition. Mechanization even in the years of Henry's boyhood, had become important to midwest farm life especially in more prosperous regions. Significant, too, was
the increasing industrialization occurring around the Ford farm in Wayne
County. But the boy's fascination with the machine and with mechanics
did not please his father who not only disliked the new industrial and
urbanized world growing up around him but also had other needs for the
boy's labor. At 16 the arguments between the two proved too much:
Ford's dislike of farming, his disagreements with his father, and the positive attraction of work in a machine shop led him to Detroit. It was
around this time, Ford himself tells us, that his dream of making something in quantity without reduction in quality began to take hold of his
imagination.

Evidence indicates not only little formal education in Henry Ford's life,
but also almost no use at all of books; further, there seems to be no sense
of any religious training or commitment. Even before Ford left home for
the first time in 1879, and though he was unaware of it, George Selden
had already applied for his celebrated patent for a gasoline-motored car.

(It would later play a significant role in the development of Ford's company.) Clearly, then, people—both in the United States and abroad—were responding to the possibilities inherent in new sources of energy. Ford himself experimented with steam engines, before he began to study the internal-combustion engine. But from a very early age his commitment was to engines and to production in quantity, not to the manufacture of luxury items for the few.

Ford did return to the farm for a period. His father, hoping to give him a worthwhile occupation that would provide independence and livelihood, bequeathed 40 acres of timberland to Henry. Ford used the opportunity to get married, to build himself a house, as well as a machine shop—and to avoid any farming whatsoever! By 1891 he had left the rural homestead for good—for a position as an engineer with the Edison Illuminating Company. He advanced rapidly and became chief engineer. In his spare time he worked at home on a small motor-driven vehicle of his own design. By 1893 the Duryea brothers successfully had demonstrated the first American gasoline automobile. Two years later, a meeting with Thomas A. Edison, perhaps Ford's only hero, encouraged him to continue work on his engine. By 1896 he had demonstrated his own first car; by 1899 the Company asked him to choose between his hobby and his job. Ford made his decision: a full dedication of his future to the automobile.

Detroit was taking young Ford seriously as a builder of automobiles and the nation as a whole was increasingly fascinated by the possibilities of the "horseless carriage." Yet Ford's first corporate venture, the Detroit Automobile Company was short-lived; within a year a new firm had been formed, the Henry Ford Automobile Company. But it, too, did not survive. Such detail is significant only because it documents Ford's intense difficulties in working under conditions in which he lacked complete control, and he vowed never again to be in a position where others could give him orders. Meanwhile, between 1899 and 1902, Ford had used his time well. He was becoming famous. He knew that one of the central propositions of the new age was self-advertisement and publicity, and that car speed was the way to it in the automobile business. Ford himself did not believe that high speed added to a car's value, but he was aware that breaking speed records made one a celebrity in the social world at large. Furthermore, such records cornered the attention of the rich and, notwithstanding his growing dream, they alone could afford this new toy—expensive as such handmade objects inevitably had to be. And when Ford began to win races at fashionable tracks such as that at Grosse Pointe, Michigan—at one event he reached the speed of 70 miles an hour—international publicity came to him. Finally, the famous driver Barney Oldfield broke all records at the Grosse Pointe course in the "999," a car Ford had built.

By 1903 the Ford Motor Company was a reality. Incorporated with basic capital investment of only $28,000 provided by a Detroit coal dealer (most of that in the form of shop, machinery, patents, contracts), the company managed to assemble an extraordinary group of business-men, engineers, etc. Within five years it had become one of the leading automobile manufacturers. There was little to distinguish the company's product. Ransome E. Olds had already pioneered in producing inexpensive cars. "Mass production" methods were available to all manufacturers. But, as Roger Burlingame tells us, the automobile of 1903 was still in an early experimental stage:

> no detail of engine or transmission was settled, no design of any part frozen; there was no standardization of tools or processes, and it was not until four years later that true interchangeability of parts even among supposedly identical cars made in a single factory was demonstrated. . . . In 1903 there were more than 25 American manufacturers of passenger cars and, with the exception of Olds, no manufacturer sold more than a few hundred cars each year. The automobile, therefore, was for the most part a strictly handmade article.

Meanwhile, the famous public fancy was increasingly captured by the possibilities of the automobile. There was clearly a rising demand although obviously most cars remained too expensive for the wide and hungering middle-class market. Woodrow Wilson in fact feared the motorcar mania because, he suggested in 1906, the automobile might very well bring socialism to America by inciting the poor to envy the rich!

In 1907, against "sound" advice, Ford announced his mission and his dream:

> I will build a motor car for the great multitude. It will be large enough for the family but small enough for the individual to run and care for. It will be constructed of the best materials, by the best men to be hired, after the simplest designs that modern engineering can devise. But it will be so low in price that no man making a good salary will be unable to own one—and enjoy with his family the blessing of hours of pleasure in God's great open spaces.

From the vantage point of the time it was issued, this extraordinarily simple statement is breathtaking in its implications. It is, in fact, a prediction of a new social order, an introduction to the world that was to be in the 1920s. It had enormous significance for the individual, the family, the mass society—and perhaps even in a sense proposed a serious redefinition of each. It hinted at a new definition of work and of production. It projected the likelihood of a new lifestyle. It implied a new kind of possible egalitarianism unheard of in the world's history—and it did all of this not in the name of needs, basic requirements of life, but in terms of possible pleasure: here, indeed, was a consumer vision of the world.

The creation of the Model T—the Tin Lizzie or the flivver as "she" was also called—is the climax of the story, the final convergence of Ford and history. It called for a series of key decisions, each Ford's fundamental responsibility no matter where the original idea came from. First, there was the matter of the huge new plant covering over 65 acres at Highland Park and the start of a major effort to cut back on dividends to stockholders, to plow some of the profits into new production. Second, there was the decision to make one car and only one car: "The way to make automobiles is to make one automobile like another automobile, to make them all alike, to make them come from the factory just alike—just like one pin is like another pin when it comes from the pin factory." In this decision, of course, Ford simply followed the well-established tradition of mass production as developed in the United States but never applied to the automobile industry. It meant the search for a car design suitable for mass use rather than one simply for cheap manufacture. Third, there was the need for low-cost production techniques. It resulted in the introduction of the famous moving assembly line, which involved an enormous financial commitment in terms of tools. The idea of continuous movement seemed simple enough and it rested on two seemingly simple principles: (1) the work must be brought to the worker and not the worker to the work, and (2) the work must be brought waist high so no worker would have to stoop. Taking almost *seven* years to perfect, the system at Highland Park was an established fact by 1914 and the production revolution had been wrought. Men and machine, through the central conveyor belt had been in effect merged into one gigantic machine. It made possible a dramatic reduction in the time required to produce a car. By 1920 one completed Model T rolled off the line every minute; by 1925 one every ten seconds. Production rose from 39,640 in 1911 to 740,770 in 1917. In 1920 every other car in the world was a Model T Ford.

By the early 1920s Ford commanded over 60 percent of the American output. Never before had such a complex mechanical process been devised or such production been possible. The achievement required a spectacular degree of synchronization, precision and specialization. Yet this in itself created newer problems that led to still further revolutionary consequences. For instance, such mechanization meant that little real skill was required by any particular worker. Only the top engineers and designers had to know anything about the total process. It suggested the possibility of an easily obtainable work force, but it had inherent drawbacks—in the form of the sheer monotony of the work, which led to an alarming turnover in the labor force.

With production methods already radically altered by 1914, Ford announced yet another daring step. He proposed a new wage scheme, a kind of profit-sharing (in advance of actual profits) in which the minimum for any class of work would be (under certain conditions) five dollars a day. At the same time, he reduced the working day from nine to eight hours. The key fact here was that in *no* sense was pay tied into productivity. There were conditions attached to the minimum-pay stipulation: certain minimum standards of conduct and behavior as outlined by the company; that is, standards by which the company judged men to be "good workers." Ford, in effect, doubled the wages of those "who could pass his sociology examination on the clean and wholesome life," stated John R. Commons, who reported on the operation of Ford's plan with considerable enthusiasm. Not only did the resultant stable work force please Ford, but he was able to show an increase in profits as well. And, as he was well aware, he had also made every workman a potential customer.

There was still one more remaining piece in the mosaic of a new order of work and life, production and consumption. Ford established a "Sociological Department" (later called the "Education Department") initially under the direction of an Episcopal minister. Its aim was paternalistic: to teach Ford's workers how to live the exemplary life, how to budget their new-found high wages, to encourage them to refrain from liquor or tobacco, to provide elemental lessons in hygiene and home management, to suggest steps helpful in the "Americanization" of the huge numbers of foreign-born in the company's work force. Under pressure from those who opposed such paternalism and charged Ford with spying or a special kind of tyranny, the scheme was eventually given up. But it was in effect replaced by the company's extraordinary trade school with perhaps more lasting effects. Nonetheless, it is important to see the social aspects of Ford's thinking about his world and to see how the whole dream finally produced a totally new order, the object of Ford's mission and dream, whether or not he fully realized it.

By the 1920s, then, Ford and his new system were being widely hailed as the American System. The miracles he had wrought in production and consumption made his name synonymous with American success. A national figure, his advice sought on all kinds of issues, Ford began to yield to pressures to go beyond the world of automobile manufacture. With war raging in Europe, he sailed off in 1915 on his famous and much maligned "peace ship," a venture in personal diplomacy by which he hoped to dramatize the crusade for peace. In 1918, at the urging of Woodrow Wilson, he ran for the Senate from Michigan and lost in a close contest in which voter fraud was later established. Ford's writings grew more voluminous on many subjects; he owned his own newspaper, the *Dearborn Independent* in which he conducted "his own" column (it was obvious that he increasingly relied on ghost-writers for much of his published work, although this dependence, of course, did not relieve him of responsibility for what was said in his name). The blatant anti-Semitic material published in the paper, for example, was one of the worst mistakes of his career. It cost him countless followers, and threatened him with court action as well.

Ford's national dreams in the 1920s led him to propose the development of Muscle Shoals (site of the later T.V.A.) under his own auspices. It was a grand scheme to bring industry to the countryside, and to decentralize industrial concentration while at the same time offering the advantages of industrial life to isolated rural areas. George Norris and others in the Senate blocked this private takeover. Ford continued to remain a much sought-after man politically. There was even talk of his running for the presidency in 1924, but he finally decided against encouraging such a move.

Meanwhile, in Ford's immediate world, potential disaster turned almost literally to gold. He had lost a stockholders' suit to compel the payment of special dividends. Company stockholders were more and more frightened by his apparent lack of interest in profits; the "socialism" of his Five-Dollar-a-Day wage scheme and the Sociology Department; the idea of profit-sharing; and the projected society of the common man. Ford was now determined to obtain complete control to carry out his plans. Taking a daring chance, he bought out all the stockholders. But he hated banks and bankers, and refused to borrow from them to achieve his goal of complete family ownership (something unique for an industrial corporation of that size and wealth). To obtain increased operating capital, he put a squeeze play on Ford dealerships. He pushed through a production speed-up, forced cars on unwilling dealers, threatened franchise losses if they didn't pay for cars, ordered or not, and forced them to go to *their* banks, leaving Ford free and clear and, finally in the 1920s, his own master.

The 1920s initially seemed to bring increased growth; Ford's organization weathered the 1921 depression better than any other company in the industry. Meanwhile, he continued his struggle for full integration in production. He sought to make his enterprise completely self-sufficient, acquiring raw materials and methods of transportation to achieve an even flow of raw materials into the processes of production and then an even flow of finished goods coming off the production line—a kind of universal and unceasing procession of the universal car, the Model T.

Ford was unable to create the final realization of his vision either on the technological side (with the system of complete integration) or the social or human side (with the reshaping of human lives by means of the Sociological Department) any more than he had been able to transcend Highland Park and later River Rouge. The wider regional or national dreams remained unfulfilled. But the impact of Ford's revolutionary mission continued to unfold in the United States and through the rest of the world. *Fordismus* had in fact created a 1920s different from what the decade would have been without it. Nevertheless, other forces had begun to threaten the basic assumptions on which Ford's radical revision of things had been partly based.

In 1927 the Ford Motor Company made its crucial decision to end production of the great Tin Lizzie, the Model T, and begin work on the replacement Model A. Ford had perhaps belatedly learned a fundamental fact about the new and affluent mass society he had done so much to shape if not to create: price and efficiency alone would not dictate consumer choice. Many of his competitors already knew as much. This new world of mass consumption was also a new world of mass communications in which national advertising and newer forms of national media (radio, film, the new journalism) helped play upon human needs and desires, hopes and fears. Ford was not familiar with the world of Bruce Barton; he did not sense the need for individual and even private fulfillment; he had not perceived that the common man did not want to *feel* common; mechanical perfection, although often desirable, was not enough.

Ironically, of course, it was profits (or the lack of them) that forced Ford's move. He himself was clearly uninterested in simply making money for its own sake; his whole career is a testament to that observation; his own simple and sometimes even austere way of life are sufficient evidence. But the Company did exist as part of a capitalist order and survival meant coming to grips with competition—no matter how much Ford might wish to rely on internal strengths and isolate himself from external dangers, and no matter how "false" for him were the values that led to the rejection of the cheap, ugly, durable, efficient, simple, and black Model T. Having in a sense created the 1920s, he failed to see what else had also been created.

The retreat of 1927—with the decision to end the Model T—was a fateful one. Except for some of the production miracles he contributed to during World War II, Ford's life was increasingly given over to a bitter series of struggles—within management and with labor, the latter often being bloody affairs. The seemingly progressive Henry Ford of 1907 to 1927 seemed unable even to understand the world of the 1930s. The Ford of the Five-Dollar-a-Day and the Sociological Department could not believe that workers really wanted unions and that strikes could ever achieve a real purpose.

Even in terms of the day-to-day operation of the business Ford could admit in 1933 that the new plant at River Rouge "is so big that it isn't any fun any more." Increasingly (again, ironically for the man who "made" the 20th century) he continued to turn to the past: new interest in rediscovered folk dancing; republication of McGuffy *Readers;* historical collecting for his special museum or for Greenfield Village, which was a kind of sentimental reconstruction of his own past, that past that he had run away from so many years ago. We face a strange portrait: the man who invented the future now carefully rediscovering the past.

Was there an answer to the fundamental problem his life so startlingly posed? Could the ideals projected by the phrases "mechanical perfection" and "common man" ever really be reconciled? Would even a totalitarian regime be able to achieve the perfect reconciliation? Ford tried and we have seen the outcome in the America of the 1920s. Yet the question continues to haunt us—partly because of how far Ford went, because we are still feeling the consequences of that accomplishment, because we still respond to the experiences of the 1920s with a continued sense of hope and fear.

*   *   *

When George Herman Ruth, Jr., died in 1947, the *New York Times* devoted more than two of its large eight-column pages to him. While each column clearly supplemented the other, they were vastly different in tone and method of presentation. The headline on the first read:

> Ruth, Baseball's Great Star and Idol of Children, Had a Career Both Dramatic and Bizarre/World-Wide Fame Won on Diamond/Even in Lands Where Game is Unknown, Baseball's Star Player Was Admired

There followed a traditional and detailed obituary, rich in sentiment of recalled moments of sorrow and joy as well as prosaic biographical fact, with strenuous effort to recount both significant achievements and re-capture an extraordinary personality. The second headline presented something else:

> Ruth Set Fifty-four Major League Records and Ten Additional Marks in American Circuit/Slugger Starred in 10 World Series/Ruth Set Major League Homer Mark on Total of 714—Hit Over 40 Eleven Seasons/Had Most Walks in 1923/All-Time Batting Great also Struck Out Most Times in Career Lasting 22 Years

The page itself had no prose story. It was simply a serial listing of all kinds of records, a careful selection of complete box scores of games important in Ruth's career, a carefully outlined and specially-headed box that listed his yearly salary from the first days in Baltimore ($600) in 1914 to the final year at Brooklyn ($15,000), for a lifetime total of $925,900.

In these two descriptions of the career of one of the great sports heroes of the 1920s (so often called "The Golden Age of American Sports"), it is perhaps possible to see two aspects of the enormous appeal spectator sports held for this decade. The mechanization of life generally, when combined with the mounting effort to rationalize all aspects of man's activities produced a particular middle-class delight in what could be measured and counted. (How fitting, then, were statistics on the "home run," with both numbers hit and distances travelled by the ball.) Americans could delight in the data that Ruth and other players provided. Athletic records provided a means of measuring achievement—success— in sport as such statistics did in other aspects of the mechanized and rationalized life. Salary figures most especially also assisted in judging success.

But no matter how fascinated a society may be with this mechanized aspect of the life that its athletes lead (and naturally transfer to the games they play or watch), it apparently was not enough. "Star," "Idol," "Dramatic," "Bizarre," were words featured in Ruth's official obituary, suggesting the public demands something more. Perhaps in an increasingly mechanized world more was called for. Grantland Rice, the sports writer, once wrote this about the great sports figures like Ruth:

> they had something more than mere skill or competitive ability. They also had in record quality and quantity that indescribable asset known as color, personality, crowd appeal, or whatever you may care to call it.

And if our sports mirror other aspects of our lives in a significant way, it might not be inappropriate to propose that what Rice suggests about sports figures was the lesson Ford had bitterly learned by 1927 when he discovered that his "common man" was no longer willing to settle for record-book cheapness, mechanical efficiency, and the like. People, he discovered, also wanted "style" (a favorite subject of Henry's son Edsel with whom old Henry constantly fought) in their cars; that is, "color, personality, crowd appeal."

Also in 1927, another major American corporation was enjoying huge success. Col. Jacob Ruppert's New York Yankees was the best baseball team in the world; there are those that claim it was the greatest baseball team of all time. Ruth hit 60 home runs that season, Lou Gehrig drove in 175 runs, the Yankees won the pennant by 19 games and swept the World Series against the Pittsburgh Pirates in four straight games. Babe Ruth earned $70,000 in 1927 for simply playing under contract with the Colonel. And Ruth was worth every penny of it to Ruppert's corporation that owned a gigantic stadium (often known as "The House that Ruth Built") with 70,000 seats to fill. This was big business for the Colonel and the Yankee organization—and seeing the Babe perform and produce was something big and special for the fans. It was more than a question of team loyalties, more than winning or losing the game. The *New York Times* account of one 1927 World Series game perhaps captures a little of this sentiment:

> his majesty the Babe had sent 64,000 folks in a paroxysm of glee by clubbing a screaming liner into the right field bleachers. . . . The big time came in the seventh. The Yanks had the game safely stowed away and the suspense was over . . . but the fans still stood up and demanded that Mr. Ruth get busy and do something for home and country. . . . "A homer,

Babe! Give us a homer!" ran the burden of the plea, and the big fellow pulled his cap on tighter, took a reef in his belt, dug spikes into the ground and grimly faced [the pitcher]. . . . Upward and onward, gaining speed and height with every foot, the little white ball winged with terrific speed until it dashed itself against the seat of the right-field bleachers, more than a quarter of the way up the peopled slope. And now the populace had its homer and it stood up and gave the glad joyous howl that must have rang out in the Roman arena of old. . . .

This description is itself revealing evidence of another pertinent aspect of the world of George Herman Ruth, Jr., perhaps an aspect helping to "make" him into the heroic Babe he would become. The new mechanized era of mass society was also one of mass communications as well, and the media demanded suitable material for copy. A new group of reporters and writers—Ring Lardner, Grantland Rice, Haywood Broun, John Kiernan among them—were ready exploiters of achievement and personalities, anxious to expand the traditional meaning of "news" for a whole series of publications, radio broadcasts, sometimes even films, which constantly demanded copy to feed a growing number of hungry consumers of this kind of news. They invented along the way an often brilliantly different and always special kind of rhetoric and style. Their unique prose delighted readers, sold more copies, appealed to more advertising agencies with products to sell—which was done through buying space in publications or time on the radio. "The Ruth is mighty and shall prevail," Haywood Broun wrote in 1923. It is still quoted by enthusiasts of the special sports' writing prose of this golden age of sports and of sports promotion.

The "mighty Ruth" of 1923 was born among the most lowly in a poor, third-floor apartment over a saloon in the waterfront section of Baltimore, Maryland in 1895. His parents, both children of immigrants, constantly struggled with poverty in a home described as an "angry, violent, desperately poor place, tense with all the frustrations of extreme poverty and shabbiness." Ruth confessed that he hardly knew them, and the major recollections of his father seem to be those of repeated and brutal beatings. "I was a bad kid," Ruth tells us in his autobiography. Unable to take care of their seven-year-old son and describing him as "incorrigible," his parents put Ruth in St. Mary's Industrial School in Baltimore. He would remain there—with occasional returns to the parental home—until he was 19.

The story of Ruth's upbringing reads like a stereotype of Victorian childhood among the lowliest urban poor, a kind of Dickensian horror tale without any cheerful relief, without any sentimental moments of escape from nightmare. The school stressed order and discipline; it tried to educate but clearly did little in the case of Ruth: he could barely read and write. There was no privacy. And there were few if any friends for Ruth who was the object of unkind verbal abuse because of his size and shape. After leaving school, he continued to have—and to retain almost until the end of his life—the most primitive of personal habits and the crudest of manners. There is little evidence that the strict Catholicism administered at St. Mary's had any significant effect on him. Ruth's excessive and obsessive interest in gambling, sex, and drinking appear to be schoolboy products he carried throughout his life. When at home, he lived near the harsh waterfront, mixing with rough sailors and bums. In effect he was an abandoned child. "I had a rotten start," he tells us, "and it took me a long time to get my bearings." But St. Mary's appears to have been of little help in getting those "bearings" and Ruth's life story leads one to wonder whether he ever really got them. Perhaps this upbringing accounts for what appears to be his genuine fondness for the countless number of children who idolized him during his great career and for his willingness to visit children in hospitals and homes throughout these later years.

St. Mary's did try to give Ruth a vocation. He was assigned to the shirt factory to learn the tailor's trade and the assignment itself indicates that the brothers noted no special potential or skills during his many years with them. But two positive things do emerge from his life at St. Mary's. First, he appeared to learn (as Ken Sobol, his ablest biographer tells us) that his "personal crudities" became "uproarious crowd-pleasers" in the presence of an audience. This was certainly important preparation for the "colorful" personality and always willing performer Ruth was to become. He would be eager to provide "good copy" and to delight fans off the field as well as on. (The shy, educated, craftsmanlike Lou Gehrig, for example, never learned to be a showman and never earned the kind of vast following or the money that Ruth did.) But St. Mary's most important gift was not any special training but a special opportunity. Baseball was about the only recreational outlet given to the boys at St. Mary's. So it was here that Ruth learned to play the game and to develop the enormous native skills, the coordination and power, that would make him the most spectacular ball player of his time.

Baseball had been a successful professional activity since the 1870s, and by 1903 it had become sufficiently developed and well organized to create the beginnings of a mass audience and the source of significant careers for many young men. For Ruth—a man without learning, traditional skills, or alternate route—it offered a miraculous escape from the treadmill of poverty. Baseball could provide him with effective social mobility. Ruth was certainly not the first nor the last of the children of fairly recent immigration and urban poverty to find their way to national status and success. But in many ways his career was among the most spectacular. One of St. Mary's Brothers recommended Ruth to the owner of the Baltimore club and he signed his first professional contract in 1914. That same year his contract was sold for $2,900 to the *Boston Red Sox* and with that organization he soon matured into a pitcher of rare ability.

While at Boston, Ruth also began to show remarkable prowess as a hitter. Baseball fans started to talk of his home runs and by 1919 he was more often in the outfield than on the pitching mound. The following year was a turning point in both Ruth's career and in the game itself. The Yankees purchased his contract for $100,000 and also guaranteed the $350,000 mortgage on the financially shaky Red Sox stadium. It was a record sum—but the Babe delivered with a record number of home runs and enthusiastic fan response. The winter of 1920–21, however, produced a scandal that rocked the entire structure of professional baseball. Gamblers had managed to buy the services of several members of the Chicago White Sox (subsequently labelled "Black Sox") to "throw" the 1919 World Series. The owners then reorganized baseball's business structure and appointed a stern federal judge, James Kenesaw Mountain Landis, as new high commissioner with unlimited power to assure the sanctity of the sport, though they still worried whether this reform would be enough, whether the fans would return. Many historians of the game attribute Ruth's brilliant performance during the following season as the most important factor in reviving spectator enthusiasm. Nine to ten million fans in the 1920s annually paid to see major league baseball.

By the end of the 1921 season (again to quote Sobol) more words were written about Ruth "than had ever been devoted to any other athlete in any single year. More people had watched him play than any other player. And more citizens of America, young and old, knew his name and could even recognize his homely round face than ever heard of Ty Cobb or John J. McGraw." Sports writers vied with one another to provide him with appropriate nicknames ("Sultan of Swat") but somehow he always remained "Babe" or "Bambino" (a change from "Nigger-Lips" he was often called at St. Mary's). He was the nation's great boy-child and Americans loved their big boy who often did so many childish things.

Whatever his achievements on the field, his growing contributions to the record books, the Babe also delighted millions of his countrymen by the sheer bigness of his affable personality and even by his awesome inability to curb his overwhelming appetites. Most Americans seemed to tolerate at least some of the indulgences of their big boy. No Ford or Barton, Ruth enjoyed spending money as well as earning it. An incorrigible gambler, and for large sums, he never seemed concerned about winning or losing. He loved expensive and fancy clothes. His interest in sex seemed limitless, and he frequented the better brothels even while in training or on tour with the ball club. His gluttony became equally legendary; he often overate and overdrank to the point of actual and severe physical illness. Like so many celebrities in our modern mechanized age, Ruth's frequent illness, physical collapse, even hospitalization became almost routine. The Babe's most publicized collapse and hospitalization occurred during spring training in 1925, and the public apparently accepted the official explanation that his illness was the result of influenza and indigestion; the real cause, it appears, was a serious case of syphilis. A much concerned public watched intensely for reports of Ruth's condition. One well-known sports writer called it "the stomach ache heard round the world."

Ruth was a heroic producer in the mechanized world of play. He was also an ideal hero for the world of consumption. Americans enjoyed the Babe's excess; they took comfort in the life of apparently enormous pleasures that Ruth enjoyed. Seldom if ever (even in this age of the rising popularity of Freudian thought) did they seem aware of what might exist behind this pattern of excess and illness. "Babe Ruth," Bill McGeehan said in 1925, "is our national exaggeration. . . . He has lightened the cares of the world and kept us from becoming overserious by his sheer exuberance."

Ruth found a way of making all of this pay; he made himself into a marketable product. In 1921 he hired an agent—or perhaps Christy Walsh snared Ruth. Walsh saw the vast possibilities in this extraordinary era of communications. He originally developed a ghostwriting syndicate especially in the sports field: writers who would sell articles and books under the name of a contracted sports figure. Increasingly the ghostwriter was becoming important in the public relations field. More and more distinguished Americans who wished to be heard or read (like Henry Ford), or whom the public would like hearing from (like Babe Ruth), contracted with professional writers to do the job. Soon there was no field without such literary talent and the number and range of such ventures increased markedly in the 1920s. Walsh provided Ruth with a great deal more than ghostwriting: as agent he worked out product endorsements for advertising; he solicited special assignments in movies (Ruth made a few but was never very successful in this field); he arranged and booked barnstorming tours during the off-season or even tours on the vaudeville circuits. In 1926, for example, Ruth played 12 weeks in vaudeville—in effect just appearing on stage so that fans in dozens of small towns could see their hero close up—for over $8,000 a week. This sum was considerably more than many notable show business people with special talents for entertaining were earning. Barnstorming around the country in 1927 and playing with hastily arranged teams of local citizens, Ruth added over $30,000 to his already sizeable income. Press agent activity was hardly new; neither was Walsh's. He served as a kind of business manager arranging investments, bank accounts, and the like in an effort to keep Ruth from squandering all his money. But what he did for Ruth added in a special 1920s way to the ballyhoo that promoted a professional athlete into a celebrity of ever exaggerated proportions.

The year 1925 marked a low point in Babe Ruth's career and few believed he could recover. His "stomach ache heard round the world" was followed later the same season by failures to maintain training and to perform effectively. Manager Miller Huggins, in exasperation, fined him $5,000 for "misconduct off the ball field," and his decision was upheld by Col. Jacob Ruppert, the Yankee owner. Ruth, with his own special arrogance, had originally taken the whole thing as a joke but now began to pay greater attention to his work, the management of his affairs, and possibly even to his image. His exceptional comeback in the 1926 season became, according to Sobol, a "symbol of continuity." Ruth was 30 and no longer a boy; he had suffered a kind of depression and the fact that he could recover gave the whole country a sense of hope. Increasingly, the writers waxed sentimental over him and his generosity to the kids. (Ruth himself may have begun to believe the new image the writers had projected of him; he even began to color his days at St. Mary's in terms of kindnesses done him by some of the Brothers.) Increasingly, the press transformed him into an older, less boyish "idol of the American boy." They began to forget the excesses and the crudities. His relationship with Mrs. Claire Hodgson may have also contributed to the change in his life. He married her in 1929 after the death of his estranged first wife. He paid greater attention to training, developing a shrewder interest in investments. The new Mrs. Ruth provided structure and order in his life; a tighter rein and necessary stability. It is difficult to avoid speculating on whether she was not providing as well the kind of love that Ruth never received from his mother so long ago in Baltimore.

But the Bambino of the 1930s and 1940s—the sentimentalized and reformed "idol" of American youth—is not the hero of the 1920s. Historian William E. Leuchtenberg may be somewhat unkind in describing him in 1934 as "a pathetic figure, tightly corseted, a cruel lampoon of his former greatness" when he took off his Yankee uniform for the last time. But Ruth by now was out of place and out of time. He might be transformed into a sentimental figure by sentimental writers. Perhaps the times called for that kind of hero. But for the 1920s he was the perfect creation for an increasingly mechanized world that still hungered as well for the extraordinary personality, that tired merely of the Model T automobiles and yet was also appreciative of their virtues—wanting only something more, something bigger than life.

What kind of personality did Ruth bring to the era he so aptly characterized? And what was the price to himself and to the kind of society that enjoyed and admired "our national exaggeration?" What does it say about our values and his values, about the tragic set of conditions and circumstances that may lurk beneath the surface of his life and as well as of the life of his nation in the 1920s?

One series of probing questions, at least, is suggested in a passage from the work of a great Dutch historian who made a significant effort to come to an understanding of American history and especially the current American culture during the First World War. He is writing, in effect, about the onset of the 1920s and is considering what will follow. I do not know whether or not he saw Ruth during his own visit to this country during the Babe's comeback year (1926) but he most certainly must have heard about him. It would be interesting to listen to him discuss this view with special reference to Ruth's career. Perhaps we can do it for him:

> One of the preeminent elements of modern civilization is sport, in which intellectual and physical culture meet. In it too mechanization seems to attain the opposite of its purposes. Gregarious modern man tries to save his individualism, as it were, in sport. But sport is not just the strictly physical development of skills and strength; it is also the giving of form, the stylizing of the very feeling of youth, strength, and life, a spiritual value of enormous weight. Play is culture. Play can pass over into art and rite, as in the dance and in sacred stage presentations. Play is rhythm and struggle. The competitive ideal itself is a cultural value of high importance. Play also means organization. But now, as a result of the modern capacity for very far-reaching organization and the possibilities created by modern transportation, an element of mechanization enters sport. In the immense sport organizations like those of football and baseball, we see free youthful forces and courage reduced to normality and uniformity in the service of the machinery of rules of play and the competitive system. If we compare the tense athlete in his competitive harness with the pioneer hunter and the Indian fighter, then the loss of true personality is obvious.
>
> Johan Huizinga
America

12

The Triumph of
Political Caution

FRANKLIN D. ROOSEVELT
NORMAN THOMAS
ROBERT TAFT

by James T. Patterson
Brown University

In the midst of the Great Depression, Socialist Party leader Norman Thomas secured an appointment with President Franklin D. Roosevelt at the White House. Thomas was angry at the effects of New Deal agricultural policy on southern tenant farmers, and he became so agitated that Roosevelt grew impatient. "Oh, Norman," he shot back, "I'm a damn sight better politician than you are." Thomas answered, "Certainly, Mr. President. You are on that side of the table, and I'm on this." Roosevelt replied, "I know the South and there is arising a new generation of leaders in the South, and you've got to be patient."

Thomas was right about sorry conditions in the rural South. But like many other prophets he was too principled to be a successful democratic politician, and in 1940 he drifted still further from the ideological mainstream by staunchly opposing American aid to England. By the end of the decade his Party had foundered so badly that the humorist James Thurber was moved to publish an apt cartoon. It showed a woman looking up from her newspaper and asking her husband, "What ever happened to the Socialist Party?"

Robert A. Taft of Ohio, seven years younger than Roosevelt and five years younger than Thomas, was hardly known outside his home state until 1939, when he rose from freshman Senator to status as a leading contender for the Republican presidential nomination of 1940. As a Hoover Republican, Taft opposed much of Roosevelt's New Deal, and he was so outspoken and impolitic in his criticism that he annoyed middle-of-the road politicians. Like Thomas, he compounded his alienation from the center by attacking the administration's drift toward intervention in Europe. Branded as a reactionary and an isolationist, he failed to get the nomination in 1940—and again in 1948 and 1952.

There were no personal tragedies here. Taft died in 1953 as Senate majority leader and at the peak of his political influence, while Thomas died 15 years later honored for his lifetime of struggle for social justice. But neither man was willing to support most of the practical compromises that made Roosevelt the supreme political mover of his times, to accept the growing power of interest groups in American society, or to approve the interventionist foreign policy which captured the minds of their generation. Roosevelt's triumphs showed that the road to political success lay in pursuing an activist course abroad and in following a slightly left of center path at home. This practical route, less consistent and less "principled" than the roads offered by the Left under Thomas or the Right under Taft, often seemed circuitous and devious. Still, it led to the overthrow of fascism abroad and to modest reform at home. And even a generation later it seemed such a sensible middle way to American voters that spokesmen of the Left or Right remained in an unhappy minority.

*   *   *

"I know that traditionally every American mother believes her son will one day be President," Sara Delano Roosevelt remarked late in her life. "But much as I love tradition and believe in perpetuating good ones, that is one to which I never happened to subscribe. What was my ambition for him? Very simple— . . . to grow to be like his father, straight and honorable, just and kind, an outstanding American."

Sara Roosevelt spoke truthfully. If she had had her way, her son Franklin Delano would never have sullied himself in politics. The daughter of Warren Delano, a wealthy merchant, Sara was an attractive, strong-willed woman of 26 when she married James Roosevelt, a widower twice her age, in 1880. Franklin, who was to be her only child, arrived in 1882, and for the next 60 years, Sara loved, attended, and overprotected him.

Franklin did not seem to mind, for his early life was idyllic. The family home in Hyde Park, New York, a comfortable estate on the Hudson River, was well-staffed with servants and nurses, for James Roosevelt was himself a rich businessman. As a man of leisure, James also had ample time to spend with his son, both at Hyde Park, where young

Franklin was free to roam the woods and to frolic on the river, at Campobello Island off the coast of New Brunswick, where the boy developed his passion for sailing and the lore of the sea, and on wide-ranging travels in the United States and Europe. Blessed with every material comfort, and educated at home by tutors until he was 14 years old, Franklin had a childhood singularly free of tension or trauma.

Four years at Groton School, which Franklin entered in 1896, widened his horizons, for the headmaster, the Reverend Endicott Peabody, developed in impressionable boys a Christian commitment to duty and service. "As long as I live," Roosevelt wrote 40 years later, "the influence of Dr. and Mrs. Peabody means and will mean more to me than that of any other people next to my father and mother." Groton also eased Franklin's path into Harvard in 1900, where he presided over the *Crimson*, the college paper.

But his eight years at Groton and Harvard did not give him much real direction, and few people could have predicted that this amiable, well-mannered, and sociable young man possessed elements of greatness. After leaving Harvard he entered Columbia Law School. But he performed spottily, and he left school (having passed the bar exams) before completing his degree. Taking a job as a clerk in a New York law firm, he showed much less interest in his work than in the politics of his "cousin Theodore," who had become President in 1901. For Franklin the six years after leaving Harvard in 1904 were a moratorium, a time when he drifted, awaiting the vocation which would give purpose to his life.

In 1910, Roosevelt began to find himself. He was then 28. Acceding to the entreaties of Hyde Park area Democrats, he agreed to run for the state senate. (Though admiring TR, Franklin followed his father, and was a Democrat). At first he appeared to stand little chance of election in a traditionally Republican district. The young candidate also seemed too aristocratic for democratic politics, especially because he had a disconcerting habit of tilting back his head when challenged and looking down his nose through his pince-nez. But he was a handsome, strapping six-footer, he worked hard, and he proved flexible enough to learn the arts of campaigning. And because Democrats ran well in 1910, Roosevelt won by more than 1,000 votes.

During the next ten years he moved rapidly to the top ranks of the national Democratic Party. Though some regular politicians continued to find him pompous and cold—"awful arrogant fellow, that Roosevelt," one commented—he quickly established himself as an opponent of bossism, an advocate of conservation, and a proponent of progressive ideas. Economic competition, he said in 1912, "has been shown to be useful up to a certain point and no further. Cooperation must begin where competition leaves off." In 1912 he campaigned hard for Woodrow

Wilson and was rewarded with the post of Assistant Secretary of the Navy. Working in Washington for the next eight years, Roosevelt gained valuable political and administrative experience, as well as sufficient recognition to win the vice-presidential nomination in 1920 by acclamation. "When parties can pick a man like Franklin Roosevelt," Walter Lippmann wrote, "there is a decent future in politics."

The next summer Roosevelt contracted polio which paralyzed him from the waist down for the rest of his life. But with characteristic drive he refused to retire. Instead, he supported New York Governor Alfred Smith in his quests for the presidency and in 1928 reluctantly accepted the Democratic nomination for Governor of New York. As a popular and successful Governor for the next four years he gathered enough support to win the presidential nomination. With Herbert Hoover leading a demoralized Republican Party, Roosevelt swept into the White House.

The new President clearly deserved the label "progressive" many supporters gave him. His support of Wilson, and then of Smith, had long stamped him as a member of the reformist wing of the Party, and his gubernatorial proposals, including unemployment insurance, conservation, and public power, placed him among the nation's most activist political leaders. Yet during the campaign Roosevelt remained vague about his "New Deal," and he even lambasted Hoover for failing to balance the budget. Americans, he said, must drop the idea that "we ought to center control of everything in Washington as rapidly as possible." Many reformers accordingly regarded Roosevelt as a pale imitation of Hoover. "Progressivism today, if we are to revaluate the term," John Chamberlain wrote in September, "must either mean Norman Thomas or [Communist candidate] William Z. Foster, ineffectual though one or both of them may be."

Critics like Chamberlain continued to be alarmed by many of Roosevelt's policies in 1933. Instead of attempting to nationalize the banks, the President merely declared a bank holiday and gradually reopened the more solvent banks. In an ultra-conservative move, he demanded successfully that Congress cut the salaries of both veterans and government workers. Progressives were particularly distressed that the National Recovery Administration (NRA), which established codes of fair competition to improve business conditions, exempted monopolies from antitrust prosecutions. On these three issues the President found himself to the right not only of most progressives but of many moderates in Congress.

Other critics complained that Roosevelt was inconsistent, that his New Deal lacked any coherent ideological principles. They noted accurately that he used one hand to slash government salaries while using the other to authorize his relief director, Harry Hopkins, to pump billions into the relief of unemployment. Though the President permitted the

NRA to protect big business from prosecution, he turned around in 1935 and angrily denounced capitalists as "economic royalists." Roosevelt readily conceded that he was a practical politician, not a doctrinaire thinker. His philosophy, he told reporters, was that of a "Christian and a Democrat." When asked for the rationale behind the Tennessee Valley Authority, he replied that it was "neither fish nor fowl, but whatever it is, it will taste awfully good to the people of the Tennessee Valley." Such statements, while frank, did not satisfy those critics who demanded that the New Deal show a more coherent philosophy.

Other observers grumbled that the New Deal stopped far short of providing the national direction the country needed. The NRA, for instance, let the dominant interests—usually big business—form most of the industrial codes, and it lacked the power to compel employers like Henry Ford to agree to codes once they were established. The Agricultural Adjustment Administration, which offered subsidies to commercial farmers who cut production, also emphasized decentralized decision-making. National referenda, not government blueprints, determined crop reductions, and farmers who refused to comply with quotas established by the referenda, while denied subsidies, still benefitted from the higher prices which ensued from nationwide declines in supply. Right-wing critics were fond of calling the New Deal "fascistic" (or, oddly, communistic), but the Left was far more accurate in pointing to Roosevelt's faith in decentralization, states' rights, and voluntarism.

To many people in the 1930s and thereafter Roosevelt appeared to be the champion of the so-called forgotten man. But here, too, critics correctly recognized inadequacies in his programs. His upbringing at Hyde Park, Groton, and Harvard had given him little opportunity to perceive the sufferings of factory workers, tenant farmers, or blacks. Indeed, Roosevelt paid much more attention to agricultural problems and conservation than he did to urban or labor questions. During his more than 12 years as President he refused to support a federal bill outlawing lynching, the primary goal of the NAACP at the time, and he recommended no civil rights legislation. His Social Security program excluded millions of citizens and allowed states to determine the level of payments to the blind, crippled, and dependent. His understanding of labor problems was so limited that he waited until the last minute—when it made little difference—to support the National Labor Relations Act which guaranteed meaningful collective bargaining. As Secretary of Labor Frances Perkins correctly put it, "all the credit for it belongs to Robert Wagner."

The most persuasive critique of Roosevelt attacks his failure to end the depression. By early 1937 prosperity showed signs of returning, but all indicators lagged behind figures for 1929, and when Roosevelt cut federal spending in 1937, the economy again plunged sharply. Not until the heavy defense spending of the war years (federal expenditures approximated $3 billion in 1932, $9 billion in 1939, and $98 billion in 1945) did the country pull out of the depression. In retrospect, it is clear that New Deal fiscal policy was far from radical, and that Roosevelt himself must bear much of the blame for the caution his administration displayed.

Though these criticisms suggest much that was unwise or unfortunate, they tend to overlook four important qualifications. First, they underplay Roosevelt's superb skill as a politician. Especially in his first term he showed excellent timing, as well as a willingness to use his powers of patronage in dealing with Congress. He proved an inspiring public speaker. Though an untidy administrator, he possessed the charisma to attract bright subordinates to Washington, and the openness (some called it the guile) to keep them inspired. He kept his promise, made in the inauguration of 1933, to "do something."

Second, the view of Roosevelt as conservative or ideologically incoherent simply ignores not only the consistent activism of his administration, but also the humanitarian premises of his major programs. Unlike Hoover, Roosevelt refused to let such dogmas as states' rights, limited government, or balanced budgets obliterate his concern for the lives of ordinary people. Accordingly, much of his legislation, especially relief spending, social security, and the TVA, were innovative measures that assisted millions of Americans, including blacks and other poor people, in memorable ways. He proved at least willing to give Wagner his way in writing a landmark piece of labor legislation, and indeed to encourage militant labor leaders like John L. Lewis to begin massive drives for members. When radicals complain that Roosevelt was a conservative whose only achievement was to "save capitalism," they forget that he was a little left of center, and that in preserving the system, he also reformed it.

Third, ideologues of the Right and Left fail to appreciate the power of entrenched institutions. One of these was the Supreme Court, which struck down the NRA and the AAA and which made Roosevelt move cautiously in formulating social security. Another was the structure of political parties, which no American president has been able to recast along clear ideological lines. Roosevelt had to deal with unsympathetic politicians of his own Party, in Washington and at every level of administration. And the President had to be especially gingerly in handling Congress, which heeded dominant interest groups and which obstructed efforts to change racial or economic relationships. "I did not choose the tools with which I must work," he explained to a group advocating civil rights legislation. "The southerners by reason of the seniority role in Congress . . . occupy strategic places on most of the Senate and House Committees. If I come out for anti-lynching, they will block every bill. . . . I just can't take that risk."

Finally, the very popularity of Roosevelt's programs suggested not only that millions of Americans appreciated his efforts, but also that he was pursuing the politics of the possible. The depression, far from radicalizing people, shocked them. It spawned fear and desperation, not the ideological critique of capitalism that consistent radicals longed for. Instead of destroying values of individualism, it merely set them temporarily aside and led people to search for security. Roosevelt could have gotten higher appropriations for relief and public works. He could have moved more purposefully to assist labor and small farmers. But any effort to promote socialistic policies would have clashed with dearly held American values about the role of the state, the primacy of the individual, and the virtues of decentralization. In pursuing the left-of-center course that he did Roosevelt modified these values but he also appealed to them. Because he became unprecedentedly popular in doing so, it is hard to argue that any alternative course, either of the principled Right or Left, would have succeeded.

If Roosevelt seemed circuitous in developing domestic policies, he was simply devious in his handling of international affairs. Temperamentally he was an activist, and ideologically he had been a Wilsonian internationalist. But politically he was super-cautious. In 1932 he waffled about the League of Nations in order not to alienate the Hearst newspapers, and in 1933 he effectively torpedoed the London Economic Conference, which was struggling, albeit clumsily so, to improve international economic relations. He also acquiesced in so-called neutrality legislation, which forced America to deny munitions to all belligerents, whether aggressors or innocent. In 1938, when British Prime Minister Neville Chamberlain agreed to meet Hitler at Munich, the President apparently approved the policy of appeasement. "Good man," he cabled Chamberlain enigmatically.

Roosevelt had grounds for caution. His primary goal remained to alleviate the depression, and he shrank from divisive confrontations with congressmen, who strongly favored neutrality laws. Like many Americans, he also hoped that the European democracies could contain Germany. Even after war broke out in September 1939, Americans continued to dream that Hitler could be stopped. During this time of tension Roosevelt successfully secured repeal of the arms embargo so that American supplies could flow to the Allies. But he also told the country, "I have said not once but many times, that I have seen war and that I hate war. I say that again and again. . . . As long as it remains within my power to prevent, there will be no black-out of peace in the United States."

This policy—sympathy to the Allies, but not American boys in battle—seemed sufficient until the spring of 1940. But Hitler then dispelled doubts about his military power by sweeping through the low countries and France. Alarmed, Roosevelt warned in June that America would "extend to the opponents of force the material resources of this nation. . . . Signs and signals call for speed—full speed ahead." He also supported America's first peace-time draft. But he continued to move very carefully, delaying several months before swapping Britain 50 overage destroyers in return for the leasing of some British bases to America. Before the 1940 presidential election he offered non-interventionists one final, extreme assurance. "I have said this before," he proclaimed in Boston, "but I shall say it again and again and again: Your boys are not going to be sent into any foreign wars."

The election safely behind him, Roosevelt called for a program of lend-lease, under which America would lend equipment to Britain and Canada. But again he avoided explaining the ultimate implications of such a policy: that to protect these shipments the United States might have to engage its naval vessels against German submarines. Gradually, of course, that is what happened, for America began radioing the position of German submarines to British warships. When a German submarine fired at an American destroyer in September, Roosevelt failed to tell the people of the destroyer's tracking activities, and ordered the fleet to "shoot on sight." Thereafter, the United States was involved in an undeclared shooting war against Germany on the Atlantic.

Was Roosevelt wise in pursuing a policy that made war with Germany likely, if not inevitable? Many critics thought not. Hitler, they argued, lacked the military technology—and probably the desire—to wage war on the United States. The Atlantic Ocean gave the western hemisphere free security. Others argued that Germany's invasion of the Soviet Union in June 1941, which left Britain safe from attack, made American involvement unnecessary. Indeed, the Soviet Union stopped Germany by 1943, a year before America landed troops on the continent of Europe. These arguments, however, overlook the revulsion many Americans were coming to feel by 1941 for the uniquely barbaric character of Hitler's regime. Roosevelt and his advisers, sharing this revulsion, could not coolly observe European events from the perspective of *Realpolitik.* And to argue that Hitler and Stalin should have been left to destroy each other, however appealing to Americans in the Cold War years, is to forget that in 1941 Hitler appeared unstoppable. In retrospect American military involvement against Germany seems to have been the surest way of destroying fascism and restoring democratic governments to western Europe.

The broader question of course concerns Roosevelt's means to that end. Should he have been more open and forthright? On this point his defenders insist that neither Congress nor the American people favored involvement in the war at any time prior to the attack on Pearl Harbor, that the President had to proceed very slowly lest he play into the hands of the isolationists. But Roosevelt was not only cautious, but also devious and deceiving. His lack of candor was probably unnecessary, for Americans would hardly have rejected him in the election of 1940, nor would they have disapproved of lend-lease. More important, his half-truths, reprehensible in themselves, set a dangerous precedent later chief executives were to abuse badly. But fortunately for his reputation, the recklessness of Japan and the greed of Germany made his deceptions seem understandable and even justified in the light of history. By contrast, the noninterventionists—men like Thomas and Taft—seemed naive and ill-informed. Such are the virtues of circumspection in the handling of public affairs.

*   *   *

What is the making of an American socialist? For Morris Hillquit, an immigrant who became a prominent socialist theoretician between the 1890s and his death in 1933, it was largely an intellectual matter of imbibing teachings in Marxism. For Eugene Debs, the long-time Socialist Party leader, it was a more evolutionary development from craft unionism to industrial unionism to socialism. And for William ("Big Bill") Haywood, a miner and leader of the Industrial Workers of the World, it was also a process in escalating radicalism, which led to his expulsion from the Socialist Party in 1913 when he urged his followers to try "a little sabotage in the right place at the right time." For these men, and for many other Americans early in the 20th century, socialism was a growing popular movement. Debs, the Party's presidential candidate in 1912, received 897,000 votes, or 6 percent of all ballots cast.

Norman Thomas was neither immigrant nor blue collar worker, and his conversion to socialism was gradual. Born in 1884, two years after Roosevelt, he grew up in a happy middle-class family in Marion, Ohio. His father, like both his grandfathers, was a Presbyterian minister, and Norman led an unexceptional small town existence. For a time he even delivered newspapers for Warren G. Harding's Marion *Star*. Though Thomas' parents were not rich—Norman needed the financial help of an uncle to attend Princeton University in 1902—the boy suffered no real hardships. Like Roosevelt, he grew up knowing little about the lives of poor people.

Thomas' moderate views also changed little during the next decade. After graduating from Princeton as valedictorian of his class, he served two years as a settlement house worker in New York City, travelled around the world, and received his training for the ministry from Union Theological Seminary in New York. Tall, lean, articulate, attractive, Thomas could well have taken a post in a fashionable Presbyterian parish, but he chose in 1911 to work with immigrants, primarily poor Italian-Americans, in East Harlem. Though this decision suggested his social concerns, the 27-year-old Thomas was then a progressive, not a radical. In college he had admired Princeton's president, Woodrow Wilson, and he was not one of the 897,000 who voted for Debs in 1912. As late as 1915 Thomas conceded in a letter to his Princeton classmates that his education "really began" when he experienced "life here in this district." But he added, "Looking back on the ten years since we left Princeton I almost marvel to think how happy they have been."

Thomas' conversion to socialism, which developed after 1914, stemmed partly from the writings of Christian socialists like Walter Rauschenbusch. "Insofar as any one book or series of books made me a Socialist," he said later, "it was probably [by] Walter Rauschenbusch." More important were Thomas' daily experiences in East Harlem, which turned him slowly away from capitalism. As late as 1916, he voted for Wilson, but America's drift toward preparedness led him to join the Fellowship of Reconciliation, a Christian pacifist group, by the end of the year. "War and Christianity," he said, "are incompatible." When America entered World War I in 1917, Thomas converted to socialism. "The only hope for the future," he wrote, "lies in a new social and economic order which demands the abolition of the capitalistic system. War itself is only the most horrible and dramatic of the many evil fruits of our life which exalt competition instead of cooperation." Thomas left the parish ministry in 1918 and joined the Socialist Party he would lead in six successive presidential campaigns from 1928 through 1948. At the time he was 33 years old, highly effective as a minister, happily married, and the father of five children. Only his wife's inheritance enabled him to manage financially over the years.

During the next decade Thomas pursued a variety of activities. He served as an editor for *The Nation,* as editor of the short-lived *New York Leader,* and for most of the period as co-executive director of the League for Industrial Democracy, an outgrowth of the Intercollegiate Socialist Society. As a Socialist nominee he ran for Governor of New York in 1924, for Mayor of New York in 1925 and 1929, and for the New York Senate in 1926. He also spoke in support of striking workers at Passaic, New Jersey, in 1926, where he was arrested on a charge of inciting to riot. Adhering steadfastly to support of democratic socialism, Thomas was quick to criticize the dictatorial features of Russian communism. "The establishment of a fellowship of free men," he wrote as early as September 1918, "does not justify—indeed it cannot be secured by—a proletarian dictatorship which denies suffrage and freedom of discussion to a middle class minority." And he repeatedly supported the civil rights of blacks. Racial discrimination, he said in 1921, "is a practical denial of the fundamental principles of brotherhood and Christianity."

Well before Thomas became the perennial Socialist nominee for President, his Party had begun to decline. Many Socialists defected when their

Party opposed American entrance into World War I, and those who took a strong anti-war position were prosecuted by government authorities. Debs, one of those jailed, garnered 915,320 votes for the presidency in 1920, but the size of this total, the highest in Party history, stemmed in part from sympathy for the still-imprisoned Debs, who was by then an almost saint-like figure. Indeed, his percentage of votes, 3.5, was well below the 6 percent he achieved in 1912. (Women, enfranchised by the 19th Amendment, voted in mass for the first time in 1920.) The end of large-scale immigration from eastern and central Europe after 1914 further deprived the Party of potential new blood, while many of the most militant radicals turned to communism. Above all, the surface prosperity of the 1920s inhibited recruitment of workers. When Debs died in 1926, he left the Party without any commanding leader. So Thomas' 1928 nomination as Socialist Party presidential candidate came almost by default. The ascendancy of Thomas, a middle-class socialist and pacifist, to the position held by Debs, a symbol of the militant working class, suggested not only the changing character of the Party but also the weakness of class-conscious politics amid the Republicanism of the 1920s.

At first Norman Thomas could do little to improve his Party's fortunes. In 1928 he received only 267,420 votes, over 100,000 less than Debs had attracted as far back as 1904. Despite vigorous organizational activity in the next two years, the Party failed to win new left-wing and liberal support. The "people's lawyer," Clarence Darrow, quipped in 1931 that he could not become a member "because I'd be too lonely." A year later the writer John Dos Passos found socialism too mild and ineffective. Joining the Socialists, he said, would have "just about the same effect on anybody as drinking a bottle of near beer."

As Dos Passos spoke, however, the nation was struggling through its third year of hard times, and socialist ideas began to get a wider hearing. During and after his 1928 campaign, Thomas avoided traditional Marxist rhetoric about the class struggle. "There is no sense in our talking revolution," he said. Instead, he called eloquently for a host of immediate reforms within the framework of capitalism. These included increased federal spending for public works, a constitutional amendment prohibiting child labor, federal old-age pensions and unemployment insurance financed by more progressive income and corporate taxes, lower tariffs, pacifism, and an end to American imperialism in the Philippines and the Caribbean. Under Thomas, the Socialist Party revealed what its members already knew for many years—that it was neither extremist nor revolutionary. It offered rather a galaxy of advanced reforms.

When Thomas ran again in 1932, he succeeded in attracting many middle-class intellectuals to his standard. These included philosopher John Dewey, pacifist editor Oswald Garrison Villard, black leader

W. E. B. Du Bois, and theologian Reinhold Niebuhr. As in 1928, he attacked Hoover and the Republicans, but he fired equally hard at the Democrats, "the party which debars Negroes from the polls in the South and makes it difficult for white workers to vote by poll tax." Roosevelt, he said, was "playing ball with Tammany Hall" and "parading under the false colors of liberalism." He described Roosevelt as a "nice person who once graduated from Harvard, has a good radio voice, and is as sincere as the old party politics will permit." Thomas did not expect to win, and he did not, polling but 884,781 of the nearly 40 million ballots. But because this was more than three times the total he had received in 1928, socialists retained some hope for the future.

During the next four years Norman Thomas occasionally offered faint praise of Roosevelt and the New Deal. The President, he conceded in 1933, "has courage, political shrewdness, a liberal point of view, and a willingness to act." Thomas approved of the Securities and Exchange Commission, the Home Owners Loan Corporation, and the TVA. He applauded the effort under Section 7-a of the NRA to guarantee workers decent wages and hours. In 1936 he admitted that Roosevelt was "probably as liberal as any capitalist administration in America is likely to be." As in earlier years Thomas continued to sound as much like a left-wing social gospeller as a Marxian socialist.

But the New Deal still left Thomas discouraged and critical. Like other left-wing spokesmen, he demanded more spending for relief and public works, generous social security, progressive taxation, and a program of racial justice. The NRA, socialists argued, could "easily become the framework of a Fascist state." Thomas grew especially angry at Roosevelt's close association with Democratic bosses like Frank Hague, who deported Thomas from Jersey City in 1938 rather than permit him to speak. The New Deal, he argued, was "hopelessly inadequate" and a "grand adventure in opportunism."

The harmful effects of the AAA on southern tenant farmers drew Thomas' most concerted fire. "No satirist ever penned such an indictment of a cruel and lunatic society," he charged, "as AAA's author, who destroyed food-stuffs while millions were still on breadlines." Thomas, no celebrator of the agrarian life, had little enthusiasm for plans to help tenants buy small plots and set up on their own. Rather, he hoped in the long run for an agrarian socialism somewhat along the lines of the Israeli *kibbutzim.* In the short run, he helped organize a tenant farmers' strike in the South, while lobbying tirelessly in the hope of getting Agriculture Secretary Henry Wallace to guarantee croppers a portion of the bonus payments provided from Washington.

Thomas' work for the tenant farmers symbolized his role during the 1930s: enlightened, humanitarian, eloquent—and unsuccessful. Neither Wallace nor Roosevelt paid him much attention, and the strikes, which were suppressed, left union leaders on company blacklists. Later, Thomas could console himself by noting that the New Deal ultimately embraced some socialist ideas. But at the time his Party suffered heavy losses in Party membership and voting support: Thomas got but 187,342 votes in 1936 (.4 percent of the vote) and 99,557 in 1940. Many problems contributed to this decline, including intra-party feuding as well as divisive tactics by communists and Trotskyites. But Thomas' message failed primarily because Roosevelt's left-of-center policies absorbed many liberal and left-wing elements which had flirted with radical solutions in 1932. What destroyed socialism, Thomas conceded later, "was Roosevelt in a word. You don't need anything more."

Because many American socialists opposed getting involved in both world wars, it is easy to describe them as isolationists or as absolute pacifists. But Norman Thomas, while joining these critics of war, fit neither label after World War I. He offered qualified support for the League of Nations in the 1920s, supported American participation in the World Court, and sought to find means of promoting international cooperation. He was a pole apart from narrow nationalists who thought always of America First.

By the mid-1930s Thomas had also become so aroused to the potential dangers of fascism that he renounced any faith in absolute pacifism. Thus he urged the administration to permit economic aid to the Spanish loyalists. "Victory by the Spanish fascists," he said, would "menace the peace of the world by the encouragement it would give to fascist aggression." Thomas even helped organize the so-called Debs Column of volunteers to assist the loyalists. This position, which appalled many of his long-time pacifist admirers, showed that Thomas, like many other American leftists in the 1930s, was aware early of the threat posed by European fascism. The Munich accord, he noted a year later, was a "logical kind of deal for capitalist powers."

Even before 1939, however, it was clear that Norman Thomas was more of a pacifist than an anti-fascist. In opposing American sanctions against Italy during the Italo-Ethiopian war, he insisted that "fascism will be brought to the countries which thus far have accepted it, more definitely through war than through any other means." The fighting that broke out on the continent in 1939, he said, merely revealed the same "age-old European power conflicts plus new imperialist struggles for oil, coal, spheres of influence and investment, and markets for exclusive trade." Thomas publicly sympathized with the Allies, but he sought desperately to stop the trend toward American involvement. For Thomas this meant appearing on platforms with conservative members of the America First organization; it meant approving the neutrality laws; it meant opposing the draft and lend-lease; and it meant adopting the "Fortress America" argument that the United States was inevitably safe from foreign invasions. When warned of the possibility of Nazi aggression, he snorted, "Nonsense! We still have two oceans to guard our ramparts."

When America entered the war, Norman Thomas offered the administration "critical support." Later in life he even conceded, "The one major stand in the past that bothers me a good deal is how sorry I ought to be that I opposed our getting into the Second World War." Yet in 1942 his Party announced that it "does not give its blessing to this war or any war." Thomas consequently attacked Roosevelt's incarceration of Japanese-Americans, his treatment of dissidents and conscientous objectors, his refusal to provide a refuge in America for European Jews, and his disregard of civil rights for blacks. The President, he believed, was too quick to overlook the imperialism of Britain and the dictatorial character of Soviet rule. Thomas was especially appalled at the policy of unconditional surrender and the neglect of progressive domestic legislation. "My case against Roosevelt," he concluded, "is that the foreign policy or lack of foreign policy is unnecessarily prolonging this war and inviting the next; . . . that, on the whole, the government's wartime policies have aided big business; that by the President's own admission there is no more New Deal."

As in the 1930s, Thomas scored some points. World War II did see rapid escalation in the power of big business; Roosevelt did tend to overlook the ambitions of his allies; America did treat Japanese-Americans cruelly and react slowly to the demands of blacks. But during World War II Americans wanted above all to *win*—as efficiently and if necessary as ruthlessly as possible—and Thomas, who was easily dismissed as a naive isolationist, barely received a hearing. In 1944, his vote sank to 78,227, even less than it had been in 1940, and Party membership practically vanished. If the New Deal helped weaken American socialism, the fascist menace smashed it to its knees.

*   *   *

When Robert Taft was born in September 1889, his proud father proclaimed him a "remarkable child. . . . I am obliged to give my judgment for those, *nemine contradicente,* who contend that the boy is one of the most remarkable products of this century."

Such effusions were of course normal enough for parents. But William Howard Taft and his wife Nellie did not let love for their children stand in the way of rigorous training for excellence. Americans, Bob's father proclaimed later, "deny to children the great and indispensable good that comes from discipline. Character is formed by the practice of self-restraint and self-sacrifice, by overcoming obstacles." More than the Roosevelts or the Thomases, the Tafts viewed life from the perspective of William Graham Sumner, the advocate of rugged individualism who had been one of William Howard Taft's favorite teachers at Yale.

As a boy Bob also could not help but be aware of his family's eminence. His grandfather Alphonso had served President Grant as Attorney General and Secretary of War, and Benjamin Harrison as ambassador to Russia and Austria-Hungary. Bob's jovial, gregarious, and ambitious father surpassed Alphonso by reaching the presidency from 1909 through 1913. As chief executive, Taft proved too judicious and too stand-pat a Republican to satisfy progressives, and both Woodrow Wilson and TR beat him badly in the three-way election of 1912. The apostasy of TR and other Republicans angered Taft, who cherished party regularity, but the defeated candidate did not retire from public activity. He was rewarded in 1921 when President Harding appointed him Chief Justice of the Supreme Court, a post he held until 1930.

With such a background it is not surprising that Bob Taft aimed for excellence. After a boyhood in Cincinnati and three years in the Philippines where his father served as Governor-General, he crossed the Pacific alone in 1903 to begin three years at the Taft School in Connecticut. Founded by Bob's uncle, the School offered disciplined rote learning and stressed, as Groton had for Franklin Roosevelt, the virtues of public service. Taft graduated first in his class. Moving to Yale, he finished first again. He then attended Harvard Law School and placed first for a third time. When he left Harvard in 1913, he seemed stiff and shy to some of his contemporaries. Then and always he lacked Franklin Roosevelt's charm and Thomas' eloquence. But there was no doubting the capacity of his intellect, his willingness to work, and his desire to achieve. Bob, Harvard's dean wrote former President Taft, showed great "faithfulness and severity . . . He is a demonstration that a legal mind is heritable."

After leaving law school Taft had an opportunity to work in an uncle's prestigious New York firm. He received a still more intriguing offer to serve as clerk for Supreme Court Justice Oliver Wendell Holmes. But to Taft New York offered little appeal. "They are so aggressive," he complained of New Yorkers. "Perhaps it is seeing so much of New York and Eastern people. I have so long decided that New York was the last place, that I spend a great deal of time in argument, uselessly." The chance to assist Holmes may have been more attractive—Taft did not reveal how he felt about it. But his father urged him to refuse the offer, and begin his career with a firm in Cincinnati. Taft, no rebel, did as he was told, and for the next four years he worked steadily in the city of his birth.

When America entered the war in 1917, Taft determined to enter the armed forces. Rejected for poor eyesight, he turned to Washington, where he secured a job as a young lawyer for the Food Administration headed by Herbert Hoover. For Taft, who had been doing menial legal work in Cincinnati, life in wartime Washington was stimulating. Gradually he grew close to Hoover, who made him a top aide and took him to Paris for the peace conference. There Taft reflected Hoover's bitterness at European power politics. "I almost wish," Taft said, "that we had let them [the Europeans] settle their own troubles when we had licked the Kaiser."

Taft's work with Hoover left him confident of his ability, and he plunged quickly into politics, first to support Hoover's unsuccessful attempt for the Republican presidential nomination in 1920, then to run as a nominee from Cincinnati for the state legislature the same year. Elected easily, and re-elected in 1922 and 1924, Taft moved rapidly to the front ranks, becoming speaker before leaving the assembly in 1926. Meanwhile, he built up a lucrative law practice in Cincinnati, battled party insurgents on the local level, and became a recognized expert on problems of state taxation. In 1930 he ran successfully for the state senate, only to lose in the Democratic landslide two years later.

Robert Taft's defeat at the polls, however, failed appreciably to overturn a strongly held philosophy of government which he had developed during the previous 20 years. Uncomplicated, it was an anti-statist philosophy that stemmed from the social Darwinian tenets of his upbringing, intensified from 1917 to 1919 (when he concluded that regulation of the economy was all but impossible except under the extraordinary conditions of war), and flourished during the Harding-Coolidge era. "Government," he had insisted in 1920, "has reached almost the limit of effective action. . . . Every government in the world is the same and every government tends to become a bureaucracy . . . there are some things which simply have to be borne until they remedy themselves." Robert Taft in 1932, like his father in 1912, refused to let the passage of time overturn his faith in conservative principles or in party orthodoxy.

The depression eventually forced Taft to accept some New Deal measures. He endorsed increased appropriations for public works, supported the Securities and Exchange Commission, and conceded the necessity for some public relief spending. But, like Thomas, he grew increasingly angry at what he considered Roosevelt's political motives. "I should hate to see Roosevelt get in," he wrote his mother in 1932, "because he seems to me to be such an opportunist." Always a partisan Republican, Taft also found the depression very frustrating politically. "I do not like to be in the position," he said, "where the returning prosperity, which I am most anxious to secure, is bound to benefit the opposite party."

With the approach of the 1934 election Taft grew increasingly strident in his condemnation of the New Deal. The present course of the administration, he wrote, "will lead directly to a government control of everything, and practical confiscation of property to effect a redistribution of wealth." The TVA, he added, was a "step in the direction of revolution," and Roosevelt's "complete recklessness with regard to governmental expenditure" would soon result in the "destruction of the system and probably a socialistic state." In 1936 Taft concluded that "if Roosevelt is not a communist today, he is bound to become one."

Such extreme rhetoric did little for Republicans before 1937. In that year, however, Roosevelt rashly tried to pack the Supreme Court and, by cutting relief spending, helped provoke a recession. Moderates as well as conservatives also blamed presidential policies for encouraging sit-down strikes in such major industries as automobiles and steel. With the Democrats on the defensive Taft ran for the Senate in 1938. Though an uninspiring speaker, he proved an indefatigable campaigner and wisely showed more ideological flexibility than he had before 1936. He denounced the Wagner Act for failing to enumerate unfair labor practices, but endorsed the principle of government guarantees of collective bargaining. He attacked the AAA's crop curtailment program, but conceded that the government ought to buy surpluses during depression, providing that it disposed of them in the same crop year. He even offered a quasi-Keynesian view of fiscal policy. "There should be a long-term public works program," he proclaimed, "which could be carried out more intensively in hard times and less actively in times of prosperity."

But such statements were concessions to the times, not changes in Taft's philosophy. Indeed, he continued to assault the administration. The farm program was "socialism with a vengeance." New Dealers were "proposing a totalitarian state which they have today in Russia." He insisted that "the whole spending program is a fraud upon the people of Ohio" and that "the regulation of wages, hours, and prices and practices in every industry is something which is, in effect, socialism; which is government regulation of the worst sort; which means a totalitarian state. . . . You cannot carry it out without the arbitrary power of a dictatorship of some kind." Such hyperbole made Taft a target of the progressive press. But 1938 was a year of Republican resurgence, and Taft won with votes to spare.

Once in office Robert Taft mellowed slightly. As early as 1939 he supported modest appropriations for public housing, and by 1945 he became co-sponsor of a broad program to provide federal funds for residential construction, public housing, and slum clearance. The bill passed a Democratic Congress in 1949. In 1945 Taft became a convert to the cause of federal aid to secondary education, which he steered through the Senate in 1948 and 1949, only to see the House defeat it. Taft never supported these measures with evangelistic fervor, for he continued to fear governmental encroachment. But he defended them as necessary to correct inequality and to preserve the capitalistic system. Ironically, at the time of his death in 1953 he was not only more progressive than he had been in the 1930s but to the left of Dwight D. Eisenhower, the so-called "modern" Republican whom he had unsuccessfully opposed for the Republican presidential nomination the year before.

But though he bent with the times, Taft gradually emerged as a leader of a conservative coalition in Congress, which as early as 1938 began cutting liberal Democratic appropriations for social programs. He fought consistently against efforts to impose more progressive corporate and income taxes. And in 1947 he led a bipartisan majority to passage of the Taft-Hartley Act. While far from the "slave labor law" that unions branded it, the measure enumerated unfair labor practices, outlawed the closed shop, and attempted to limit the authority of the National Labor Relations Board. Enactment of Taft-Hartley made Taft more than ever the hero of the Republican Right.

Taft, like Thomas, paid a price for sponsoring ideas that affronted moderate voters and powerful interest groups. Indeed, he suffered much more grievously than Thomas, for Taft yearned for the presidential nomination his father had gained so easily. In 1940, 1948, and 1952 he failed to win that cherished prize, in part because the more liberal eastern wing of his Party thought him too conservative and concluded he could not win if he ran. That was the price he paid for his refusal to line up with his times.

His views on foreign policy hurt him most of all. Like Thomas, he had not been a thoroughgoing isolationist earlier in life, and as late as 1935 he supported American participation in the World Court. But the intrigues at the Versailles Conference proved unforgettable. "European quarrels," he said in 1939, "are everlasting. There is a welter of races there so confused that boundaries cannot be drawn without leaving minorities which are a perpetual source of friction." Like other Republican noninterventionists, he believed that a strong defense, including a powerful air force, could protect the country against all opponents. America, he said, "need not and shall not be involved. We have an isolated location, and it is still isolated in spite of all the improvements in air transportation."

Though never a pacifist, Taft shared some of Thomas' attitudes. "Modern war," he said, "has none of the glamour which we were taught to associate with war in our childhood. It is nothing but horror and mechanical destruction. It leaves the victor as exhausted as the vanquished, and a train of economic distress in its wake." America's policy, he repeated endlessly prior to World War II, "should be to preserve peace with other nations, and enter into no treaties which may obligate us to go to war. Our army and navy should be designed to provide an adequate defense against attack."

Taft's views most closely approached Thomas' in two major ways. First, both men feared that World War II would lead to wholesale destruction of civil liberties. Thomas, who remembered the persecution of leftists 20 years earlier, revealed a humane concern for free speech. Taft, an economic conservative, wished also to protect capitalistic freedom. "We have moved far toward totalitarian government already," he said in 1939. "The additional powers sought by the President in case of war, the nationalization of all industry and all capital and all labor, already proposed in bills before Congress, would create a Socialist dictatorship which it would be impossible to dissolve once the war is over."

The two critics, one on the Left, the other on the Right, also opposed what both men repeatedly called American "imperialism." "We should be prepared to defend our own shores," Taft said in 1939, "but we should not undertake to defend the ideals of democracy in foreign countries. . . . No one has ever suggested before that a single nation should range over the world, like a knight-errant, protect democracy and ideals of good faith, and tilt, like Don Quixote, against the windmills of fascism. . . . Such a policy is not only vain, but bound to lead to war." During World War II Taft elaborated on this theme by attacking proposals that America join a postwar alliance to police the world. "Our fingers will be in every pie," he predicted. "Our military forces will work with our commercial forces to obtain as much of the world trade as we can lay our hands on. We will occupy all the strategic points in the world. . . . How long can nations restrain themselves from using such force with just a little of the aggressiveness of Germany and Japan? . . . Potential power over other nations, however benevolent its purpose, leads inevitably to imperialism."

With his eyes on retaining his Senate seat and ultimately on reaching the presidency, Taft ordinarily was careful to temper such criticisms. He backed Roosevelt's military policies during the war and voted unenthusiastically for the United Nations. Later, amid the Cold War, he offered reluctant support even for the Truman Doctrine and, in 1948, for a peace-time draft. But his stand against intervention before 1941 enabled opponents to identify him with isolationism, and his assaults on "imperialism" and "crusading" distressed liberal internationalists, who heard only more carping from an unreconstructed midwestern nationalist. Moreover, for all his perceptiveness concerning the potential dangers of a military-industrial complex, he never struck Republican president-makers as "safe" or responsible. Taft's critical view of the New Deal hurt him with liberal eastern Republicans, but his unrepentant attitudes about the world damaged him still more.

*   *   *

Robert Taft, like Norman Thomas, was a prominent spokesman for a consistently held world view. But both men reached limited audiences because they could not help but criticize the two major political developments of their time: a capitalistic welfare state, and an activist, far-ranging foreign policy. And because Roosevelt, master of the art of the possible, promoted both to items of faith with the majority of American people, critics of the Right and the Left became spokesmen for ever dwindling minorities.

13

McCarthyism: Everyman as a Potential Subversive

HARRY S. TRUMAN
WHITTAKER CHAMBERS
JOSEPH MC CARTHY

by Athan Theoharis
Marquette University

In February 1950 a relatively obscure junior Senator from Wisconsin, Joseph McCarthy, catapulted into national prominence by charging that communists had successfully infiltrated the State Department. His recklessness, failure to document his charges, and disregard for the reputations of innocent individuals, became familiar tactics. They produced the term "McCarthyism," which described the distinctive anti-communist politics of the 1950s, its inflammatory rhetoric and obsessional, even irrational fear of communism. Yet, in 1953, at the height of McCarthy's influence, the level of popular concern for the issues the Senator exploited appears strikingly limited. A poll in that year asking "What kinds of things do you worry about?" revealed that only one percent considered the threat of communism as a major concern and only eight percent foreign affairs. Moreover, when the question was rephrased to elicit a direct response—"Are there other problems you worry about or are concerned about, specifically political or world problems?"—concern about communism increased to six percent and about foreign affairs to 30 percent. Of those polled fully one-third could not name a single congressman or senator prominent in the investigation of communism.

The relative popular indifference to communism indicated by this poll closely correlated with the Communist Party's actual influence in American society. Indeed, communism had never been a major political force and its appeal had been principally limited to alienated intellectuals. Even during the height of the Great Depression, the Communist presidential candidate in 1932 polled only slightly over 100,000 votes. Formal Party membership increased from 10,000 to 12,000 in 1930 to 50,000 by January 1938 and to 82,000 at its highest in 1947. But the onset of the Cold War and the resultant adoption of stringent anti-radical measures virtually decimated the already-fragile American Communist Party: by 1951 the circulation of the communist *Daily Worker* declined from a postwar high of 23,400 in 1949, to about 14,000 (slipping further to about 6,000 in 1958); Party membership in 1954 totaled 25,000.

In contrast to the relative indifference of the general public, when confronted by the alleged domestic threat of communism, political elites—whether liberal or conservative—became highly sensitive to the issue during these post-war years. In 1950 and 1951, for example, President Truman's Attorney General, J. Howard McGrath, undertook a nationwide speaking effort to arouse the nation to the communist danger. A partisan Democratic Senator, McGrath had been elevated to the Attorney Generalship after engineering Truman's successful election campaign in 1948. Highly ambitious, insensitive to civil liberties, like many Catholic leaders McGrath was a rabid anti-communist. In his speeches seeking both to defend the Administration's internal security record and alert the nation to the seriousness of the communist "threat," the Attorney General informed his audiences: "There are today many communists in America. They are everywhere—in factories, offices, butcher shops, on street corners, in private business—and each carries in himself the germs of death for society." "The communist conspiracy," he warned, "—at this very moment—is . . . busy at work—undermining your government, plotting to destroy the liberties of every citizen, and feverishly trying, in whatever they can, to aid the Soviet Union."

Concomitantly, many liberals and socialists were gradually subordinating their libertarian principles in behalf of the effective prosecution of communists. In 1952 Merlyn Pitzele, one board member of the American Civil Liberties Union, objecting to the Union's sponsorship of a book on blacklisting in the movie industry, argued that the volume failed to emphasize that communism, rather than McCarthyism, was the real danger to America. In 1950, the socialist periodical *New Leader* lamented that "Those who agree with Senator McCarthy's basic thesis that innocents and fellow-travelers often can prove more dangerous in objective fact that the bona fide Communist Party member cannot be grateful to the Senator for the carelessness with which he prepared his case." And the Democratic liberal, Senator Hubert Humphrey of Minnesota, urged enactment of an anti-communist bill in 1954. "Either senators are for recognizing the Communist Party for what it is," said Humphrey, "or they will continue to trip over the niceties of legal technicalities and details."

Since the 1930s, Republican leaders had sought to discredit liberal Democrats by red-baiting. Republican Senator Robert Taft of Ohio, respected for his intellect and integrity, contended in the 1930s that "If Roosevelt is not a communist today he is bound to become one." Seven years later Taft, "Mr. Republican," was advising his fellow Republicans to concentrate on the anti-communist issue, arguing that "We cannot possibly win the next election unless we point out the utter failure and incapacity of the Truman Administration to conduct foreign policy . . . We cannot possibly win on domestic policy, because every domestic policy depends entirely on foreign policy." In the 1944 presidential campaign, GOP presidential nominee Thomas Dewey represented Franklin Roosevelt's re-election as "essential" to the communist cause. "In Russia," he explained, "a communist is a man who supports his government. In America, a communist is a man who supports the fourth term so our form of government may more easily be changed."

Both the Republican and the Democratic leadership shared a common anti-communist consensus. They differed only over methods not fundamental objectives: the degree to which (and not whether) individual liberties should be restricted to safeguard the "domestic security" and the extent of foreign aid and diplomatic commitments essential to containing and then rolling back "communism." Given this consensus, far-reaching and politically repressive loyalty/security measures were not unexpectedly adopted. In 1947, a federal employee loyalty program was established. Under this program, individuals were questioned about their reading interests (one was asked whether he subscribed to the *New Republic* or had books about the Russian government in his library), were denied clearance because of their relatives' political activities (a vice-president of an engineering firm performing classified work for the Navy Department was denied a security clearance in 1953 because his former wife—whom he had divorced six years earlier—allegedly had been active in communist-front activities). Applicants for all Atomic Energy Commission fellowships (including non-classified research) had to receive an FBI clearance after 1949. And the Navy Department in 1952 advised its personnel to "seek wise and mature counsel prior to associating with persons or organizations of any political or civic nature, no matter what their apparent motive may be, in order to determine the true motives and purposes of the organization."

Given the national climate, the Navy Department's advice seemed eminently sensible. A 1951 speaking invitation of a Washington, D.C. college to Marquis Childs, the widely syndicated columnist, was rescinded after the college's president discovered that the FBI had a file on him. Similarly, another invitation to the eminent China scholar, Owen Lattimore, to speak in New Hampshire was canceled in the summer of

1950 because Senator McCarthy had accused him of being a subversive. The action was justified on the grounds that "Just now with the critical condition of the country, anyone about whom there is any question should not be allowed to speak."

State and local legislative bodies were moving vigorously, and sometimes ridiculously, to suppress the dissemination of radical ideas. After 1945 over 30 states and two United States territories required teachers and public employees to take loyalty oaths. Indiana even required loyalty oaths from those seeking a license to wrestle. The New York City Department of Sanitation was designated a "security agency." Loyalty oaths were required of those wishing to fish in the city's reservoirs. Birmingham, Alabama, adopted an ordinance warning communists to leave town within 48 hours; New Rochelle, New York, directed communists to register with the police; Detroit barred the sale of communist literature on the streets; and Alabama stipulated that all written instructional material used in the public schools carry a statement that the author was not a member of the Communist Party, an adherent of Marxian socialism, or a member of an organization listed by the Attorney General or by any congressional committee. Fear of communism even led a private foundation in 1951 to offer $100,000 to fund research for the purpose of detecting "traitors." By such standards, every man was a potential subversive; no restriction was so gross that it violated the national interest.

Significantly, during these postwar years, public figures like Harry Truman, Whittaker Chambers, and Joseph McCarthy helped trigger a McCarthyite politics. Neither charismatic leaders nor powerful thinkers, they shared a common anti-communist consensus, and differed only over tactics, not fundamental goals. They were colorful as personalities, acting at times as adversaries, at times as unwitting collaborators. Indirectly and almost fortuitously, they activated the issue of subversion. Indeed, their political careers reflected the issues and concerns shaping American politics in the postwar years.

*   *   *

Born in Lamar, Missouri, on May 8, 1884, Harry S. Truman's early values and outlook were shaped by the limited educational and social opportunities of a small Midwestern town. Influenced by the associational and conformist pressures of a closed, isolated community, with its emphasis on patriotic duty and order, and by his family's anti-Republican biases, the young Truman soon joined numerous fraternal organizations as well as the National Guard, and was active in the local Democratic Party. Encouraged and protected by his mother, Truman turned not to sports but to reading and music during his youth. Ambitious but constrained by his family's economical status, Truman could not afford to attend college. His post-high school work experiences varied from bank clerk to dirt farmer until the opportunity provided by World War I both broadened his background and experiences. Enlisting in the Army, Truman fought in Europe and eventually rose in rank to captain an artillery battery where he acquired valuable political contacts (including the nephew of Kansas City political boss, Tom Pendergast). Returning to Missouri after the Armistice, he became co-owner of a Kansas City haberdashery, a venture that failed in 1922. Bankrupt and with no future plans, Truman was approached by representatives from the Pendergast machine and agreed in 1922 to run for, and was elected, a commissioner of Jackson County.

An indefatigable worker and an incorruptible and able administrator, Truman compiled an outstanding record in the county. Yet this record brought him no particular distinction. At best, he had demonstrated political astuteness and developed a solid political base deriving from his membership in numerous social and fraternal organizations (the Moose, Elks, Lions, Eagles, Shrine, American Legion, and Baptist Church). Truman's honesty and administrative abilities and the extensive statewide contacts he gained through his fraternal activities made him an attractive candidate and prompted "Boss" Tom Pendergast to urge him to seek the Democratic nomination for the United States Senate in 1934. Elected after an uninspiring campaign, Truman arrived in Washington a freshman Senator who, like many others in the depression decade, had abandoned his former conservative predilections to emerge a loyal New Dealer.

Missouri's junior Senator—disparagingly dismissed by some political commentators as "the Senator from Pendergast"—was not embraced by Franklin Roosevelt. Nor did Truman's loyal New Deal voting record particularly enhance his standing with the White House. But his party regularity and attractive personality had won for Truman entry into that small group of powerful solons known as the Senate club. This alone constituted Truman's main political asset until 1941, when he attained national prominence as chairman of a special Senate committee investigating waste and favoritism in the defense program.

The combination of this recently acquired reputation, a solid New Deal voting record, close relations with the congressional leadership, and the rift over Henry Wallace's renomination between Party conservatives and liberals at the National Convention resulted in Truman's selection in 1944 as the Democratic vice-presidential candidate. He was a compromise choice. Basically conservative in conviction but with a liberal voting record, he was acceptable to the conservative wing of the deeply divided Party and the congressional leadership as well as the liberals and to organized labor.

In the campaign, Truman was neither consulted on strategy nor was involved in Administration policy decisions. He met with Roosevelt only five times during the campaign and three times between the inaugural and Roosevelt's death on April 12, 1945. A not altogether impressive Senator and a poorly informed Vice President had suddenly become President.

Harry Truman brought to the presidency distinct assets and liabilities. An able, if highly partisan, politician and capable administrator, he soon further consolidated presidential powers. But he was hardly a profound thinker and tended to be a liberal more out of necessity than conviction. Moreover, he had no specific program addressed to the complex international and domestic problems confronting postwar America. His conservative predilections and distrust of planning would lead to reliance on two practices designed to sustain his Administration's initiative in foreign affairs: (1) unilateral and secretive actions, and (2) provocative, if not alarmist rhetoric to win support for often controversial decisions.

On becoming President in 1945, Truman had inherited an assertive Congress led by an informal coalition of Republicans and conservative Democrats, mostly from the South. Since 1938, the conservative-controlled House Committee on Un-American Activities (HUAC) had "red-baited" the New Deal, either by questioning the loyalty of its personnel or by representing Roosevelt's extension of presidential powers as leading to socialism or to communism. Wartime investigations of federal employees and postwar revelations of seemingly inadequate security procedures intensified the conservatives' demand for a thorough housecleaning of the executive branch. Capitalizing in part on this issue during the 1946 congressional elections, the Republicans secured control of both houses of Congress for the first time since 1930, insuring that the subsequent Congress would concentrate its efforts on investigating the loyalty of federal employees. (During 1947 and 1948, Congress instituted no less than 35 separate committee investigations of federal personnel and policies.)

Lacking Franklin Roosevelt's political capital and alarmed by leaks of classified information in 1945 and 1946, Truman moved quickly to take control of the loyalty issue. On November 25, 1946, he appointed a special presidential commission to investigate the loyalty problem, and on March 22, 1947, he formally instituted a permanent federal employee loyalty program. As Truman told a political confidant in mid-1947, the establishment of a presidentially-directed loyalty program was intended in part "to take the ball away from Parnell Thomas [the Republican chairman of HUAC]." In part, too, it suggested his antipathy toward the ardent New Dealers whom he had initially been hesitant to challenge. (He privately referred to them as "crackpots and the lunatic fringe.") The departure of Harold Ickes and Henry Wallace from the Cabinet in mid-1946, combined with the 1946 election results which seemingly confirmed a rightward shift in the national mood, ended Truman's uneasy relations with New Deal liberals. Already basically sympathetic to the more conservative anti-communist advisers in his Cabinet, Truman thereafter more openly accepted their policy recommendations in both the international and internal security areas. What this meant in substance was captured in the lament of White House aide Admiral William Leahy regarding the diplomacy of Secretary of State James Byrnes at the Moscow Foreign Ministers Conference in December 1945. "Byrnes," he complained, "was not immune to the communistically inclined advisers in the State Department."

Not surprisingly then, the President enacted a loyalty program that sought "absolute security." (Existing legislation indeed provided more than adequate authority to dismiss suspect employees holding sensitive security positions. Moreover, the *Amerasia*° episode in 1945 did not involve actual espionage; it simply highlighted the sloppiness of existing security controls over classified documents.) What was required, Truman affirmed, was to insure that not "even one" person of doubtful loyalty or "potentially subversive" was employed in the federal government— whether as janitor or atomic scientist. To disarm congressional opposition still further, Truman appointed conservatives to the loyalty program's major administrative positions. As chairman of the Loyalty Review Board, he selected Seth Richardson. A former Assistant Attorney General during Herbert Hoover's Administration, Richardson believed that "the government is entitled to discharge any employee for reasons . . . sufficient to the government, and without extending . . . any hearing whatsoever." The Loyalty Review Board, in fact, actively lobbied to revise standards for dismissal—so as to reduce the need to prove disloyalty. Many appointees to lower level loyalty boards were even more reactionary; during loyalty hearings they focused not only on the political activities but also the ideas of liberal federal employees. The effect of such appointments was to undermine those very procedural safeguards Truman had instituted in 1947, hopefully to balance individual rights and security considerations.

Seeking to sustain their initiative in the internal security field, the President and his close advisers also acted in ways that indirectly exacerbated popular fears and legitimized an anti-communist politics. In December 1947, the Administration publicly released the Attorney General's list of "subversive" organizations, thereby establishing a litmus test for ascertaining the "disloyalty" of individuals who might have engaged in

---

° *Amerasia* was a journal of Far Eastern affairs edited by prominent radicals. In June 1945 the offices and residences of the journal's editors and certain governmental officials were raided by FBI agents and hundreds of classified governmental documents were found. Yet, those arrested were only indicted for illegally possessing government documents (for they were not engaged in espionage but seeking to influence official policy by critical reporting and leaks). Ultimately the case never was prosecuted owing to governmental illegality in pre-arrest investigations (including break-ins, wiretapping, and bugging).

radical politics during the 1930s and 1940s. Earlier that year, Truman acceded to the recommendations of Attorney General Tom Clark and FBI Director J. Edgar Hoover and instituted a nationwide propaganda campaign to alert the nation still further to the seriousness of the internal security threat.

Truman's attitudes then were not completely unlike those of an American Legionaire, though he was restrained by the responsibilities of office and the exigencies of Democratic politics. No statement more revealingly captured his attitudes than the emotional speech he personally drafted in response to the 1946 rail and coal strikes, one that his advisers convinced him to revise. In his draft, Truman charged "Every single one of the strikers and their demigog [sic] leaders have been living in luxury. . . . Now I want you who are my comrades in arms . . . to come with me and eliminate the Lewises, the Whitneys, the Johnstons, the Communist Bridges [all important union officials] and the Russian Senators and Representatives . . . Let's put transportation and production back to work, hang a few traitors and make our own country safe for democracy."

The need to sell costly and controversial foreign policy proposals (such as the Truman Doctrine and Marshall Plan) to a fiscally conservative and suspicious Congress impelled the President to resort to similar alarmist rhetoric. Truman's St. Patrick's Day address of March 17, 1948, captured the tone of most of his foreign policy speeches:

> We must beware of those who are devoting themselves to sowing the seeds of disunity among our people. . . .
> We must not be confused about the issue which confronts the world today. . . .
> It is tyranny and freedom. . . .
> And even worse communism denies the very existence of God. Religion is persecuted because it stands for freedom under God. The threat to our liberties and to our faith must be faced by every one of us.

Such themes were reiterated during the Korean War in 1950 and 1951: "Our lives, our Nation, all the things we believe in are in great danger." "We are fighting for freedom, for the right to worship as we please, in any church that we choose to attend, [for] the right to read what we please, and the right to elect public officials of our own choosing."

The President's desire to avert an intensive public debate over his administration's national security decisions was clearly one reason for such inflammatory rhetoric. Criticism of the Administration, he continuously argued, adversely affected the national security by dividing the nation. On the one hand, Truman characterized criticisms from the left as ultimately disloyal, an argument repeatedly made during Henry Wallace's 1948 presidential campaign on the Progressive Party ticket. On the other hand, he dismissed the foreign policy attack of conservative Republicans as "appeasement" and "isolationism," and described Senator McCarthy as "the best asset the Kremlin has." In April 1950 he attacked GOP criticism as an effort to "sabotage the foreign policy of the United States [which] is just as bad in this Cold War as it would be to shoot soldiers in the back in a hot war." In the same vein, Truman dismissed Republican attacks on the Administration's loyalty procedures as prompted by partisan and publicity-seeking motives. In August 1948, he described HUAC's investigation of the charges of Whittaker Chambers (that communists had successfully infiltrated the New Deal and had thereby promoted communist policies) as a "red herring" to divert public attention from the "reactionary" record of the 80th Congress. Democratic National Committee chairman J. Howard McGrath repeated this denunciation of HUAC in December 1948: "At the very moment that the federal grand jury is acting against spies and spy rings, the committee is racing to milk the situation of its last headline . . . They have done everything to cripple legal, proper investigations and they do all this in highly political atmosphere." Confronted after the Korean War by growing support for a Republican-sponsored internal security measure, the President in August 1950 proposed an alternative bill. Contrasting both proposals, he assailed the "excessive" and "arbitrary" provisions of the Republican-sponsored measure.

From 1947, then, Truman's foreign and internal security policies had evolved into a politics of unthinking anti-communism. By the 1950s, and as a result, he could not effectively rebut the McCarthyites in Congress. Confronted by their challenge of 1950 and by domestic and international developments that seemed to confirm inadequate security procedures, Truman lamely and belatedly extolled the need to safeguard constitutional and libertarian principles. More importantly, his presidential style, especially his refusal of March 1948 and again in the 1950s to allow congressional committees access to loyalty records of federal employees on the grounds of executive privilege, enabled some conservative lawmakers to accuse him of attempting a "cover-up."

With the accepted need to insure adequate internal security safeguards in the tense atmosphere of the 1950s, Truman's rhetorical concern for civil liberties and emphasis upon deference to the executive branch appeared unwise if not irresponsible. Not surprisingly, the President's popularity, as measured by public opinion polls, plummeted to a low of 23 percent in November 1951. His low esteem was precipitated in great part by the dramatic revelations of the House Committee of Un-American Activities following its interrogation of Whittaker Chambers.

*   *   *

Whittaker Chambers was born on April 1, 1901, in Philadelphia, Pennsylvania, and grew up on Long Island, New York, in an atmosphere of family instability and financial insecurity. A commercial artist, his father was estranged from his mother and also from him. Chambers' early family situation was abnormal as his father had left home briefly though returning to live in the same house but physically apart from the rest of the family. Chambers' mother lived in dire fear of marauders, whether real or imaginary, and kept an axe for protection. His maternal grandmother, who lived with the family, had gone insane and had to be carefully watched. The young Chambers acquired few friends, had an uneven school record, and developed an unreal sense of his own cultural superiority and uniqueness. Attracted to theological explanations (but not to formal religion), Chambers was a misfit in suburban Long Island both in his cultural alienation and messianic, despairing view of the world. Decidedly nonconformist and unconventional, Chambers had an embittered youth.

After an unsuccessful effort to reach Mexico upon graduation from high school, Chambers came back, worked in an advertising agency for a time, and then enrolled in Columbia College (commuting to school to reduce expenses). Though possessing recognized literary abilities, he was neither a disciplined nor a successful student. He did become associated, however, with a group of talented writers who, like many other intellectuals of the 1920s, were troubled by conditions throughout the world but particularly those of their own society. Forced to withdraw from Columbia because of an atheistic play he had published during his junior year, Chambers traveled to Europe where he saw little that improved his regard for the existing social order. Upon returning to New York, he successfully appealed for reinstatement to Columbia where he irregularly attended classes and dropped out by the end of the semester. In February 1925, he joined the Communist Party.

Chambers' personal life, troubled family relations (which were further complicated by his younger brother's suicide), and conviction that the world was bent for destruction attracted him to the communist prescription for radical change. Chambers was not a factional or intellectual leader within the Party, though he steadily rose in influence. Variously, he served as editor of worker's correspondence, foreign news and copy editor of the *Daily Worker,* and editor of *New Masses,* the intellectual organ of the American Communist Party. (Chambers supplemented his meager party income by free lance translating—one of his most famous efforts being the popular children's book *Bambi.*) Becoming a paid Party functionary in 1932, Chambers attempted to recruit members in Greenwich Village. In 1934, he was assigned to Washington, D.C., where at some point he switched from his older roles of recruiter and supervisor to a new one of courier for the espionage activities conducted by Communist functionaries or sympathizers within the federal government.

Chambers later broke decisively with the Communist Party. His attraction to communism had always been more cultural and psychological than political and ideological. Thus, when breaking with the Party (the specific reason or reasons for the break remain inexplicable), he became deeply religious and a fanatical anti-communist. Chambers did not then hesitate to intimidate those who were vulnerable (such as Julian Wadleigh) because of having provided him with government secrets. He asked them for financial aid. Desperately in need of money, Chambers also sought unsuccessfully in 1939 to publish a manuscript dealing with his experiences in the Party. Employed finally as book reviewer for *Time* magazine, he gained respectability, and the opportunity to test his abilities as a writer. His easy if florid style and his flair for the dramatic fit in with the magazine's distinctive style of journalism. Rising steadily, Chambers became a senior editor in 1941, for a while edited the foreign news section, later headed the magazine's special projects section. By August 1948, he was one of *Time*'s top editors (receiving an annual salary of $30,000).

Ironically, it was only Chambers' former communism that led to his national prominence. Following his break with the Party, he had shifted sharply rightward, attacking not only radicalism but also the New Deal. By then, however, Chambers was distinctly nonpolitical, attempting, in fact, a withdrawal from a society he believed morally corrupt. He definitely did not seek leadership of the anti-communist right, a role thrust upon him by events beyond his control but especially by his public charges against Alger Hiss—in August 1948—that Hiss was a communist who had sought to promote communist interests in the Roosevelt New Deal and then, abruptly changing his testimony, in late 1948 and 1949 that Hiss was engaged in espionage. The timing and impact of these charges helped create the atmosphere that made credible McCarthy's charges of "Communists in the State Department."

Even so, Chambers' own attitudes toward McCarthy were ambivalent and suspicious. Writing to the conservative publicist William Buckley, Jr., on August 6, 1954, Chambers commended the Senator's contribution as "repeatedly [calling] the attention of the antisocialist masses to the fact that the Socialist and Communist apparats co-exist, . . . it is that seizure of power that the Senator alone on the Right, at this moment, visibly imperils." While encouraged by McCarthy's ability to identify reform with subversion and to attract a mass following, Chambers remained disturbed by his demagogic and publicity-seeking methods. In the course of declining Buckley's invitation to write a blurb for his sympathetic book on McCarthy, Chambers wrote (on February 7, 1954): "One way which I can most easily help Communism is to associate myself publicly with Senator McCarthy; . . . all of us, to one degree or another, have slowly come to question [McCarthy's] judgment and to fear acutely that his flair for the sensational, his inaccuracies and distortions, his tendency to sacrifice the greater objective for the momentary effect, will lead him and us into trouble. In fact, . . . we live in terror that Senator McCarthy will one day make some irreparable blunder which will play directly into the hands of our common enemy and discredit the whole anti-Communist movement for a long while to come."

Although his distrust of McCarthy centered on the Senator's irresponsible uses of anti-communism (irresponsible because it was both carelessly thought-out and sensationalist), Chambers himself had no superior claim to leadership of the anti-communist right. For much like the Wisconsin Senator, his own impact on national politics had been circumstantial, the product of a series of fortuitous developments that had swept ex-communists like him along in their wake.

In a basic sense, Chambers was a silent witness against communism. His testimony that led to the trial and conviction of Alger Hiss was reluctantly given; it was precipitated by the exigencies of the electoral politics of 1948. The immediate catalyst in fact was Harry Truman's re-election strategy of running against the 80th Congress and questioning the sincerity of the Republicans' commitment to their relatively moderate 1948 platform. At the Democratic National Convention, Truman had announced the recall of the 80th Congress into special session to enact needed legislative reforms, and thereby to contrast the disparity between the GOP legislative record and the Party's platform. The Congress convened on August 3, 1948.

Responding to pressure from the Chairman of the Republican National Committee, J. Parnell Thomas, then Chairman of HUAC, initiated public hearings on July 31, 1948, into communist infiltration of the New Deal. As its first witness, HUAC called Elizabeth Bentley. A courier for the Communist Party during the war years, Ms. Bentley began telling her version of this role to the FBI in late 1945. In early July 1948, the *New York World-Telegram* publicized her story that she had successfully operated a wartime communist spy ring in Washington and portrayed her as the "red spy queen."

Elizabeth Bentley's dramatic but unsubstantiated charges made her a not altogether credible witness. The crude partisanship displayed by the Committee members who questioned her served further to defuse the impact of her charges. Seeking to corroborate her testimony, HUAC turned to Whittaker Chambers, then a respected senior editor of *Time* and not so easily dismissed as the flamboyant and unstable Ms. Bentley. Adding to this credibility was the fact that Chambers was not a willing informer; in fact, he had to be subpoenaed to testify. The Committee first examined Chambers in executive session on August 3. Encouraged by this testimony, it immediately went into public session, delaying its questioning until press and radio coverage was assured.

HUAC originally subpoenaed Chambers because of charges he had earlier made to federal officials. In 1939, in an attempt to secure a publisher for a proposed book on his break with communism, Chambers had contacted Isaac Don Levine, a right-wing journalist who had recently assisted a former Soviet military attaché to serialize his memoirs in the *Saturday Evening Post*. Levine expressed interest in Chambers' book. Upon reading the manuscript, however, Levine advised Chambers that it required considerable reworking. Later that year Levine visited Chambers (then employed by *Time*) and urged him to tell his story to officials in Washington. Chambers hesitated, but after considerable pressure agreed to a September 1939 interview Levine had arranged with Assistant Secretary of State Adolf Berle. At that meeting, Chambers named 18 individuals (including Alger Hiss) whom he contended were part of a communist cell in Washington. Chambers did not then charge that these individuals were communists or were engaged in espionage, but only that they were fellow-travelers who sought to promote communist influence in the federal government—a standard right-wing charge of the time.

In 1942, FBI agents interviewed Chambers. Their visit had not been prompted by Berle's notes of the September 1939 meeting but by charges of another defector from communism, Ludwig Lore. He advised the FBI that Chambers was knowledgeable about communist espionage activities. In this interview, Chambers reiterated his 1939 testimony, adding two names to the list. Subsequently, he was questioned by FBI agents in 1943, 1945, and often between 1946 and 1948; by civil service investigators during the war years; and by a State Department security officer in 1945 and 1946. His sole charge to all of these officials was that these (now 20) individuals had sought to promote communist influence within the federal government. Chambers in fact assured FBI agents that his testimony had been forthright and complete and further that he possessed no documentary evidence to support his allegations.

This allegation of communist infiltration of the New Deal greatly interested the Committee and was the basis for its subpoena. In his opening statement before HUAC on August 3, Chambers identified only eight persons whom he contended were communists (Alger Hiss was one of the eight). Chambers again did not charge that they had engaged in espionage. In fact, he denied that such was their purpose. By promoting communist infiltration of the federal government, Chambers stressed, they had sought to implement communist policies. Hiss's name was singled out only as the result of questions from Committee members; HUAC was then more interested in having Chambers' testimony about the activities of Harry Dexter White, a high-level Treasury official.

The matter could have died here. For while Chambers had made these charges publicly for the first time in August 1948, his earlier private statements involving Hiss had been circulating in Washington since 1941.* In-

---

* Hiss had first accepted a position in the State Department as an assistant to Assistant Secretary of State Francis Sayre in 1936. In subsequent years, Hiss's influence and role increased, eventually attending the Yalta Conference of 1945 as an assistant

deed, in 1945 and 1946 these charges triggered a State Department investigation of Hiss, and he had been able to establish his own loyalty and good character. Hiss, no longer a public employee (in 1948, he was President of the Carnegie Endowment for International Peace), nonetheless decided to respond directly, telegraphing the Committee on the very afternoon of the day of Chambers' testimony and requesting an opportunity to deny the charges under oath. Hiss's initiative then, and not Chambers' testimony, alone produced the dramatic Hiss-Chambers confrontation.

When seeking a hearing before HUAC, Hiss intended to deny that he had been a member of the Communist Party (the sole positive charge against him made by Chambers). Confronted by his denial, the Committee on August 5 sought to ascertain whether he had known Whittaker Chambers during the 1930s. Responding to the Committee's questions, Hiss evasively affirmed that he had not known anyone "by the name of Whittaker Chambers" and "to the best of my knowledge" had not known of Chambers until the name came up during an interview with the FBI in 1947.

Hiss's August 5 testimony was a masterful performance and demoralized the Committee. Some Committee members felt that Chambers had duped them and argued that the matter should be dropped and given over to the Justice Department to determine who had committed perjury. However, Richard Nixon, then an ambitious freshman congressman from California, urged the Committee to pursue the investigation. Instead of focusing on whether Hiss had been a communist, Nixon argued, the Committee should investigate whether Hiss and Chambers knew each other during the 1930s. If such an acquaintance could be established, HUAC could challenge Hiss's veracity and indirectly corroborate the communist-infiltration theme.

Accordingly, the Committee's hearings shifted from the question of communists in the New Deal to the relationship between Hiss and Chambers. While differing over the nature of this relationship, both men testified to the fact and to considerable contact during 1935 and 1937. But this was no world-shaking development. The Committee failed to establish that Hiss had been a communist or had done anything treasonable. Again on Hiss's initiative, however, the case assumed a new form as he challenged Chambers to repeat his charges outside of the Committee room where they were not protected from libel. Chambers complied during a *Meet the Press* interview on August 27, and Hiss filed a libel suit a month later. The gist of Chambers' charge, repeated in his October 1948 grand jury testimony, was summarized in his responses to pointed questions on *Meet the Press* when

---

to Secretary of State Edward Stettinius and serving as Secretary to the San Francisco Conference (where the United Nations was formally organized). His principal responsibility and interests were in the international collective security realm; thus his role at Yalta, San Francisco, and selection to head the prestigious Carnegie Endowment.

he emphasized: "I think what needs clarification is the purpose for which that group was set up to which Hiss belonged . . . not, as I think is in the back of your mind, for the purpose of espionage, but for the purpose of infiltrating the government and influencing government policy by getting communists in key places." Influencing policy, Chambers added, was "very much more important than spying." Moreover, on a subject that would become important, Chambers had then dated his own break from the Communist Party in late 1937 or early 1938.

On November 17 and December 2, 1948, Chambers dramatically altered his testimony against Hiss. He produced four notes in Hiss's handwriting and 65 typewritten pages of State Department documents. Hiss's attorneys had these materials turned over to the Justice Department. At the time a grand jury was in session and, as part of its work, was considering whether to indict Hiss or Chambers for perjury for their testimony before HUAC. Responding to a leak on December 1 that the grand jury would not indict Hiss, HUAC counsel Robert Stripling and Congressman Richard Nixon visited Chambers at his Maryland farm that night. On December 2, the Committee subpoenaed Chambers to produce any other relevant documents he might have and the excommunist led the HUAC investigators to his pumpkin patch where, after opening a hollowed-out pumpkin, he produced two strips of developed microfilm (the so-called Pumpkin Papers) containing 58 frames of eight classified State Department documents stamped April 1, 1938. Chambers then claimed to have received the microfilm and the other documents from Alger Hiss during the 1930s while acting as a courier for the Communist Party. After breaking with the Party, Chambers stated, he had given those documents in a sealed envelope to a nephew to preserve them as a safety measure. Producing them now, he fundamentally changed the character of the confrontation. On December 15, 1948, a federal grand jury indicted Hiss on two counts of perjury (the statute of limitations precluding an espionage indictment): that he had lied in denying before the grand jury that he (1) had given classified State Department documents to Whittaker Chambers, and (2) he had met Chambers after 1937.

These documents, however, did not clearly establish Hiss's guilt, especially in view of the abrupt, actually contradictory shift in Chambers' charges. Chambers had clearly committed perjury: either in his testimony before HUAC in August 1948 and the grand jury in October 1948 when he had denied under oath that Hiss had engaged in espionage or in his testimony before the grand jury in December 1948 and during the Hiss trials of 1949 when he had described Hiss as one of the most zealous communist spies in Washington. Another question involving Chambers' veracity centered on the date of his break from the Party, which he revised. Since one of the typed documents was dated on April 1, 1938, Chambers could not have received them from Hiss had he left the Party in late 1937 or early

1938—as he claimed during his HUAC testimony. During the first Hiss trial, he thus dated his departure as April 15, 1938. Chambers' failure of memory on this point was particularly striking in view of his precise HUAC testimony about Hiss's activities during the 1930s (which included itemization of Hiss's numerous residences and hobbies, and even the disposition of an old Ford).

Chambers' penchant for dramatizing his story and his instability (he unsuccessfully attempted to commit suicide in December 1948) also diminished his credibility. As one consequence, the first Hiss trial resulted in a hung jury. In the second trial, Thomas Murphy, the government prosecutor, significantly changed his summation to the jury. From his affirmative statement during the first trial that "if you don't believe Chambers then we have no case under the federal perjury rule, . . . where you need one witness plus corroboration," Murphy now only directed the jury to consider "the immutable evidence," and notably the typewritten documents.

Yet the evidence was not necessarily "immutable," though the jury did convict Hiss in his second trial. Subsequent disclosures about an old Woodstock typewriter that had once belonged to the Hisses and the date of Chambers' break from the Communist Party have raised questions about Alger Hiss's guilt, creating further doubts about the veracity and motives of the government's star witness. In a 1952 motion for retrial, Hiss's attorneys raised the issue of forgery by typewriter—and argued that the typed documents, which were crucial to securing conviction, had been forged on a typewriter deliberately manufactured to resemble the Hisses' Woodstock. Their motion was denied. Since then, however, further questions about the typewriter have arisen, centering principally on whether particular typing characteristics might have been due to miscasting during manufacture, thus common to that year's model, and who *first* found the Woodstock. For example, although the FBI had 263 agents on the Hiss case, 30 assigned specifically to locate the typewriter, defense attorneys themselves found and produced it at the first trial. Surprisingly, despite the FBI's considerable efforts, the government made no attempt then to ascertain the Woodstock's authenticity. More strikingly, in Richard Nixon's book *Six Crises*,* in a 1951 HUAC report, and in an article (in the *American Weekly*) by Win Brooks, who had access to privileged information from the FBI and the government prosecutor, it was baldly claimed that the FBI had located the typewriter. When these disclosures created a furor, it was explained that there had been a factual error (indeed, the first edition of Nixon's book was recalled and this reference altered). If the FBI had

---

* During his taped conversation of February 28, 1973, with White House counsel John W. Dean III, then President Richard Nixon referred to the Hiss case and claimed "We [HUAC] then got the evidence, *we got the typewriter*, we got the Pumpkin Papers. We got all of that ourselves." (Italics added.)

indeed found the typewriter, it rather mysteriously lost it only to be found again by Hiss's attorneys. In addition, there was the matter of Chambers' break with the Party. Correspondence with a publisher with whom he was under contract to do a free-lance translation, Mrs. Esther Chambers' November 1948 testimony, which specified her husband's denunciation of communism occurred at the time of a move from a Baltimore apartment, and Chambers' first public listing of his apartment and telephone number under his real name—all place the date around February 1938, well before the April 1 date affixed to one of the State Department documents.

Recently released FBI documents raise another question: the nature and extent of the covert relationship between the FBI and HUAC during 1948. A December 9, 1948 FBI memorandum records a conversation between HUAC member Nixon and two former FBI agents wherein the Congressman "voluntarily stated . . . that he had worked very close with the Bureau and with [FBI Assistant Director Louis] Nichols during the past year on [the Hiss] matter." The closeness of this Nixon-Nichols relationship is further confirmed by Nixon's actions following his December 1, 1948 visit to Chambers' farm. Upon returning to Washington, Nixon telephoned Nichols in the middle of the night to apprise him of Chambers' claim to possessing additional documents and of Nixon's plan to initiate HUAC hearings on this development. Nichols' memorandum on this conversation records that Nixon "specifically urged that we [FBI] not tell the Attorney General that we were told of this information as the Attorney General would try to make it impossible for the Committee to get at the documents. He [Nixon] also asked that the Bureau also not look for the documents themselves." To justify this audacious request, the freshman congressman explained that HUAC planned to subpoena the documents "and the purpose of his call, which he reiterated was strictly personal and highly confidential, was merely to apprise the Bureau so that the FBI would not be caught off base. He stated they [HUAC] were handling the matter so there will be no criticism of the FBI and he particularly urged that we do nothing about the information which he has just furnished as he feels the statute of limitations has run out." If this partisan congressman had urged that the FBI both mislead the Attorney General and not seek this information, FBI Director Hoover nonetheless concurred with this recommendation, directing Nichols: "Do so & let me know result."

Whether or not Hiss was actually guilty of giving State Department documents to Chambers, the latter's charges had major political consequences during the early 1950s. Because of Hiss's pre-war employment and wartime and postwar prominence in the State Department, his conviction came to symbolize the existence of a serious internal security problem. Truman's August 1948 intemperate dismissal of HUAC's probe of Chambers' charges against Hiss, which the President characterized as a "red herring," indirectly established the necessity for independent congressional investigations of executive branch internal security procedures. Chambers' principal contribution, then, made it impossible to dismiss demands for a purge of the federal government as irresponsible red-baiting on the part of anti-Roosevelt partisans. In a very real sense, therefore, there was more than a chronological relationship among Chambers' charges, Hiss's conviction (January 21, 1950), and Joseph McCarthy's Wheeling, West Virginia, speech (February 9, 1950). This Hiss-Chambers contretemps served as catalyst to the McCarthyite politics of the early 1950s.

* * *

Born into a poor Wisconsin farm family on November 14, 1909, Joseph R. McCarthy early demonstrated great drive and a nimble mind. His early educational and vocational experiences were typical of an isolated, rural community. Ambitious to succeed despite his poverty and his undistinguished high school record, young McCarthy enrolled in Marquette University in 1930 and eventually elected to study law. Upon graduation, he returned to his home county to practice law and enter politics. Active at first in the Young Democrats, McCarthy switched to the Republican Party and in 1939 was elected to a circuit court judgeship. McCarthy's record on the bench suggested a flair for publicity and a casual disregard for established legal and judicial procedures.

With the outbreak of World War II, McCarthy secured a commission with the Marine Corps where he served behind a desk as an intelligence officer (and not, as his later campaign literature represented, as a tail gunner). While still in military service, he entered Wisconsin's Republican primary as candidate for United States Senate against the incumbent, Alexander Wiley. McCarthy was defeated, but the campaign had familiarized the State's voters with his name and his military "exploits." Consequently, after being reelected circuit judge in late 1944, he successfully secured nomination in the Republican primary by 5,400 votes out of 410,000 cast (he defeated the progressive incumbent Robert La Follette, Jr.) and won election to the Senate in 1946. Notwithstanding this meteoric rise, McCarthy's political career had not been marked by intellectual ability or widespread popularity but rather by simple good luck. He capitalized on La Follette's vulnerability in 1946 and profited from the nationwide voter reaction against the Truman Administration, which Republicans captured with the slogan "Had Enough? Vote Republican."

As the junior Senator from Wisconsin, McCarthy compiled a decidedly undistinguished record. Owing to his poor legislative and attendance record, he was voted the "worst" Senator by the Washington press corps in 1951. McCarthy was also closely identified with lobbying interests: in 1947 his efforts on behalf of Pepsi Cola to end wartime sugar rationing won him the title, the "Pepsi Cola Kid," and his attempts to gut public housing legislation involved questionable relations with a prefabricated housing corporation (Lustron). Moreover, McCarthy was not identified with any major legislative measure. He voted with conservative Republicans on domestic policy questions (except for farm supports) and with liberal Republicans on foreign policy matters. His principal national exposure prior to 1950 stemmed from a Senate Armed Services Committee investigation of the United States Army's treatment of German SS troops accused of murdering 250 American troops and Belgium civilians in 1944. Ironically McCarthy charged the Army and the Committee with covering up the brutal treatment of these imprisoned SS troops. When pressed by the Committee and by reporters to document such accusations, the Senator, despite earlier claims to evidence, produced nothing.

McCarthy's broadside against the Armed Services Committee investigation indirectly revealed his Senate status as an independent maverick not then aligned with the Republican leadership or part of the informal Senate "club." By his attacks on both the Army and the Committee, McCarthy found himself at odds with the conservative Democratic and Republican leadership (including Republicans Styles Bridges and William Knowland and Democrats Millard Tydings and Richard Russell). Nor was the Wisconsin Senator then the darling of the anti-communist right.

Wisconsin newspapers, and particularly the *Milwaukee Journal* and *Madison Capital Times*, had disparagingly reported McCarthy's senatorial "exploits" and in 1949 began investigating his pre-senatorial career. Both newspapers publicized the Senator's questionable conduct while circuit court judge and his condemnation by the Wisconsin Bar Association—which narrowly averted voting for his disbarment—for campaigning for the Senate while still a judge (in violation of both the Wisconsin constitution and the ethics of the bar). In addition, Wisconsin's press disclosed that McCarthy had not paid a state tax on income received from stock market investments in 1943. Given the fortuitous circumstances of his 1946 victory and the Democrats' success in carrying Wisconsin in the 1948 presidential election, McCarthy appeared to be in deep political trouble.

Indeed, McCarthy's record was such that his domination of national politics from 1950 through 1954 seemed inconceivable. So, too, that his name would become a familiar descriptive phrase "McCarthyism," or that he would become the national political symbol of the American right. That McCarthy and McCarthyism so evolved was the consequence of his timely exploitation of a burgeoning climate of doubt about the priorities and wisdom of Harry Truman's leadership as well as the Senator's own aggressive style of operation. In great part, these doubts were the product of an emotional, unthinking fear of the Soviet Union and a conviction that the Kremlin leaders were bent on world domination. By the 1950s, many Americans viewed the Soviet Union as the Antichrist, believed that the Soviets were winning the Cold War, and attributed Soviet postwar gains to the diplomatic errors or treason of American policymakers (resulting in the "loss" and "sell-out" of Eastern Europe and China). A sense of American omnipotence and omniscience, encouraged by the Truman Administration, made many Americans ripe for the simplistic conspiratorial explanations of the origins of the Cold War crisis offered by the junior Senator from Wisconsin.

McCarthy's political difficulties partially explain his enthusiastic adoption of the anti-communist issue in 1950. Not that the Republican Senator had failed to exploit this issue before. He had red-baited his opponents in the 1946 campaign and the *Madison Capital Times* in 1949. During the congressional debates of 1947–48, he had callously associated communism with public housing, price controls, and labor unions. And he had called for legislation outlawing the Communist Party in 1947. Unthinkingly raising the issue of "communists in the State Department" in early 1950, then having found himself backed into a corner by Democratic efforts to discredit him, McCarthy audaciously pressed the attack. There were obvious credits to be had: his charges provided him with national publicity and, furthermore, he had no political choice but to establish the correctness of his position.

The immediate occasion for McCarthy's exploration of the "Communists in the State Department" theme was in Wheeling, West Virginia, on February 9, 1950, where he delivered a now-famous speech before the local Republican Women's Club. In that address, the Senator got very specific and held up a sheet of paper which he claimed was a list of 205 "known" communists in the State Department. The speech was not part of an orchestrated strategy to gain national prominence; it lacked careful research or advance publicity. Furthermore, it was not original, whole excerpts having been lifted from an earlier speech by Richard Nixon, newspaper stories from the conservative *Chicago Tribune* and *Washington Times-Herald*, and a 1948 report on State Department loyalty procedures by a subcommittee of the House Appropriations Committee. That it created any furor resulted from its bald claims and timing, for it came in the aftermath of Alger Hiss's conviction and Secretary of State Dean Acheson's highly publicized press conference response that he would not "turn [his] back" on Alger Hiss.

McCarthy's Wheeling speech was Republican Lincoln Day oratory, and it was the first of three speaking commitments he had been assigned by Republican Party officials (with subsequent addresses in Salt Lake City and Reno). His charges at first were virtually ignored; although the Associated Press and the *New York Times* inexplicably published them three days later. Responding to the *New York Time's* story, the State Department cabled McCarthy (then in Denver en route to his Salt Lake City speaking commitment) for this list so that it could promptly undertake an investigation. Unprepared for this reaction, lacking even a copy of the speech or clearly remembering just what numerical figure he had cited, the Senator brazened out reporters' questions by stating that he would only turn the list over to the President if so requested and by claiming to have mentioned not 205 known communists but "known security risks." Speaking in Salt Lake City later that day, McCarthy scaled down the charge to 75 "known communists," and later markedly reduced even this number.

The specific identification of this issue with McCarthy, however, derived only from a decision by the Democratic Senate leadership to call his bluff as one method of discrediting the developing Republican strategy of attacking Democratic foreign policy decisions, a strategy that dated from early January 1950. Challenged to develop his charges more fully, McCarthy complied on February 20, 1950, by delivering a rambling, sometimes incoherent speech on the Senate floor (then claiming to read from a list detailing 81 communists in the State Department). In response, on February 22 the Democratic Senate leadership introduced a resolution (S. Res. 231) to create a Subcommittee of the Senate Foreign Relations Committee to investigate McCarthy's charges.

Appearing before the Subcommittee on March 8, McCarthy only divulged six names. In time the Subcommittee shifted from investigating these six to other more prominent Foreign Service personnel or advisers (John Stewart Service, Philip Jessup, and Owen-Lattimore), whom McCarthey subsequently named. Despite his failure to produce evidence confirming that these men were communists or had committed espionage (at best his documentation consisted of listing the political organizations to which they had belonged or meetings they had sponsored), and despite the abrupt shifts in his accusations, McCarthy successfully preserved his credibility by responding aggressively to his critics and by brazenly ignoring his own contradictions. From charging on March 21 that Owen Lattimore was the "top of the whole [Soviet espionage] ring of which Hiss was a part" and that he would "stand or fall" on that charge, the Wisconsin Senator was asserting by March 30 that he "may have perhaps placed too much stress on the question of whether or not [Lattimore] had been an espionage agent." And when the Subcommittee issued its majority report on July 17, 1950, branding his charges a "fraud and a hoax," McCarthy countered by pledging that "Communists will be dug out one by one, regardless of how frantically Tydings [the Democratic Chairman of the Subcommittee] screams for their protection. . . . The job will be a long and difficult one in view of the fact that all of the power of the administration is dedicated to the task of protecting the traitors, Communists, and fellow travelers in our government."

In addition to McCarthy's raw assault, there was the recent arrests of Klaus Fuchs and Julius and Ethel Rosenberg on the charge of atomic espionage, the outbreak of the Korean War, and the devastating defeat of the Chinese Nationalists by the Chinese Communists—and all combined to create an atmosphere conducive to a McCarthyite politics. More importantly, McCarthy was sustained by most conservative Republicans.*

At first, Republican leaders had neither encouraged nor endorsed McCarthy. But his notoriety and the Democratic counterattack prompted them to move quickly to neutralize Administration and Senate Democratic efforts to discredit him—and so to commit themselves despite McCarthy's failure to produce solid evidence and the crudity of his charges (during the 1950 congressional campaign he attacked Democrats as the "Commiecrat party"). Accordingly, following a March 22, 1950, Republican Senate Policy Committee meeting, where it had been decided not to make McCarthy's charges a party issue. Senator Robert Taft privately argued that the Senator should "keep talking and if one case doesn't work out, he should proceed with another one." Publicly, Taft countered Truman's attacks on McCarthy describing the Senator as "a fighting Marine who risked his life to preserve the liberties of the United States. The greatest Kremlin asset in our history has been the pro-Communist group in the State Department who succumbed to every demand of Russia at Yalta and Potsdam, and promoted at every opportunity the Communist cause in China until today Communism threatens to take over all of Asia." Taft's standard for judging McCarthy's methods was not then and would not in the future be very exacting. He later contended that "whether McCarthy has legal evidence, whether he has overstated or understated his case, is of lesser importance. The question is whether the communist influence in the State Department still exists." And he further charged that years of FBI intelligence gathering on communists in government had been ignored because of the Truman Administration's attitude that communists were merely "just another form of Democrats."

Taft's tolerance of McCarthy was based ultimately on political expediency. For McCarthy's charges, as a 1954 *Fortune* poll of prominent business executives revealed, succeeded in keeping "the albatross [of disloyalty] hung about the neck of the New and Fair Deals." Yet McCarthy's tactics—particularly his intemperance and failure to research his charges thoroughly—made him politically unreliable while threatening to discredit an anticommunist politics.

In any case, the Republicans could not always skirt the McCarthy issue, particularly in the aftermath of their 1952 political successes, when they gained control of the presidency and both houses of Congress. Still disdain-

---

* Additionally, FBI Director Hoover not only commended McCarthy's "Americanism" but supplied FBI reports (although not raw files) to the Wisconsin Senator. When McCarthy publicly broke with Eisenhower's Attorney General, Herbert Brownell, the Senator ceased open contact with Hoover, limiting himself to guarded association with trusted Hoover aides.

ful of McCarthy's methods, the newly elected Eisenhower administration and the Republican Senate leadership nonetheless respected his value to the Party. After 1952 their main concern was how to channel and control his activities. For one, Taft (as Republican majority leader) sought to curb McCarthy by appointing Senator William Jenner to head the Internal Security Subcommittee (McCarthy became Chairman of the Government Operations Committee and its Permanent Investigations Subcommittee) and by requiring that all investigations be cleared through the Party leadership. Taft confided to an associate: "We've got McCarthy where he can't do any harm." For its own reasons, the Eisenhower administration, through Vice President Richard Nixon and White House congressional liaison Maj. Gen. Wilton B. Persons, urged McCarthy to continue to expose communists but to do so in cooperation with fellow Republicans in the White House.

But McCarthy was not to be so easily controlled. Indeed, he came into conflict with the administration almost immediately, and as Chairman of the Permanent Investigations Subcommittee conducted investigations of the Voice of America, the State Department's International Information Agency, and the Army's loyalty/security procedures. In addition, McCarthy's divergent conceptions of adequate internal security procedures and foreign policy priorities led him to challenge the administration's (1) appointment of Charles Bohlen as Ambassador to the Soviet Union, (2) its opposition to legislative control of foreign policy (such as with the Bricker Amendment), and (3) the unilateral drafting of internal security safeguards. The inevitable showdown came over McCarthy's October 1953 investigation of the Army's security procedures at Ft. Monmouth, New Jersey.

In its initial response to McCarthy's arraignment of high-level Army personnel, the Eisenhower administration had sought to reach some compromise. This effort failed and the humiliated Secretary of the Army Robert Stevens threatened to resign unless the executive branch supported his efforts to preserve the Army's integrity. Counterattacking, the Army accused McCarthy of conducting a vendetta to secure favorable treatment for G. David Schine, a recent inductee and former member of the Senator's staff. This charge led to an investigation of the Army's complaints. The resultant nationally-televised Army-McCarthy hearings, which began on April 22, 1954, and lasted 35 days, dramatically exposed McCarthy's questionable methods and undercut his popular following.

Responding to the adverse popular reaction to McCarthy and to his misuse of power, Republican Senator Ralph Flanders, on June 11, 1954, introduced a resolution calling for McCarthy's removal as chairman of the Permanent Investigations Subcommittee. Finding the Senate leadership unresponsive to his proposal, particularly Southern Democrats who feared this attack on the seniority principle, Flanders amended his resolution to censure McCarthy for 46 counts of misconduct. This resolution, S. Res. 30, was further amended on the floor, with a provision added that established a special Select Committee empowered to investigate Flanders' charges and to permit McCarthy to defend himself. After tightly controlled hearings, in September 1954, the Committee (chaired by conservative Republican Senator Arthur Watkins of Utah and known as the Watkins Committee) recommended McCarthy's censure on two counts: (1) his failure in 1951 to cooperate with a Senate committee investigating campaign violations during the 1950 election, and (2) his abuse of General Ralph Zwicker during the February 1954 Ft. Monmouth hearings.

The Senate vote on this Committee report was delayed until after the 1954 congressional elections. When Congress did reconvene, in late November, McCarthy and his supporters (notably William Jenner, Barry Goldwater, and Herman Welker) went on the offensive. They argued that the real purpose behind the censure was the destruction of McCarthy because of his efforts against communists and subversives. Accordingly, copies of a pamphlet that contained excerpts from the *Daily Worker* demanding McCarthy's expulsion were placed on the desk of every Senator. And McCarthy publicly accused the Watkins Committee of conducting a "lynching bee," charging further that it was the "unwitting handmaiden" of the Communist Party.

The Senate subsequently voted to drop the count censuring McCarthy for abuse of General Zwicker (citing lack of cooperation by the Army and the broad use of executive privilege, both of which frustrated the Committee investigation). However, the Senate added another count—which condemned McCarthy for his attack on the loyalty and integrity of the Watkins Committee. And on December 2, 1954, by a vote of 67 to 22 McCarthy was condemned for misconduct against the Senate.

By the end of 1954, McCarthy had become anathema to many conservative and moderate Republicans, although he still commanded a significant following among anti-communists. Thereafter, and until his death on May 2, 1957, he remained an isolated political figure. Yet his death or condemnation did not mean the end of McCarthyism, for the powerful anti-communist politics to which the Senator had given his name remained a basic aspect of the national political culture until the 1970s. Only then, following the reaction to the Vietnam War and to the Nixon administration's abuses of "national security," was McCarthyism effectively neutralized.

14

Seeking Equality in White America

WALTER WHITE
MARTIN LUTHER KING
MALCOLM X

by August Meier and Elliott Rudwick
Kent State University

Walter White, Martin Luther King, and Malcolm X rank among the most important black protest leaders in the 20th century. Walter White was the chief executive of the NAACP for a quarter century prior to his death in 1955, the very year in which Martin Luther King emerged to national prominence as the leader of the Montgomery, Alabama bus boycott. For the next dozen years, until his assassination in 1968, King did more than any other single person to popularize nonviolent direct action as a technique of black protest and was, in fact, the most celebrated Negro in America. For a few brief years prior to his murder in 1965, Malcolm X, who was King's contemporary, had emerged as the most important spokesman for black nationalism since Marcus Garvey.

For a half-century after its founding in 1909, the NAACP was the preeminent protest advancement organization for Negro equality in the United States. It was created during a period of extreme racial oppression by a group of prominent black intellectuals and white Progressives. Rejecting the accommodating approach epitomized by Booker T. Washington, they sought to secure the Constitutional rights to which Negroes were entitled under the 14th and 15th Amendments. In accordance with the strategy of Progressive reformers, they employed a three-pronged approach—educating white public opinion through investigations and propaganda; lobbying in state legislatures and Congress; and ultimately most significant, mounting in the federal courts a sustained legal attack against disfranchisement, segregation, and mob violence. The Association began as a little organization chartered by the State of New York and run by a small staff and board of directors in New York City. Significantly, at its top levels the NAACP was avowedly interracial and consciously used its prominent white members to strengthen its appeal in an exceedingly hostile white environment. Gradually the organization established branches across the country. By 1918, when Walter White joined the staff, the Association had grown to about 9,300 members in 80 cities and towns. This membership was overwhelmingly black as were the great majority of branch officers.

*   *   *

Walter White, a 25-year-old graduate of Atlanta University, had been born into Atlanta's tiny black elite. His father was a mailman, an occupation which Negroes regarded at the time as very prestigious. All the members of his family were exceedingly light-skinned; Walter White himself had fair hair and blue eyes and was physically indistinguishable from a Caucasian. His most vivid childhood recollection was the 1906 Atlanta race riot, when he witnessed mobs chasing and killing defenseless blacks, and when his own neighborhood only narrowly escaped attack because Negroes fired at the invaders. Subsequently, while a student at Atlanta University, Walter White met a different kind of Caucasian; years later he warmly recalled a number of his white professors.

As a young man, White exhibited a flair for leadership and public speaking. Active in black Atlanta's civic life, he played a prominent role in setting up that city's branch of the NAACP in 1916. Through this work, White met James Weldon Johnson, the noted writer who was the NAACP's Negro field secretary. While on a tour organizing branches in the South, Johnson observed and was deeply impressed with his efforts, and at the beginning of 1918 White, then a young employee of the Atlanta Life Insurance Company, accepted the post of assistant secretary at the NAACP in New York City.

The NAACP had a half dozen key leaders at the time: W. E. B. Du Bois, editor of the *Crisis*, the organization's monthly magazine; John Shillady, a white social worker who held the post of Secretary; James Weldon Johnson; Joel Spingarn, a wealthy white man who occupied the central position of chairman of the board and helped to project the Association nationally through his militant speeches; his brother, Arthur Spingarn, a New York lawyer who for years would be working closely with Walter White as chairman of the NAACP national legal committee; and Mary White Ovington, a financially independent white social worker who made the NAACP her major interest. Up to the time that Walter White arrived in New York, Du Bois and Johnson were the only Negroes who held positions of authority in the organization. The top executive post of Secretary, for example, had always been occupied by a white but the NAACP did not really grow until Johnson became field secretary in 1916. Johnson proved so effective in this post as well as in his work as Acting Secretary, that the board of directors appointed him permanently to the job in 1920. He thus became the first black to have that position. Johnson and White, who continued to serve as assistant secretary, were a remarkably successful team. Under their administration, the Association grew rapidly, sank deep roots into the black community, and clearly became the dominant Negro racial advancement organization. Moreover, the rise of Johnson and White marked the advent of a black bureaucracy within the NAACP, which not only gave Negroes a key voice in policy-making but also tied the national office more closely to the branches and to local Negro communities throughout the country.

The two men complemented each other exceedingly well. Johnson brought to the NAACP an enormous range of political and civic contacts, a distinguished reputation as a cultivated intellectual and author, and an extraordinary tact and diplomacy in working with people which had served him well during his earlier years as a United States Consul in Venezuela and Nicaragua. While not lacking in administrative talents, Johnson functioned superbly as the organization's ambassador to white and black America, attracting numerous local black leaders to the Association's ranks, conferring with presidents, lobbying with congressmen, and symbolizing the Association's unalterable determination to secure first-class citizenship for Negroes in America.

White, on the other hand, who was an unknown young man, proved a bureaucrat par excellence. Possessed of a quick mind and a passion for detail as well as enormous drive and ambition, he quickly made himself indispensable to Johnson and the board of directors. Although the NAACP spent a great deal of effort agitating for the enactment of a federal anti-lynching law, it was evident by the 1920s that the organization's most important work would lie in the courts. And Walter White's major arena of operations was in the legal program. His first dramatic and dangerous assignment was to investigate lynchings whose perpetrators the NAACP wished to bring to court. Passing as a Caucasian journalist, he investigated mob murders in Estill Springs, Tennessee, and Elaine, Arkansas. In Elaine, he himself barely escaped being lynched by a mob that had discovered his true identity. In the nick of time he jumped aboard a train that was just pulling out of the station, only to have the conductor inform him, "Mister, you're leavin' town just as the fun is about to start. They're after a yaller nigger down here passin' for white."

Less dramatic but more important, White proved adept at mastering complicated legal matters and functioned as administrator for the NAACP's legal committee. He himself was not a lawyer, but working closely with Arthur Spingarn, he handled negotiations with local lawyers and carried out much of the committee's routine business. His influence grew steadily, and by the mid-1920s all important decisions regarding legal work were in practice made jointly by the two men. Having become indispensable to the board, he was the obvious choice to succeed Johnson as Secretary of the NAACP in 1931.

Walter White took over at a time when the onset of the Great Depression presented the NAACP with its most serious crisis since its founding. Income plummeted at the very time that the Association had to grapple with the black community's catastrophic economic problems. As a result of several internal developments, which will be discussed below, Walter White was able to bring the NAACP through these critical years; indeed, it emerged with greater prestige and a more solid record of achievement than ever before. He presided over modifications in the organization's program and structure, so that the local branches gained greater influence at the national policy level. The Association paid increasing attention to the economic problems of the black workers. Finally, White emerged with unprecedented personal control of the organizational machinery owing to the fact that the busy members of the board of directors quite naturally tended to accept his advice and ratify his decions. Consequently, he exercised a degree of power in the NAACP's affairs that no single person had ever before enjoyed.

The NAACP's first response to the Depression was simply to try to keep alive and solvent. With income from memberships declining disastrously, White spent considerable time raising money among white philanthropists. At his recommendation the board of directors cut staff substantially. This action led to an unprecedented rebellion with most department heads from Du Bois down, criticizing White in a sharply worded complaint to the board. Never before in the organization's history had staff thus challenged the Secretary. The board, however, sided with White, and most of the staff backed down. A few, most notably the Director of Branches, were dismissed; White emerged with undisputed control over all staff except Du Bois and the *Crisis*.

From the beginning, Du Bois had run the *Crisis* as an autonomous unit within the NAACP. More than once his editorial independence had brought him into conflict with the board, but his personal prestige and eminence had prevented an open break. Both White and Du Bois were men of strong ego, but they would have undoubtedly tolerated each other and their sharp differences of opinion, if the Depression had not produced serious competition between them for the scarce resources available to the Association. The *Crisis,* which had been virtually self-supporting, had become a deficit operation draining badly-needed funds from an organization already fighting for financial survival. Under the circumstances, Du Bois's espousal of a black separatist editorial position that ran counter to the NAACP's basic ideology, precipitated a head-on clash that ended in Du Bois's resignation from the Association. Management of the *Crisis* came under White's jurisdiction, with the appointment of Roy Wilkins, the new assistant secretary, as editor.

Wilkins had resigned as Managing Editor of the black weekly, the Kansas City *Call* to join the Association staff. White's relationship with him was quite different from the one he had with Johnson. White exercised a tighter rein over the organization's bureaucracy and did not follow Johnson's policy of permitting the assistant secretary a virtually independent sphere of operations. Under Wilkins, the *Crisis* now faithfully articulated the organization's official policies. And to a considerable extent Wilkins performed White's earlier function of handling the routine administration of the legal work. But unlike Johnson, White very directly involved himself in the important litigation undertaken by the Association, continuing to make key decisions with Arthur Spingarn. In fact, the contrast between the two administrations was so marked that hostile critics unfairly referred to Wilkins as White's "errand boy."

Throughout Walter White's administration, the NAACP remained basically committed to fighting for enforcement of the Negro's constitutional rights. However, the Depression and the New Deal provided it with new challenges and opportunities. Despite the Roosevelt Administration's limited perspective regarding the problems of black America, it proved more responsive to its needs than any previous presidency. Prominent New Dealers, most notably the President's wife, displayed a genuine interest in Negro Americans, one that was rooted in a humanitarian concern for the welfare of all of the underprivileged in American society. At the same time, the black vote had reached sizable proportions in many northern cities, creating an additional motivation for the attention to Negro welfare among New Deal politicians. After 1935, the rise of the Congress of Industrial Organizations (CIO), with its explicit policy of organizing unskilled and semi-skilled workers regardless of race, also helped to establish a climate more favorable to the NAACP's mission. Blacks were included in the emergency relief and job programs, and subsequently in other federal programs such as public housing. The Roosevelt Administration appointed an unprecedented number of Negroes to prominent positions in the federal bureaucracy. These policies raised the hopes of blacks, who now demanded additional gains. For example, in 1933 under NAACP initiative, various race organizations established the Joint Committee on National Recovery (JCNR), an agency that would fight discrimination in the administration of many New Deal Programs. The JCNR was especially effective in exposing the unequal wage rates provided by the National Industrial Recovery Act codes.

Although the NAACP had broadened the scope of its efforts, critics complained that it was still dominated by a concern for the black middle class that prevented the development of meaningful projects addressed to alleviating the desperate plight of the black masses. This criticism was not new, but it had a greater effect during the Depression. Pressures came most importantly from a group of young black intellectuals that included Abram Harris and Ralph Bunche, both professors at Howard University. They wanted the NAACP to encourage the unionization of black workers and to build a close alliance with progressive elements of the labor movement. And they also denounced the oligarchic character of the NAACP's self-perpetuating national board of directors in whose selection the branches had no voice.

While the NAACP fought discrimination on several fronts, its critics were essentially accurate in contending that White and the most influential board members wanted the organization to maintain its emphasis on securing enforcement of the Negroes' constitutional rights. Both board chairman Joel Spingarn and White basically agreed that the Association, while seeking to fight as many kinds of discrimination as possible, lacked the resources and skills to develop a labor organizing program. Nevertheless, White, the astute bureaucrat, and Spingarn, the skillful interpersonal leader, felt that the NAACP had to respond in some positive manner. In 1933 Spingarn hosted a conference of NAACP leaders and its critics among the black intellectuals at Amenia, New York, to provide a forum for a free exchange of ideas. More important, the Association appointed a committee chaired by Abram Harris to propose new directions for the organization. The Report of this Future Plans and Program Committee asked the Association to democratize board elections, recommended that the organization encourage Negroes "to view their special grievances as a natural part of the large issues of American labor as a whole," and urged the Association to create industrial and agricultural councils that would educate workers for economic and political action.

White regarded the Report's goals as laudable but noted that the Harris Committee had failed to indicate where the financial resources for this approach would be obtained. Privately, he questioned the effectiveness of the idea of workers' councils (which had been advanced even before the CIO was born). Certainly the implementation of such a proposal would have drastically altered the NAACP's character and downgraded the fight against disfranchisement and segregation in the South.

On the other hand, NAACP leadership did institute some significant changes in both organizational structure and programmatic direction. Election procedures were modified, providing the branches with some voice in the selection of board members. And in the following years the NAACP gradually forged an alliance with the new CIO labor unions. The final turning point came in 1941. Requested by the United Automobile Workers to help get Negro scabs out of the Ford automobile plants, White secured assurances that the union would cease discriminatory policies against black members. White personally went to Detroit and successfully urged many black strikebreakers to leave the factories.

Responding to the rising criticism of NAACP policies and practices Joel Spingarn decided to step aside. He resigned as chairman of the board in late 1935, occupying the ceremonial position of President until his death a few years later. He was replaced as board chairman by an old and close friend of Walter White, the distinguished black surgeon, Louis Wright. Although Spingarn was under no pressure to resign, his withdrawal was significant organizationally both because it symbolized the ending of the crucial role white leaders had played in the Association from the outset and because it further consolidated White's control. Spingarn and White had always worked well together and had been in basic agreement. But even more than Spingarn, Wright deferred to White's judgment in administering the NAACP.

Also in 1935 the Association was enormously strengthened by creation of a legal department headed by Charles Houston, a brilliant black lawyer who had received his LLB at Harvard in 1920, where he was the first Negro on the *Harvard Law Review*. He came to the NAACP from an administrative post at Howard University, where he had dramatically upgraded the law school into a fully accredited institution geared toward providing black lawyers with expertise in civil rights litigation. Houston's arrival at the NAACP was the result of many years of work by White. Previously the NAACP had followed a conscious policy of usually using prestigious and non-paid white lawyers to conduct its most important cases, a policy to which White fully subscribed. Because of the extreme racism of the period, black lawyers frequently were at a disadvantage in their training, experience, and standing in the courts. Nonetheless, Walter White, even before becoming NAACP Secretary, both personally and for the good of the Association, wished to see Negro counsel utilized at the highest levels of its legal work. Aided by pressures from black lawyers who felt that they themselves should be leading the struggle for Negro rights, White pushed in this direction during the early 1930s. He had secured the services of both Houston and his law partner, William H. Hastie, for several key cases in 1933 and 1934, and finally succeeded in obtaining a foundation grant to enable the NAACP to add Houston to its staff in 1935.

Houston's appointment as special counsel was important in several ways. Coming almost simultaneously with Joel Spingarn's withdrawal, it marked the final consolidation of black dominance in the NAACP. It also solidified NAACP ties to the black community by increasing support among the Negro bar. Secondly, even though the NAACP legal department exhibited greater autonomy than any other department, its establishment was another step in enhancing the organization's bureaucracy; the post of special counsel greatly diminished the significance of the chairman of the legal committee. Arthur Spingarn welcomed these developments, and upon his brother's death in 1939, assumed the powerless position of Association President. Thirdly, Houston shared the concern of men like Harris for making the NAACP more responsive to the black working class. White greatly respected Houston's judgment, consulting him on a wide range of organizational concerns beyond the legal work. Accordingly, although Houston consciously deferred to White's authority as Secretary, his influence fortified the NAACP's growing interest in labor and economic matters. Houston's contacts with the more radical intelligentsia, like his standing among black lawyers, greatly strengthened the organization.

Yet Houston's most significant contribution was in developing the NAACP's campaign for constitutional rights, particularly the fight against school segregation. He conducted the first battles for equalization of salaries of school teachers in the South, and the admission of blacks to advanced study in the southern universities. Victories in these cases raised enormously the NAACP's public standing and gained for it thousands of members among the largest professional group in the Negro community—the southern school teachers. As vulnerable public employees, they had hitherto been mostly indifferent to the organization.

Thus, by the time of World War II, the NAACP under Walter White's leadership was more vigorous and influential than ever before. He had built up the NAACP's traditional program, while successfully adapting the organization to meet the challenge of the changing times. He had not only successfully weathered the financial crisis precipitated by the Depression but had made the NAACP a voice of protest that federal agencies had to reckon with. White established vital ties with the newly-organized CIO industrial unions and forged new bonds with influential groups in the black community.

Ironically, Walter White eventually lost control of the organizational machinery he had done so much to develop. Walter White had made the NAACP into a superb and efficient organizational mechanism. Thus, largely because of his work during the 1930s, the NAACP was able to play an increasingly successful role in the struggle for equal rights in succeeding years. In turn, it was the NAACP that made White a figure of national reputation. Well known not only in the black community, but among white elites as well, Walter White, although a fluent speaker and possessed of considerable personal charm, was neither a charismatic leader nor a man of prominence independent of his role in the NAACP. Unlike Du Bois or Johnson, both distinguished men who brought great prestige to the Association, White became a celebrity through the NAACP, and through the work he did in it to make the organization a significant force in American public life. During these years there were always a few dissident board members who were hostile toward him and critical of the concentration of power in his hands. They charged him with operating a "one-man show." As he became more and more of a celebrity, he spent increasingly less time in the office, lecturing for pay to other organizations. To some extent he lost his close grip on the handling of administrative detail, at the same time that he made himself vulnerable to charges that he was using his position as NAACP Secretary for personal gain. To his opponents both on the board and in several of the NAACP branches, Walter White appeared to be a self-centered publicity-seeker. When he divorced his black wife of nearly 28 years to marry a white woman, his critics, exploiting his domestic problems, claimed he embarrassed the Association. When he returned from a year's leave in 1950, he found the board polarized over whether to keep him in office or replace him with Roy Wilkins, who had been Acting Secretary in his absence. After an acrimonious debate the board voted to retain White with the title of Executive Secretary but to delegate authority to Wilkins over all internal matters and to make him responsible directly to the board. He received the title of Administrator. White, however, continued to formulate broad organizational policy and act as the Association's spokesman. Yet in reality his power had substantially withered away. He died in 1955, just after the NAACP had achieved its most famous victory in the school desegregation cases.

During the last dozen years of Walter White's life the NAACP had helped bring about significant changes in the status of black Americans. Desegregation of the armed forces was begun by President Truman's order. In several northern states the NAACP and other organizations won the enactment of laws designed to obtain fair employment practices, access to public accommodations, and nondiscriminatory housing. Piling up victory after victory in the courts, the Association successfully attacked the South's white primary, racially restrictive housing covenants, segregation in interstate transportation, and discrimination in publicly-owned recreational facilities. *Brown vs. the Board of Education* in 1954 brought to a triumphant climax the NAACP's legal campaign against segregation in Southern schools. These achievements encouraged a new militancy among southern blacks and set the stage for Martin Luther King.

*   *   *

Martin Luther King was catapulted into national prominence by the Montgomery, Alabama, bus boycott of 1955–56. Son of a prominent Atlanta Baptist minister, King had graduated from Morehouse College, and after studying at Crozer Theological Seminary and Boston University, became pastor of a black Baptist church in Montgomery. When in Decem-

ber 1955, Montgomery's Negro citizens initiated a boycott against segregation in the local buses, King was asked to head the movement. He
was chosen primarily because as a newcomer, he was acceptable to all
groups in the Negro community. He was an impressive man, dignified,
well-educated, and enormously eloquent. These qualities helped to project him and the movement into national prominence, made him attractive
to the mass media, and elevated him as the foremost symbol of the black
protest in America.

The Montgomery bus boycott represented a new method—nonviolent
direct action—that had slowly been gaining adherents since the founding
of the Congress of Racial Equality in 1942. CORE, a tiny, predominantly
white organization until the 1960s, had been founded by pacifists who
sought to apply Gandhian techniques of nonviolent direct action to
America's race problem. Concentrating on desegregating places of public
accommodation in northern and border cities, CORE chapters had originated the sit-in technique that would become famous in 1960 when used
on a wide scale by Southern black college students. King was like the
founders of CORE, though unlike the great majority of participants in
direct action demonstrations. He possessed a Gandhian faith in the principles of pacifism and nonviolence. Speaking of the creation of a "beloved
community," King maintained that love was more powerful than hate
and that civil rights demonstrators who were beaten and jailed by hostile
whites transformed their oppressors through the redemptive character
of their suffering.

King and his supporters won in Montgomery when a judicial ruling
desegregated the buses. Even before this victory, a similar boycott had
started in Tallahassee, Florida, and after it, another began in Birmingham, Alabama. Such developments heralded the emergence of a militant
"New Negro" in the South, no longer afraid of white hoodlums, police,
or jails, and ready to act boldly and collectively. Seizing upon this new
mood, King in 1957 established the Southern Christian Leadership Conference (SCLC), a federation of local direct action groups usually led
by Baptist ministers.

Although King's appeal does much to explain the growing popularity
of direct action in the late 1950s, the fact was that legalism had revealed
its limitations. Blacks were ready for a new approach. Despite impressive
advances since the end of the second World War, the great majority of
Negroes were still disfranchised in the South, and Supreme Court decisions desegregating transportation facilities were still largely ignored.
The region had responded to the school decision of 1954 with the rise
of racist White Citizens Councils, attempts to outlaw the NAACP, massive
resistance to court decisions, and forcible curtailment of black voter
registration. Discrimination in employment and housing abounded, even
in those northern states that had model civil rights laws.

Nonetheless, what was occurring among black Americans was a revolution in expectations. There were the successes of King and his followers, the increasingly favorable new laws and court decisions, the growing recognition by white elites of the legitimacy of black demands. Moreover, Negroes were developing a new confidence in the future as they watched the birth of independent African nations and the growing influence of non-white peoples in international affairs. They no longer felt the need to accept the humiliations of second-class citizenship. Consequently such humiliations—somewhat fewer though they now were—appeared more intolerable than ever. Paradoxically, the NAACP's success in the legislatures and the courts, more than any other single factor, led to this revolution in expectations and to the resultant dissatisfaction with its program. Increasing black impatience and disillusionment accounted for the rising tempo of nonviolent direct action—including some campaigns initiated by NAACP branches—that culminated in the student sit-ins of 1960.

For the next five years, nonviolent direct action dominated the civil rights struggle, and the dramatic events and victories that followed were aptly described as the "Civil Rights Revolution" or the "Negro Revolt." Direct action was widely practiced in the South in the battle against segregation and disfranchisement, as well as in the North against housing, employment and school discrimination, and police brutality. These tactics were employed by many groups—by local ad hoc organizations and committees, by NAACP branches, by CORE chapters and by the Student Nonviolent Coordinating Committee (SNCC), which originally had been formed to "coordinate" the college student sit-ins of 1960. King and SCLC were associated with some of the most famous of these campaigns, notably the struggle to desegregate places of public accommodation in Albany, Georgia, in 1962, the celebrated 1963 Birmingham campaign, which precipitated the great and climactic demonstrations across the country that spring and summer, and the 1965 confrontation in Selma, Alabama, over the issue of voter registration. The efforts of King and SCLC, along with those of other activist organizations, and the pressure brought by the NAACP-led lobbying group, the Civil Rights Leadership Conference, produced the Civil Rights Act of 1964, as well as the Voter Registration Act of 1965. All of this activity in the streets and in Congress practically eliminated segregation in places of public accommodation in the South and enfranchised millions of new black voters.

King functioned in a paradoxical manner. Regarded by the outside world as leader of the nonviolent direct action movement, he actually was criticized by many activists within the movement. Although he was a symbol of militant direct action, his critics denounced him for what seemed, at times, as indecisiveness, and more often for a tendency to accept compromise.

In a movement that defined successful leaders as those who shared in the hardships of their followers, in the risks they took, in the beatings they received, in the number of arrests and the length of time they spent in jail, King was suspect. He tended to leave prison for other important engagements relatively quickly rather than remaining and suffering with his followers. In a movement that usually gave leadership to those who mixed democratically with their followers, King remained isolated and aloof. In a movement that prided itself on militancy and "no compromise" with racial discrimination or with the white "power structure," King maintained close relationships with, and appeared to be influenced by, Democratic presidents and their emissaries. He seemed amenable to compromise, considered by some half a loaf or less, and willing to postpone or avoid direct confrontations in the streets.

King's career was marked by failures that, in the larger sense, must be accounted triumphs. The buses in Montgomery were desegregated only after lengthy judicial proceedings conducted by the NAACP Legal Defense Fund. Nevertheless, Montgomery was a triumph for direct action and gave this tactic a popularity unknown when identified solely with CORE. King's subsequent major campaigns—in Albany, Georgia; Danville, Virginia; Birmingham, Alabama; and St. Augustine, Florida—ended as failures or with only token accomplishments. But chiefly because of his presence, each of them dramatically focused national and international attention on the plight of the Southern Negro, thereby facilitating overall progress. In Birmingham, in particular, demonstrations that fell short of local goals led directly to passage of a major Federal Civil Rights Act. This same pattern of local failure and national victory was repeated later at Selma, Alabama.

In the Gandhian tradition, King was ideologically committed to disobeying unjust laws and court orders, but generally he followed a policy of obedience to federal court orders. He called for a genuine union of black and white common people, ascribing race prejudice primarily to capitalists playing white workers against black. Yet, in practice, he was amenable to compromise with the white political and economic establishment.

In short, King was a "Conservative Militant." In combinations of militancy with caution and righteousness with respectability lay the secret of his enormous success.

Certain important civil rights leaders privately dismissed King's position as the product of mass media publicity. But the same could be said of the successes of the civil rights nonviolent action movement generally. In fact, contrary to the official nonviolent direct action philosophy, demonstrations secured their results not by changing the hearts of hostile whites through a display of nonviolent love, but through the national and international pressures generated by the publicity arising from mass arrests and incidents of violence. No one employed this strategy of securing publicity through mass arrests and precipitating violence from white hoodlums and law enforcement officers more than King himself. He abhorred violence: as at Selma, he constantly retreated from situations likely to result in the deaths of his followers. Yet he was precisely most successful when his demonstrations precipitated violence from southern whites against black and white demonstrators.

Publicity alone does not explain the durability of King's image nor why he remained for the rank and file of whites and blacks alike the symbol of the direct action movement, the most charismatic leader that the civil rights movement produced. At the heart of King's continuing influence and popularity were two facts. First, better than anyone else, he articulated the aspirations of Negroes who responded to the rolling cadence of his addresses, his religious phraseology, and the vision of his dream of freedom and a just society for them and for America. He intuitively adopted the style of the old fashioned Negro Baptist preacher and transformed it into a new art form. Second, he communicated black aspirations to white America more effectively than anyone else. His religious terminology and manipulation of the Christian symbols of love and nonresistance were partly responsible for his appeal among whites. To talk in terms of Christianity, love, and nonviolence was reassuring to the mentality of white America. By uttering Christian pieties in magnificent displays of oratory, King became enormously effective.

If Martin Luther King's success with blacks was largely due to the style of his utterance, his success with whites was much more complicated. He unerringly knew how to exploit to maximum effectiveness their growing feeling of guilt. Here, of course, King was not unique; novelist and essayist James Baldwin is perhaps the most conspicuous example of one who achieved success with this formula. But King went beyond the guilt motif. With intuitive, but extraordinary skill, he not only castigated whites for their sins, but in contrast to angry young writers like Baldwin, he explicitly stated his belief in their salvation. Not only would direct action bring fulfillment of the "American Dream" of freedom and justice to Negroes, but direct action by blacks would help whites to live up to their Christian and democratic values; it would purify, cleanse and heal the sickness in white society. King had faith that the white man would redeem himself. Hence, Negroes must not hate whites but love them.

King thus gave white men the feeling that he was their good friend, that he posed no threat to them. This was the same feeling white men received from Booker T. Washington, the noted early 20th century accommodator. Both men stressed their faith in the white man and the belief that he could be induced to accord Negroes their rights. Both stressed the importance of whites recognizing the rights of blacks for the moral health and well-being of white society. Like King, Booker T. Washington had an extraordinary following among whites. Like King, Washington symbolized for most whites the whole program of Negro advancement. Even though their philosophies were in fundamental disagreement, there were these important similarities in the way both men functioned vis-a-vis the white community.

King's very tendencies toward compromise and caution, his willingness to negotiate and bargain with White House emissaries, his hesitancy to risk violence upon demonstrators, further endeared him to whites. He appeared to them a "responsible" and "moderate" man. But black militants, as has been noted, were less satisfied with him. Illustrative of their dissatisfactions was King's caution in the famous symbolic march from Selma, Alabama, to Montgomery, the State capital, in 1965. The march was intended to focus national attention on the State's disfranchisement of blacks. In the face of a federal court injunction barring this march and with almost certain prospect that the county sheriff and his deputies would violently assault the demonstrators, King proclaimed his determination to go ahead. Pressed by the White House and Department of Justice, he privately accepted a compromise in which he would lead his followers a short distance down the highway until asked to halt by state troopers, whereupon he would conduct a prayer service and then turn back. He carried out the agreement to the surprise and anger of the marchers, who were prepared to defy the federal court and to risk their lives in a major confrontation. King's acceptance of face saving accommodations in this and other instances was fundamental to the particular role he was playing, and it was essential for achieving and sustaining his image as a leader of heroic moral stature in the eyes of white men. His caution and compromise kept open the channels of communication between the activists and the majority of the white community.

The March on Washington of August 1963—a mass demonstration of 250,000 people held to press Congress to pass the bill that eventually became the Civil Rights Act of 1964—had made direct action respectable. Selma, which attracted thousands of white religious and civic leaders from across the country, made it fashionable. More than any other force, Martin Luther King impressed the civil rights revolution on the American conscience.

This picture had another side: King might not have been either respected or respectable if on his left there had not been more militant activists engaged in more radical forms of direct action. Without CORE and, especially, the Student Nonviolent Coordinating Committee (SNCC) to serve as contrasts, King would have appeared "radical" and "irresponsible" rather than "moderate" and "respectable."

Martin Luther King, then, occupied a position of strategic importance as the "vital center" within the civil rights movement. Though King had lieutenants who were far more militant and radical than he, SCLC acted as the most cautious, deliberate, and conservative of the direct action groups because of his leadership. As a consequence, King and the SCLC functioned—almost certainly unintentionally—not only as an organ of communication with the establishment and white public opinion, but also as something of a bridge between the activist and more traditionalist or "conservative" civil rights groups. It appears unlikely, for example, that the NAACP would have participated in the March on Washington if King had not done so. The March was the brainchild of the civil rights movement's ablest strategist and tactician, Bayard Rustin, and the call was issued by the veteran and respected protest leader, A. Philip Randolph. SNCC and CORE enthusiastically approved of the project, but the NAACP held back, fearing that the militant activists would turn the March into a display of massive civil disobedience. King found himself subjected to cross-pressures from the activists and the Kennedy administration. But when he finally decided to participate in the March, the NAACP considered it necessary to join. King's identification with the March was also essential for securing the support of large numbers of white clergymen and their moderate followers. Thus the March would have been a minor episode in the history of the civil rights movement without King's support.

Yet, curiously enough, despite his charisma and international reputation, King was more a symbol than a power. Indeed his strength in the civil rights movement derived less from an organizational base than from his symbolic role. In the period after the Montgomery bus boycott, King developed no program and revealed himself as an ineffective administrator. He failed badly to capitalize on his popularity among blacks. SCLC did not develop an overall sense of direction or a program of real breadth and scope. Although the leaders of SCLC affiliates became the race spokesmen in their communities—displacing the established local conservative leadership of teachers, old-line ministers, and businessmen— SCLC did little except to advance the image and personality of King. Until Birmingham, King appeared not to direct but rather to float with the tide of militant direct action. He did not supply the initiative for the bus boycott in Montgomery but was pushed into the leadership by others. Similarly, in the late 1950s and early 1960s, he appeared to let events shape his course.

Under King's leadership SCLC called the conference in April 1960 that gave birth to SNCC. But within a year, most of the SNCC youth had lost faith in the man they satirically called "De Lawd" and had struck out on their own independent path. By that time, the spring of 1961, King's power in the southern direct action movement had been further curtailed by CORE's stunning freedom ride project to dramatize interstate bus segregation in the deep South.

From the point of view of the civil rights movement, it was probably fortunate that King had not obtained a predominance of power commensurate with his prestige. Organizations with different and even competitive approaches actually proved helpful in securing the movement's victories. Disunity was thus functional rather than dysfunctional. The movement needed those who viewed the struggle chiefly as a conflict situation in which the power of demonstrations and the power of blacks would force recognition of the race's humanity and citizenship rights as well as the achievement of equality. Equally necessary were those who saw the movement's strategy to be chiefly one of capitalizing on the basic consensus of values in American society by pricking the conscience of the white man to the contradiction between his professions and the facts of discrimination. And equally essential to the movement were those who operated skillfully, recognizing and yet exploiting the deeply held American belief that compromise among competing interest groups is the best *modus operandi* in public life.

King was unique in that he maintained a delicate balance among all three of these basic strategy assumptions—of confrontation, compromise, and moral appeal—that stressed commonly shared values. The traditional approaches of the Urban League (conciliation of the white businessmen) and of the NAACP (appeal to the courts and to the sense of fair play in the American public) basically exploited the consensus in American values. But it would of course be a gross error to say that the Urban League and the NAACP strategies were based simply on attempting to exploit the consensual values, while SNCC and CORE acted simply as if the situation were one of pure conflict. Implicit in the actions of every civil rights organization were all these assumptions. The NAACP especially encompassed a broad spectrum of strategies and activities, ranging from time-tested court procedures to militant direct action. Sophisticated CORE militants knew very well when a judicious compromise was necessary or valuable. But King was in the middle; in effect, he seemed to be acting on all three assumptions described above. His was both a purely moral appeal and a militant display of power. He talked of the power of Negro demonstrators in the streets, but unlike CORE and SNCC activists, he accepted some compromises that consisted of token improvements while calling them impressive victories.

Viewed from another angle, King's failure to achieve a position of power on a level with his prestige was functional because rivalries between personalities and organizations remained an essential ingredient of the dynamics of the movement. They were a precondition for its success as each current tried to outdo the others in effectiveness and in maintaining a militant public image. Without this competitive stimulus, the civil rights revolution would hardly have accomplished as much as it did.

Major newspapers like the *New York Times* and the Washington *Post* were sympathetic to civil rights and racial equality. Though more gradualist than the activist organizations, they congratulated the nation upon its good luck in having a "responsible and moderate" leader like King at the head of the nonviolent action movement. In point of fact, they over-estimated his power and underestimated the symbolic nature of his role. It would probably be more appropriate however to have congratulated the civil rights movement for its good fortune in having had King as its symbolic leader. Traits that many activists criticized in him actually functioned not as sources of weakness, but as the foundations of his strength.

King's influence was at its peak between 1963 and 1965. In 1964 he was awarded the coveted Nobel peace prize. Yet at that very time, de-velopments were underway that would erode King's effectiveness and stature as a civil rights leader. By 1964 and 1965, the continuing revolu-tion of expectations had alienated many militants in CORE and espe-cially in SNCC to the point where they questioned the value of integra-tion and nonviolence. When SNCC leaders articulated the slogan, "Black Power," in 1966 and denounced white liberals, integration, and the philosophy of nonviolence, it marked the end of an era. King was no longer able to bridge the divergent wings in the black protest movement.

Meanwhile, with victory largely achieved in the struggle for consti-tutional rights in the South, King and SCLC, like the other protest or-ganizations and leaders, sought to tackle the enormous problems of the black urban poor. But the massive demonstrations he led in Chicago in 1966 achieved no concrete results. King's open and early criticism of the Vietnam War, moreover, lost him the financial support of some civil rights sympathizers and undermined his cordial relationship with the White House. In the midst of his declining fortunes, King sought to con-tinue the struggle to achieve world peace and alleviate the plight of the black poor. Although he had premonitions that he would be killed, King refused to retreat from his activist role. In early 1968 he went to Memphis to lead demonstrations in support of black garbagemen seeking a living wage. There on April 4 he was felled by an assassin's bullet.

King was the great symbol of nonviolent direct action, and he elo-quently voiced the black man's aspirations for full equality and integration into American society. But paradoxically, the civil rights revolution of the 1960s also produced a growing sense of black nationalism. There were several reasons for this development. One important product of the dra-matic achievements of the protest movement was a new pride in being black. Heightened militance encouraged overt expression of anger and hostility against whites, thus fostering a continued sense of alienation from American society at the very time that more white Americans than ever before were recognizing the legitimacy of the black man's demands. This alienation was strengthened by the rapid escalation of expectations that flowed from the victories in the streets, courts, and legislatures.

Accordingly, the rate of social change seemed painfully slow, especially because it became increasingly clear that even after constitutional rights were secured, the legacy of discrimination and poverty would still leave the black masses an enormous distance from the goal of genuine equality. The resulting disillusionment stimulated a belief that blacks would have to go it alone and provided strong encouragement for separatist impulses. No one articulated these tendencies better than Malcolm X.

*   *   *

Malcolm X, born Malcolm Little in Omaha, Nebraska, came from a background that contrasted sharply with that of Walter White and Martin Luther King. Where they were raised in solid southern middle-class families and enjoyed the benefits of a college education, Malcolm, the son of a lower-class Baptist preacher, grew up in poverty in a northern ghetto and never finished high school. His father was killed by racist whites, and Malcolm turned into a street-wise youth. He moved to the East and became a petty criminal in New York and Boston. Convicted on a burglary charge, Malcolm served six years in a Massachusetts prison where he became converted to the teachings of the Nation of Islam (more popularly known as the Black Muslims). Founded in 1930, this small lower-class sect led by Elijah Muhammad predicted that Allah would destroy the white devils and usher in the ascendancy of the black man. It demanded a separate territory within the United States where black people could establish their own state and offered its followers an immediate and practical program of acquiring wealth through hard work, thrift, and racial unity. Like the integrationist civil rights organizations, the Black Muslims manifested both the Negroes' quest for recognition of their human dignity and the blacks' rejection of gradualism.

After leaving prison in 1952, Malcolm X, like other members of the sect, shed his "slave" surname and became an important leader in the movement. His extraordinary gifts as a public speaker attracted a host of new recruits for the Nation of Islam. Although his strength lay in his abilities as a spokesman and agitator rather than as an administrator, he served as head of the Harlem Mosque and organized a number of new congregations of the sect. Unquestionably, he deserves major credit for the significant growth of the movement in the late 1950s and early 1960s. Malcolm was also mainly responsible for making the Nation of Islam known to a larger public, both black and white. His barbed rhetoric, denouncing as hopelessly incurable the racist sins of white society, and his militant advocacy of racial separatism and retaliatory violence made exciting copy for the media. Moreover, many blacks who would never join the Black Muslims or subscribe to their program, resonated to his denunciations of white society and his advocacy of black retaliation.

Even dedicated black pacifists and convinced integrationists were moved by Malcolm X. As one official of CORE wrote after hearing him in a 1962 debate with Bayard Rustin:

> I came away . . . with mixed feelings. . . . Being a pacifist, a Negro, and one who has been involved in the racial struggle lately I expected to be "with" Bayard all the way and "against" Mr. X completely. My mixed feelings were the result of the discovery that I was applauding more for Malcolm X than I was for Bayard Rustin. . . . There is no question in my mind but that Bayard presented the saner attitude, but the amazing thing was how eloquently Malcolm X stated the problems which Negroes have confronted for so many years. . . . I must confess that it did my heart a world of good to sit back and listen to Mr. X list the sins of the white man toward the black man in America.

Indeed, Malcolm X struck an even more responsive chord among activists in the militant integrationist organizations like CORE and SNCC, which were becoming increasingly disillusioned with the pace of social change and the efficacy of nonviolent direct action techniques.

Had it not been for the Nation of Islam, which had given him a forum, Malcolm X undoubtedly would have been just one more angry black. But by 1963 he had become such a celebrity that in the public mind he overshadowed the organization and its leaders. Both his public image and his effectiveness in recruiting new members made him a threat to high ranking officials who feared that he would take over the sect when the ill and aging Elijah Muhammad died. Even Elijah himself, whose appreciation for Malcolm X's services had led him to name the latter chief minister, had shown some fears of his prominence. Thus it is clear that in spite of all the movement had done for him and all that he had done for the Nation of Islam, serious tensions had developed within the organization. By the end of 1963 only a pretext was required to produce an open break. Malcolm X's sardonic comment on President Kennedy's death—it was "the chickens coming home to roost"—provided this pretext. Malcolm was suspended for this remark. A few months later, having concluded that Elijah Muhammad's mind had been irrevocably poisoned against him, Malcolm left the organization.

For the less than a year that he was still alive, Malcolm was groping for a viable program from which to build a new movement. He established his own Muslim sect and also reached out for a broader non-Muslim black following. While retaining his nationalist ideology, he simultaneously softened his anti-white stance. He returned from a pilgrimage to Mecca in May 1964, announcing that he had found a new insight after meeting white Muslims who displayed no racial prejudice. Fundamentally, however, Malcolm X's new program called for race unity and solidarity among American blacks regardless of class and ideological differences as well as a working alliance with African nations which he hoped would mount an attack on American racism through the United Nations. The Organization of Afro-American Unity which he formed in June stressed above all the necessity of black folk in America working together in the struggle against racism and discrimination. Its platform, which in many ways prefigured the thrust of the black protest movement in the late 1960s, explicitly justified acts of retaliatory violence as a constitutional right of self-defense and it outlined an eclectic program ranging from voter registration and black political unity, through local community control of the public schools, to a cultural revolution that would create a distinctive black literature and art. Yet at the very time that black separatism, anti-white sentiment, and justification for violence were becoming increasingly important in the most militant sectors of the black protest movement, Malcolm X was unable to attract a large membership or establish a viable organization. Nor did his intense efforts to convince the African nations to exert pressure on the United States through the United Nations prove successful.

During his last months Malcolm X had only a handful of active followers and had to face the growing harassment from the Nation of Islam. Not only was Malcolm denounced as a traitor, but he believed that the Nation was responsible for the bombing of his house and for physical attacks on his followers. His fears for his own life were confirmed in February 1965 when he was assassinated in New York. Three Muslims were subsequently convicted of his murder. Malcolm X died at the lowest point in his career since leaving the Massachusetts prison in 1952. Only after his death, in the mood of intense disillusionment felt by many Negroes in the late 1960s, the wave of ghetto riots, and the surge of black nationalist sentiment did Malcolm X join Martin Luther King and W. E. B. Du Bois in the pantheon of modern black heroes.

White, King, and Malcolm X struggled against racism and discrimination and for the attainment of justice, equality, and human dignity, but individually they were highly varied. Presenting different ideologies and operating with highly contrasting styles, all were agitators and protesters. One, Walter White, was a bureaucrat and administrator who for three decades functioned superbly in an organizational milieu, while the other two were charismatic spokesmen who transcended their organizational base. Both Martin Luther King and Malcolm X were to a remarkable degree projected by the mass media, while Walter White, who was far less celebrated, was fundamentally a product of his organization. Two were integrationists who sought the complete inclusion of blacks in American society and sought to enlist white allies in the attainment of this goal; the third was a black nationalist who maintained that to integrate with American society was to board a sinking ship, and who believed that blacks must go it alone and control their own destiny. Both White and King possessed a passionate faith in the Judeo-Christian tradition and the "American creed" of equality and liberty for all, although they differed as to means—White relying on lobbying in the legislatures and litigation in the courts, while King was committed to the tactic of nonviolent direct action. Malcolm X, on the other hand, profoundly distrusted white America, and although his position during the last months of his life was ambiguous, his speeches espoused an ideology of separatism and retaliatory violence.

Each man epitomized a phase in the history of the black protest movement in the 20th century. Walter White flowered in a period when Negro protest centered on a strategy of legalism conducted by a professionalized elite in a highly structured organization. King flourished when it became evident that legalism despite its undisputed achievements in the courts and legislatures, had only limited success in battering down the walls of discrimination. With King nonviolent direct action emerged as the principal instrument of the black protest movement. Malcolm X came to prominence on the periphery of the black revolt of the early 1960s and was canonized only after it became evident that nonviolent direct action was no more of a panacea than legalism. All three men not only thrived in their respective milieus but each had an enormous influence in strengthening the black protest strategy and ideology with which he was identified. White pushed the legal struggle and made the NAACP a more effective instrument for leading this fight at a time when the Association was the only national black protest organization. King, associated with the dramatic victories of nonviolent direct action, played a key role in bringing to a successful conclusion the NAACP's decades-long campaign against disfranchisement and segregation in the South. Malcolm X stimulated separatism and pride in blackness, at the same time that his strident rhetoric and talk of retaliatory violence helped legitimize the integrationists in the eyes of white America by making them look like moderates.

All of these three men died (two by assassination) while still pursuing their careers as Negro protest leaders. At the time of their deaths each of them had passed the peak of their public careers. Both White and Malcolm X had lost influence as a result of organizational factionalism, while Martin Luther King's prestige was waning because the method with which he was identified had lost its vogue. Yet each had had an enormous impact on the black man's struggle for racial equality in America.

15

The Presidential Mystique

JOHN F. KENNEDY
LYNDON B. JOHNSON
RICHARD M. NIXON

by Christopher Lasch
University of Rochester

The origins of the welfare-warfare state lie in the underlying crisis of advanced capitalist society. The industrial system long ago reached the point where it was capable of satisfying the material needs of society many times over. Now it depends for survival on the creation of new markets abroad, on state subsidies, and on the continual generation of new consumer demand. By the turn of the century it was already clear that the state would have to play a greatly expanded role in the capitalist economy to guarantee favorable conditions for investment abroad and to prevent cutthroat competition at home. The reforms of the progressive period did not, however, remove the system's underlying irrationalities, and in the '30s the American economy suffered a breakdown more serious than any in its history. Prosperity was restored only by means of war spending.

Thereafter state intervention became a regular and indispensable feature of the system. Concealed subsidies to the auto industry in the form of the federal highway program; direct subsidies to the oil industry in the form of the depletion allowance; socialization of the indirect costs of production such as education, research, and development; military spending; and the maintenance of political stability in Europe, Latin America, and Asia were the most obvious of the many ways in which the state served the corporate system in its dotage. The government also paid the repair bills and doctor bills and cleaned up the garbage, the social and material waste left by a system that thrived on waste and to which waste was of the essence, its very life blood—a steadily accumulating torrent of disposable goods, throwaway items of every description, products designed for instant obsolescence, prematurely worn out wreckage both material and human.

All this required an unprecedented expansion of the powers and prerogatives of the executive branch of the federal government, especially the presidency itself. As commander-in-chief, the President headed a vast army deployed throughout the world and kept in constant readiness. A far-flung intelligence establishment served, or was meant to serve, as his eyes and ears. As the federal bureaucracy grew and threatened to become unmanageable, the White House staff expanded, ostensibly to keep the President in touch with the various departments but in reality with the effect of rendering him increasingly independent of them. The cabinet as a body lost its traditional advisory role. The President now treated the heads of executive departments as specialists in their fields, consulting them only about matters falling within their respective jurisdiction, not about general policy. Policy at the highest level was increasingly made by the President and a handful of trusted subordinates chosen for their ability, real or imagined, to act with vigor and dispatch in emergencies, in crises affecting national "security."

Congress, like the cabinet, ceased to function effectively as an advisory body. It lacked access to important information—so it was told, at any rate—and the tradition of bipartisanship in foreign policy, established after World War II, stifled debate on central questions in a period when those questions were almost invariably defined as matters of foreign policy. Lacking not only the means but the will to act, Congress acquiesced in executive encroachments on its rights, and it even surrendered its war-making power. The cult of the presidency had no more zealous devotees than the members of Congress; many of the latter's more enterprising leaders hoped to use their congressional careers as a springboard to the exalted heights of the White House.

The President of the United States thus emerged as one of the most powerful officials in the world, second only to the greatest socialist dictators. But he was also one of the most dangerously isolated from the world around him. The growth of the office had the effect of shielding its occupant from controversy, from conflicting opinions, from criticism, and from the moods of the country. The Kennedy, Johnson, and Nixon administrations show the effects of this isolation of the chief executive— the delusions of grandeur to which it gave rise, the sense of omnipotence combined with an almost paranoid concern with security, the obsession with crisis and with rising to crisis, the cult of toughness and of the moral value of "survival"—the survival of the office and its prestige—as an end in itself.

The presidents of the '60s and '70s were representative men not only in being products of the political system in which they had risen to the most rarefied heights but also in articulating values that were indispensable to success within that system. These values were widely shared, no matter how far political success, in the long run, had carried these men beyond the common run of humanity. If Kennedy, Johnson, and Nixon were out of touch with public opinion at many points—for instance, in overestimating the lengths to which the country would go in supporting petty dictators in Vietnam—they nevertheless embodied popular expectations of what a bold and fearless leader ought to be. Their careers in office, therefore, tell us something not only about the expansion of the presidency to "imperial" dimensions but about the changing value system that made this expansion possible or at least put no insurmountable obstacles in its way.

*   *   *

At his birth in 1917, John F. Kennedy inherited advantages—charm, good looks, and above all, money—that made his political success, at least in retrospect, appear almost inevitable; especially when combined with his father's fanatical devotion to that objective. The son of an Irish Catholic immigrant, Joseph P. Kennedy went to Harvard, married into Boston's powerful Fitzgerald family, and made a fortune in financial speculations, in Hollywood promotions, in the liquor business, and in a number of other lucrative but somewhat questionable enterprises. He served as head of the Securities and Exchange Commission and as Ambassador to England under Franklin D. Roosevelt. His accomplishments in business and politics were less impressive, however, than his achievement as the founder of a dynasty—the ambition that was clearly closest to his heart.

Snubbed by their rich neighbors in Brookline, Bronxville, and on Cape Cod, the Kennedys withdrew into a life of strenuous domesticity, centering after 1926 on the family compound at Hyannisport, Massachusetts. "We decided that our children were going to be our best friends," Rose Kennedy has said. ". . . Since we couldn't do both, it was better to bring up our family than go out to dinners"—especially when dinner invitations from the proper people were rarely forthcoming in any case.

Rose and Joseph Kennedy may be said to have brought up their family with a vengeance, closely supervising every detail of the children's training, testing them in sports, instilling a fierce will to succeed. If one of the boys came in second in a sailing race, the fatherly admonition was sure to follow: "Next time come in first." Winning was held to be more important than the methods used to win, providing that one never trusted in the loyalty or good will of persons more highly placed in the social hierarchy. One might seek to impress them, but one must never trust them. Urging his second son to publish his Harvard honors thesis, a study of English appeasement in the '30s entitled *Why England Slept,* Joseph Kennedy wrote: "You would be surprised how a book that really makes the grade with high-class people stands you in good stead for years to come." Thirty years later, just after his election to the Presidency, John Kennedy passed this advice along to Richard Nixon in a significantly altered form: "Every public man," according to Nixon's account, "should write a book at some time in his life, both for the mental discipline and because it tends to elevate him in popular esteem to the respected status of an intellectual.") The only high-class people one could trust completely, however, were the Kennedys themselves. Each child was brought up to a sense of the overwhelming importance of the family tie, the responsibilities of being a Kennedy, and the need to do credit to the family name.

Arthur Schlesinger, Jr. has suggested that childhood sicknesses—diphtheria, scarlet fever, appendicitis, stomach trouble—developed in John Kennedy a "sensitivity that set him somewhat apart from the extroverted and gregarious family." Alone among the other children, he read a great deal—mostly books of adventure, biography, and history. The principal effect of this reading, however, must have been to strengthen the will to excell, to do great things, and to test his fortitude against adversity. In this manner he also strengthened his identification with a family whose distinguishing mark, in any case, was not so much extroversion and gregariousness as a sense of its own destiny. The combination of great wealth, the social rejection that great wealth had been unable to prevent, and the "staged social withdrawal" (as Burton Hersh has called it) that followed this rejection, had left the Kennedy family with a strong belief not only in its own distinctiveness but in the need to assert this distinctiveness against often hostile surroundings. To keep alive the awareness of "being a Kennedy" was the underlying object of a strenuous family code that idealized struggle, not sociability.

There was the danger, moreover, that wealth would serve as a temptation to dissipation. To combat it, the children were restricted to very small allowances and made to appreciate the value of a dollar, as Joseph Kennedy would have put it. It was his father's "toughness," John Kennedy believed, that had prevented his younger brother Edward from becoming a "playboy." "My father cracked down on him at a crucial time in his life, and this brought out in Teddy the discipline and seriousness which will make him an important political figure."

Whether he himself experienced similar temptations to a life of frivolity, John Kennedy does not say; nor is it clear when it occurred to him that he had a future as "an important political figure." His education was conventional and his early development unremarkable. After a year at Canterbury, a Catholic school in Connecticut, he spent three undistinguished years at the Choate School, and then entered Princeton—a minor act of rebellion, since his father preferred Harvard. An attack of jaundice forced him to leave in the middle of his freshman year, whereupon he dutifully transferred to Harvard. There he worked on the *Crimson* and injured his back playing football.

Harvard left him with the "patrician ease of manners" so admired by Schlesinger and others. But it probably contributed less to Kennedy's intellectual development than several visits to England and the continent —excellent vantage points from which to observe the dissolution of the western European empires and the paralysis of England and France in the face of the fascist threat. Perhaps during such trips abroad, he also began to glimpse the possibility (to which the elder Kennedy, an isolationist, remained permanently oblivious) that the United States would inherit world leadership from these European nations. Back in America in 1941, Kennedy was rejected by the army because of his back injury but talked his way into the Navy. In the Solomon Islands in 1943, he and his crew survived for five days following the wreckage of their boat, the famous PT-109. This heroism, together with the war death of his elder brother Joseph, Jr.—for whom the patriarch had projected a brilliant career in politics—made John Kennedy heir to the family's political ambitions.

Two terms in the House of Representatives were followed, in 1952, by a Senatorial victory over that quintessential Brahmin, Henry Cabot Lodge, Jr., all the more convincing because it came in a year of Democratic defeat. Six years later Kennedy was elected to a second term in the Senate, rolling up the biggest majority in Massachusetts history. Much more than his meager accomplishments as a legislator, his demonstrated ability as a vote-getter made him the leading Democratic candidate for President in 1960. All his campaigns were characterized by the expenditure of large amounts of money, by fanatically thorough organization supervised by his brother Robert, and by skillful use of the media. In 1960, Kennedy won the Democratic nomination by defeating Hubert Humphrey in the important primaries in Wisconsin and West Virginia and by holding off a last-minute effort on behalf of Adlai Stevenson. The latter had contributed to Kennedy's rapid rise in 1956 by arranging for him to deliver the principal nominating speech on behalf of himself and then by throwing open the vice-presidential nomination, in which Kennedy made a strong showing, impressing people with his youth, attractiveness, and air of self-confidence.

These qualities again proved their usefulness in the election of 1960, the first in which television may have played a decisive part. In his celebrated debates with Nixon, Kennedy said little of substance but projected an "image" of candor, poise, and sincerity. The chief issues of the campaign were almost wholly imaginary. Kennedy criticized the Eisenhower administration for tolerating the presence of Fidel Castro in Cuba, whereas in fact (as he himself knew) the administration was secretly planning the Bay of Pigs invasion. Kennedy also criticized Eisenhower for permitting the growth of a non-existent "missile gap" between the United States and the Soviet Union. His call to "get America moving again" seemed to boil down to the suggestion that a Democratic administration would be even more zealous in fighting Communism than a Republican administration headed by Richard Nixon.

Kennedy's Churchillean calls to national greatness and personal self-sacrifice nevertheless made a strong appeal to those who longed to savor the taste of world leadership after the torpor of the Eisenhower years. The Democratic platform, moreover, contained a strong civil rights plank, and although civil rights was hardly an issue during the campaign, this idealism was attractive at a time when the civil rights movement still commanded broad liberal support. Meanwhile the nomination of Lyndon Johnson, a Texan, as vice-president nullified the possibility of a Southern revolt against the national ticket. It was a master stroke of the Kennedy strategists, though undertaken, it appears, almost inadvertently.

With all these advantages, Kennedy won by a very narrow margin—a testimony, probably, to lingering anti-Catholic prejudice, to popular apathy about assuming a larger share of the world's work, and perhaps also to a vague apprehensiveness that has always surrounded the Kennedys—a fear that their "charismatic" leadership would divide the country, exacerbate social tensions, and unleash violence. This presentiment—which turned out to be quite accurate—had nothing to do with the substance of Kennedy's programs; rather it reflected the legend that was already taking shape around the Kennedy family, the source both of John Kennedy's appeal and of the irrational fear and hatred of the Kennedys.

In many ways the most important event of the Kennedy administration—its high point, from which everything else was a decline—was the inaugural, memorably captured by the television cameras. This event solidified the myth of Camelot before "Camelot" had even come into being. At Kennedy's insistence a black singer, Marian Anderson, sang the National Anthem—seemingly a gesture that the new administration intended to take bold and vigorous action in contrast to Eisenhower's dilatory policy on civil rights. Robert Frost gave the occasion added drama and poignancy. While reading his inaugural poem he first lost his place in the glare of the sunlight and then expressed the hope that Kennedy would usher in "a golden age of poetry and power." The inaugural address itself was a superb performance. "The torch has been passed to a new generation of Americans, born in this century, tempered by war, disciplined by a hard and bitter peace ..." The Kennedy preoccupation with discipline, testing, and "tempering" were hereby invoked on behalf of a whole generation's belief—so soon to be shattered—that it stood poised on the brink of greatness: "Ask not what your country can do for you; ask what you can do for your country."

It would be difficult to exaggerate the importance of this spectacle, and of the symbolic meaning of Kennedy's presidency in general, in setting the political tone of the '60s. Though Kennedy's legislative record was meager and his foreign policies mostly a disaster, his call for idealism and self-sacrifice made a deep impression. It particularly appealed to the Eastern liberal establishment, which felt vindicated in its long-standing attempt to persuade the nation to live up to the responsibilities of world leadership. It also attracted the liberal left—the peace movement, the civil rights movement, the young. Through his words and gestures much more than his actions, Kennedy appeared to have created a new opening in American politics and to have widened the available space for dissent —even, indeed, to have given dissent a new legitimacy.

In doing so, however, he raised expectations of vigorous executive leadership that even truly vigorous leadership would not have been able to satisfy. When these expectations began to turn sour, they contributed to the transformation of left liberalism into a radicalism increasingly bitter and despairing, sweeping in its rejection of official pretensions and of authority in general. Nearly all of the revolutionaries of the late '60s began their careers as enthusiastic adherents of the New Frontier. Their hopes for America, even when those hopes turned to rejection of everything the New Frontier had stood for, were indissolubly linked to the Kennedys. The spectacle of Tom Hayden weeping at the coffin of Robert Kennedy makes all this unforgettably clear. Similarly the black militants of the Johnson period came out of SNCC and CORE, where an indispensable ingredient of their political initiation had been the idealism of which President Kennedy so brilliantly made himself the spokesman.

What attracted people to Kennedy was the quality that made Norman Mailer suppose, for a brief moment, that Kennedy's presidency would be an "existential event." It was this same quality that made many people fear that his presidency would prove to be more strenuous than the country could bear. And in the first reaction to his murder in 1963, it was again this quality that made it so easy to believe that his assassin had been a man of the Right, a racist, an embittered reactionary moved by hatred of Kennedy's ebullient liberalism.

To activate the country—necessarily also (though unintentionally) to divide it—were Kennedy's important contributions to American politics. His record, as distinguished from his reputation, was far from brilliant.

In domestic concerns, he proved an ineffective leader of Congress, possibly because he felt overly inhibited by the narrowness of his electoral margin. In foreign affairs, his misguided activism justified whatever public apathy might have contributed to the inconclusiveness of that margin. The Kennedy administration clearly took enormous risks, not on behalf of American interests but on behalf of American "prestige." If there was a common pattern running through the administration's response to a succession of international crises—the Bay of Pigs, the Berlin crisis of 1961, the Cuban missile crisis—it was a tendency to weigh alternatives without much regard for their military, strategic, or political consequences, but with enormous regard for their effect on American "credibility."

The Bay of Pigs fiasco—itself the product of a haunting fear that the Cuban revolution had undermined American prestige in Latin America—appeared to have left an impression of American weakness, which Kennedy sought to overcome in his meeting with Khrushchev in Vienna in June 1961. In the face of Soviet threats to sign a peace treaty with East Germany, Kennedy overreacted, rejecting the diplomatic responses recommended by the British and by a few of his own advisers, calling up the reserves, urging the country to build fall-out shelters, and characteristically proclaiming Berlin "the great testing-place of Western courage and will." The immediate result was that the East Germans walled off West Berlin and the Russians resumed atmospheric testing of nuclear weapons.

In this era of deteriorating relations with the communist bloc, the vogue of games theory, popularized by Robert McNamara's bright young men in the Defense Department and by pundits like Herman Kahn, gave an intellectual gloss to what was essentially a theatrical conception of international politics. Everything depended on the "credibility" of a nation's "postures." The Cuban missile crisis exemplified this conception in a highly developed form. Leaving aside the recklessness of the Soviet decision to arm Cuba with short-range missiles, the fact remained that this step in no way altered the military balance of power; yet everyone in the Administration agreed on the need for a tough and vigorous response. Debate was confined to the question of whether the United States should remove the missiles by a surprise attack or resort to a blockade—the second policy being hardly less provocative, reckless, and irresponsible than the first.

The best that can be said of this episode, in which the world hung for five days on the edge of nuclear war, is that the consequences of his own recklessness sobered Kennedy. The immediate fruit of this sobriety was the nuclear test-ban treaty of 1963, the first step toward détente with Russia and the liquidation of the European phase of the cold war. Yet in retrospect one can see that détente merely left the United States free to embark on the still greater folly of Vietnam; and Kennedy himself took the decisive step of increasing American commitments to the point where disengagement from Vietnam could only appear as a national defeat.

*   *   *

Lyndon B. Johnson was imprisoned from the beginning of his presidency in this fateful act of his predecessor. To make matters worse, Johnson retained as many of Kennedy's advisers as he could, especially in foreign policy. Johnson's eagerness to preserve "continuity" with the Kennedy administration, misguided though it may have been, was understandable. The country was suffering from the shock of Kennedy's assassination and needed to be reassured that orderly governmental processes were intact. Deeply resentful of the Kennedy mystique, the cult of the Kennedy "style," and unflattering comparisons to himself as a boorish provincial, Johnson nevertheless made no break with Kennedy's foreign policies, now drifting toward a full-scale engagement in Southeast Asia.

Shorn of the rhetoric of the New Frontier, those policies in any case accorded with his own inclinations. Lyndon Johnson, though by no means a simple man, took a very simple view of American foreign policy, one that was rooted in his provincial origins. Born in central Texas in 1908, Johnson grew up in genteel poverty, in a part of the country where the populist movement had once flourished. His father was a farmer and schoolteacher who served five terms in the Texas House of Representatives. His mother also taught school. After graduating from high school, Johnson worked at manual jobs for three years. He then entered Southwest Texas State Teachers College on a loan, working as a janitor to pay his way, taking an active part in school debates and in student politics. At one point he dropped out for lack of funds and taught school for a year in Cotulla, near the Mexican border. After graduating in 1930, he taught public speaking and debate in the Houston high schools.

Johnson's political career began in 1932, when he went to Washington as secretary to Representative Richard M. Kleberg, owner of the huge King Ranch. Thereafter he rose slowly through the harsh world of Texas politics, thanks to his skill in political intrigue, his connections with the oil interests, his own growing fortune in land, cattle, and later in communications, and finally to the patronage of the Roosevelt administration. He served as state administrator of the National Youth Administration from 1935 to 1937. In the latter year he went to the House of Representatives in a special election, serving three more terms during which he supported Roosevelt loyally (even in his court-packing plan), backed important New Deal reforms, and brought the Rural Electrification Administration to Texas.

In 1948 he was elected to the Senate and began his illustrious career as a master-manipulator of the legislative process, first as minority leader and later as leader of the Democratic majority. His success in these positions depended on an elaborate network of Senatorial friendships, his ability to overwhelm colleagues with non-stop monologues, and his understanding of the importance of backstairs intrigue as compared with the total non-importance of formal Senatorial debate. His years in the Senate confirmed habits of secrecy and deviousness acquired earlier in the notoriously Byzantine politics of his native state.

It is hardly necessary to add that these habits carried over into Johnson's conduct of the presidency. Again and again Johnson misled the country about the extent of American commitments to Vietnam or the lengths to which he was prepared to go in defending American "credibility." During the presidential election campaign against Barry Goldwater in 1964, at a time when he had already decided on a greatly expanded American role in Vietnam, he assured the country, "We are not about to send American boys nine or ten thousand miles away from home to do what Asian boys ought to be doing for themselves." Kennedy had told similar lies, of course, and Johnson could legitimately claim that here again he was blamed for the same things his predecessor had done more "stylishly"; yet at the same time it cannot be denied that Johnson not only did nothing to close the gap between pronouncements and policy, he widened it to unprecedented lengths.

Johnson had a strong sense of himself as a member of a disfranchised minority—the South. He was convinced that a southerner could never be elected President, a belief that helps to explain why he decided to settle for the vice presidency in 1960; he was convinced that he had exhausted the possibilities of the Senate and regarded himself as blocked from a national career. It also helps to explain his resentment of the Kennedy cult, which seemed to be directed not only against himself but against his entire region. But this same sense of belonging to a persecuted minority gave Johnson a certain sympathy with other minorities. In his first race for the Senate, the support of Mexican-Americans was crucial to his close win. In the Senate and later as President, Johnson was instrumental in the passage of the civil rights laws—notably the Civil Rights Act of 1957 and the Voting Rights Act of 1965—which have had such an important effect on American politics. The War on Poverty, the most imaginative venture of his administration, stemmed also from his feeling for the problems of minorities as well as from a certain populist sympathy for the underdog. It has become a cliché to say that only a southern President elevated to the office by accident could have done for racial minorities what Johnson did. What is perhaps not so obvious is that his being a southerner not only placed Johnson in a strategic position to win southern acceptance to measures the South would not otherwise have tolerated but it also enabled him to grasp the seriousness of the racial problem in the first place. It was his deep sense of the reality of discrimination in American life that gave rise to Johnson's passionate wish for "consensus." Indeed he appeared to be the ideal instrument for such a consensus until the war in Vietnam, which he himself escalated to catastrophic proportions, wrecked his presidency and created new and deeper divisions in American society.

There were definite limits to Johnson's sympathy for minorities. Shortly after becoming President, he said to a group of reporters, *à propos* of the latest crisis in Latin America: "I know these Latin Americans. I grew up with Mexicans. They'll come right into your yard and take it over if you let them. And the next day they'll be right up on your porch, barefoot and weighing one hundred and thirty pounds and they'll take that too. But if you say to 'em right at the start, 'hold on, just wait a minute,' they'll know they're dealing with somebody who'll stand up. And after that you can get along fine." If poverty and provincial origins had given Johnson a taste of what life was like for those doubly cursed by poverty and a dark skin, his own white skin—and his spectacular rise to affluence and power—meant that it remained no more than a taste. His social vision did not go beyond the classic prescriptions for dealing with injustice: give everybody an equal start, above all an education, and meanwhile keep the niggers off your porch.

Carried over into foreign affairs, the same attitudes yielded a conventional intransigence in the face of Communism, which Johnson instinctively saw, it would seem, in the form of hordes of little men threatening to encroach on the prerogatives of their betters. This was a view of the world that left little room for complexity, especially when shored up by well-worn historical analogies to "Munich." Communist threats had to be nipped in the bud by a strong show of force, after which the adversaries might be able to "get along fine." In a fine show of bipartisanship, Johnson, as majority leader, regularly lined up the Senate behind the blustering policies of John Foster Dulles. To anyone familiar with Johnson's thinking on the subject of Latin Americans—to say nothing of his general record on the cold war—his unpremeditated response to the Santo Dominican crisis in 1965 should have been entirely predictable. "What is important," he said after dispatching troops to put down a rebellion led by liberals, "is that we know, and that they know, and that everybody knows, that we don't propose to sit here in our rocking chair with our hands folded and let the communists set up any government in the Western Hemisphere."

When in the very first days of Johnson's presidency, Ambassador Henry Cabot Lodge, Jr. returned from South Vietnam to warn that the political and military situation there was deteriorating and that hard decisions would soon have to be made, Johnson's immediate reply was equally predictable: "I am not going to lose Vietnam. I am not going to be the President who saw Southeast Asia go the way China went." (Later Richard Nixon repeatedly made essentially the same statement; he too did not intend to be the first President to lose a major war.)

The more his "consensus" eroded, the more Johnson tended to see every event as a test of his own fortitude. By the end of 1967, Vietnam and the riots in Watts, Newark, and Detroit had polarized the country. The peace movement had evolved "from dissent to resistance." The civil rights movement had given way to "black power." Important sections of the establishment itself were in revolt against the war. Senator Eugene McCarthy of Minnesota declared his intention to contest the Democratic nomination. As his popularity waned and the country fell apart, Johnson increasingly took refuge in the delusion that his position was comparable to that of earlier presidents faced with opposition to unpopular wars. On one occasion he called in congressional leaders and read passages from Bruce Catton's *Never Call Retreat*, describing how Copperheads in Lincoln's party had tried to get rid of him in 1864. Again and again Johnson announced his refusal to be swayed by opposition. The President would stand firm; the nation would stand firm. "We must not break our commitments to freedom and the future of the world ... Make no mistake about it. America will prevail." This harping on survival, standing firm, and honoring "commitments" was a measure of the emptiness of American policy in Vietnam and of Johnson's failure as a war leader: he was never able to convince the country that American interests were at stake or American security endangered. Instead, the war was presented as a matter of abstract "honor" and "credibility"—this at a time when the "credibility" of the White House had reached an all-time low.

In his last months in office, Johnson lived in beleaguered isolation. The threat of demonstrations, together with fear of violence, prevented him from moving about the country. As a result, he was increasingly out of touch with popular opinion. McCarthy's strong race in the New Hampshire primary in March 1968 (in which he carried 42 percent of the vote) showed how badly Johnson had underestimated popular opposition to the war. Meanwhile the Tet offensive showed how badly the President's advisers had underestimated the military strength of the North Vietnamese. On March 31, 1968, Johnson announced a modified bombing halt, initiated negotiations with Hanoi, and declared that he would not run for re-election. Five days later Martin Luther King was assassinated in Memphis and the black ghetto in Washington (and in many other cities as well) went up in flames. The impression of a be-leaguered government, no longer able to govern even in the rudimentary sense of keeping the local peace, was unmistakable.

*   *   *

The violence and turmoil of the '60s culminated in the spring and early summer of 1968. Johnson's withdrawal from the presidential race and the King riots were followed by a long student strike at Columbia University, still more serious student-worker uprisings in Paris, and the latest in a series of political assassinations, the shooting of Robert Kennedy in Los Angeles. Some observers concluded either in hope or despair that the old order was collapsing, but this impression was misleading. In fact the political turbulence of the period had given rise to a deep longing for peace and quiet. A growing "white backlash" manifested itself in the emergence of politicians like Louise Day Hicks of Boston and George Wallace of Alabama, no longer a sectional figure but a man with a na-tional following. "Law and order" became an important political issue. Student radicalism, perceived by the working class as a movement of spoiled children of the rich, the so-called counter-culture, drugs, and permissive sexual morality, were deeply resented, especially by white ethnic groups. Such groups, moreover, saw themselves as the chief victims of racial integration and welfare programs aimed at improving the posi-tion of racial minorities.

The growing reaction made itself felt on national politics. Both parties emphatically repudiated the "new politics" in choosing their presidential candidates—the Democrats in a setting of unparalleled official violence at Chicago, the Republicans in the artificial seclusion of Miami. In the campaign that followed, Richard Nixon and his running-mate Spiro Agnew, emphasized the law-and-order issue. In spite of the disadvantage of his ties to the unpopular Johnson administration and of his own insipid campaign based on the "politics of joy," Hubert Humphrey finished strongly, barely averting victory by waiting until the last moment to qualify his support of Johnson's policies in Vietnam. Nixon was thus elected by a smaller margin even than that of Kennedy in 1960.

Nixon's election was a triumph of persistence and of his capacity to recover from seemingly conclusive defeats. After losing to Kennedy in 1960, he was badly beaten in a race for governor of California in 1962. Immediately following this second defeat he berated the press, in a memorable display of petulence, for its allegedly unfair treatment of his career, pointing out that one consequence of his retirement from politics would be that reporters "won't have Richard Nixon to kick around any more."

That Nixon still became his Party's nominee six years later reflected the fact that the "liberal" Rockefeller and "conservative" Goldwater wings of the Party had fought each other to a standstill. His comeback would not have been possible, however, without his remarkable ability to suffer public abuse and indignity and even to turn them to his political advantage. In his own view, his entire career had been a succession of "crises," each more harrowing than the last, which he had survived in spite of recurrent temptations to quit. In the process he had mastered to perfection the techniques of political survival—the most important, in his eyes, being a recognition that "the ability to be cool, confident, and decisive in crisis is not an inherited characteristic but is the direct result of how well the individual has prepared himself for the battle."

Born in 1913, the son of a California grocer of moderate means, Nixon seldom lost an opportunity to remind audiences of his humble origins. This, of course, is a time-honored ritual of American politics, but Nixon carried it much further than most politicians. Thus in the famous Checkers speech in 1952, in which he defended his right to stay on the Republican ticket against charges of financial improprieties, Nixon labored to present himself as more average than the average man with his mortgages, his wife's cloth coat, and his faithful dog Checkers. It was all very well, Nixon said, "that a man like Governor Stevenson, who inherited a fortune from his father, can run for President," but it was essential "that a man of modest means can also run for President." On this occasion, as on so many others, Nixon threw himself with enthusiasm into the role of the common man. He was the poor Quaker from Whittier, who began laboring at odd jobs at ten, worked his way through Whittier College, went to the Duke University Law School on a scholarship, and rose to political eminence by dogged tenacity and without the advantages of inherited wealth and an illustrious family name. All of this does not mean that he found the role altogether uncongenial or regarded his performance as in any way a distortion of the truth, any more than his carefully rehearsed allusions to the social privileges enjoyed by his adversaries were not prompted by genuine resentment of the rich and well-born. This resentment, indeed, ran throughout Nixon's embattled career, in the course of which he repeatedly pitted himself against rich, well-educated opponents: Alger Hiss, Stevenson, Kennedy, the "Eastern liberal establishment," and the media which, in Nixon's eyes, faithfully reflected the establishment's views. But whereas Johnson's scorn of this same Eastern establishment was the scorn of a man who had made it big in Texas and was confident of his own abilities, Nixon's hatred reflected an outsider's uneasiness in the presence of his social superiors. Johnson compensated for his provincial origins by developing an egregious egoism. Far from attempting to conceal his achievements, he broadcast them far and wide. Nixon, on the other hand, repudiated his own gifts

—which include intelligence, imagination, and (as Gary Wills convincingly argues) a certain sensitivity to suffering—and wrapped himself in groveling humility. Where Johnson's vanity was utterly unpremeditated (some found it almost endearing for that reason) Nixon's humility, like all his other public poses, had about it a theatrical quality that should by no means be confused with the absolute insincerity of which he was often accused. The point, rather, is precisely that Nixon could throw himself into an almost any performance with total conviction. All public men adopt roles of one kind or another, but Nixon lost himself in those roles. This was what made it so hard to locate the "real" Nixon. Nixon not merely performed parts, he was his parts.

In college, Nixon won debating awards and was elected president of the student government, but it is more to the point that he enjoyed acting in student theatricals. According to Ola-Florence Jobe, his sweetheart of adolescence, he was an accomplished actor, with an "almost instinctive rapport with his audience." His interesting account of his political career, *Six Crises,* is full of passages, as Bruce Mazlish notes, in which political confrontations are described in theatrical terms. For example, Nixon prided himself on his ability to distinguish a convincing performance from a poor one, as in the Hiss case, when he became certain that Whittaker Chambers was telling the truth because "I did not feel that [his performance] was an act." On the other hand Hiss, he thought, "had put on a show when he was shown a picture of Chambers" that he professed not to recognize. After watching the Army-McCarthy hearings on television, he remarked scornfully, "I prefer professionals to amateur actors." During his famous "kitchen debate" with Nikita Khrushchev, Nixon "was sure that he was going through an act," and he later reproached Marshal Georgi Zhukov with underestimating the intelligence of the Soviet people. "They aren't dumb. They know when somebody is acting and when it's the real thing—particularly when the acts have been so amateurish."

A remarkable instance of Nixon's acting ability occurred during one of his televised debates with Kennedy in 1960, when Kennedy demanded more active support of the anti-Castro forces in Cuba. Although Nixon knew that Kennedy himself had been briefed on the preparations for the Bay of Pigs invasion, considerations of official secrecy prevented him from exposing Kennedy's demagoguery. Most politicians in such a predicament would have evaded the issue or even joined Kennedy in demanding more vigorous measures against Castro—a seeming criticism of Eisenhower's inactivity that would nevertheless have been eminently forgivable under the circumstances. Instead, Nixon threw himself into a vigorous and entirely convincing denunciation of Kennedy's position —that is, the very position that was already being carried out, partly at Nixon's own instigation, by the Eisenhower administration. "I think,"

Nixon said, "that Senator Kennedy's policies and recommendations for the handling of the Castro regime are probably the most dangerously irresponsible recommendations that he's made during the course of this campaign." As Nixon writes in *Six Crises,* "I was in the ironic position of appearing to be 'softer' on Castro than Kennedy—which was exactly the opposite of the truth..." Nevertheless, he predicted, with great astuteness, the way in which the Bay of Pigs invasion laid the groundwork for the Cuban missile crisis. If the United States followed Kennedy's policy, Nixon said, she would not only lose all her friends in Latin America but issue an "open invitation for Mr. Khrushchev... to come into Latin America."

Even more remarkable than this performance itself, in which Nixon formulated the most telling criticisms of a policy in which he himself fully believed (if one can say that he fully believed in any policy), is the detachment with which Nixon discusses it in his book. He comments on his own performance with the same objectivity with which he comments on the performances of Hiss and Chambers, noting with some pleasure—but with complete indifference to the irony of the situation—that he spoke "the exact opposite of the truth" so effectively that several important papers, including the *New York Times,* strongly commended him. Not only that, they reproached Kennedy with such vigor that he was obliged to modify his position. That they had been completely misled as to the nature of Nixon's own position does not seem to have occurred to Nixon; if it did, it did not greatly trouble him. What mattered was that his act had been found altogether convincing.

Such triumphs, however, have been rare in Nixon's career. In spite of his absorption with acting, or perhaps because of it, his reputation for deviousness and insincerity remained the most enduring thing about him. He himself unwittingly gave the reason for this. "From considerable experience in observing witnesses on the stand," he writes, "I had learned that those who are lying or trying to cover up something generally make a common mistake—they tend to overact, to overstate their case."

Nixon's policies as President can be briefly summarized. Their overriding objective was to restore peace and quiet at home, while quietly expanding American influence abroad. By ending the draft and relying more heavily on air power, Nixon successfully defused Vietnam as a political issue. He managed to withdraw American forces while averting a humiliating defeat. Abandonment of messianic anti-Communism made possible a partial accommodation with the Soviet Union and China. At home, the reformist programs of the '60s were scrapped, thereby reassuring the South, the ethnics, and "Middle America" in general. Big business, meanwhile, was allowed to do very much as it pleased, and businessmen showed their gratitude by making large contributions to the Republican campaign in 1972.

In the short run these policies were brilliantly successful. The turmoil of the '60s was forgotten, prices soared, and a series of spectacular diplomatic successes engineered by Henry Kissinger brought the Nixon administration international acclaim. These achievements, however, did nothing to reverse the long-term decline of the American economy or the long-term decline of American power throughout the world. In any case they were quickly overshadowed by the Watergate scandals.

Watergate grew out of an obsession with internal security by no means peculiar to the Nixon adminstration. The tremendous growth of presidential power since the 1930s, as we have seen, has had the curious effect of isolating the presidency not only from public opinion but from political reality. The picture of Nixon shrinking from the sight of demonstrators, so convincingly described by John Dean during the Watergate hearings, epitomizes the new state of affairs. As the Presidency expands, the range of experience available to the President steadily contracts.

Kennedy and Johnson had already excluded not only Congress and the cabinet from their traditional advisory roles but the newer intelligence agencies as well. One of the most remarkable aspects of Vietnamese policy was the way in which intelligence reports predicting the failure of that policy were systematically ignored. The decision-makers listened to the intelligence agencies only when their reports appeared to reinforce conclusions already arrived at.

The Nixon administration simply carried this administrative absurdity to its logical conclusion. When the existing intelligence agencies failed to support the presidential theories that Daniel Ellsberg was a psychopath and a traitor, that George McGovern's campaign had ties to radical movements, or that these movements in turn were financed by foreign enemies, the White House concluded that the intelligence itself, not the White House theories, was defective. From this it followed that the White House had no choice but to set up its own intelligence operations for the purpose of spying not only on the political opposition but on the other branches of government, including, presumably, the intelligence agencies themselves.

The expansion of the presidency occurred simultaneously with the rise of the art of mass promotion, which tends to submerge the distinction between truth and falsehood in a blur of plausibility. Several times reference has been made to the fact that recent presidents have seemed to care more about their "image" than about the substance of their policies. This tendency cannot be attributed to the psychological peculiarities of the men who have sat in the presidency. Indeed, the fact that men as different from each other as Kennedy, Johnson, and Nixon should all have acted in similar ways and worried about the same things—their ability to rise to crisis, to project an image of decisiveness, in short to give a convincing performance of executive power—shows that whatever prompted these concerns is endemic in American culture. It was not only Kennedy, Johnson, and Nixon who acted as if credibility were more important than truth. Their critics resorted to the same standards. Thus when doubts finally began to be raised about the leadership of the Johnson administration, they focused on the "credibility gap." Public relations and propaganda have created a society in which "the image," in Daniel Boorstin's words, has "itself become the original" and people "talk constantly not of things themselves, but their images."

In politics, the Nixon administration carried these tendencies, once again, even further than preceding administrations. Inheriting the domestic tensions and confusion that had been generated by the war, Nixon did not limit himself to trying to stifle opposition and destroy the left—deplorable measures that are nevertheless easily intelligible. Instead he mounted a full-scale attack on a single individual (Daniel Ellsberg), instituted an elaborate security program to prevent further leaks of what was regarded as vital security information, and convinced himself that Ellsberg was somehow in league with the leading Democratic contender for the presidency.

These actions led more or less directly to Watergate and the Watergate cover-up; and since they apparently defy rational explanation, it is tempting to dismiss Watergate as the work of one lonely psychopath, as the Warren Commission said of the assassination of John Kennedy. Where was the danger, even to Nixon's popularity, which these actions were intended to counter? The Pentagon Papers contained no state secrets of any importance, certainly none relating to the country's "defense posture." The public response to them was one of indifference. In any case the report covered only the actions of earlier Presidents, most of them Democrats. Nevertheless, the panic touched off by publication of the Pentagon documents was entirely predictable and even appropriate. It was not the substance of these disclosures but the fact of their having been made at all that was disturbing to the administration. They threatened the executive's control over information and raised the terrifying prospect that other officials would follow Ellsberg's example.

For all the apparent excessiveness of his response, Nixon had grasped the central fact that presidential power has come to rest on the ability to manipulate information and that this power, to be completely effective, must be recognized by everyone else as indivisible. Any other administration, confronted with a threat to its monopoly over information, would have acted along the same general lines.

The Watergate disclosures, followed by innumerable other disclosures of official wrongdoing, provided the country with a vivid demonstration of the dangers of unchecked presidential power and with an opportunity to arrest its growth. Although these disclosures and the threat of impeachment forced Nixon out of office, it is abundantly clear that there is little enthusiasm for curbing the powers of the executive. Four decades of unremitting turmoil, domestic and international, have created in the people a willingness to grant almost unlimited powers to the President, now in the hope that he will boldly attack the crisis and "get America moving again," now in the hope that he will clamp down on malcontents and dissidents, the putative source of all the troubles that afflict the nation and disturb the peace.

The mood of the country changes, but what does not change is the belief that only the President can deal effectively with crisis, whatever the crisis of the moment happens to be. The simple fact that Presidents are now elected to deal with crisis, which underlies the cult of the presidency, makes it impossible for most Americans to contemplate any steps that would weaken the office. The sheer size of the country and the magnitude of the problems facing it make the United States almost ungovernable. The Presidency provides at least the illusion of government.